PERSONAL & PROFESSIONAL DEVELOPMENT FOR BUSINESS STUDENTS

PRAISE FOR *PERSONAL AND PROFESSIONAL DEVELOPMENT FOR BUSINESS STUDENTS* BY PAUL DOWSON

The first thing I really love about Paul Dowson's hugely comprehensive *Personal and Professional Development for Business Students* is its clarity; he takes complex themes and turns them into accessible learning outcomes for students and academics. The other thing to love about this book is its humanity – it is insightful and borne of a deep concern about how students transition from higher education to working life and citizenship.
Jane Artess, HECSU Director of Research

Paul Dowson's *Personal and Professional Development for Business Students* clearly approaches the 'twenty-first-century century skills-issue' and stresses the importance of personal development in relation to higher education in a fast changing globalizing employment market. Hands-on, reflective, thorough: this book is already a definite must-have both for HE institutions' professionals and students.
Nieke Campagne, Careers/Policy Advisor, Leiden University, The Netherlands

This is a thought provoking invitation to students engaged in the management of their careers. It steps way outside the tired banalities of what is called 'career guidance'. And that means facing career-management issues ranging from the personal to the planetary. The author invites students into a process of critical and self-critical engagement with the issues. Some of these are moral and ethical. The material points to the uses of narrative in making sense of the resulting complexity. All of this moves into territory deeper and wider than what are recited as economic, psychological and political 'facts'. The inclusion of episodes from the author's experience help to draw each student into her or his own experience not just for its functionality but also for its humanity.
Dr Bill Law FRSA, the career-learning café, www.hihohiho.com

Paul Dowson's encouraging book connects depth of thought and analysis with a clear perception and an empathic understanding of the needs which students and graduates have in their search to find their career and their position in life. The ways introduced and explored open up practical steps and perspectives during higher education which will be truly empowering. The text is making clear that there is common ground between the author and the reader in the latter's struggle for a position of responsibility in business and human existence. I assume this fresh, pragmatic and at the same time deep approach will inspire students' career development and debates on the subject among academics and professionals in the UK and elsewhere.
Dr Gerhart Rott, University of Wuppertal, Germany. Representative formerly from FEDORA and now the EAIE at the European Lifelong Guidance Policy Network (ELGPN)

This book is unique in the areas of personal development, employability and responsibility in business. First, it brings all these areas together in a coherent and rigorous fashion. Second, it recognizes what is needed for the twenty-first-century business student in an environment which demands both integrated thinking and integrity. Third, it is focused in practice, recognizing the different functional areas and outlining what responsibility looks like in each of these. Fourth, it acts as a credible means of integrating the business curriculum by embedding personal development in each of the professional areas. The book is for students, academics and practitioners, setting up a dialogue that will enable the most effective career development.
Simon Robinson, Professor of Applied and Professional Ethics, Director of Research Centre for Governance, Leadership and Global Responsibility, Leeds Beckett University

Personal and Professional Development for Business Students makes accessible to the student reader a wealth of scholarly riches, setting employability in a wider critical context, that of the development of the ethical and integrated self. Packed with fresh perspectives and through provoking concepts and practical ideas, the book grapples with the challenges of how to become an employable professional in the protean world of postmodernity. While refusing simplistic conclusions and naive optimism, the book provides ample grounds for a belief in the lasting benefits that come from intellectual enlightenment and reflective learning.
Dave Stanbury, Director of Employability, University of Essex

In this wonderful book, Paul Dowson presents an excellent and accessible overview of theories on identity development. It offers a wealth of theoretical information and practical exercises, aiming at the integration in business of the personal, the moral and the organizational level. It will be a great help to business students in becoming competent, authentic and responsible professionals.
Professor Hetty Zock, University of Groningen

PAUL DOWSON

PERSONAL & PROFESSIONAL DEVELOPMENT FOR BUSINESS STUDENTS

LRC Stoke Park
GUILDFORD COLLEGE

Los Angeles | London | New Delhi
Singapore | Washington DC

SAGE

Los Angeles | London | New Delhi
Singapore | Washington DC

SAGE Publications Ltd
1 Oliver's Yard
55 City Road
London EC1Y 1SP

SAGE Publications Inc.
2455 Teller Road
Thousand Oaks, California 91320

SAGE Publications India Pvt Ltd
B 1/I 1 Mohan Cooperative Industrial Area
Mathura Road
New Delhi 110 044

SAGE Publications Asia-Pacific Pte Ltd
3 Church Street
#10-04 Samsung Hub
Singapore 049483

Editor: Kirsty Smy
Assistant editor: Nina Smith
Production editor: Sarah Cooke
Copyeditor: Gemma Marren
Proofreader: Lynda Watson
Indexer: Judith Lavender
Marketing manager: Catherine Slinn
Cover design: Shaun Mercier
Typeset by: C&M Digitals (P) Ltd, Chennai, India
Printed and bound by CPI Group (UK) Ltd,
Croydon, CR0 4YY

Library of Congress Control Number: 2014947470

British Library Cataloguing in Publication data

A catalogue record for this book is available from the British Library

ISBN 978-1-44628-220-5
ISBN 978-1-44628-221-2 (pbk)

At SAGE we take sustainability seriously. Most of our products are printed in the UK using FSC papers and boards. When we print overseas we ensure sustainable papers are used as measured by the Egmont grading system. We undertake an annual audit to monitor our sustainability.

I dedicate this book to my daughter and two sons, Hana, Alexander and Luke who in their twenties are still near the beginning of the adult life course.

CONTENTS

LIST OF TABLES

ABOUT THE AUTHOR

This is Paul Dowson's second business title following *Business Ethics in Practice* which he co-authored with Professor Simon Robinson (CIPD, 2012). The themes of responsibility and comprehending the contemporary age are again present but applied to personal and professional development. Paul gained his MBA from the University of Leeds and is a Fellow of the Royal Society of Arts. He is currently working with the Centre for Governance, Leadership and Global Responsibility at Leeds Beckett University as well as Bath Spa University.

FOREWORD BY DR VICTORIA HANDS

We live in momentous times. No matter what their area of expertise, the leaders of tomorrow will be the first generation ever to face the triple crises of global climate change impacts, diminishing oil and the scarcity of other natural resources such as water and the majority of minerals we take for granted today.

Today's decisions shape our tomorrow – what is at stake now is no less than the very existence of the human species on the planet. It's a bit surreal and can be likened to standing at a historical crossroads. The responsibility for the future rests with all, including young adults, with a particular emphasis on the role of women (currently 30 per cent female representation in 46 global parliaments). This constitutes quite a weight to put on, what Dowson coins, '19-something' adults and others born around the new millennium.

The 'new normal' under which we are increasingly operating is characterized by velocity, uncertainty, complexity and ambiguity (VUCA) at a global scale. This book makes a great companion for any young person or educator wishing to maximize their resources and resourcefulness for a resilient future.

The role of education providers (institutions and individuals alike) is crucial in not only delivering relevant information, but also in facilitating transformational learning approaches. This adds cognitive dissonance to cognitive development and through social learning permits the co-creation of new knowledge focusing on myth-busting, as well as both challenging and transforming the status quo.

Essentially this involves the appreciation of an individual's existing competency, which is what this book encourages: the exploration of personal identity and creativity, reflection and self-awareness; to become self-conscious in the true sense of the word (at the individual, group and global scale); to see ourselves as unique parts of a thriving, ever-changing global system. The process, as Dowson explains, leads to enhanced self-esteem, which is essential when inevitable obstacles arise. This in turn enhances social learning and generates innovation for global good, bringing individual good as a happy by-product.

Cognitive development must focus on understanding how we arrived at our current global state by contextualizing the present in relation to history, at the same time as anticipating the future and appreciating emerging trends – taking a bird's eye view. Unlike the majority of those in power over the last 50 years, who seem to have adopted something closer to a mouse's myopic view, young people will need highly developed critical thinking skills to be able to distinguish between bankrupt theories that make it untenable for human existence on planet Earth, and those which will make humanity's future not just possible but bright.

Young people need the knowledge, skills and behaviours to move from the predominant short-term thinking and doing embraced by many of their role models to appreciating and expanding upon the *long-term, global well-being* focus which is starting to characterize resilient business practice. They will need to be able to integrate self-knowledge and knowledge of the world in continuous, life-long action learning and reflection to be 'future-fit', ethically robust, sustainability literate and implementation ready. Which employer is going to say no to that skills package if they want to be around for the rest of the twenty-first century?

Dowson introduces signposts and urges the mastery of skills including the ability to embrace interdisciplinary, intergenerational and integrated thinking and most importantly, translate theories into practice through interdependence, collaboration and creativity. What he hints at is nothing short of an evolution of human consciousness.

So this book, which aims to guide the young adult embarking on business studies (and other degree courses) in their own personal development is a timely and a critical asset. It is based on the belief that changes in consciousness are about personal development, that there is a strong relationship between personal development and business responsibility, that accepting and valuing plurality in oneself and in others enables us to access our inherent creative resources which will support the development of a global consciousness within which humanity can thrive. *Personal and Professional Development for Business Students* embeds in education the potential of a most welcome pedagogy of hope.

Dr Victoria Hands

Director, Sustainability Hub, Kingston University

ACKNOWLEDGEMENTS

I would like to acknowledge here everyone who, one way or another, played an important part in the publication of this book. Firstly, I extend my thanks to Kirsty Smy and Nina Smith, the editorial staff at Sage Publications. It was a pleasure to work together on producing this book. Secondly, I would also like to acknowledge the anonymous panel of academic reviewers for their valuable comments. Next, the countless students who have helped me to develop my thinking and teaching on Personal and Professional Development and its integration with corporate and global responsibility. There are also a number of people to mention by name in supporting the research and writing of this textbook including: Jane Artess, Steve Barry, Nieke Campagne, Victoria Hands, Nicky Hirst, Jacomijn van der Kooij, Bill Law, Hannah Marsland, Phil Marsland, J. Richard Middleton, Carolynn Rankin, Simon Robinson, Gerhart Rott, Ismail Mesut Sezgin, David Stanbury and Hetty Zock. My thanks also to Philip Doyne and Ruth Fidler for reading large sections of the book and providing comments.

QUICK REFERENCE – KEY IDEAS

This is a list of 64 key themes examined in the book, four for each of the 16 chapters, many of which are brand new for a personal development textbook. Take some time to review these and using the chapter numbers find material that particularly interests you. By using this book you will become familiar with all these important subjects or concepts.

QUICK REFERENCE – KEY THINKERS/AUTHORS

Here is an index by chapter number of 40 minds whose thinking has contributed significantly to this textbook.

1 INTRODUCTION

● ● ● ● ● ● ● ● ● ● ● ● ●

PROLOGUE – FROM THE AUTHOR

We are living in a time significantly impacted by the global financial crisis. Historically it has been referred to as the beginning of the *post-post war period* (Sloterdijk, 2011), or as *late* or *'liquid', modernity* (Bauman, 2000). There is certainly no denying the growing influence of globalization. We might say that all these things are combining to turn the world upside down, impacting us all in profound ways, both professionally and personally.

The adaptation required adds to the anxiety and disorientation of many (Bauman, 2008). This encompasses you if you are studying at university, at the beginning of your journeys as adults, in search of many things including desirable and meaningful employment. You are facing a cacophony of voices and narratives to comprehend, in both wider environs and academia. You are required to develop particular skills and characteristics to progress. It is a big ask. This book will help you.

What is *different* about this time that students are currently experiencing, studying in higher education institutions? And how is the world likely to re-shape over the coming years? This book aims to examine personal and professional development in the contemporary context.

Also at this time, there is much scope to produce a PD resource that attaches as much significance to values and virtues as to skills development. In a highly competitive job market students are differentiated not just by their skills development and portfolio but also by their experiences and personality, reflecting in great measure their values.

In an age where business has to be seen to be responsible as well as aim to be responsible in all its ways of operating, a new generation of responsible business practitioners is called for. Professionalism in business practice is increasingly tied to responsible action. This book is among the first of its kind to link personal and professional development with corporate responsibility.

It is also valuable in recognizing the challenges faced by students, expressed in many ways – emotionally, socially, financially. Many students find it far from straightforward to transition through university; and to define and find a fulfilling career pathway. The book also seeks to offer some encouragement and resources to students whose progress is not as straightforward as hoped for.

THE CHAPTERS

There are 16 chapters and following this introduction the book is divided into four parts.

Part I – The land of opportunity

The five chapters constituting Part I will communicate a sense of the great opportunities which lie ahead for graduates who make the most of the time of learning and development at university.

2 Where you are now

The time at university will be presented as a key time of *transition* with students setting out to find and build new futures for themselves. University usually provides a time of what Erikson refers to as *moratorium* (Welchman, 2000) – some 'time out' to work out what students want, and to define direction. As well as studying to gain knowledge of a specific subject, intrinsic to a higher education is the notion of personal development planning (PDP). The purpose of a higher education will be examined as will the contemporary context in which we find ourselves.

   Key idea: o life stage   o postmodernity   o transition   o values

3 An A to Z of skills development

This chapter will introduce students to the significance of skills acquisition and development in higher education. Having provided an A to Z overview of all the skills defined and desired by employers the chapter will outline the most strategic specific skills to be developed at university. Employers are on the look-out for graduates with higher skills and skill levels. The student who deliberately sets out to enhance their skills portfolio at university will be better placed to meet this skills requirement.

   Key idea: o critical thinking   o independent learning   o skills gap   o teams

4 Graduate skills

What makes a 'graduate' and what skills are particularly associated with graduate jobs? Futuretrack (2012), a recent key piece of UK research, defines three groups of graduate jobs requiring high level skills. The *experts* group of jobs focus on specialist knowledge gained from a degree course. The *orchestrators* group of jobs draw on a host of strategic skills including managerial skills, problem-solving skills, planning skills and decision-making skills. The *communicators* group require high level communication skills, whether oral or written. The smart student will soon see that the above skills groups are not mutually exclusive and graduates need to provide a skills offering that encompasses all three skills areas to gain graduate employment.

Key idea: o graduate skills   o networking mentality   o skills development   o skills offering

5 Competencies and ways of operating in the twenty-first century

Having thoroughly dealt with skills, this chapter takes us one step further by introducing competencies, which are particularly bound up with professionalism. Helen Haste's thinking is central to this chapter's presentation of her key competencies for twenty-first-century living and working. Added to this, any book on personal development must address the central issue of gaining confidence, which permits the person to become an effective practitioner in any professional context. The chapter concludes with looking at what it means in practice to be a so called *ethical practitioner*.

Key idea: o agency   o competencies   o confidence   o ethical practitioner

6 Going global

This timely chapter on globalization looks at the global potential and relevance for every business, as well as its implications for personal and professional development. The chapter examines how to relate positively to matters global and outlines what it means to be a global practitioner. An introduction to worldviews prepares business students for the diversity of outlooks found both within and beyond national boundaries. Global consciousness stretches individuals and businesses to get past the strangeness associated with encountering and befriending people who think in a different way from us.

Key idea: o ecozoic   o global   o strangeness   o worldview

Part II – Self-awareness and development

The five chapters of Part II take the reader on a journey from self-profiling (founded upon self-understanding) through to self-presentation. It will be argued that these aspects of personal and professional development are mutually supporting.

7 Self-development and profiling

The student committed to self-study and examination will be best equipped to select an appropriate career path. A couple of intriguing yet powerful aids to self-profiling will be presented in this chapter, namely the enneagram and Myers-Briggs. At university you may hear for the first time the expression 'reflective practice'. It has grown up in the world of professional practice and is associated with the theorist Donald Schön. The chapter includes a whole gallery of theorists that help us to understand what is encompassed by the term 'personal development'.

Key idea: o *Bildung*   o enneagram   o Myers-Briggs   o reflective practice

8 Integrity matters: the integrated self and organization

The book will be unique in its deep consideration of what is integrity and in presenting virtues as central to what a student can offer. We will examine not only personal integrity, but also organizational integrity. Both the individual and the organization are called upon to find their 'moral compass'. As Jack Whitehead's 'living contradiction' model will show, this suggests integrity is more about moral authenticity than moral perfection (Barnett, 2009).

Key idea: o integrity   o living contradiction   o moral authenticity o multiple identities

9 Career and life planning

The notion of planning underlies the importance of looking before you leap and making career (and life) decisions based upon a foundation of accurate self-awareness. Edgar Schein's career anchors are introduced in this chapter. Planning, however, doesn't equate to boring and Mark Savickas' thoughtful, yet inspiring thinking is an appeal to our imagination and creativity in putting together a career and life plan. The reader will learn how to story themselves forward.

Key idea: o career anchors   o career planning   o narrative   o self-concept

10 The nuts and bolts of career communication

So much of securing wanted and meaningful employment rests on the individual making it happen. This chapter will focus on the critical area of career communication which is a *work in progress* matter for all adults in the job market. This is an extremely practical chapter which examines important communication elements at every stage of the job application process from CV to assessment centre.

Key idea: o assessment centre   o body language   o first impressions o group work

11 Volunteering and internships

In a highly competitive job market differentiators are even more significant. Here extra-curricular activities and responsibilities, as well as volunteering placements and internships are sources of competitive edge. This chapter will provide pointers as to how to reflect on work and other experiences of all kinds and the significance of gaining insights into how organizations operate.

Key idea: o cooperant   o internship   o social entrepreneur   o volunteering

Part III – The responsible practitioner

Many students now express a desire to 'make a difference' in terms of their career destinations. This coincides with a move towards businesses meeting customer and employee expectations to act responsibly. The three chapters of Part III examine what it means to be responsible.

12 Freud & Sons: a vocabulary for understanding psychosocial development

What happens when the metaphorical wheels don't turn, or at times come loose? And why does life so often feel like 'two steps forward, one step back' – or sometimes something even less progressive? This chapter takes us beyond metaphors to a vocabulary we can both examine and use to understand ourselves and other people. Personal development draws significantly on psychoanalysis for much of its vocabulary and core concepts. Here we outline the core ideas of four great thinkers in this area, beginning with Freud himself, followed by Carl Jung, Melanie Klein and Erik Erikson.

Key idea: o identity crisis o individuation o intergenerational o projection

13 Responsible business practice

CSR (corporate social responsibility), more recently termed CR (corporate responsibility), has over the past three decades become more and more integral to business practice and a business education. This relates to the same growth in business ethics reflected in dedicated business school modules on this important subject. Adopting the 'quadruple bottom line' framework, this chapter in a timely way examines the impact of business in four areas: economic, environmental, social and existential. An exciting second half to the chapter then looks at responsibility applied to the three major business functions in which responsible practice can be developed: responsible marketing, responsible accounting and responsible human resources management (HRM).

Key idea: o employee engagement o quadruple bottom line o responsible business o responsible marketing

14 Responsible leadership and governance

What does responsible leadership look like in practice? This is examined in this chapter through looking at a number of leadership theories culminating in the inspiring concept of self-leadership. The chapter goes on to look at leadership's so often 'invisible' sister, governance. An important thinker in the area of responsible governance is Mervyn E. King, who masterminded South Africa's so called

'King reports': King I, King II and King III. Attention is also given to looking at ethical coding including codes of ethics, codes of practice and codes of conduct.

Key idea: o governance   o King III   o responsible leader   o self-leadership

Part IV – Humanity and futures

University life is not without its stresses. Indeed, for many reasons it can include personal challenges of all kinds. Personal and professional development is a resource to help adults come to terms with these difficulties. Part IV uniquely outlines some of the issues students face and where to gain some support and help. Placed alongside this is a useful chapter providing a window to the future.

15 Supporting resources

There are a number of issues that can cause an adult to feel 'stuck', and start to hamper their progress. The anxiety surrounding identifying a suitable career path and employment is a common concern. Added to this relationship problems, family difficulties, debt and depression are common issues that adults struggle with. The good news is that universities have professional support services to help students facing such challenges. A review of this chapter will reveal that all manner of difficulties faced by students are reassuringly common and help is never far away. The chapter also incorporates a fascinating overview of 'Generation Y'.

Key idea: o Generation Y   o relationships   o self-discovery   o storying oneself

16 Futures

How can we gain a greater handle on where the world is heading and what is the significance of this for both individuals and business organizations? And if we could anticipate the future, would it change what we would do in the present? This chapter shows that so called futures thinking or futures studies certainly amount to something more concrete than staring into a crystal ball. What of the economy becoming 'circular' rather than linear? What might be the consequences of rising inequality? And what is the future for employment?

Key idea: o circular economy   o futures consciousness   o futures trends o post-Freud orientation

KEY THEMES

When introducing another textbook for a market that is already occupied by a number of competing titles it is important not to 'reinvent the wheel'. It is clear that a new book should cover the areas students and staff would expect to find in turning to a textbook concerned with personal development, employability and careers. However, at the same time this new title is being written to respond to where competitor texts are weak. *Personal and Professional Development for Business Students* has four key themes encompassing a plethora of new and very timely subjects.

A new globality

The first of these is a full treatment of the contemporary context which is both extremely challenging but at the same time possessing great opportunity. This is what Bauman refers to as a new 'globality' (Bauman, 2001) – that is, a world that is now subject to the phenomenon of globalization. This raises a number of significant issues for business students: anticipating continued economic and cultural change in terms of their own futures; being able to understand and handle a diversity of world-views; and appreciating the move towards 'global responsibility' in business.

Responsible business

The second key theme centres around businesses being called upon by consumers and governments to act responsibly in every way – the movement towards responsible business. This is not often presented as being a shared enterprise where businesses and businesspeople work together with other stakeholders to become more responsible in their business practice. This has a number of dimensions not covered in competitor textbooks: the linking of responsible business with professionalism; its outworking in terms of leadership and management; and the importance of it being distinctively evident in the business functions of accounting, HRM, sales and marketing.

The responsible practitioner

The application of this movement to the individual produces the third key theme – the concept of the responsible practitioner. Responsible business requires responsible business professionals and employees. In the same way that businesses are more explicit of their values reflected in codes and policies, individuals too are wanting to express their values in what they do. The book will uniquely look at what integrity is and its significance for the individual. It will also underline the empowering significance of individuals taking responsibility for their development and career pathways.

Good transitions

The fourth key theme will be the book's recognition of the humanity of adults, particularly in their searching for good transitioning. We must avoid a computer manual approach to personal development. Real life is way more exhilarating and perilous than many books on personal development seem to suggest. Students as young adults face a significant time of life transition in going to university. This is the first of a number of transitions that will follow, all requiring adaptation and usually involving some difficulties. It is not unusual at university to face a whole gamut of challenges that can all too easily interrupt momentum. Positively, there are excellent resources at university to help.

ADDITIONAL FEATURES

In addition to these key themes there are a number of additional features to the content of the book that are timely and will be appreciated by all.

The timing of the new book will permit an examination of the multi-faceted nature of all the things professionally the student should seek to embody. In addition to a range of core skills, the book covers competencies, responsible virtues and values.

The financing of doing a degree has necessitated students working in paid employment alongside studying. The great competition for graduate jobs calls for students to differentiate themselves from others, particularly in terms of not only work experience, but also the areas of interests pursued and volunteering. The book dedicates a chapter to students making the most of responsibilities fulfilled in work, placements and clubs and societies.

Finally, the book uniquely incorporates business ethics and corporate responsibility in personal and professional development. This is particularly helpful where students are not able to take a core or elective module in ethics or CR.

Corresponding to these key themes and additional features, set out below are a number of introductions to concepts core to the book. They arise naturally from questions that may already have emerged for you while reading this first chapter.

WHAT IS PERSONAL DEVELOPMENT?

Many students who arrive at university are surprised to discover that the learning includes personal and professional development. Furthermore, students often question its validity and its usefulness. This often betrays the fact that it isn't a priority for many students. It is natural that the highest priority is one's choice of core subject (whether this is Business or History or Chemistry or Fine Art). Then there are the understandable priorities of seeking to get through university financially, which leads many students to part-time employment; and also just enjoying this chapter of one's life to the maximum.

Nevertheless, personal and professional development forms a part of the whole and many students through time begin to see more and more its relevance for their lives and for their futures. In a nutshell, personal and professional development (PD) is about being the best that you can be. In the world in which we live that is no automatic or easy feat. Table 1.1 shows an example syllabus and summarizes the subject matter covered in PD.

Table 1.1 An example personal development syllabus

Study and Communication Skills	Supporting resources
	Writing skills and essay writing
	Giving presentations
	Referencing
	Learning with dialogue
Employability and Careers	Personal development planning
	Personal development portfolio building
	CV and careers communication
	Careers definition and destination
	Job applications and interviews
Personal Development and Awareness	Reflection and reflective practice
	Identification of skills and capacities
	Self-awareness and self-presentation
	Awareness of 'other'
	Meta-awareness and meta-cognition
Professional and Advanced Development	Leadership and management
	Project management
	The responsible organization
	Vision and values formulation
	Volunteering/placement experience

It is easy to think of one's entire education from early childhood as being about subjects and knowledge, but from our earliest school days educationalists and educational establishments have been seeking to develop us as people. An education implies a preparation of some sort; so it is relevant to ask, 'What am I being prepared for?' The answer is for many things: for all our interactions and relationships with others; to help us to get the maximum from life's opportunity; to develop our character, our values and our skills; and to facilitate us in finding our place in the world and in the world of work. You can see here that the overarching notion of PD centring around being the best that we can be fits so well.

Employability is a term we are often introduced to at university. Accepted, it isn't the most inviting of terms, but it captures an important reality. Employability means virtually what it says. It raises the question of how employable one will be as a graduate in your subject with your university experience now complete. The times we are currently living in where a university education costs a lot of money, where there are usually dozens and dozens of people chasing every job and where recession in the western world has made the search for desired job opportunities even tougher than it ever was, means that we all as adult individuals must face this issue of how useful or desirable or just plain marketable we might be to potential employers. If we are not the best we can be, then the jobs might always be going to someone who has worked a little harder on this dimension of who they are and what they have to offer an employer.

At this point it is important not to panic. The average job holder even in the most desirable of occupations and fields is not the complete item. People are both developed and flawed in an alarming way. They will offer some specialist knowledge, skills and expertise that have enabled them to secure their roles. At the same time, like all adults, we are a 'work in progress' and therefore in need of further learning and development as both people and professionals. This learning and development never stops. This book will outline all the areas that adults need to address in their personal and professional development, particularly in our contemporary twenty-first-century and global context.

WHAT IS A PROFESSIONAL?

In the world of work one of the highest compliments one can receive is to be described by one's clients (or customers) or colleagues as being 'a professional'. Traditionally, there were only a few people who could describe themselves as professionals, but with the advent of management education and thinking we now look at virtually every role in the world of work through the lens of professionalism.

Professionalism is bound up with going about one's job in the correct way. Again, this is no easy or automatic task. Firstly, there are what are known as professional practices. As the word suggests, this is allied to what one does as a professional – to one's practice. For every role there are standards that one must achieve in a number of areas. Secondly, we probably hear more about professional behaviour and its shadow, which is 'unprofessional' behaviour. The latter is where the professional slips every now and again. This should not surprise us. What matters here is the professional's attitude to where he or she could have done better. Through what is known as reflective practice it is important to be professionally aware and learn from these experiences.

Professionalism can be likened to driving a car well. A good driver through their latent ability and their driving experiences comes to a place where they can drive both consciously, but also automatically. Along the way even good drivers make mistakes – underestimating different driving conditions, miscalculating in certain situations or not fully allowing for an out of the ordinary happening.

Professionalism is also aspirational. In the same way as one might want to be a good driver, it is natural for many to want to be good in their jobs – to be a professional. To find a job where one fits and one performs can have a 'rollerball effect' upon an individual.

WHAT ABOUT OUR UNCERTAIN WORLD?

Ours is a watery world. Yes it is full of opportunity, but at the same time it is fundamentally dynamic or, put another way, shifting and uncertain. This has many implications for the way we lead our lives and operate in our organizations. There are at least four dimensions to this fluid dynamism which can be seen everywhere.

The first is what we might term shifting patterns. Little it seems is fixed in stone. People rarely now gain jobs for life, even in the spheres and circles that are most appropriate for them. Our employer today may very well not be our employer tomorrow. Employing organizations themselves seek to be flexible, meaning that re-structuring and inevitable lay-offs and severance are never too far away.

In the face of such uncertainty workers need to become more flexible themselves and a key concept we will develop in this book is one of 'adaptation', a second dimension. Adaptation is the ability to stay light on your feet and to be able to respond to the information all around us which we can both see and sense; and to be able to change and adopt, if needed, a new path. It is a critical step further than what is termed as adjustment, which unlike adaptation, can be achieved without personal development. The adaptive self is able to manage recurrent transitions. The adaptive self never stops learning. The adaptive self is protean and capable of hybridity, all things I shall enlarge upon in the book.

A third dimension I have called 'authorship'. This is the stark reality that no one is going to be able to manage your life and career for you. You cannot expect even your nearest and dearest, or most noble of mentors to do that. How your life unfolds is in so many respects down to you. Because of the uncertain world that I have been describing this requires that we all toughen up and develop a stronger sense of ourselves: what we can do, alongside the sense of what is not in 'our bag'. What we can achieve when we are activated and determined to do so. You are your own story and authorship enables you to respond positively to this reality.

The fourth dimension is how this watery world with its lack of security and stability leaves a lot of people thinking. Very apparent is that there are both winners and losers in this environment. Some people are in the right place at the right time. Others adapt to the new reality. Others are both in the wrong place and are unable to adapt. Their maladaptation may be costly. The disparity between the winners and losers (some would call it inequity), ushers in a lot of pressure for adults to contend with. Certainly there is much uncertainty in our watery world. But added to this we find anxiety, distress, frustration, anger and denial. It would be good to not have to state this, but these are realities in contemporary western society and they even explain lifestyles and patterns of consumption.

WHY ALL THIS TALK OF GLOBAL?

There are a few terms we will hear more and more over the years to come. The first is the term global and its associated concept of globalization. The second will follow on behind global and globalization: *global responsibility*. We shall be looking at all these terms in the book and their huge implications for our futures.

In his book *The Future* (2013) Al Gore lists a number of 'drivers of change' at work in the world at large:

- ever increasing globalization
- the shifting of the global balance of power in the direction of the east
- the revolution in biotechnology and life sciences
- the depletion of natural resources
- climate change.

It should be noted that while these things pose great challenges for all, including businesses, they also present many opportunities. Smart individuals and organizations will work towards a 'future picture' incorporating rather than denying these things.

Where were you on 11 September 2001? We live in a world where big things happen and bring on many changes. There are many who would argue that 9/11 shifted everything (Hall, 2009). It was as momentous, perhaps more so, than Pearl Harbour. Such events and happenings cannot be anticipated, however, they do point to a need for people and businesses to be aware that the business environment is dynamic and requires concerted analysis to see more clearly into the future.

Prabhu Guptara (2006) speaks of the distinction between pro-market and anti-market groups of people, which is partly explained by the dividing fortunes of people in the new global epoch. The former can envision where they and business fit into with the new global environment and ethos. The latter may have been left behind or even culturally for various reasons may be resistant to change. It is sometimes a protest position in relation to inequity of all kinds.

WORLDVIEW AND LATE MODERNITY?

A radical inclusion in this book is extensive content relating to the concept of worldview or *Weltanschauung* as it is known in Germany. A worldview is simply seeing the world in a certain way. It could alternatively be labelled as 'world ways' reflecting the fact that the west sees the world through different spectacles than does the east. There are myriad ways to 'divide the cake', so to speak.

In a global business context it is important to remember that people from other parts of the world, from other cultures, don't view the world in the same way that you do. The implication for matters like business strategy, sales and marketing, corporate responsibility and HRM are enormous. Here we also need to remember that because of globalization the world lives literally next door in our towns and cities. We do not need to travel abroad to encounter global diversity and different worldviews.

We are also living in a specific historical age. The book will outline what is meant by the terms modernity and postmodernity, which help us to both map and explain where we have arrived in terms of world history. Again the significance of this for business is enormous. Most commentators in this area refer to our being located in what is known as 'late modernity', which suggests we are transitioning from one age into another. A central feature of our contemporary lives is the place occupied by technological and communications media, which includes as Alan Kirby so ably puts it 'computers in every house powerful enough to put a man on the moon' (Kirby, 2006).

WHY PERSONAL TRANSITIONING?

In the same way that the world as a whole and the business environment are transitioning from one state to another, significantly the same can be said of adults; and particularly the huge transitions associated with young adulthood and going to university. In the space of only a few years many young adults leave school, often locate in a new city (or even country) when going to university and then following a few years of concentrated study at university venture into the world of work, and that search for a graduate job.

This book has been written with the particular opportunities and challenges associated with this journey in view. Students need to remember that this is a big ask for all sorts of reasons. Financially, it's a difficult journey for many. Relationally, it isn't plain sailing for everyone. And then there's the challenge of finding meaningful and desired employment. University is also for many a time when students are looking to find themselves. It is an opportunity (away from home) to start a new chapter and discover what they want and don't want; what they like and don't like; and perhaps most significantly who they want to be and don't want to be.

The book will highlight the thinking of psychologist Terri Apter (2001) who maps many of the challenges that are faced by students at university. An important message here is that all these challenges are not unusual, and support services are available to help. For example, within the space of a few weeks of commencing university many 'homebound' romantic relationships (often from school days) very quickly break down. For some this is timely and about moving on. For others, it can be devastating. Life can be cruel, but one is able to come to terms with such difficulties and discover new life.

In addition to the great opportunity to meet new friends and enjoy all the collegiate potential in one's university, college or department, university provides a range of advice services to help students past all manner of challenges.

PEDAGOGICAL FEATURES

Each chapter will be written to have stand-alone significance in its treatment of a particular subject. Here the aim is to make each chapter so relevant and differentiated from competitor texts that the book would be an attractive resource even for just a number of its 16 chapters. It is intended for students to acquire the book in their first year of university and refer to it as a PD resource throughout their course of studies.

According with the book's function as a learning resource, the chapters will incorporate a number of pedagogical features and boxes. These highlight some important topics and are noticeable as one flicks through the book. These include:

CASE STUDIES

Case studies will point to real life examples of subjects being presented. Often these will highlight good practice in the world of business. This will enable the students to associate a business with a particular approach, sometimes worthy of emulation and sometimes not.

ETHICS

This unique feature deals with ethical issues related to personal development, making philosophical and conceptual matters more accessible.

EMBODIMENT

This unique feature presents somebody or something that embodies a certain quality or principle, making philosophical and conceptual matters more accessible.

EMPLOYABILITY FOCUS

This feature acts as a so called 'so what' focus, relating to careers and employability. The intention with the book is always to keep one eye focused on employability, and these foci, present in every chapter, are a reminder of the connection of the subject matter to the world of work and the competitive job market.

THE BOOK'S AUDIENCE AND PURPOSE

This textbook, as reflected in the title and as will become clear from the language, is written for and addressed to students. At the same time, the content of the book and its level makes it an appropriate reference for business people. The author himself completed an executive MBA while working in business and there is much material in the book that will interest the business practitioner as much as the business student. Notes on the use of the book can be found below.

Undergraduates and postgraduates

- The book will help students see how personal development is intrinsic to both study and experiences at university.
- It presents how personal development applies to employment and life in general.
- It is a resource for thinking about the future.
- It will help students identify career and development pathways.

Business people

- The level of the book and its content are also applicable for those already working in the business world.
- It will generate ideas for planning professional and career development.
- It will contribute to practitioners making the most of their employment situations and help develop organizations.

REFERENCES

Apter, T. (2001) *The Myth of Maturity: What Teenagers Need from Parents to Become Adults*. New York: W. W. Norton & Co.

Barnett, R. (2009) 'The postmodern university: prospects of the ethical', in J. Strain, R. Barnett and P. Jarvis (eds), *Universities, Ethics and Professions: Debate and Scrutiny*. London: Routledge.

Bauman, Z. (2008) *Does Ethics Have a Chance in a World of Consumers?* Cambridge, MA: Harvard University Press.

Bauman, Z. (2001) 'The great war of recognition', *Theory, Culture and Society*, 18 (2–3): 137–150.

Bauman, Z. (2000) *Liquid Modernity*. Cambridge: Polity Press.

Futuretrack (2012) 'The changing relationship between higher education and the graduate labour market: evidence from Futuretrack', conference paper, Manchester, 7 November.

Gore, A. (2013) *The Future*. London: W. H. Allen.

Guptara, P. (2006) 'Tackling poverty: the roles of business, government and NGOs'. Available at: http://ethix.org/2006/12/01/tackling-poverty-the-roles-of-business-government-and-ngos (accessed 2 June 2013).

Hall, J. R. (2009) *Apocalypse: From Antiquity to the Empire of Modernity*. Cambridge: Polity Press.

Kirby, A. (2006) 'The death of postmodernism and beyond', *Philosophy Now*. Available at: http://philosophynow.org/issues/58/The_Death_of_Postmodernism_And_Beyond (accessed 2 June 2013).

Sloterdijk, P. with Heinrichs, H. (2011) *Neither Sun Nor Death*, trans. Steve Corcoran. Los Angeles: Semiotext(e).

Welchman, K. (2000) *Erik Erikson: His Life, Work and Significance*. Buckingham: Open University Press.

PART I
THE LAND OF OPPORTUNITY

WHERE YOU ARE NOW

A NOTE FROM THE AUTHOR

The inspiration for the title of this chapter is David Bowie's similarly titled song 'Where are we now?' Many of you will be reading this for the first time in one of your early weeks at university. It's a new start and everybody's hope for you, including all the staff at the university from the lecturers to those who look after security, is that this will constitute for you 'the time of your life'. Remember that all the staff are there to help you in every way they can. It's an all adult environment, which inevitably means you have a more collegiate relationship with the teaching staff than you will have enjoyed at school.

This chapter has three broad elements. The first element will cause you to focus on what's new about arriving at a university. It will ask you to think about why you're here, how that might differ from other students and how university constitutes a new life stage. University is not without its challenges and we shall look at the transition you experience before you truly settle into university life.

In the second element of the chapter the focus switches from you to the university itself and looks at the purpose and content of a higher education, which again shows some departures from your previous schooling and education. There will be aspects to this content that will surprise you – probably because you will have not anticipated or thought about what a university education is all about. This element ends with looking at a business school so you can compare it with your own university or department. Universities like other organizations and businesses differ enormously as do individual business schools and departments. In every university and business school, community can be found and enjoyed. I urge you to get involved here and make the most of this aspect of your university experience.

The third element looks at the fascinating issue of the contemporary context you find yourselves in. The world today is very different from the one your parents and older relations ventured into as young adults. I have spent some time unravelling the conundrum of what it means for us to be living now, in what is termed late modernity. This is extremely relevant for our

(Continued)

(Continued)

futures and future business activity. The chapter closes with looking at how a university positions itself in this time of great transition and uncertainty.

Which only leaves me here to outline the learning outcomes for the chapter which are as follows.

Learning outcomes

When you have completed this chapter you will be able to:

- describe, analyse and critique your rationale for coming to university
- locate and describe your current life stage
- comprehend and evaluate the purposes and content of a higher education
- locate and describe the contemporary context of late modernity
- define and evaluate your values.

CASE STUDY – LEARNING TRIBES

A piece of research by *The International Graduate Insight Group (i-graduate)* surveyed some 25,000 international students from more than 190 nations and plotted student affiliation across five learning tribes as follows:

The Surfers – these students prioritize living life over work and would like to have fun doing it. Account for 11 per cent of the student population.

The Seekers – students seeking primarily to get a job and see study as a means to that end. Account for 24 per cent of the student population.

The Gekkos – in essence these students are in pursuit of status, recognition and money. Account for 23 per cent of the student population.

The Bonos – those students who want to make a difference and who put personal development above any other group. Account for 22 per cent of the student population.

The Kids – as the name suggests these have plenty of youthful enthusiasm and want to delay taking personal responsibility. Account for 20 per cent of the student population.

There was no significant gender difference among the tribes (Spencer, 2008).

Questions

1   If you had to place yourself in one of the categories, in all honesty which one comes closest to you and why you are at university?
2   Are you aware of other students having other motivations from you to be at university?
3   What do you think of this way of looking at the student population? How do you respond to the framework presented?

Responses to these questions from former students included one who said he'd like to add the following tribes:

- The Unsure
- The Knowledge Thirsty
- The Traditionalists

Another student remarked that she expected students to shift tribes through time spent at university.

It's difficult to imagine any young adult students admitting to being in *The Kids* category. This pejorative descriptor seems to stand in the way of a critical research approach.

WHY I CAME TO UNIVERSITY?

A good question to ask, particularly at the beginning of one's university experience, is why you came to university? From years of asking first year students this question the most common responses are outlined below. It is important to recognize here that people's motives differ, as do their combinations of the most important factors. Actual reasons given are recorded as stated by students.

Occupational

The occupational motive has at least three dimensions:

Deferral: to delay getting a job, to put back having to hold a job until I am sure what I want to do, not ready for work yet.

Positional: to get a job I want to do, to expand employment opportunities for the future.

Aspirational: higher job prospects and job fulfilment, get respect in a chosen career, widen future opportunities, to get the job that I want and to move to a successful career.

(Continued)

(Continued)

Educational

To expand my knowledge, to learn more, to become more educated on the world around me, to gain knowledge about the world, I wanted to study something I'm interested in, wisdom over knowledge.

Independence

To create my own viewpoint, to move out (from family home) and become independent, to branch out, to be my own boss in relation to living away from home.

Vocational

To (go on to) help others, to put me in a place to make a difference.

Expected of me

Expected of me, because my parents wanted me to, the thing to do from my background.

Progression

To (go on to) get a Masters, to open more opportunities up, finding links for the future.

Social

To meet like-minded people, fun, social, I want to make new friends, to socialize and get smashed, to have a laugh

Experiential

For the Uni experience.

Graduate status

For the status of obtaining a degree, for the kudos of having a degree, to gain the respect of peers, family and friends.

Developmental

For development on a personal level, to make something of myself, widening my horizons, cultural knowledge and understanding, a time of preparation.

A NEW LIFE STAGE

Life consists of certain stages. One of the first exponents of this notion was Isidore of Seville (c. 560–636) who in his Etymologies divides the human life into the following parts:

Table 2.1 Isidore of Seville's life stages

0–7	Infantia (infancy)
7–14	Pueritia (childhood)
14–28	Adolescentia (adolescence)
28–50	Inventus (youth)
50–70	Gravitas (maturity)
70+	Senectus (old age)

We obviously would differ with his descriptions but how he divides the lifespan is interesting.

The more famous William Shakespeare also divided the life – into ages. In Jaques's famous 'All the world's a stage' speech in the play *As You Like It*, he describes seven ages of man (Friedman, 2000) as follows:

1 Infant
2 Schoolboy
3 Lover
4 Soldier
5 The justice
6 Pantaloon (clown)
7 'Second childishness'

However, perhaps the most famous scheme of life stages was conceived by the US psychoanalyst and thinker, Erik Erikson, who suggested that life consisted of eight psychosocial stages, each of which centres around a struggle (termed a 'crisis') between two conflicting personality outcomes.

Table 2.2 Erikson's eight life stages each with its crisis

First year	Infancy	Trust v. mistrust
2–3	Early childhood	Autonomy v. shame and doubt
4–5	Play age	Initiative v. guilt
6–11	School age	Industry v. inferiority
12–18	Adolescence	Identity v. role confusion
20s and 30s	Young adulthood	Intimacy v. isolation
40–64	Middle adulthood	Generativity v. stagnation
65+	Late adulthood	Integrity v. despair

A brief examination of Table 2.2 will lead to the observation of significant life-change from being a young teenager to becoming a young adult. George Boeree (2006) speaks of how in the traditional society of the Oglala Lokota native Americans an adolescent boy was sent off on his own, weaponless and with minimal clothing, on a *dream quest*. The expectation was that the youth's life path would be revealed on the fourth day in a dream. University in some way now serves that 'coming of age' purpose where away from home the young person becomes a young adult and works out, in a fashion, in which direction they are going to head.

Returning to Erikson, his sixth stage – encapsulating the crisis of intimacy versus isolation – the key relationships are love relationships, friendships and work or university connections and the key issues are intimate relationships, work and social life.

Intimacy has both broad and narrow connotations here applying to both close relationships (including friendships) through to sexuality. David Elkind suggests the issue at stake here is the search to 'share with and care about another person without fear of losing oneself in the process' (Elkind, 1970).

Erikson's theory suggests that for each life stage struggle there are two possible outcomes. Where people adapt positively to the challenge a specific virtue is the developmental prize. In the sixth life stage the actual virtue is love. If on the other hand one maladapts to the challenge the outcome is less favourable – in this stage, an isolation of sorts. It is a common human experience to maladapt to life's challenges as much as adapt.

There will be an opportunity to focus in greater depth on Erikson (and other development theorists) in Chapter 12. First, it is important here to mention Erikson's concept of *moratorium*, a term which denotes a delay or pause given by our culture to young people in their late teens and early twenties before they take on more adult responsibilities.

Society sanctions this key transitional time, often coinciding with the university years, so a young adult can begin to search for what Erikson referred to as a 'compelling idea' (Erikson, 1975) to work towards. The thinking of Erikson here relates to that of the Danish philosopher Søren Kierkegaard who, like Erikson and many young adults, didn't find a rapid route-way to the centre or focus for his life. Even so, Kierkegaard argued for the need to discover an idea or 'life-view' to unreservedly identify oneself with (Gardiner, 1988).

Another, theorist Dan McAdams (1997), built his own thesis on Erikson's thinking and like Erikson is concerned essentially with identity development. However, the focus for McAdams was a person's creation of a life story. This McAdams suggests is a personal myth that an individual starts working on in late adolescence and young adulthood in order to give the individual a sense of his or her life having a unity and a purpose and to enable the individual to have a sense of place in the psychosocial world (Sugarman, 2001).

McAdams' thinking begins to raise the important issue of not only how we story our lives, but also the extent to which life narratives are a *self-creation* with its important implications for personal responsibility.

KEY CONCEPT – TRANSITION

Naomi Golan (1981) defines transition as 'a period of moving from one state of certainty to another, with an interval of uncertainty and change in between'. Starting at university is a huge transition for most students, often geographically and in other ways, leaving behind one way of life and venturing out in search of a new one that will consist of new patterns and new friendships. There is usually a period of great change and uncertainty in transitioning between the former and the new.

William Bridges in his book *Managing Transitions* (1995) speaks of three phases of transition:

- first, an ending
- second, a time in between the old and the new, which he calls the 'neutral zone'
- and third, a new beginning.

Transition he argues is a peculiarly 'psychological process people go through to come to terms with the new situation' (Bridges, 1995). The ending can easily feel like loss and often involves having to let go of something. The neutral zone is not a comfortable place and seems like 'limbo' – a 'nowhere between two somewheres' as Bridges puts it. Potentially, the neutral zone can leave people feeling lonely, isolated and unsure about what is happening to them. If your new university experience feels like this you are not alone or peculiar. As D. H. Lawrence puts it, 'the world fears a new experience more than it fears anything' (Lawrence, 2003). Give the process time, the limbo and its associated feelings are transitional.

Edmund Sherman (1987) usefully distinguishes between two types of strategy for coping with transition. The first of these is the *instrumental* strategy. This has to do with practical, concrete steps a person must take to come through to a new beginning. Bridges would argue that 'showing up' for events and other opportunities (both academic and social) is important, as is an attitude of 'being present' when one does show up.

The second of these strategies for coping with transition is the *expressive* strategy. Sherman says that this is about handling a whole range of emotions and feelings that might include anxiety, tension, fear, sadness, frustration and anger. It is important here to be honest with oneself and with others you can trust, about such thoughts and feelings. Good friends, family and the university counselling service can help here.

Sherman suggests the concurrent use of both instrumental and expressive strategies as the most effective way to transition to a new beginning. Given time and support the uncertainty gives way to a new pattern of living and friendships.

VIEWS OF HIGHER EDUCATION

Richard Tawney saw education as a kingdom of ideas in which all can participate (Tawney, 1931). Michael Oakeshott argues for student-centred critical conversation as a means of achieving higher learning.

Education should provide a place where conversation is explicitly given priority. The distinctive mark of a university, Oakeshott argues, is a place where the undergraduate 'has the opportunity of education in conversation with his teachers, his fellows and himself'. He calls this conversation an 'unrehearsed intellectual adventure' (Oakeshott, 1989).

Jonathan Sacks places this conversation in the context of the plurality and new tribalism that has emerged from globalization. Interestingly conversation is also at the heart of business in a globalized world. In his book *The Dignity of Difference* (2002), Sacks highlights a number of significances to good conversation:

- When respectful, engaged and reciprocal it creates the dignity of *difference*.
- It calls forth our greatest powers of empathy and understanding.
- It sustains overarching community in the face of difference.
- It demands that we open ourselves to others' stories, which may conflict with ours.
- Through listening, we may hear something that will help us face the dilemmas that confront us.

Robert Palmer argues for the importance of a holistic approach and environment for learning, seeing it not purely as an intellectual exercise but also as having emotional and spiritual dimensions. The emotional dimension recognises the importance of feelings in learning which will 'either enlarge or diminish' the exchange between students with teachers (Palmer, 2007). The development of consciousness and significant life meaning is encompassed by the spiritual dimension (Dowson and Robinson, 2009).

THE PURPOSE OF A UNIVERSITY

There is no question that in recent times universities have taken on more and more the character of a business organization. This of course makes a university of even more pertinent interest to business students who gain first-hand experience of and insight into a significant business organization. All the things that a business student is studying, whether business strategy or marketing or finance (and so forth), can be seen in the life of the university.

Alongside this reality as a business organization a university is an institution of learning, suggesting perhaps the existence of some sort of spectrum ranging from universities that have adopted a profit maximizing pragmatism all the way through to ones that see themselves as preservers and transmitters of all that is best in society's cultural traditions.

Commonly held purposes of a university, which are by no means mutually exclusive, include the following:

- creating and advancing knowledge through research
- passing on this knowledge through teaching
- transferring this knowledge to wider society including business
- transforming lives for the benefit of society.

In addition to these polymorphous purposes universities also embody powerful organizational values.

Relating to this is the more detailed examination of Ronald Barnett's (1990) general aims of higher education.

EMBODIMENT BOX – THE GENERAL AIMS OF HIGHER EDUCATION (RONALD BARNETT)

Ronald Barnett has been described as 'probably the foremost authority on the purpose of higher education in the UK' (Cowan, 2005). Below are listed his general aims of higher education (Barnett, 1990):

- the pursuit of truth and objective knowledge
- research – about the expansion of knowledge
- liberal education (see below)
- institutional autonomy
- academic freedom
- a neutral and open forum for debate
- rationality
- the development of the student's critical abilities
- the development of the student's autonomy
- the student's character formation
- providing a critical centre within society
- preserving society's intellectual culture.

In addition to his general aims Barnett focuses on the nature of a *higher* form of learning that is practised in higher education (Dowson and Robinson, 2009). This encompasses the development of higher-order thinking that involves: 'analysis, evaluation, criticism and even imagination' (White, 1997).

- An important piece of research is provided by Walter McMahon in his book *Higher Learning, Greater Good* (2009) about a major skills deficit in OECD countries owing to technical change and globalization.
- McMahon posits that the answer to this shortfall is what he terms *human capital formation* consisting of the acquisition of knowledge, skills and attributes demanded by knowledge-based economies subject to the intense competition that is central to globalization.
- Businesses are acutely aware, McMahon says, of skill deficiencies and the emerging mission of higher education is to respond to this shortfall. For students this has important implications.
- Firstly, students should seek to *embody* the new knowledge, including new technologies, by taking every opportunity at university to develop and absorb the new knowledge on offer. Skills particularly sought after, McMahon argues, include capacities to reason, to critically evaluate evidence, and to create new knowledge (through research). English and mathematics he adds are 'basic to other fields and vital to almost all jobs' (McMahon, 2009).
- Secondly, this involves a commitment to continually update knowledge, skills and attributes through continued learning and development through the life cycle in the workplace and in other contexts. McMahon's research suggests not only that those with lower skills earn less but also the emergence of a widening 'gap' in the fortunes of those embodying the new knowledge and those left behind.

WHAT IS A LIBERAL EDUCATION?

A clear statement of what is meant by a liberal education comes in Patrick Keeney's book *Liberalism, Communitarianism and Education: Reclaiming Liberal Education* (2007).

A liberal education is a somewhat 'polymorphous' concept but it is possible to pick out its strands. Firstly, it presupposes an ideal of civil association. The individual is being prepared to take their place in wider society and appropriate their public inheritance.

Secondly, a liberal education is bound up with the development of the mind and the acquisition of a worthwhile knowledge over and above or irrespective of any vocational end. Thirdly, this knowledge is intended to transform the entire outlook of the learner.

CHARACTER FORMATION

How do you respond to Ronald Barnett's notion that one of the general aims of higher education is character formation? Do you see this in a different light if you consider that it is one of the general aims of education as a whole?

As is highlighted by George Howie's book, *Aristotle on Education* (1968), this aspect of education has a very long history. Howie argues that education is 'concerned with the inner resources of individual persons' and that from the days of antiquity philosophers aspired to impart *wisdom*, which he differentiates from teaching subjects (Howie, 1968).

Aristotle's contribution to the philosophy of education in this area should not be underestimated. Below are outlined some of the hallmarks of his thinking in this area:

- Every living organism is working towards its self-actualization in line with its purpose (known as a teleological outlook).
- Potentialities latent in an organism are progressively realized (provided that they are not inhibited by the environment).
- People have the power to control their own development.
- The happiness of the individual is bound up with the happiness of others.
- Diversity rather than unity is the mark of meaningful community.
- Character emerges from natural endowment, from habit formation and from teaching.

EMBODIMENT BOX – CAN YOU MANUFACTURE GOOD CHARACTER?

An article by Richard Reeves (2008) in the BBC News magazine examines the issue of character – considering what shapes it and the political and cultural agendas in this area.

Firstly, Reeves says character is a 'loaded term' and that it sounds 'Victorian, judgemental' and even 'a bit dull'. Do you agree?

Secondly, perhaps it naturally leads us to thinking about good and bad character. What do you think about this way of categorizing people?

Thirdly, formative influences on character include 'our genes, our parents and our peers'. Can you detect these influences on your own character and can you think of any others?

Fourthly, if you accept that education has a role to play in character formation, how would you envisage a university teaching character?

Fifthly, in the same article Julia Margo suggests that character has become significantly more important to career opportunities and earnings. Does this adjust the way you view it?

Sixthly, confidence, responsibility and self-control are particularly valued in the workplace and beyond. How do you think university might help you forward in these areas?

A CONTEMPORARY BUSINESS SCHOOL

Piper, Gentile and Daloz Parks' (1993) title *Can Ethics Be Taught* provides an inside-out perspective on what's going on at one contemporary business school – Harvard. There are ten points here, all of which you should be able to observe in your own university business school.

1 In addition to helping students connect with their capacity for high achievement (reflected in career ambitions) the teaching staff are also seeking to support students in finding a sense of purpose and to forge connections between self and social issues – between self-realization and societal concerns.

2 At a time when increasing attention is being given to the social responsibility of business, a business education must necessarily focus not just on skills acquisition and development, but also on the attitudes and values of future businessmen and women.

3 Because the large corporation has become in the west the definitive contemporary institution in much the same way that the church dominated the medieval world, this effectively raises the bar for future business managers and for leadership and management training. Business schools are seeking to equip graduates for more complex and wider ranging management responsibilities.

4 This necessitates an enlarging of business school students' consciousness. Not just social consciousness, but consciousness of the complexity of business and business management in the twenty-first century. Managerial leadership, Daloz Parks argues, needs to be 'capable of engaging complex relationships among conflicting loyalties within a vision of the common good'.

5 Reflection (covered in Chapter 7) is at the heart of contending with this greater complexity. Students need to be able as future managers to see the benefit of pulling back from activity and observing what is happening and why. Students should be able to ask themselves, 'what am I doing here?' and 'what is it achieving?'

6 Daloz Parks speaks of a certain 'cultural insulation' which shows little awareness of anybody outside our own circle of people like us. Such insulation and individualism delimits the capacity to manage in a globalizing context where people are invariably not like us and often think quite differently.

7 This highlights the significance of the business environment with its social-economic-political fabric in which the contemporary business or corporation sits. A perspective that recognizes the interdependent complexity of the business environment is also called for.

8 The development of virtues, such as the formation of moral courage, is increasingly part of a business management education. That is, being enabled to act not only legally, but justly; not only defensibly, but compassionately; not only efficiently, but consistent with a moral vision.

9   Harvard sees the need for a cultivation of diverse perspectives grounded in a 'more empathic imagination'. The capacity for empathy is not about pity. It is an ability to see with, stand with and sometimes suffer with another – given less consciousness, you'd probably overlook them.

10 All these things lead to a broad way of approaching what is termed *business ethics* in a business school context encompassing not just individual values and the individual's role as future manager and decision maker, but also corporate purpose and responsibility, the complex and interrelated business environment and even comprehension of socio-political and economic systems.

ETHICS BOX – VALUES

Coicaud and Warner (2001) have identified three roles that values play in ethics.

1   Values define what is good versus bad and what is right versus wrong.
2   Values permit us to engage in 'ethical mapping' – differentiating principles we wish to abide by from courses of action to avoid.
3   Values permit people to better relate to themselves, to other people and to society at large.

University represents a time when you are given an early opportunity as an adult to think about, test and determine your values. A value might be defined as a tightly held belief upon which a person or an organization or a culture acts by choice. Or more simply, they reflect what people value.

Values can be divided into three categories:

Individual values are our private meanings reflected in an individual's actions, goals, relationships, personal possessions and preferences.

Cultural values are the values held by groups of people in families, organizations, professions and nations.

Universal values are the values that unite us all.

Values are expressed in all sorts of ways, but are particularly evident in the constant flow of decisions and choices people make – in how time is allocated, how money is spent, choices about home life and choices about work life.

Lore (1998) distinguishes between ideals, standards and work values.

Ideals are ultimate aims that people strive for and constitute a reference point pulling them towards a desired life for oneself and others.

Standards denote 'a level of performance or attainment used as a measure of adequacy' (Lore, 1998). They always contain a 'should'

(Continued)

(Continued)

and a judgement or conclusion as to whether the standard has been achieved.

Work values, Lore argues, may be quite different from values one applies to other areas of life. Their congruence with organizational values is significant.

Reivich and Shatté (2002) discuss the related concept of underlying beliefs which they see as deeply rooted and deeply held beliefs about how the world ought to operate and how you feel you ought to operate within that world. Many people they argue have underlying beliefs that fall into one of three categories as follows:

People who are achievement oriented

The underlying belief for this group is that success is the most important thing in life. It is given away in such comments as:

- 'I must never give up'
- 'Failure is a sign of weakness'
- 'Being successful is what matters most'

People in this category set very high standards for themselves and often protect those standards with an accompanying perfectionism.

People who are acceptance oriented

The underlying belief here is the need to be 'liked, accepted, praised and included by others'. If they voiced this they would be saying things like:

- 'I want people to think the best of me'
- 'What matters most in life is being loved'
- 'I must please people and make them happy'

Such people are often sensitive souls. They can jump to insecure conclusions and overreact in interpersonal dealings.

People who are control oriented

This group of people have an underlying belief about being in control or being in charge. They might say:

- 'Only weak people can't solve their own problems'
- 'Asking for help shows you can't cope'
- 'You must at all times remain in control'

Such people would tend to put lack of control down to personal failure.

Reivich and Shatté suggest the application of a cost–benefit ratio to ascertain how useful or harmful an underlying belief is to the individual. The following questions are relevant here:

- What is this belief costing me to sustain?
- How is it helping me?
- What adjustments can I make such that it costs me less and helps me more?

THE CONTEMPORARY CONTEXT

There are different ways of mapping history and labelling historical eras. In terms of western civilization, Jonathan Sacks (2002), for example, says that today we are living through the sixth universal order – global capitalism – which is essentially about the great significance of a number of institutions: the market, the media, multinational corporations and the internet. The five former orders were ancient Greece, ancient Rome, medieval Christianity, Islam, and the Enlightenment.

Alan Kirby (2006) cuts the cake in a different way and speaks (more recently) of romanticism, then modernism, then postmodernism, then post-postmodernism. Some undergraduates will already be familiar with these terms. If not, it is well worth taking some time to get to grips with what they describe – because this enables one to map the journey of different nations and to gain insight into where we are today and how different a world it is, particularly for young adults, from the one experienced by the same age group only a couple of generations ago.

Modernity

Modernity was a product of the Enlightenment and conceived the universe naturalistically (Naugle, 2002). This spelled the end of a preoccupation with the supernatural. Modernity was bound up with the scientific domination of nature which promised, according to Harvey, 'freedom from scarcity, want, and the arbitrariness of natural calamity' (Harvey, 1992).

Middleton and Walsh (1995) argue that modernity was founded on two grounding convictions:

- a mythic belief in progress
- the autonomous self's quest to understand and control the world.

Modernity displayed an extraordinary self-confidence and produced what Christopher Lasch (1984) describes as an 'imperial self'. An able summary of the spirit of the age of modernity is captured in the following quote:

Autonomous subjects, scientifically grasping and technologically controlling and transforming the world, unimpeded by threats such as tradition, ignorance and superstition, devise their own remedy ... This is the heart of modernity's historical self-confidence. (Middleton and Walsh, 1995)

The ultimate outworking of modernity was, however, inherently violent in a number of respects. The postmodern author Jean-Francois Lyotard famously remarked that modernity gave us 'as much terror as we can take' (Lyotard, 1984).

As Ziauddin Sarder has commented, modernity produced the Holocaust (Inayatullah and Boxwell, 2003) as well as other violence such as positing western civilization 'as the norm, the sole repository of truth, the yardstick by which all "others" are to be measured' (Inayatullah and Boxwell, 2003).

Postmodernism

Postmodernism was born out of disillusionment with modernity. It is a difficult phenomenon to pin down but the following authors cast light on its nature and shape.

Akbar Ahmed describes eight characteristics of postmodernism as follows:

1 Postmodernity assumes a loss of faith in the project of modernity. It embraces pluralism instead of totalising orthodoxies.
2 The media is the 'central dynamic' of postmodernity and shapes the way we see the world.
3 Ethno-religious revivalism or fundamentalism feeds on postmodernity.
4 Postmodernity remains connected to modernity.
5 The metropolis is central to postmodernity.
6 The postmodern project is driven by those with access to the media and to means of communication.
7 Postmodernity celebrates hybridity – the mixing and mingling of styles and ideas.
8 Although postmodernity sees itself as self-explanatory its language is often paradoxical and enigmatic.

The writer and designer David McCandless in his book *Information Is Beautiful* (2012) presents an alternative perspective on postmodernism, which is useful to place alongside that of Akbar Ahmed's. McCandless' characteristics include:

Embracing complexity – as well as 'contradiction, ambiguity, diversity, interconnectedness and criss-crossing referentiality'.

Truth as assembled – or constructed, not as a single thing 'out there' to be discovered.

Resisting 'order' – which in modernism did violence to difference and excluded those different from the norm.

'Mini-narratives' – are embraced. Grand narratives are rejected. The small story can reflect the global pattern of things.

Interconnectedness – reflected in our technology and communications.

Self-expression – as well as participation and creativity are postmodern personal values.

A couple of Sardar's observations (Inayatullah and Boxwell, 2003) complete our overview here of postmodernity. Firstly, because of its rejection of all grand systems of thought, Sardar argues, postmodernism effectively dismantled all the dominant value and ethical systems, leaving in place a vacuum.

Secondly, whereas modernism marginalized, even oppressed all non-western cultures, postmodernism, Sardar says, opened 'the door for their re-entry into humanity and rejoices in the diversity and plurality of ethnic cultures' (Inayatullah and Boxwell, 2003).

Late or 'liquid' modernity

Particularly since 9/11 (Hall, 2009; Kirby, 2006) the sense has been one of transition to a new age, beyond postmodernism. This has caused key thinkers in the area to speak of the current age as late or 'liquid' modernity (Bauman, 2000).

Richard Middleton's (2012) penetrative observation about late modernity is that it constitutes 'a culture which has lost the mythic rootedness in the modern metanarrative, but which still exhibits a great deal of continuity with the modern'. Here Middleton argues that late modernity has given up its overarching faith in progress but holds onto the autonomous self's quest to understand and control the world with a vengeance.

Zygmunt Bauman adopts the primary metaphor of liquid to describe this transitional time. Young people, he argues, want to keep their options open rather than settle their loyalties like former generations. This avoidance of fixation expresses itself in all sorts of ways including marriage, employment, faith systems and consumerism (Bauman, 2000).

Bauman speaks of two distinctive features of liquid modernity. Firstly, that this is a time of anxiousness. Uncertainty is everywhere, which makes looking beyond the challenges of the now a difficult, some would even say a futile, task (Bauman, 2008). Secondly, this is very much a consumerist time where happiness is sought in the great turnover of commodities, encompassing not only their creation and acquisition, but also their disposal (Bauman, 2008).

It is more difficult to define who are the quintessential late modernists. For Kirby (2006) the essential generation gap roughly separates those born before and after 1980. Those born post-1980, Kirby argues, might see their peers as 'free, autonomous, inventive, expressive, dynamic, empowered, independent, their voices unique, raised and heard'. Those born pre-1980 will view contemporary texts (not the people who generate them) as 'alternately violent, pornographic, unreal, trite, vapid, conformist, consumerist, meaningless and brainless'.

The cultural phenomenon par excellence of late modernity is the internet (Kirby, 2006), consisting of a self-determined journey through a pathway of cultural products. This also allows for a certain *hybridity* (Bauman, 2008), which is a distinctive feature of late modernity giving the individual the sense that they are creating, combining and managing their involvement with the cultural product. It is intrinsic to the internet, Kirby argues, that 'you can easily make up pages yourself (e.g. blogs)'.

Kirby also highlights the triteness and shallowness of this transitional period. A piece of communication is often exceptionally brief by historical standards and this invites his comment that the era of late modernity amounts to a 'cultural desert' (Kirby, 2006).

CASE STUDY – A YOUNG ADULT'S PERSPECTIVE

On deferred responsibility

'Youth is protracted and responsibility (including marriage, mortgage, etc.) is deferred. *NOT NOW.*'

'The situation is linked to finances. Many young adults have returned (following Uni) to living with their parents. There is a message to young adults saying "*go home*".'

'Living back at home generates new issues and challenges for both parents and their children. The (old) family dynamic has changed.'

'Adults are treated like children, but they're not contributing as they might – a confused dynamic.'

The (only) thing to do

'School leavers and young adults feel they have to go to Uni – not only job-wise but also socially. It's the thing to do.'

Anxiety surrounding jobs

'There is anxiety surrounding job pathways. Many friends have opted for deskilled jobs.'

Living in the now

'This generation is living for the now.'

'This generation is disillusioned with authority and kicking against it in many respects – but it is not disillusioned with consumerism and leisure pursuits.'

'This consumption is narcotic.'

THE POSTMODERN UNIVERSITY

Perhaps the best statement of the place of a university in our contemporary and postmodern context is provided by Ronald Barnett (2009). For Barnett, our pluralist world finds its echo in higher education, resulting in what he describes as the 'age of the ethical university'. It is worth spending some time deconstructing Barnett's claim because it will cast light upon some of the things you will see at work in your own university.

Firstly, Barnett argues that universities have a history of concern for the 'other' written into their life as institutions and reflected in their key activities. This makes them inherently ethical. This is not to deny what may be termed as an 'instrumental' counter force at work, effectively combatting the significance of ethics.

Secondly, Barnett adds that this conflict is always at the heart of the aim to be an 'authentic university'. Like an individual or business organization that seeks to be authentic, this does not imply that it always succeeds in this and doesn't fall short of its own standards. Rather to be authentic is to keep trying to live out its chosen ethical virtues. Authenticity is evident not in following ethical rules, but in its people being generous and hospitable to one another and embodying an ethical way of living and behaving.

Thirdly, there are some who say that a more market-driven university sector will put the squeeze on ethics, however, Barnett argues that the neo-liberal world with its multiple income streams brings autonomies and choices to the university that its predecessors did not enjoy.

Fourthly, because of the multiple stakeholders that form the life of a contemporary university, representing between them contrasting and even opposed points of view, a university must handle what Barnett calls this supersaturation with values. This value complexity actually enables the university to be ethical.

Fifthly, a university therefore becomes, as Barnett puts it, 'a space in which difference is played out', which makes it a 'supremely tolerant institution'. It therefore has the potential, in postmodern society, to model a way of operating that individuals can learn from and take as future managers and leaders into business organizations.

Sixthly, Barnett leaves us with four key concepts that flow out of this notion of the ethical university:

- the formation of 'virtue' among students (and staff)
- the idea of community in academic life
- the significance of dialogue
- the aim of excellence in the ethical development of students.

DEVELOPMENT POINTER – VALUES EXERCISES

From the following 15 values commonly shared by many people pick out the
five you rank most highly. State why you have selected them.

Compassion	Respect for elders
Devotion	Responsibility
Fairness	Reverence for life
Freedom	Self-respect
Generosity	Social harmony
Honour	Tolerance
Humility	Truth
Preservation of nature	Any others

Think about the charities that you like to support and follow or where you
might potentially volunteer. How do they reflect your values?

APPLIED PERSONAL DEVELOPMENT

We started the chapter by looking at the issue of why you came to university.
Here you could be anywhere on the spectrum from not really having given the
matter much thought, all the way through to having definite ideas about why
you wanted to come to university and what you're hoping to achieve. The
critical point is that there is a lot more to universities as organizations and in
terms of their purpose than one could appreciate until you become a part of the
university and a member of its learning community.

This of course puts the onus on what you make of university now that you
have started this new chapter in your life. And of course there is no reason why
you can't make more of some aspect of it that you hardly even knew about
before you arrived.

Look upon starting at university as a rehearsal for starting in any organization –
for example, your first graduate job. Give yourself some time to find your
feet. Appreciate that every organization has its own character and culture.
Where possible, try not to adopt a peripheral (on the margins) positioning in
relation to all that is going on in your school or department, both academically

and socially. It's a good idea to 'opt in' rather than 'opt out'. The same applies in the workplace.

I utilized the words 'moratorium' and 'transition' to communicate that university provides you with a bit of space to work out what you want out of life and that university is often the first of a number of significant transitions in one's adult life. Both these notions are positive and provide you, the individual, with opportunities – opportunities to learn and develop as a person and to make good decisions. University is an adventure and most young adults would value this opportunity that you have secured.

We spent some time locating ourselves in late modernity as it is termed. We learned through this that you are likely to look upon life in a different way from how a parent might have looked upon it at your stage. There is not only a historical and generational issue here, but also a geographical one and students from different parts of the world arrive at university with very different life experiences of where they call 'home'. Difference is at the heart of the university experience and you have a further opportunity to handle differences responsibly. This is a fantastic preparation for an interrelating world of differences, not just culturally but also commercially (in business).

The development of criticality is important, as is conversation. Learn to develop your listening as well as speaking skills and, as Harvard has underlined, try to break out of what it describes as 'cultural insulation' – which is a defensive posturing in the face of diversity.

Differences apply to all and we saw when looking at values that people are oriented in different ways. It is essential to comprehend this if you aspire to be a good manager. People are variously motivated and it takes skill and an astute quality to get the best out of everyone in a team context.

REFERENCES

Barnett, R. (2009) 'The postmodern university: prospects of the ethical', in J. Strain, R. Barnett and P. Jarvis (eds), *Universities, Ethics and Professions: Debate and Scrutiny*. London: Routledge.

Barnett, R. (1990) *The Idea of Higher Education*. Buckingham: Open University Press.

Bauman, Z. (2008) *Does Ethics Have a Chance in a World of Consumers?* Cambridge, MA: Harvard University Press.

Bauman, Z. (2000) *Liquid Modernity*. Cambridge: Polity Press.

Boeree, C. G. (2006) 'Erik Erikson 1902–1994'. Available at: http://webspace.ship.edu/cgboer/erikson.html (accessed 5 June 2013).

Bridges, W. (1995) *Managing Transitions: Making the Most of Change*. London: Nicholas Brealey Publishing.

Coicaud, J. and Warner, D. (2001) *Ethics and International Affairs: Extent and Limits*. Tokyo: United Nations University Press.

Cowan, J. (2005) 'Atrophy of the affect in academia or what next, after 40 years in the wilderness', in S. Robinson and C. Katulushi (eds), *Values in Higher Education*. St Bride's Major: Aureus Publishing.

Dowson, P. and Robinson S. (2009) 'Higher education, personal development and coaching', *Annual Review of High Performance Coaching and Consulting*. Hockley: Multi-Science Publishing.

Elkind, D. (1970) 'Erik Erikson's eight ages of man'. Available at: www.pdx.edu/sites/www.pdx.edu.ceed/files/sscbt_EriksonsEightAgesofMan.pdf (accessed 5 June 2013).

Erikson, E. H. (1975) *Life History and Historical Moment*. New York: W. W. Norton & Co.

Friedman, L. J. (2000) *Identity's Architect: A Biography of Erik H. Erikson*. Cambridge, MA: Harvard University Press.

Gardiner, P. (1988) *Kierkegaard*. Oxford: Oxford University Press.

Golan, N. (1981) *Passing Through Transitions: A Guide for Practitioners*. New York: Free Press.

Hall, J. R. (2009) *Apocalypse: From Antiquity to the Empire of Modernity*. Cambridge: Polity Press.

Harvey, D. (1992) *The Condition of Postmodernity*. Oxford: Blackwell.

Howie, G. (1968) *Aristotle on Education*. London: Collier Macmillan.

Inayatullah, S. and Boxwell, G. (eds) (2003) *Islam, Postmodernism and Other Futures: A Ziauddin Sardar Reader*. London: Pluto Press.

Keeney, P. (2007) *Liberalism, Communitarianism and Education: Reclaiming Liberal Education*. Aldershot: Ashgate.

Kirby, A. (2006) 'The death of postmodernism and beyond', *Philosophy Now*. Available at: http://philosophynow.org/issues/58/The_Death_of_Postmodernism_And_Beyond (accessed 2 June 2013).

Lasch, C. (1984) *The Minimal Self: Psychic Survival in Troubled Times*. New York: W. W. Norton & Co.

Lawrence, D. H. (2003) *Studies in Classic American Literature*. Cambridge: Cambridge University Press.

Lore, N. (1998) *The Pathfinder*. New York: Simon & Schuster.

Lyotard, J. (1984) *The Postmodern Condition: A Report on Knowledge, Theory and History of Literature*. Minneapolis: University of Minnesota Press.

McAdams, D. (1997) *The Stories We Live By: Personal Myths and the Making of the Self*. New York: Guildford Press.

McCandless, D. (2012) *Information Is Beautiful*. London: Collins.

McMahon, W. W. (2009) *Higher Learning, Greater Good: The Private and Social Benefits of Higher Education*. Baltimore: The John Hopkins University Press.

Middleton, J. R. (2012) Email to Paul Dowson, 10 April.

Middleton, J. R. and Walsh, B. J. (1995) *Truth Is Stranger Than It Used to Be: Biblical Faith in a Postmodern Age*. London: SPCK.

Naugle, D. K. (2002) *Worldview: The History of a Concept*. Grand Rapids: William B. Eerdmans.

Oakeshott, M. J. (1989) *The Voice of Liberal Learning*. New Haven, CT: Yale University.

Palmer, P. J. (2007) *The Courage to Teach: Exploring the Inner Landscape of a Teacher's Life*. San Francisco: Jossey Bass.

Piper, T. R., Gentile, M. C. and Daloz Parks, S. (1993) *Can Ethics Be Taught*. Boston: Harvard Business School.

Reeves, R. (2008) 'Can you manufacture good character?', BBC News magazine, 9 July. Available at: http://news.bbc.co.uk/1/hi/magazine/7497081.stm (accessed 6 June 2013).

Reivich, K. and Shatté, A. (2002) *The Resilience Factor*. New York: Broadway Books.

Sacks, J. (2002) *The Dignity of Difference: How to Avoid the Clash of Civilizations*. London: Continuum

Sherman, E. (1987) *Meaning in Mid-life Transitions*. New York: State University of New York Press.

Spencer, D. (2008) 'Global: learning tribes and the new youth market', *University World News*, 30 March, 21. Available at: www.universityworldnews.com/article. php?story=20080327105946510 (accessed 6 June 2013).

Sugarman, L. (2001) *Life-span Development: Frameworks, Accounts and Strategies*. Hove: Psychology Press.

Tawney, R. H. (1931) *Equality*. London: Allen and Unwin.

White, J. (1997) 'Philosophy and the aim of higher education', *Studies in Higher Education*, 22 (1): 7–19.

3 AN A TO Z OF SKILLS DEVELOPMENT

A NOTE FROM THE AUTHOR

A key term in the vocabulary of a recruiting employer is the word *skills*. It is not difficult to work out that employers want a plurality of skills – and that they are on the lookout for so called 'higher-order' skills when employing graduates. Strangely, students are often not as deliberate as they could be about seeing university as an opportunity to upskill and consciously seize every opportunity to develop a marketable skills set sought by employers. To assist with the planning and process of skills development universities offer personal development planning in some form or another.

Skills development at university is a huge subject and the next couple of chapters are dedicated to this. In this chapter I am hoping to differentiate between skills and strengths, which are often grouped together. The A to Z provides a panorama of the many skills that one can develop. We will also take a look at some specific skills and how they are grouped.

Finally, along with skills another word that will pop up more and more at university and beyond is self-awareness. Tristine Rainer, in her book *The New Diary* (1979), rightly presents this as a far from straightforward path of development. Seeing ourselves in our entirety with clarity is a continuing journey. However, of all the things to recognize in oneself perhaps the easiest dimension of us to grasp fairly quickly is our skills set. Even here, however, we must view ourselves fairly and realistically.

Learning outcomes

When you have completed this chapter you will be able to:

- define and identify skills
- comprehend how skills relate to personal development planning and employability

- understand the significance of teamworking skills including team roles
- define critical thinking and independent learning skills
- summarize how to prepare for a presentation.

THE NEXT TRANSITION

In the last chapter we introduced the concept of transition and particularly focused on the transition of arriving at university. However, in the space of just a few years there will be yet another transition as graduation leads to other significant changes. This may involve moving. Most will hope it leads to desired job opportunities. This may of course take time and that's part of the transition process.

In Lisa Perrone and Margaret Vickers (2003) Australian case study, 'Life after graduation', there is a little phrase tucked away at the back of their article – speaking of the likelihood of 'student procrastination'. This is the notion of putting off doing something or looking at something now, when it can be left until later. This particularly applies to the notion of working towards one's future and one's career when frankly there are other things to occupy one's time and thinking. This book will try to persuade students not to procrastinate about their futures, but to build into university life elements that permit engagement with such matters without taking away from other areas which it recognizes may currently have a higher priority.

Perrone and Vickers add a number of poignant points all of which are worth taking note of and can be summarized as follows:

- They speak of the university years as a significant life transition that for various reasons is underestimated.
- Organizational downsizing, delayering and outsourcing combined with a much larger supply of graduates often pushes students into work outside graduate occupational destinations.
- Relevant business and work experience while at university is an important factor recruiters look for in graduates. One student responded that he would have been better placed with this experience, paid or even *unpaid*.

As far as skills are concerned the article suggests that the development of effective learning, language and communication skills were most highly sought after by employers.

This article accords with another by Geoff Mason (2002) where the theme is high skills utilization under *mass* higher education – the latter denoting the high proportion of people now attending university. Mason speaks of the higher levels of employer demand for the analytical and communications skills associated with the possession of a degree. Added to this he highlights a confluence between the growth of project-type working in the employment market and the kinds of skills students are developing at university – 'problem solving, highly numerate, able to articulate thoughts well on paper' (Mason, 2002). He also adds critical thinking, data gathering and analysis.

SKILLS CENTRICITY

One tends to hear more about the *skills* employers are seeking in graduates than any other single thing, including a student's knowledge, strengths, competencies, talents and even character. With this in mind we are going to start with an in-depth overview of the skills particularly valued by employing organizations.

First of all, it is important to define what we mean by skills and then unpick these from the related entities of strengths, competencies and talents, which along with knowledge and character constitute much of what a student is offering any potential employer.

A skill may be defined as 'an ability to do an activity or job well, especially because you have practised it' (*Cambridge Advanced Learners Dictionary*). Alternatively, I've defined a skill as 'something you learn to do, which can be improved or developed so you become *good at it* through practice and experience'.

Skills should be differentiated from strengths, which are covered in Chapter 5 which will highlight the key resource of Strengths Finder 2.0 by Tom Rath. A strength is closer to a capacity than an ability and it provides a potential for effective action. Strengths are bound up with character and attitude.

Ellis speaks of competencies being a 'package of skills, knowledge and values' (Ellis, 1989). Competencies are central to professionalism, both of which we shall cover in Chapter 5.

Finally, a talent can be defined as an innate or 'God given' ability that allows you to do something well. Talents are central to individual identity but critically are not chosen.

Turning now to concentrating on skills, there are a number of preliminaries we should cover relating to the importance of what is often referred to as skills acquisition at university.

Firstly, university provides ample opportunity to acquire and develop new skills. It is better that students approach skills acquisition intentionally and develop a strategy through PDP for acquiring and developing specific skills. At the same time, full engagement with your university course and studies, supplemented by part-time employment, volunteering and activity in university societies all can lead to skills acquisition.

Secondly, skills acquisition and development is not just something young adults are engaged with at university. This is a priority for working people of all ages and is a concern that continues throughout working life. Related to this, the pace of change necessitates that people continually update their skills offering. Even the proverbial 'old dog' is required to develop so called 'new tricks'.

Thirdly, certain skills are more highly prized and therefore more marketable than others. Again, this highlights the importance of setting out to acquire certain skills in a deliberate fashion.

Fourthly, employers speak of a mismatch between the skills they need and what graduates often offer. This is even referred to as a 'skills gap' and implies that students who set out to develop the skills most wanted by employers will be best placed to secure employment opportunities.

Fifthly, it is almost as important to profile and evidence a skills offering in your CV, job applications and social media (such as LinkedIn) as it is to have skills.

SKILLS ACQUISITION

Skills acquisition is a three stage process consisting of skills analysis, skills match/identification and skills training.

Skills analysis

This involves an honest and critical evaluation of one's current skills offering or profile. We must get beyond a *tick-box* approach to skills. This would be the equivalent of ticking a box entitled 'Tennis Skills'. Yes, you may play tennis, but the key here is to what standard and also the profile of your tennis skills broken down into forehand, backhand, serve, agility and so forth.

Some good questions to ask oneself here are:

- What skills have I acquired and to what level of standard?
- Looking at specific skills, how might I further develop these?
- What skills strategic to my future and my development are underdeveloped?

Skills match/identification

A second part of the process is placing one's current skills offering or profile alongside one that would be required for a target career opportunity or simply a personal skills-centred development target. For example, you might want to develop people management skills as an integral element of your career choice; or it may be that you want to further your skills in a particular language whether or not this coincides with a career aim. Updating one's skills is ever a professional issue and here you may ask:

- Which skills and what kind of expertise will in the future be required in my area of interest?

Skills training

This is the third aspect of the process and requires that you appropriate a given skills training opportunity. This might be embedded as part of your university course and learning or it may involve a discrete training opportunity. For those students with part-time jobs or volunteering responsibilities these all constitute possible ways to be trained in skills development.

PERSONAL DEVELOPMENT PLANNING (PDP)

Personal development planning is 'a structured and supported process undertaken by individuals to reflect upon their own learning, performance and/or achievement and to plan for their personal, educational and career development' (Quality Assurance Agency, 2009).

PDP forms an intrinsic part of UK higher education and other nations have their own equivalents. It is intended to equip students in a number of areas including the following:

- becoming more effective and self-directed (independent) learners
- relating their learning to a wider context
- improving their study and career management skills
- formulating personal goals and evaluating progress.

The ideas that underpin these conceptions according to Norman Jackson (2001) mean that PDP is:

- integral to *higher* level learning
- concerned with all aspects of learning
- supported with a view to it becoming self-sustaining
- a process involving reflection as well as planning, recording and monitoring of progress towards the achievement of personal objectives
- intended to facilitate the capacity of individuals to communicate their learning to others.

Although PDP focuses very much on skills development, Valerie Metcalfe writes that 'actual skills development is ... determined on an individual level and influenced by the opportunities and experiences of learning found in specific course programmes, stand alone and linked modules as well as co and extra-curricular activities' (University of Westminster, 2006).

SKILLS SWOT ANALYSIS

A simple way to get started along the path of skills acquisition is to do a SWOT (strengths, weaknesses, opportunities and threats) analysis.

The suggestion would be to give yourself plenty of paper space and write down your answers to the four questions in Table 3.1. Remember the importance of *accurate* assessment, avoiding the twin errors of underestimating and overestimating one's skills offering and opportunities/threats.

Table 3.1 Skills SWOT analysis

Where do your present **strengths** in skills lie?	What are your **weaknesses** in terms of skills?
What **opportunities** do you have to develop skills?	What **threats** are presented to you by your current skills offering?

AN A TO Z OVERVIEW

You've probably never seen an A to Z of skills before. There are a surprising number of personal and professional skills, all having value in different contexts, as shown in Table 3.2.

Table 3.2 An A to Z of skills

A	Accounting skills	
	Action planning skills	
	Advisory skills	
	Analytical skills	
	Skills of appearance	An aspect of presentation
	Skills of appraisal	
	Artistic skills	
	Assertiveness	
B	Business skills	
C	Caring skills	
	Chairing skills	
	Change management skills	
	Clarifying skills	
	Coaching skills	
	Cognitive skills	
	Comedic skills	
	Commercial awareness	
	Communication skills	
	Concentration skills	
	Conflict-prevention/resolution skills	
	Confrontational skills	
	Consultation skills	
	Coordination skills	
	Counselling skills	
	Creative thinking skills	
	Critical thinking skills	'Criticality'
	Cultural awareness	
	Customer-focused/customer service skills	

(Continued)

Table 3.2 (Continued)

D	Data collection skills Decision-making skills Delegation skills Design skills Dialogue skills Diplomacy skills	
E	Editing skills Empathic skills Employability skills Engagement skills Enterprise skills Entrepreneurship skills Essay-writing skills Evaluative skills	
F	Financial management Flexibility skills Focusing skills Friendship skills Fund-raising skills	Not subject to procrastination and distraction
G	Goal-setting skills Group skills Guidance skills	
H		
I	ICT skills Impacting skills Skills of influence Influencing skills Initiating skills Skills of using initiative Inspection skills Skills of the intellect Interactive skills Interpersonal skills Interview skills	
J	Job search skills Skills of judgement	
K		
L	Language skills Leadership skills Learning skills Library skills Listening skills	Highly prized, encompasses command skills To be a skilled listener; highly prized – late modernity
M	Management skills Marketing skills Mediation skills Meeting skills Meeting and greeting skills Mechanical skills Mentoring skills Musical skills	Highly prized

N	Negotiating skills	
	Networking skills	Highly prized – late
	Note-making skills	modernity
	Numeracy skills	
O	Oral communication skills	Highly prized and
	Organizational skills	transferable
		Highly transferable
P	Pastoral skills	
	People skills	
	Personal management skills	
	Persuasive skills	
	Skills of persuasion	
	Photographic skills	
	Planning skills	
	Political awareness	
	Presentation skills	
	Problem-solving skills	
	Professional skills	
	Project management	
	Public relations skills	
Q	Querying skills	
R	Reading skills	
	Recording skills	
	Reflective skills	
	Relationship skills	
	Report-writing skills	
	Research and investigative skills	
	Resource management	
	Recruiting skills	
	Reviewing skills	
S	Self-awareness skills	
	Self-development skills	
	Self-management skills	
	Self-marketing skills	
	Self-promotion skills	
	Selling skills	
	Social skills	
	Soft skills	
	Specialist skills	
	Strategic management skills	
	Study skills	
	Stress management skills	
	Supervisory skills	
	Supporting skills	
	Staff development skills	
T	Teaching skills	
	Team-working skills	
	Team leadership skills	
	Technical skills	
	Telephone skills	
	Time management skills	
	Training skills	

(Continued)

Table 3.2 (Continued)

U		
V	Vision-making skills	Highly prized
W	Work-related skills	
	Writing skills	Including spelling and grammar
X		
Y		
Z		

SKILLS CLASSIFICATION AND GROUPING

There are various ways of classifying and grouping this extensive list of skills. Table 3.3 compares three example groups of skills.

Table 3.3 Comparison of three example groups of skills

Houghton (2005)	Windmills (2004)	University of Westminster (2006)
• Organization	• People	• People
• People	• Processing	• Learning and study
• Personal strengths	• Enterprise	• Self-management
• Analytical	• Practical	• Professional working
• Practical/physical	• Exploring	
• Intuition/innovation/ creativity	• Creative	

A couple of things emerge from this comparison. Firstly, the overlap between the different frameworks. And secondly, that it is very difficult to meaningfully sweep up all the skills into just a few groups.

Table 3.4 University of Westminster's four skills model

People skills and attributes	Learning and study skills and attributes
• Group working	• Problem solving
• Leadership	• Information literacy
• Group effectiveness	• Management of information quality of work
• Working with others	• Research techniques
• Communication	• Writing skills
• Others relating to this area	
Self-management skills and attributes	**Professional working skills and attributes**
• Self-evaluation	• Ethics
• Autonomy	• Law
• Time management	• Systems
• Focus on task	• Professional bodies
	• Other considerations

We are going to adopt the University of Westminster's four dimensional and interrelated skills model here because it offers four simple building blocks of success for graduate employability. It is presented as a quadrant in Table 3.4.

ACTION PLANNING SKILLS

Action plans form an integral part of personal development planning as indeed they do in any form of planning. They are not complicated to understand. The art to them is rather how to usefully complete an action plan and to implement the plan through action. They usually consist of three to five columns headed aims, action, support/resources, timescales/dates and comments/review.

Table 3.5 Example action plan

Aims/Goals	Action	Support/ Resources	Timescales/ Dates	Comments/ Review
1	a	a	a	a
	b	b	b	b
	c	c	c	c
2	a	a	a	a
	b	b	b	b
	c	c	c	c

For every action plan there are a number of aims or goals (the example in Table 3.5 for illustrative purposes has two). This states what one is aiming for or what one intends to achieve (expressed as goals).

For every aim or goal this in turn is broken down into a number of actions. In the example action plan in Table 3.5 there are three (a, b and c) for each aim.

For every action, as the example shows, there is its own support/resources detail and its own timescale.

EMPLOYABILITY FOCUS – EMPLOYABILITY SKILLS

Graduate employability is about developing the necessary skills, attributes and experiences to secure suitable and rewarding employment. A questionnaire devised by Ray Wolfenden, as part of the Skills *plus* project, identified 39 aspects to employability divided into core skills (12), process skills (17) and personal attributes (10) (Higher Education Academy, 2000).

As a package of things that characterize the employable graduate we might include:

(Continued)

(Continued)

- self-knowledge and awareness
- ability to reflect on experience
- an all-round ability to communicate
- accompanying work and volunteering experience
- self-starting and self-reliance
- personal development planning
- career and professional development skills
- enterprise skills, both personal and professional

Distilling this into employability *skills* as such, will result in a list like this one:

- analytical
- assertiveness
- communication
- critical and reflective ability
- decision making
- flexibility and adaptability
- interpersonal
- learning skills
- lifelong learning
- networking
- problem solving
- taking responsibility
- teamworking

The Bradford NHS Care Trust produced an employability summary sheet entitled *People who are paid to work with us*, which has three elements. Following 'we want someone who' it lists:

- is down to earth
- is happy
- gives you a pat on the back
- looks nice
- gives you choice
- is trustworthy

Under 'important things to think about when supporting people' it includes:

- caring
- to listen
- being helpful
- understanding
- looking after each other
- common sense
- has some fun with me
- respects
- to work as a team member

Under 'talking to people …' it says:

- good manners
- praise
- to have a good attitude
- be pleasant
- sense of humour
- say 'please' and 'thank you'

Reflecting on this section it is clear employability is a wide-ranging concept and overall a big ask. It isn't always meaningful to separate skills out from attributes – the two interrelate and a positive attitude enlivens any skill.

TEAMWORKING SKILLS

One distinctive aspect of the workplace is working in teams. This contrasts with a more individualistic emphasis often created by schools. At university there are more and more opportunities to learn and be assessed in teams. Added to this, a business or management degree often includes input on understanding teams.

Three things are immediately evident about working in teams:

Synergy – teams can produce a quantity and quality of work far higher than the sum of what the individuals would have produced on their own.

Span of skills – the skills that are called for in successful organizations can be found within a balanced team. Successful teams are not collections of similar people. They contain people with a mixture of skills and qualities.

Team roles – different people, sometimes by choice and sometimes automatically, adopt a variety of roles when working in a team.

Belbin's team roles

Belbin's (2004) team roles (as follows) are all positive.

- Implementer

  - translates plans into action
  - systematic in approach
  - meets targets
  - practically supportive

- Coordinator

  - controls and organizes activities
  - makes use of resources
  - encouraging in style
  - delegates well and effectively

- Shaper

  - gives shape to group efforts
  - keeps team on track
  - able to unite ideas
  - results oriented

- The plant

  - prime source of ideas
  - refreshes team discussion

- creative orientation
- most effective when self-disciplined

- Resource investigator

  - brings in outside resources and contacts
  - positive influence on team relationships
  - sociable in orientation
  - can get too involved with their own ideas

- Monitor-evaluator

  - evaluates feasibility against objectives
  - critical thinking ability evident
  - can build on others' suggestions
  - fair-minded and practical

- Completer

  - ensures nothing is overlooked
  - an eye for mistakes and weaknesses
  - maintains standards
  - can be nervously driven

- Teamworker

  - affirms and supports others
  - improves communication across team
  - a helpful influence
  - fills gaps in team weakness

- Specialist

  - self-regulating
  - responds to team appreciation
  - motivated by respect
  - offers rare skills

Benne and Sheats' team roles

Another framework from Benne and Sheats (2007) divides roles into personal and social roles, task roles and dysfunctional roles.

- Personal and social roles

  - *Encourager* – affirms and supports others, maintains a positive attitude.
  - *Harmonizer* – helps keep the peace, sometimes uses humour to diffuse tension.

- ○ *Compromiser* – gives in for the sake of the group's progress, will meet others half-way.
- ○ *Gatekeeper/expediter* – keeps communications open, encourages participation from all.
- ○ *Observer/commentator* – provides helpful and timely feedback to the group about how it is functioning.
- ○ *Follower* – more of a listener than a contributor, will go along with the group's decision.

- Task roles

  - ○ *Initiator/contributor* – proposes new or different ideas for discussion and approaches to problems.
  - ○ *Information seeker* – seeks expert information and facts, comments on missing information.
  - ○ *Information giver* – a source of factual information to the group, an authority on their subject.
  - ○ *Opinion seeker* – encourages different perspectives, interested in the opinions and values of others.
  - ○ *Opinion giver* – doesn't hold back from giving their own opinions, sometimes with 'shoulds'.
  - ○ *Elaborator* – builds on others' contributions, also good at seeing consequences.
  - ○ *Coordinator* – gathers things together, sees the relationship between different contributions.
  - ○ *Orienter* – maps the group's progress, sensitive to where the group is losing its course.
  - ○ *Evaluator/critic* – can evaluate a group's progress or decision making and its reasonableness.
  - ○ *Energizer* – injects energy into group meetings and processes, a stimulating and challenging influence.
  - ○ *Procedural technician* – displays logistical strengths and concerns.
  - ○ *Recorder* – acts as secretary to the group, recording discussion and decisions.

- Dysfunctional roles

  - ○ *Aggressor* – criticizes and puts down others, an aggressive and belittling influence.
  - ○ *Blocker* – resists the ideas and contributions of others, without offering constructive points of their own.
  - ○ *Recognition seeker* – adopts a range of tactics to gain attention and derails progress.
  - ○ *Self-confessor* – uses meetings to air their own issues and feelings.
  - ○ *Disrupter* – seeks fun, sometimes to avoid work, irrelevant and disruptive content is a speciality.

- *Dominator* – assumes control and sees themselves as the authority on the topic in question.
- *Help seeker* – expresses inadequacy and helplessness stemming from a weak self-regard.
- *Special-interest pleader* – makes their own suggestions based on what others supposedly think or feel.

Teamworking considerations

The following questions should be considered when working in teams for university assignments and activities. This is followed by the characteristics of an effective team.

Strategy

How are teams increasingly important in learning and completing assignments?

Do you know other team members' strengths and weaknesses?

Leadership

Have you appointed a team leader?

Are you permitting and enabling the person to fulfil the role?

Role clarity

Is everyone clear about what his or her role is?

Does everyone in the team understand everybody else's role?

Achievable targets

Does everyone have targets to achieve and are they happy about them?

Do the targets of various members of the team stem from the overall targets of the group?

Issues

Are there any issues to resolve?

How can these be resolved in the interests of both the individuals and the team?

Ten characteristics of an effective team

1 The purpose is clear.
2 There is role clarity.
3 Team members support, respect and trust one another.
4 When conflict occurs it is managed and resolved.
5 There is open and effective communication.

6 Performance is targeted, recognized and reviewed.
7 Team members get feedback.
8 Team time is well spent (rather than wasted).
9 There is good decision making.
10 Effective team leadership is provided.

A team contributor

Robert Bacal's (2013) reflections on assessing oneself and others as team contributors are useful learning points.

- Recognize team members are 'different in style, attitude, commitment and work ethic'. In other words, others will not approach responsibilities and issues exactly like you.
- It's easy to blame others when things go wrong. Focus energy instead on solving or preventing problems.
- Don't dwell on the past. Look instead to the future and its possibilities.
- Stop back channel talk – talking in private about other team members.
- Take responsibility for your behaviour and focus on your contributions.

ETHICS BOX – INTERPERSONAL AND SOFT SKILLS

Looking first at interpersonal skills, we can draw out a number of these from an address given by famous psychoanalyst, Donald Winnicott, to the Association of Caseworkers (Lee, 1973) where the focus is interpersonal skills in the context of professional care.

- Give your attention to the other person.
- With empathy, see and feel from the other person's point of view. Listen to them.
- Be reliable, as far as this is reasonable.
- Conduct yourself with dignity.
- Be interested in the other person.
- Stay grounded.
- Accept love.
- Accept hate, but meet it with strength.
- Be tolerant of the other person.
- Do not show fear.

Erikson's ethical adult is depicted by seven terms he uses (Hoare, 2002). All of these have an interpersonal outworking.

(Continued)

An a to z of skills development   57

(Continued)

Actuality – close to participation and the notion of being present. Actualizing and actualization suggest the releasing of one's own and another's ability to participate effectively.

Mutuality – this term suggests 'mutual activation' in which two people are active and are activated by one another.

Adaptation – this is a positive, active term whereas adjustment is in essence passive. It means moulding the environment to meeting both one's own needs and the needs of others in society.

Insight – an understanding of difficulties or behaviours gained through seeing into oneself in unison with seeing 'other' (either another person or an external situation).

Spirit – the activator that promotes vitality and repels stagnation.

Soul – humility, charity in one's attitude, awareness of a certain grace at work in the world as well as human weakness.

Virtue – a potent quality that makes and keeps a person 'strong, vital, healthy, and whole' (Hoare, 2002).

Soft skills are the personal traits and social adeptness techniques you need to work with others. Conrad and Leigh (1999) divide them into four categories as follows:

- problem-solving and other cognitive skills
- oral communication skills (including both speaking and listening skills)
- personal qualities and work ethic (including self-management skills)
- interpersonal and teamwork skills (including conflict resolution skills).

CRITICAL THINKING SKILLS

Critical thinking skills form the foundation to what we build in our lives and in our organizations. Paul and Elder (2003) define critical thinking as 'that mode of thinking – about any subject, content, or problem – in which the thinker improves the quality of his or her thinking by skilfully taking charge of the structures inherent in thinking and imposing intellectual standards upon them'.

'Shoddy thinking' they argue, is actually costly and is reflected in loss of quality of life and resources. It might be compared to leaving a garden to its own devices. It would soon be overtaken by bias, distortion, partial perspectives, being uninformed and even downright prejudice. In contrast the cultivated critical thinker can be characterized as follows:

- They raise vital questions and issues, stating them clearly and precisely.
- They collate and assess relevant information and strive to interpret it accurately.
- They arrive at well-reasoned conclusions and solutions, checking them against criteria and standards that are relevant.
- They are open-minded in their thinking within a span of different systems of thought and, as needed, recognize and assess their assumptions, implications and practical consequences.
- They communicate with others in the search for solutions to complex problems.

It is useful here to spin these characteristics around in profiling Paul and Elder's so called 'shoddy thinker':

- They don't raise questions and they take information as 'given'.
- They don't seek more information.
- Their conclusions are not well reasoned.
- They are closed-minded in their approach and unaware of their own assumptions.
- They are not committed to finding solutions with others and communicating effectively.

Critical thinking skills are applied to all sorts of things and situations, including the handling of information, for example in a newspaper or journal article. Rationality is key to such an endeavour and Paul and Elder discuss the process of analysing the logic of an article or source of information by applying eight questions to it:

1 What is the purpose of the source?
2 What is the question that the author is addressing?
3 What is the most important information?
4 What are its main conclusions or inferences?
5 What are the key concepts included?
6 What are the author's underlying assumptions?
7 What are the implications of the line of reasoning?
8 What are the main points of view?

Critical thinking skills are applied also to problem solving and, finally, Paul and Elder's nine-point template for problem solving effectively is noteworthy.

1 Look on problems as 'emergent obstacles' to fulfilling one's goals, purposes and needs. Keep the latter clear before you.
2 Wherever possible tackle problems one by one. What *exactly* are the problems?
3 Separate out the aspects of the problem over which you a) have some control and b) have no control. Concentrate on the former.
4 Figure out what information you need.
5 Carefully handle this information, drawing out reasonable inferences.

6 What are the options for action? In the short and in the long term? Be realistic.
7 Evaluate options.
8 Adopt a strategic approach – either centred on actions or strategically delaying action.
9 When you act, constantly monitor the implications of the actions. Be prepared to revise the strategy or shift in terms of your analysis of the problem or your statement of it.

INDEPENDENT LEARNING SKILLS

Independent learning is called by various names, which are all variations on essentially the same thing. Some might refer to it as being a 'self-starter'. Others call it self-management. It calls for the ever familiar notion of self-discipline and is bound up in something called self-realization.

The transition from school to university is for some no more acutely felt than in this area, for two reasons. Firstly, one is accountable in a different way at university from how one was at school. There isn't a sense of someone checking up on you and regulating your actions. Secondly, it is for many an introduction to what could be referred to as the adult-order. It is an almost frightening realization for many students that *essentially*, what happens from now on is down to them. No one else will plot your future for you.

University is concerned with producing self or independent learners. These are not people who don't draw on all the input and learning that one can gain from one's lecturers and fellow students – rather independent learning has the following characteristics:

- Students work in an independent way by drawing on a collection of resources available on the net, from the library and other sources such as good newspapers and whole of life's gleanings and conversations.
- Contact with lecturers and fellow students is integral to the process of independent learning. The learning environment fulfils a strategic part of the whole, but the responsibility for what is learned and produced is the student's.
- This approach permits the student to combine their learning with their individual lifestyle and life experience and relate the learning to their own needs.

Below is a list of ten ways in which students as independent learners take responsibility for their own learning:

1 setting goals
2 planning learning
3 sourcing resources
4 working with others
5 selecting specific learning projects
6 choosing when and where to work
7 drawing on the support of teaching staff as needed

8   reflecting on learning
9   engaging with learning opportunities beyond university.
10   working towards career and future goals.

There are a number of good reasons why independent learning is encouraged.

- It develops the student so they are able to operate without close supervision.
- It develops self-reliance on the part of the student.
- It permits the student to work out a way of combining commitments to study, part-time employment, relationships and leisure.

CASE STUDY – WRITING SKILLS

The best way to write better is (like a lot of things) to practise doing it. Look upon every university assignment as an opportunity to improve one's writing. It is always helpful to write with a good dictionary to hand. Not only does this enable you to spell correctly, which is critical to looking professional on paper, but it will also enhance your word power. When uncovering a new word, look it up to understand what it means. It will not be long before you will be able to add it to your writing vocabulary.

Alongside a dictionary an accessible reference book covering grammar, punctuation and common English language errors is also a must. *Grammar for Grown Ups: A Straightforward Guide to Good English* by Katherine Fry and Rowena Kirton (2012) is the sort of reference to have to hand. While there is truth in the statement that 'nearly all of our knowledge of grammar and spelling is acquired and absorbed through extensive reading' there are so many aspects to the lifelong task of mastering a language that even the most confident writer often requires clarification in these areas.

In Fry and Kirton's book, Chapter 5 entitled 'To America and beyond' looks at the use of English in the United States, Australia, New Zealand, South Africa and Canada. It is well known that the use of so called Americanisms would not be favoured in certain contexts. Here are ten examples:

- '24/7' (rather than '24 hours, 7 days a week')
- 'touch base'
- 'gotten'
- 'takeout' (rather than 'takeaway')
- 'a heads up'
- 'train station'
- 'you do the math'
- 'period' (instead of 'full stop')
- 'I could care less' instead of 'I couldn't care less'.

(Continued)

(Continued)

A helpful resource particularly in relation to writing persuasively, which is so central to the presentation emphasis of business, is Ian Atkinson's (2012) guide *Business Writing*. His seven principles of persuasive writing are outlined below:

1 Be natural and personal.
2 Use specific words that capture attention.
3 Be specific, not vague.
4 Talk about solutions, not problems.
5 Highlight benefits.
6 Be lyrical and lively.
7 Ooze credibility.

These principles very much apply also to giving presentations.

REFERENCING SKILLS

An important aspect of completing assignments including essays, reports and other written pieces is correct and professional citation and referencing. Lecturers insist upon this and it's one of those things that if done properly really enhances an assignment.

There are different referencing styles, however, the university will advise which style they want their students to follow. A well-known referencing style is known as the 'Harvard' style. The important thing to note here is that whether your source is a book, an E-book, a journal article, internet site, newspaper article or television programme (to name only a few sources) there is a particular way of formatting these references to conform to the referencing style being used.

An extremely clear and comprehensive quick-reference guide in this area is *Cite Them Right* by Richard Pears and Graham Shields (2010). These authors point to three main reasons to perfect this skill and practice:

1 It reflects all the reading the student has done.
2 It enhances the student's credibility in relation to their ideas and arguments.
3 It demonstrates time spent in sourcing, reading and analysing material.

Another important reason to follow an exacting standard of referencing is to demonstrate that there is no aspect of plagiarism in one's work. Plagiarism, whether intentional or not, is presenting another person's work or ideas as your own (Pears and Shields, 2010). Here are a few examples that Pears and Shields provide:

- copying and pasting material from the internet without crediting (citing) the source
- presenting someone else's work as your own
- not using quotation marks when quoting
- summarizing and paraphrasing without citing the source
- citing sources that were not used.

Universities regard plagiarism as cheating and its detection is therefore a disciplinary matter. University lecturers are often adept at spotting it.

EMBODIMENT BOX – SKILLS OF APPEARANCE

We live in a highly visual culture. It is also a culture that has proliferated many options and styles of personal presentation. Our culture is heterogeneous rather than homogeneous, reflecting globalizing diversity with its innumerable people groups and range of fashions. Given this array of ways of styling and presenting ourselves, are there any general principles we can draw out under the heading of skills of appearance?

Firstly, skill of appearance is reflected in a *deliberate* approach. This is someone who has given thought as to how they will appear. This is often recognizable on the part of the person or people beholding the individual.

Secondly, skill of appearance is reflected in an *integrative* approach. All the things that make up a person's appearance including, for example, their hair, glasses, clothes and shoes can either integrate, or not.

Thirdly, skill of appearance is reflected in an *embodied* approach. Here the issue is whether the way someone presents themselves fits with who they are. It is as important to be comfortable in what you are wearing as much as being comfortable in your own skin.

Fourthly, skill of appearance is reflected in a *presentational* approach. This raises the issue of shoes and clothes being clean and extends to personal hygiene.

Fifthly, skill of appearance is reflected in a *communicative* approach. This is reflected in the person choosing to present themselves with other people in mind as well as themselves. For example, this would mean wearing appropriate clothes for a particular event or occasion, where lack of consideration might communicate the wrong thing to others.

Sixthly, skill of appearance is a *creative* approach. There is much scope with appearance to do something interesting or pleasing for others.

PRESENTATION SKILLS

University students have the potential to become the most skilled presenters for the following reasons:

- Giving presentations forms an integral part of learning and assessment.
- This means that university students get to both give presentations and practise giving them.
- A presentation is obviously a form of communication requiring high level language skills.
- Presentations are often supported by technology that students have both exposure and access to at university.

When starting out at university what stands in the way of giving presentations for many students, as is the case with anyone, is usually the student's lack of confidence. With some experience, with individual feedback and learning from others and with practise, presentation skills can be developed.

It is worth pausing to consider why any adult may be wary of giving a presentation. For many, it has something to do with *exposure* – the person is afraid to put themselves 'in the spotlight', because naturally they do not want to look stupid or perform badly. Many people are naturally shy and not accustomed to putting themselves forward in any manner. Giving a presentation runs contrary to these instincts.

For a presentation to be successful requires a number of building blocks, none of which the presenter can afford to neglect or under-resource. These are listed below.

Purpose

- What is the overall purpose of the presentation?
- To whom will the presentation be delivered and how can it be geared for this audience?
- How long is the presentation?
- Is it an individual or group presentation?
- Where is the presentation being delivered?
- What technologies can support the presentation?

Research

- What should form the content of the presentation?
- How can it be both informative and interesting?
- Is there a question to answer?
- What do the audience know already?

Preparation

- Is the structure simple and clear?
- Is there an introduction and conclusion?

- Am I prepared for questions?
- Is the handout helpful and interesting?
- Have I practised delivering it?
- Have I decided what I'm going to wear?

Delivery

- Do I sound enthusiastic?
- Do I appear upbeat and positive?
- How can I eliminate signs of nervousness?
- Am I standing still?
- Am I maintaining good eye contact?
- Do I use aids and equipment ably?

Evaluation

- How did it go?
- What feedback was given?
- What would I change next time?
- Is there anything else that stood out from doing the presentation?

Bridging the gap

There is often a 'gap' between what a presenter intended to communicate or intended to achieve through the presentation and what for the audience is communicated and achieved. This is not to suggest that every presentation falls short, not by any means. Rather that communication contains the inbuilt challenge that the communicator encodes a message that always must be decoded by the listener.

There are ten factors to try and overcome when giving a presentation. These, as it were, stand in the gap between the presenter and the audience:

1. physical noise
2. message ambiguity (open to other interpretations)
3. 'in group' language
4. language
5. cultural differences
6. status differences
7. value judgements
8. semantics (specific words used)
9. selective listening
10. time pressures.

Negative non-verbal communication

Hidden feelings are often expressed non-verbally in the exposed situation of giving a presentation. These can be eliminated with awareness (sometimes through feedback) and practice. There are a number of non-verbal gaffes that classically emerge in presentations.

- staring
- little eye contact (looking into space)
- inappropriate attire
- nervous mannerisms
- sweating
- looking disinterested
- proximity issues (too close or too far)
- blushing
- aggressive (defensive) action
- over movement of hands or feet.

EMBODIMENT BOX – TIPS FOR MEETING NEW PEOPLE

- Remember, they may be in the same situation
- A less friendly face can betray nerves
- Smile (naturally)
- Initiate (don't wait for them)
- Ask questions (it shows interest)
- Use their name, but don't be overfamiliar
- Stay with the group
- Don't dominate the conversation
- Be yourself
- Accept differences

NETWORKING SKILLS

Networking consists of individuals adopting a strategic approach to developing and maintaining relationships that will support their personal, professional and career goals. In the contemporary employment context where there is decreased job security, increased movement (or mobility) between jobs and rapid technological change, looking at relationships strategically, both at work and beyond work, has become increasingly important. Networking is not only an important influence in finding and keeping jobs, it also influences career success and fulfilment. Rather than just suggesting that students grow their social media networks, a more deliberate approach of relationship management is proposed here.

Guidelines for networking

Forret and Sullivan (2002) outline five guidelines for networking:

1 Determine your goals. What are your career aims? What balance between work and non-work activities would you like?
2 Assess your network. How large is it? When you visually depict it, what do you make of its structure and the composition of its members? How connected are its members? Or is it diverse? How fit for purpose is it in relation to your career goals?
3 Align your network efforts. Look out for networking opportunities that would help you developmentally and that would permit you to build relationships with key individuals.
4 Remember reciprocity. Network relationships are centred on this. What help and assistance can you give to the other person?
5 Evaluate your network. Do you need to spend more time and effort strengthening certain relationships? Consider whether there are additional individuals with whom you should build relationships.

Sociometrics

A language to describe networking is provided by sociometrics, which is the study and measurement of interpersonal relationships in a group of people. It is based on the fact that people make choices in these relationships on some basis or criterion. The criterion may be subjective (whether they like or dislike a particular person) or may be more objective, to do with the person's expertise, knowledge or experience.

A sociogram is a tool for mapping networks and Table 3.6 gives a list of some network types associated with sociometric data.

Table 3.6 Sociogram network types

Stars (or hubs)	People who are positively regarded or esteemed by many. They are the centre or 'hub' of attraction. Often they act as 'informal leaders' in an organization
Negative stars (or pains)	The contrary of stars – negatively regarded by many
Gatekeepers	People who serve as information bridges between different groups
Connectors (or glues)	People who have a cementing influence in networks
Ghosts	People who receive few or no positive or negative nominations
Influentials	People who are personally closest to the senior manager or CEO
Power bridges	People who have a direct personal link to someone higher in the organizational hierarchy

In addition to sociometric types there are sociometric terms used in network analysis. *Mutuals* are where two people choose each other. Then there are *negative mutuals* where two people have each recorded a negative regard for each other. *Clusters* or *cliques* are where people have chosen each other. In organizations there may be a recognizable *in-group* and an *out-group*.

KEY CONCEPT – TRANSFERABLE SKILLS

These are skills, to use Anita Houghton's words, that 'can be applied in more than one setting' (Houghton, 2005).

An extraordinarily inspirational aspect of skills development is that they can be developed in a wide variety of contexts. What this means is that if you need to work part time while at university, perhaps doing the sort of job you wouldn't want to be doing in the future, this time is by no means wasted. Not only will employers have a regard for the work experience, but also this will encourage the development of skills that are transferable.

For example, say you find yourself working in a bar or waiting on tables. This experience could help you develop many of the skills listed in the A to Z of skills in Table 3.2. Customer service skills are not complicated, however, they are much sought after and because they essentially involve the exercise of people skills, they are highly transferable.

It is a great skill to be able to handle irate and edgy customers. The outcomes for the individuals involved and the organization in question are very different depending on how the bar assistant or waiter handles the situation.

Skills are developed in a great many contexts including volunteering and even in one's personal life. As stated earlier in the chapter a key here is to recognize this as happening and use it astutely as evidence when completing a job application or summarizing skills gained in a CV. No experience is wasted. It's just a matter of how you view it and the positives you take from it.

APPLIED PERSONAL DEVELOPMENT

There is no escaping the significance of using university as a time to develop skills and to go about this in a deliberate way through personal development planning. A key aspect to this is concentrating attention on skills that are much sought after by employers, such as being able to work well in a team context. Employers expect graduates to have such skills, putting the onus on the student to develop these at university.

Employability may not be a word one would hear before going to university, but it is certainly a concept that has a high profile now in higher education. A lot of employability is to do with keeping one eye on the future and working towards it. Students often remark how quickly their time at university goes, which is all the more reason to plan for one's future throughout the time at university.

A hallmark of university is its potential to train students in critical thinking. This is at the very heart of the higher education 'project' – to expose students to learning and the viewpoints of many and support them through a process of utilizing and developing their powers of reasoning.

Developing communication skills to a high level is also a key opportunity at university. Even the inclusion of giving presentations as a part of one's course and assessments will take students forward in this area.

REFERENCES

Atkinson, I. (2012) *The Financial Times Essential Guide to Business Writing: How to Write to Engage, Persuade And Sell*. Harlow: Pearson Education.

Bacal, R. (2013) 'Teamwork file – how to be a better team contributor'. Available at: http://work911.com/articles/teamcont.htm (accessed 9 June 2013).

Belbin, R. M. (2004) *Management Teams*. Oxford: Elsevier Butterworth-Heinemann.

Benne, K. D. and Sheats, P. (2007) 'Functional roles of group members'. Available at: www.iaf-world.org/Libraries/IAF_Journals/Functional_Roles_of_Group_Members.sflb.ashx (accessed 21 June 2014).

Conrad, C. A. and Leigh, W. A. (1999) 'Soft skills: a bridge or barrier to employment'. Available at: www.aecf.org/initiatives/jobsinitiative/policy-feb99.htm (accessed 25 February 2004).

Ellis, Roger (ed.) (1989) *Professional Competence and Quality Assurance in the Caring Professions*. London: Chapman and Hall.

Forret, M. and Sullivan, S. (2002) 'A balanced scorecard approach to networking: a guide to successfully navigating career changes', *Organisational Dynamics*, 31 (3): 245–258.

Fry, K. and Kirton, R. (2012) *Grammar for Grown Ups: A Straightforward Guide to Good English*. London: Square Peg.

Higher Education Academy (2000) 'Aspects of employability: a tool for appraising programmes and modules'. Available at: www.employability.ed.ac.uk/Encourage/atSchool/Audit%20tools/HEA%20-%20Tuning%20Tool.pdf (accessed 21 June 2014).

Hoare, C. H. (2002) *Erikson on Development in Adulthood: New Insights from Unpublished Papers*. Oxford: Oxford University Press.

Houghton, A. (2005) *Finding Square Holes: Discover Who You Really Are and Find The Perfect Career*. Carmarthen: Crown House Publishing.

Jackson, N. (2001) 'Personal development planning: what does it mean?' York: The Higher Education Academy. Available at: www.heacademy.ac.uk/assets/documents/resources/database/id465_pdp_what_does_%20it_%20mean.pdf (accessed 10 June 2013).

Lee, R. S. (1973) *Principles of Pastoral Counselling*. London: SPCK.

Mason, G. (2002) 'High skills utilisation under mass higher education: graduate employment in service industries in Britain', *Journal of Education and Work*, 15 (4): 427–456.

Paul, R. and Elder, L. (2003) *The Miniature Guide to Critical Thinking Concepts and Tools*. Tomales, CA: Foundation for Critical Thinking.

Pears, R. and Shields, G. (2010) *Cite Them Right: The Essential Referencing Guide*. Basingstoke: Palgrave Macmillan.

Perrone, L. and Vickers, M. H. (2003) 'Life after graduation as a "very uncomfortable world": an Australian case study', *Education + Training*, 45 (2): 69–78.

Quality Assurance Agency (2009) 'Personal development planning: guidance for institutional policy and practice in higher education'. Available at: www.qaa.ac.uk/Publications/InformationAndGuidance/Documents/PDPguide.pdf (accessed 21 June 2014).

Rainer, T. (1979) *The New Diary*. Los Angeles: Tarcher.

Rath, T. (2007) *Strengths Finder 2.0*. New York: Gallup Press

University of Westminster (2006) *Skills in the Curriculum: A Guide*. London: University of Westminster.

4 GRAItUATE SKILLS

● ● ● ● ● ● ● ● ● ● ● ● ●

A NOTE FROM THE AUTHOR

Many of you will be well aware of intelligent and talented graduates who have not secured what we might term befitting employment. These are young adults who have got their university degrees but these have not led them as of yet into graduate work. Some may be doing work that could have been secured without a university degree. Others may even be unemployed and living again with their parents in their early twenties. This all goes to show that there is more to securing a desirable graduate job than going to university and getting a degree. What are the reasons for this?

There are a number of things at play here. Firstly, there are more qualified people chasing fewer jobs. In the economic downturn the supply of graduates is outstripping demand. In this extremely competitive environment employers can and will seek ever *more* from prospective employees. For example, they might start by only considering those who have secured a top classification from a top university.

Secondly, it has always been the case that employers attach much significance to what are known as employability skills. This causes them to value work experiences and other responsibility experiences which permit graduates to slot into employment openings more easily. Added to this certain university courses more overtly than others offer the skills development that employers seek.

Thirdly, much responsibility still rests with the graduate themselves to make the very most of the opportunity at university. This applies not only to looking on a university education as a chance to develop significant skills but also being more deliberate about documenting and evidencing such skills development in job applications.

Fourthly, it may be the case that in certain sectors and with certain jobs some degrees would be more highly regarded than others. For a whole manner of reasons sometimes graduates are not able to offer employers the most appropriate specialized degree with a skills development most attuned to the specific employment opportunity. All other things remaining equal, the employer will probably select the candidate with the most relevant degree subject.

Learning outcomes

When you have completed this chapter you will be able to:

- evaluate the job opportunities available to graduates
- profile the skills offering graduates are expected to offer employees
- define the options that give graduates employability edge
- appreciate the significance of planning in making progress
- understand and define differentiating factors for the contemporary age.

GRADUATE JOBS

For the majority of occupational areas there is a starting job suited or exclusively designed for graduates as the examples in Table 4.1 show.

Table 4.1 Graduate jobs and their job titles on entry

Accountancy	trainee accountant
Advertising	trainee account executive or trainee account handler
Architecture	architectural assistant
Armed Forces	officer cadet
Banking	graduate trainee
Charity	project assistant, fundraising assistant or admin assistant
Chemical and pharmaceutical	graduate scientist
Civil Service	fast streamer
Construction	construction trainee
Energy and oil	trainee analyst
Engineering and industry	graduate engineer
Film and TV	production assistant or programme assistant
Hospitality	trainee manager
Human resources (HR)	HR trainee
Insurance	graduate trainee
Investment banking	trainee analyst
IT and telecoms	IT trainee
Law	trainee solicitor
Management consultancy	analyst
Marketing and social media	marketing assistant
Medicine	foundation doctor
Pilots and air traffic control	first officer or student air traffic controller
Police and Fire Service	probationer constable or trainee firefighter

Recruitment	trainee recruitment consultant
Research and development	postdoctoral or research associate
Retail	trainee manager
Sales	trainee sales executive
Surveying and property	trainee surveyor
Teaching	newly qualified teacher

Susanne Christian in her book *Top Jobs: Discover the Best Graduate Jobs and How to Get One* profiles 29 graduate job areas. As you can see from Table 4.1, which lists these jobs along with the respective graduate job title on entry, there is no shortage of options. Speaking to business students, if you consider that virtually all these job areas consist of organizations that are run as businesses there are even more possibilities. The challenge here is possibly knowing where to start, or just getting started. For a whole manner of reasons it is easy while at university to put off career enquiries and research and not doing justice to the opportunity one has to be working towards a satisfying job opening, no matter how competitive the current situation is.

All the job areas above offer graduate schemes often referred to as graduate development programmes. Information about such schemes is available at your university careers service. Obviously there is competition and a limited number of places, but if you are successful this is an ideal introduction to a specific job area and will consist usually, over two years, of gaining vital experience of the employing organization and being rotated in a number of roles or departments, where your performance will be assessed. This enables the trainee to gain an understanding of what they're most suited to. Very helpfully it also involves on-the-job training supported by more formal classroom training, in some cases studying for more qualifications.

Christian is right to point out that you need to be determined to secure one of these graduate places reflected in the following process:

- Enquiring about such openings towards the end of your first year at university. Some schemes have application processes in your final year but others may be during the second year and it is important not to miss out through lack of planning.
- Graduate scheme employers look for candidates offering not only graduate knowledge and aptitude but also demonstrating varied interests and early responsibilities in sporting and other leisure activities. Former and existing part-time work experience is also valued as is demonstration of employability skills.
- The selection process almost always includes what is known as an assessment centre where candidates are required to do a number of things including: give a presentation; do group and individual exercises; sit psychometric tests; be interviewed; and consider case studies.
- Like applying to any organization it is essential to research it. This is an expectation on the part of the employer.

Paul Redmond (2010) developed the graduate jobs formula which is:

E = Q + WE + S x C

Where:

E = employability
Q = qualifications
WE = work experience
S = strategies
C = contacts

It is a very concise way of bringing together all the elements needed for a graduate to access a desirable career in what Redmond refers to as the job market 'AD' (after the downturn). How Redmond understands these essential elements is summarized below:

Employability – Redmond's 'employability redux' (Redmond, 2010) as he calls it is the recognition that employability is essentially about self-sufficiency. Added to this he fleshes out (see embodiment box) the important distinction between being in employment (which is good) and being 'employable' (which is even better).

Qualifications – Business degrees have the great potential to deliver commercial awareness which Redmond says, is an 'essential skill sought by thousands of recruiters' (Redmond, 2010). If you're not doing a business degree you may want to plan how you can alternatively gain this significant employability skill.

The biggest recruiters of business students are in order:

- The retail sector, with some retailers offering two-year graduate management training programmes
- The professional services sector including management and human resources
- Financial services including accountancy, baking, insurance and investment banking

Work experience – 'It is now widely recognised,' Redmond argues, 'that work experience is the *key* to employability' (Redmond, 2010). Work placements are particularly useful making students who have gone on them more marketable and where of a good quality deliver:

- personal development
- new learning and skills development

- assessment and feedback
- clear aims and objectives
- on-going support and contact.

Strategies – In Redmond's strategies section he deals with applications and CVs, interviews and assessment centres. Here he emphasizes how the growth of the internet and the drive to reduce recruitment costs on the part of the employer are changing the rules of engagement as far as recruitment is concerned. But as ever, successful candidates will be those who are well prepared and have approached the recruitment process strategically.

Contacts – Redmond argues, 'It's not what you know, it's not who you know. It's who knows you' (Redmond, 2010). The key to networking for Redmond is knowing exactly what you're wanting to achieve through it and the resulting interaction – what you might call adopting a very deliberate approach. Students he says should have business cards not only because they are more likely to be retained than say CVs and emails, but also because they are a symbol of being professional and prepared.

GRADUATE SKILLS

In this section we shall present the findings of three pieces of research about what constitute what we might term as graduate skills. The reader will note that there is some contrast in the results. Rather than suggesting that one piece of research has more validity than another, in this case, we should probably pool the findings and reflect on their implications.

INSTITUTE FOR EMPLOYMENT STUDIES (2000) RESEARCH

A piece of Institute for Employment Studies research summarized in a report entitled *The art of getting started: graduate skills in a fragmented labour market* (La Valle et al., 2000) highlights a number of relevant things in this area of graduate skills.

Firstly, the notion of what employers refer to as a 'skills gap' – this is the gap between what an employer looks for in hiring an employee by way of their skills offering and what skills the successful candidate actually brings. It is also the case that graduates themselves, securing employment, can be become conscious of this skills gap and would like to be in the position of offering more.

Secondly, the research lists the skill areas as follows:

- self-confidence and self-esteem
- decision making
- time management

- self-promotion
- problem-solving skills
- motivation/commitment to learning
- developing creative ideas
- pro-active/entrepreneurial skills
- visual/verbal/written communication
- cope with uncertainty
- specific craft/technical skills
- networking
- teamwork
- negotiating.

While one can immediately see that these skills are by no means *exclusive* to graduates, at the same time it is undoubtedly the case that university provides an opportunity to develop these skills not just in relation to the course of studies, but also in the life the student leads around their study in leisure, part-time employment and volunteering.

Thirdly, the research suggested that all these skills were important in the graduates' employment activity but their relative importance is reflected in the order of the above listing. This is not the same as the 'skills gap' which was much more significant in certain areas than others. The largest gaps related to negotiating and networking. Smaller, but still significant gaps related to self-confidence, self-promotion, entrepreneurial skills, time management and the ability to cope with uncertainty.

FUTURETRACK (2012) RESEARCH

The Futuretrack research (2012) headed by Professors Peter Elias and Kate Purcell (2013) casts important light on what skills are particularly associated with graduate jobs and defines three groups of graduate jobs requiring high level skills.

- The *expert* group of jobs focus on specialist knowledge gained from a degree course. Examples include chemical scientists, civil engineers, pharmacists, solicitors, physiotherapists, chartered surveyors and airline pilots.
- The *orchestrators* group of jobs draw on a host of strategic skills including managerial skills, problem-solving skills, planning skills and decision-making skills. Managers and Directors often occupy this group as do senior officers from the armed forces and other public sector organizations. Since it requires extensive experience of the particular field in question to operate as an orchestrator Elias and Purcell suggest that it is not an area occupied by many recent graduates (Elias and Purcell, 2013).
- The *communicators* group require high level communication skills, whether oral or written. Examples include web design and development,

marketing associate professionals, journalists, actors, conference and exhibition organizers. Communicators use interactive skills whether interpersonal, creative, technological or about manipulating and directing information.

PRINCE'S (2013) NEW SKILLS FOR THE WORLD WE NOW LIVE IN

Emma-Sue Prince's book *The Advantage: The 7 Soft Skills You Need to Stay One Step Ahead* endorses the development of the skills highlighted already. In addition to these, and because of a number of trends and changes, she advocates seven more, to strengthen ability to focus, communicate and collaborate as follows:

1 adaptability
2 critical thinking
3 empathy
4 integrity
5 optimism
6 proactivity
7 resilience.

Prince's understanding of these skills is outlined below:

Adaptability – this is not just about being flexible and able to change to fit altered circumstances but also about being open to new ways of operating and venturing outside our comfort zone. She outlines ten ways to become more adaptable.

1 Challenge limiting beliefs and 'mental scripts' and be prepared to open yourself up to new ways of thinking and responding.
2 Develop resilience and complete tasks through focus and self-discipline.
3 Travel more and so gain confidence in handling varied situations.
4 Seek to learn something new, be prepared to try new things and draw conclusions from new situations.
5 Look for ways to expand your comfort zone and through time reinvent yourself.
6 Practise being spontaneous and improvising. Take an opportunity now rather than putting it off.
7 Try exercising three types of flexibility: cognitive flexibility, or new ways of thinking; emotional flexibility, adjusting how you deal with your emotions and those of others; and dispositional flexibility, balancing realism and optimism.
8 Train yourself to respond more positively to changes and even setbacks.

9 Be more creative and experiment with different ways of problem solving.
10 Develop a survivor rather than a victim mentality.

Critical thinking – we introduced critical thinking in Chapter 3. As you will recall critical thinking is all about how we evaluate a situation or come to a judgement incorporating rationality, creativity and reflection. Prince describes six ways in which critical thinking is changing.

1 Making sense of information is increasingly significant in view of our being constantly bombarded with so much of it. This necessitates high level thinking skills.
2 Most high-skill jobs now demand what is known as 'situational adaptability' – the ability to respond quickly to the unexpected.
3 So called 'computational thinking' is required to correctly interpret large amounts of data.
4 New media literacy is a must, reflected in, for example, user-generated media like blogs and podcasts.
5 Optimum cognitive functioning will be required through discriminating and filtering information.
6 Being 'T-shaped' as a worker means having depth of expertise in at least one area but having the capacity to apply critical thinking and reasoning across a breadth of fields.

Empathy – Prince suggests this is 'the ability to enter the internal world of the other person' and understand their situation, feelings and motives (Prince, 2013).

Empathy is now a much sought after quality reflected in how people want to connect with others, even relative strangers, via social network sites. It has become something which one would wish to find in friendships and even collegiate relationships in the workplace. Finally, managers and leaders who can extend empathy are also appreciated and more likely to be followed.

Integrity – we shall be dedicating a chapter to integrity (Chapter 8) but this also makes Prince's list of essential soft skills. As Prince highlights, integrity is derived from the Latin word *integer*, meaning whole or intact. Her profile of integrity (as follows) is also useful in building up a picture of what integrity looks like:

- demonstrating authenticity – a life aligning with a person's values
- displaying consistency
- taking responsibility
- following through – doing what they said they would do
- being accountable
- communicating truth respectfully
- actively listening and seeking to understand 'other'
- being emotionally receptive and articulate
- acting without hidden agendas.

In the workplace, this might look like this:

- not just saying what others want to hear
- displaying depth of character
- 'walking the talk'
- being reliable
- keeping promises
- being up front in a respectful way.

Optimism – the hallmarks of optimism for Prince are threefold:

1 realistically and accurately assessing a situation
2 an 'overcoming' attitude to problems
3 a sense of empowerment to tackle something.

Prince's distinction between optimism and the cult of positive thinking is a helpful one. She warns of an 'irrational optimism where mind-set is all that matters' (Prince, 2013) and adds that 'we cannot change outcomes by thoughts and affirmations alone'. Optimism isn't blind positive thinking but looks for the big picture – all the facts and possibilities in a given situation.

Being proactive – for Prince being proactive has four elements as follows:

1 Self-awareness – this is about becoming aware of your reactions, seeing your-self if you like – so you can choose to act differently.
2 Willpower – this has to be built up over time and practised.
3 Responsibility – this is the ability to respond with conscious choices.
4 Self-mastery – this is having complete control not only of your actions but the thoughts, emotions and beliefs that underpin actions.

Resilience – how resilient someone is, Prince argues, comes down to two things and their interaction:

1 Resilience is a factor in someone's personality and, as Prince remarks, some people are just 'far better able to handle set-backs than others'.
2 Resilience also depends on your environment – not only what happens (your experiences), but also the strength of support in the form of family, friends and the social environment.

Resilience, Prince argues, is essentially about taking control given inevitable adversity or problems. It is a quality that is associated with contemporary senior leaders forever facing business and operational uncertainties and competitive-ness. It is supported by having strong social networks expressed in sites such as LinkedIn.

Pulling together these three pieces of research, what observations can we make about so called 'graduate skills'? Firstly, the research may suggest that the term graduate skills means different things to different people and critically to different employers. It could indicate at least three things:

1 An expected standard – skills an employer would expect to come with employing a graduate. It is, for example, reasonable that employers should expect graduates to spell well and show a good standard in their written communications.
2 High order skills – as well as possessing all the skills that an employer would expect to find in a graduate, there is often an added expectation of graduates possessing high order skills, for example critical thinking skills.
3 Cutting edge skills – because universities are often at the forefront of new thinking reflected in the latest research, it would be reasonable for employers to expect to find the latest and most progressive thinking in university graduates, particularly in the sort of areas highlighted by Prince above.

Secondly, looking at this research another way, perhaps to be highly skilled is a multifaceted and expanding notion – the idea that a lot of things come with a highly skilled individual who is often the product of a good and prolonged education and/or upbringing.

Thirdly, the research raises the issue of how skills are acquired and developed. Some skills development is progressed through practice even without being particularly conscious of this, for example, what is gained by practising working in small groups. At the same time, training input and strategy takes skills development forward in a deliberate fashion.

EMBODIMENT BOX – THE EMPLOYABILITY EDGE

Paul Redmond's (2010) distinction between what it means to be employable and how this trumps in many respects being purely in employment is a useful tool for reflection, as shown in Table 4.2:

Table 4.2 A comparison of being employable and being in employment

Being Employable	Being in Employment
career	job
contacts	contract
who knows you	what you know
ongoing training	previous qualifications
works with …	works for …
global worldview	'local' worldview

Employers look upon graduates who have volunteering experiences very favourably. Not only does this communicate other interests on the part of the student, it also can help students develop the employability skills so sought after by employers. A key here is for students to demonstrate the added value of their time given to volunteering. This distils down into how the student is going to ably communicate and summarize what their volunteering experience consisted of and what skills and other learning they acquired through the volunteering placement.

There are innumerable opportunities to volunteer both in one's country of study and internationally. Perhaps the best way to make the most of any volunteering experience is to select an organization working for a cause that is a genuine area of interest to the student. We cannot identify with all needs and all causes, but there are some that would be more inspirational than others depending on the individual.

There are options regarding the length of the placement. This could occupy a year out or university summer vacation or it is something students can do part-time to coincide with their studies. Charities are now very much businesses in their own right and some of them are extremely large and influential. There may be future employment opportunities in such charities and volunteering is sometimes a way into employment.

Consider some of the advantages of volunteering summarized below:

- network contacts and potential referees
- skills development opportunities
- trial responsibilities to define performance areas
- CV and application enhancement
- demonstration of commitment and motivation
- application of subject area learning in the workplace
- widening of experience
- potential intercultural learning.

GRADUATE NETWORKING

University represents a near perfect training ground for professional networking and therefore it is included in this chapter on graduate skills. Divan defines networking as 'developing and maintaining contact with people who work in the same field as you or in a related field' (Divan, 2009).

From the very beginning of university it is both professional and sensible to adopt a networking mentality for the following reasons:

1 It is a means by which you can share, develop, refine and revise your ideas. Conversations and meetings yield useful feedback and information that you may not otherwise acquire.
2 Networking constitutes a resource base for a whole manner of things including references, recruitment opportunities and the latest news and developments in your field.
3 It can also be a source of support and even fun, meeting with like-minded people.

There are a number of ways of networking and students should consider their prospects for adding new spheres to their network activity. Below are a number that are outlined by Divan:

Departmental networking – this is obviously a natural place to start, in your own department or business school. Don't limit yourself to talking with friends, but find out what other students are doing and are interested in. Don't be afraid to approach researchers and other staff attached to your school or department.

Attending added seminars and events – in addition to the academic timetable with its lectures and seminars there will be a host of added events and seminars not only in your department, but in the university and at neighbouring universities. As far as priorities allow these all have potential for developing your network.

Attending conferences – sometimes there are opportunities to attend conferences. Like the above opportunity these are also useful for your studies as well as for networking. Be sure to note down contact details and exchange cards if possible.

Other networking opportunities – these might include joining a professional society relevant to your subject area and getting involved in any relevant local groups pertinent to your academic specialism and interests.

In addition to face-to-face networking there are of course opportunities to network through web-based media.

DEVELOPMENT POINTER – USING LINKEDIN

Launched in 2003, LinkedIn is regarded by many as the number one business social networking site (Peregrin, 2012). A social media specialist, Kristina Jaramillo argues that LinkedIn has great significance as a job networking site (Peregrin, 2012), but it also doubles as a tool to stay connected to professional contacts. Marisa Moore adds in Tony Peregrin's (2012) article, 'LinkedIn profile makeover: optimizing your professional online profile', that the site is a 'great way to get your name out there and to increase your exposure and visibility'.

The article proposes eight ways to optimize your LinkedIn profile as follows:

1 Highlight only the most relevant information – avoiding the temptation to include everything about yourself.
2 Build a complete profile – where LinkedIn records it is 100 per cent complete and not missing sections.
3 Always include a picture – one, Marisa Moore adds, that 'puts your best face forward'.
4 Develop guidelines for adding individuals to your network – approach this strategically avoiding a catch all 'numbers game'.
5 Limit recommendations to people you trust – approach only people best able to endorse your skills.
6 Join groups – this increases your visibility in relevant and strategic areas.
7 Provide credible, accurate information when contributing to discussions and answering questions.
8 Maintain e-professionalism.

The advice from Peregrin's article sits well alongside Susan Joyce's (2013) piece, 'Be visible on LinkedIn', which outlines how to get 'good' LinkedIn visibility. Joyce speaks of playing nice on LinkedIn (Joyce, 2013), resisting any temptation to slip into negativity, crankiness and profanity. This is linked to Joyce's advice to practise smart self-promotion on LinkedIn, involving taking responsibility to be your own publicist. The art of doing this well is how to profile yourself and highlight your accomplishments without resorting to something which comes across as 'bragging' (Joyce, 2013).

Joyce, an online job search specialist, suggests LinkedIn is not optional for job seekers and sets out three targets for using LinkedIn to this end:

1 Establish a LinkedIn profile and connect with 100 people you know, building your network from there.
2 Join 20 LinkedIn groups relevant to your job search.
3 Connect with recruiters.

Blogs where information is posted on a regular basis are one means of professionally connecting and gaining information. Since content is not peer reviewed you need to be both critical and discerning. Authoring a blog is another option, but like all dealing with information, time spent is key.

Contributing to discussion forums, wikis and mailing lists constitutes other electronic opportunities for networking. Mailing lists have the disadvantage that they can deliver too much information.

On many degrees there is an opportunity to have a spell where you study abroad, sometimes for a whole academic year. In Europe we have what is known as the Erasmus scheme which permits a period of time in another European university. There are a number of reasons why students often don't pursue this opportunity as follows:

- they don't get around to organizing it
- relationships and friendships (at university) make it appear too radical
- fear of it being an isolating experience
- they are unaware of what is available
- they don't appreciate its contemporary value and significance.

Enlarging on the latter point, time spent studying abroad will differentiate you from the next student and its potential for enhancing a CV and job applications is significant. From the perspective of your personal development it also has great promise. It demonstrates that if you are able to adapt to living and studying in a foreign country, then you will feel more confident about the next challenge in life. But the point to really emphasize is the relevance of such a venture in a globalizing world – a chance to encounter 'other', another country, another experience, other ways of looking at the world (worldviews), other ways of living. This is not an easy option and it can bring on all sorts of challenges. However, if you talk to students who have done this you can see that it has often enlarged them as people – given them more confidence, a greater ability to cope and adapt, sometimes it has been great fun and a wonderful opportunity to experience as a young adult. An experience of another culture often changes your outlook, if only the way you now look at yourself.

Make enquiries early with your course as to the provision of exchange opportunities. You may consider doing this with another student, who you may or may not know really well before you in some sense share this experience.

ETHICS BOX – A NEW ORDER OF DISCOURSE

Sarah Mann writes in *Study, Power and the University* (2008):

> in choosing to study a 'new' subject, an individual enters a new order of discourse, that of higher education and academic practice and that of their chosen discipline. The encounter will challenge their existing representation of the world, their social relations and their sense of identity. While this challenge may potentially undermine the ground the

student stands on, if their engagement with it is constructive, it will produce a richer ground, a more differentiated understanding, new ways of acting, and new ways of being. But the negotiation of this new discourse is complex.

This is a lengthy quotation but Mann here takes us to the very heart of what it means to be a graduate. We enter a new world when we become students of higher education – and universities have their own particular ways of thinking, vocabularies (ways of talking), and cultures (ways of being). As Goldberg (2007) points out, it is not possible to stand outside such systems and as the quotation from Mann suggests this changes the student in some way.

Goldberg takes us a step further by highlighting that the discursive framework found in such places as universities is 'defined by the contradictory discourses it contains', that is, all manner of ways of thinking and of talking and of being. He continues, 'discourses are multivalent and intertwined, and … at any given time an individual may be positioned differently depending on which discourses she is at any given time enmeshed in' (Goldberg, 2007). This is characteristic of a university and what it means to be a graduate – to be exposed to difference and to graduate with a broader understanding and comprehension of such differences.

THE GLOBAL GRADUATE

An important aspect of becoming a graduate is having been a part of a genuine global community. The force of Clement Katulushi's (2005) chapter in the book *Values in Higher Education* is expanding on the significance of this important dimension of what it means to be a university student.

Katulushi cites Roger King (2003) who says, 'historically universities are more global than national in their academic and intellectual orientations'. The presence of international students is one dimension of this adding to the range and diversity of a university's clientele.

Added to this Katulushi argues that 'most universities see themselves as part of a global community' – a community where the appreciation of diversity is central to the substance of being a university. This is powerfully summarized by Katulushi where he writes, 'a genuine experience of higher education is that which enables interaction between and among the diversities of learning communities, respecting their idiosyncrasies while at the same time holding true to the tradition of university education, helping individuals and societies to transcend themselves'.

The ideal here from an educational perspective is tolerance and dialogue between students and staff from different cultures – 'enabling different types of literacies' as Katulushi puts it and resulting in genuine collaboration.

In the second half of Katulushi's chapter majoring on this idea of the university as a global community, he builds on the thinking of Whitehead (2002) who considers the intrinsic values which characterize higher education (as listed below) as essentially the values of *humanity*:

- critical and original thinking
- enquiry
- learning
- freedom
- loving relationships
- the education of social formations.

This takes Katulushi to his argument that the twin functions of a university, teaching and research, 'are both activities of humanity transcending cultures and boundaries'. In other words, university is the place where we can overcome difference and learn together. He closes his chapter with the following challenge, 'to genuinely embrace the global dimension demands effective partnership at the level of learning, and management, in terms of global collaboration and global responsibility'.

The implications of Katulushi's thinking in relation to the global graduate, as we have termed it, are as follows:

1 To have a university education is to participate in a global community.
2 To have a university education is an opportunity to inculcate tolerance and learn dialogical skills.
3 To have a university education is not just about crossing and negotiating boundaries but seeking the transcendent thinking and answers that can arise from cross-cultural collaboration.
4 To have a university education is to be exposed to the values of what it means to be (more) human.
5 The end of all this, to have a university education means that we can pursue global collaboration and global responsibility.

CASE STUDY: JAMIE SMART'S DEEP DRIVERS

Jamie Smart in his book *Clarity* (2013) identifies eight what he calls deep drivers – these are qualities and traits people already possess and can remain purely innate resources if not drawn upon. The eight drivers are:

1 clarity
2 direction
3 resilience
4 creativity
5 connection

6 authenticity
7 intuition
8 presence.

There are two aspects to this thinking by Smart. The first is to more fully comprehend what exactly is meant by these terms. This permits one to identify this innate resource within oneself. The second is to more fully appreciate the profound application of each of these resources to drive all manner of professional and personal activity.

The essence of Smart's thinking is outlined below:

Clarity – achieving a clear mind and being fully present in the moment, discerning the way forward without getting distracted by the 'noise' and complexity in the system. Clarity drives many things including effective leadership, insight, detecting opportunities and decision making.

Direction – a clear sense of direction and a motivation to pursue something without a sense of undue pressure. Direction drives strategic planning, authentic leadership, resolving uncertainty and achieving shared vision and purpose.

Resilience – an ability to bounce back after (inevitable) setbacks and implicitly involving security and trust in oneself and the world. Resilience drives dealing with change, thriving through uncertainty, responsiveness and confidence.

Creativity – not the exclusive domain of 'creatives' but the driver behind innovation and problem solving. Creativity drives strategic thinking, product and service design, brand narrative and customer delight.

Connection – strong connections and relationships that are genuine and warm extending to colleagues, suppliers and customers. Connection drives collaboration, employee engagement, persuasion and influence and effective teams.

Authenticity – being who you are, speaking and doing what is genuine, differentiating those that 'walk the walk' from those who only 'talk the talk'. Authenticity drives trust and credibility, transparency, authentic leadership and integrity.

Intuition – often associated with 'gut feel', an internal guide it is risky to ignore. Intuition drives effective decision making, opportunity identification, strategic thinking and innovation.

Presence – associated with enhanced awareness and characterized by connectedness to one's mind, body and the world around. Presence drives charismatic leadership, influencing others, clear view of reality and trend detection.

THE GRADUATE IDENTITY APPROACH

A piece of research funded by the UK Higher Education Academy entitled 'Employer concepts of graduate employability' (Higher Education Academy, 2009) sought to define what skills, competencies, attributes and personal qualities were most valued by employers from a full range of organizations in Norfolk, England.

Overall what emerged from the research was a search for graduates with four identity elements as follows:

1 values
2 intellect
3 performance
4 engagement.

What exactly these labels encompass is outlined below but some of the other details from the research are also both illuminating and significant.

Turning first to the top ten employer expectations on appointment of a graduate, these were the things that employers expected all graduates to display from day one:

1 Demonstrates honesty and integrity.
2 Is someone I can trust.
3 Is able to listen to others.
4 Is able to integrate quickly into a team or department.
5 Is able to present ideas clearly, both verbally and in writing.
6 Can assimilate information quickly.
7 Works safely.
8 Demonstrates good time management.
9 Can plan and manage their time.
10 Can demonstrate attention to detail and thoroughness.

A point to emphasize here is that these ten expectations came ahead of 37 others.

The expectation is for graduates to be 'able to fit quickly into a team' and to be good communicators, both verbally and in writing.

Another part of the research asked employers to rank groupings of employability skills relative to one another. This 'forced' ranking produced the following results in rank order of importance:

1 interpersonal skills
2 written communication skills
3 IT skills
4 experience of work environment
5 commercial/business awareness
6 numeracy skills
7 presentation skills.

This, of course, does not suggest that presentation skills are not important. Rather, that the most important skill area for these employers was interpersonal skills. Note also how written communication skills came out ahead of IT skills.

Turning now to the four elements of 'graduate identity':

Values – the research found that values which universities are concerned to foster were also valued by the employers. This included:

- diversity awareness
- citizenship
- environmental awareness
- an interest in culture.

An important point here is that such values also have significance from an employer's business perspective, encompassing customers and clients and relating to business opportunities in the areas of environmental and global awareness.

Intellect – employers look to the subject discipline to deliver cognitive abilities and to furnish graduates with a body of knowledge that both the graduate and the employer can draw upon. It is important for the graduate to be able to articulate the intellectual value of their degree.

Performance – although graduate performance in employment is essential, when they select graduates employers only assess potential and here the research discovered that employers conceive this potential through the idea of graduate identity.

Engagement – according to the research, employers expect graduates to have the ability to interact with others in a whole variety of situations. Employers were suspicious of graduates who had chosen a narrow student experience and valued those graduates who made the most of opportunities available to them, who had gained a broad-based experience through volunteering, university societies and events.

APPLIED PERSONAL DEVELOPMENT

What skills do you have or are you going to develop that mark you out as a graduate – and not just a graduate, but a graduate of distinction? What can you do to differentiate yourself from the next intelligent and talented student chasing the same opportunity? What is going to be distinctive about you?

Looking at the expectations of employers, is there anything here that makes you feel a little 'exposed' – a skill area where you are not up to standard. There is likely to be at least one or two things to work on. The time to work on these things is not later or towards graduation, but now. It is something you could mention to your personal tutor and it is something you could incorporate into your personal development plan. Beware of any suggestion or temptation to think of oneself as the 'complete item'. Everybody has what you might call a profile.

This is not just about plugging gaps but developing into excellences where your greatest potential lies. You may be exceptionally analytical. You might have the potential to be an outstanding communicator (like many of the people we see in the media). Otherwise, you might have the makings of being an inspirational leader. From the list of graduate skills you can see there are many areas where you might excel.

It is good to be working out from your first year onward which industry sectors or business cultures you find yourself most drawn to. Get hold of some highlighter pens (a green one, a yellow one and a pink one) and run down the list of job areas at the beginning of the chapter. 'Traffic light' your interest areas as follows. If you are naturally drawn to an area highlight it green. If you are naturally disinterested by another area colour it pink. If you are unsure either way highlight it yellow. Analyse the pattern this produces. Do any of those areas you have highlighted the same colour have anything in common and what does this suggest about you? Or ask yourself why you are particularly attracted to a certain area?

What can you do to start to explore your areas of interest? Could you secure a work placement in that area? Or perhaps you could do some volunteering? If you want to explore a particular responsibility, for example a leadership or communication role, consider exercising this in the context of a university club or society. Set yourself the objective of doing one thing in addition to your studies and your social life and think of this one thing as your opportunity to enhance your CV, explore an area of interest and experiment with developing skills and confidence.

Some of the skills covered in this chapter would be a big ask for any adult. Some of them which are metaphorically in line with the current of where the contemporary river is flowing – 'skills' such as collaboration, dialogue, empathy and integrity – have enormous potential. If at first you don't fully comprehend the significance of something or don't completely understand it, don't just dismiss it. Try your hand at becoming an early adopter of a certain skill or technology. Give it a go. You may surprise yourself.

For example, why not be the first person from your year group or school to study abroad at a specific university? By all means follow certain trends, but why not lead or innovate in other things. Sometimes risk takers are more highly rewarded than the risk averse. Don't let fear rob you of great opportunities.

Finally, work out what you want. Don't be tempted just to please others with your career selections and the interests you pursue. For some of you this will come naturally. For others, you may have to work really hard to figure this out or work this through. Seek support and guidance from the career service and your personal tutor. Explore in conversation with friends and fellow students the possibilities.

REFERENCES

Christian, S. (2012) *Top Jobs: Discover the Best Graduate Jobs and How to Get One*. Richmond: Trotman Publishing.

Divan, A. (2009) *Communication Skills for the Biosciences: A Graduate Guide*. Oxford: Oxford University Press.

Elias, P. and Purcell, K. (2013) 'Futuretrack working paper 5: classifying graduate occupations for the knowledge society'. Warwick: Institute for Employment Research, University of Warwick. Available at: www2.warwick.ac.uk/fac/soc/ier/futuretrack/findings/elias_purcell_soche_final.pdf (accessed 15 July 2013).

Futuretrack (2012) 'The changing relationship between higher education and the graduate labour market: evidence from Futuretrack', conference paper, Manchester, 7 November.

Goldberg, M. L. (2007) 'Discourse'. Available at: https://faculty.washington.edu/mlg/courses/definitions/discourse.html (accessed 16 July 2013).

Higher Education Academy (2009) 'Employer concepts of graduate employability'. York: HEA.

Joyce, S. P. (2013) 'Be visible on LinkedIn', *Career Planning and Adult Development Journal*, Fall: 88–90.

Katulushi, C. (2005) 'Diversity, values and international students in higher education', in S. Robinson and C. Katulushi (eds), *Values in Higher Education*. St Bride's Major: Aureus Publishing.

King, R. (2003) 'Globalization and the national context: finding a balance', *The Bulletin*, May.

La Valle, I., O'Regan, S. and Jackson, C. (2000) *The Art of Getting Started: Graduate Skills in a Fragmented Labour Market*. Brighton: The Institute for Employment Studies.

Mann, S. J. (2008) *Study, Power and the University*. Maidenhead: McGraw-Hill Education.

Peregrin, T. (2012) 'LinkedIn profile makeover: optimising your professional online profile', *Journal of the Academy of Nutrition and Dietetics*, 112 (1): 23–25.

Prince, E. (2013) *The Advantage: The 7 Soft Skills You Need to Stay One Step Ahead*. Harlow: Pearson Education.

Redmond, P. (2010) *The Graduate Jobs Formula: How to Land Your Dream Career*. Richmond: Trotman Publishing.

Smart, J. (2013) *Clarity: Clear Mind, Better Performance, Bigger Results*. Chichester: Capstone Publishing.

Whitehead, J. (2002) 'Transforming embodied values of humanity into educational standards of judgement for use in creating the new disciplines approach to educational theory', draft paper, 11 June, University of Bath Department of Education.

5 COMPETENCIES AND WAYS OF OPERATING IN THE TWENTY-FIRST CENTURY

● ● ● ● ● ● ● ● ● ● ● ● ● ●

A NOTE FROM THE AUTHOR

This may be the first time that you have heard the phrase the 'agentic individual', which is associated with the research of Helen Haste that we shall be reviewing in this chapter. Agentic derives from the term agency, which conveys the notion of being able to handle a situation or a challenge – to be in control of oneself and one's own responses and contribute positively rather than negatively to what happens or what transpires.

Twenty-first-century living and working will present all sorts of new opportunities and challenges and this chapter explores some of what will be the most sought after competencies for the years ahead.

It is difficult to be agentic if you lack confidence and the issue of gaining confidence is profiled as key to employability. The same can be said of individuals who are not aware of or utilizing their most significant talents. A popular new framework is introduced in this context.

In Chapter 2 we introduced values and you were able to think about your personal values. In this chapter we develop this further by looking at values in the workplace. This will culminate with outlining what is meant by the term the 'ethical practitioner'.

Learning outcomes

When you have completed this chapter you will be able to:

- define competencies needed for twenty-first-century success
- navigate a well-known framework of talents with its associated vocabulary
- appreciate the significance of self-confidence

- understand and apply the concept of values in the workplace
- outline what is meant by an ethical practitioner.

COMPETENCIES

Haste argues the term 'competence' implies 'good enough' functioning (Haste, 2007). She adds that a competence is not just a collection of skills as it is sometimes considered, but 'a way of approaching problems and issues within which certain skills are required' (Haste, 2007). Haste's research, however, emphasizes what she terms a 'generative adaptation' – of responding creatively to 'the management of inevitable ambiguity and uncertainty' (Haste, 2007). She underlines a tendency to associate all these things with the new replacing the old. In practice, it is far more complex, requiring a simultaneous management of both continuity and change and finding ways of 'dealing constructively with irreconcilable multiple perspectives'. This takes us to a place where exercising competencies approximates an ethical task.

Haste proposes a number of key competencies needed for twenty-first-century life and these we shall look at in detail below.

Haste's key competencies for twenty-first-century life

- managing ambiguity and uncertainty
- agency and responsibility
- finding and sustaining community
- managing emotion
- managing technological change.

Managing ambiguity and uncertainty

The need to be aware of a distance between oneself and 'other' (the other person or someone with a different and other cultural background) is at the heart of Haste's managing ambiguity and uncertainty competence. This involves handling dialogue with 'other', comprehending multiple perspectives and being able to adapt to the disparity between one's expectations and one's experience.

In addition, this competence is also about managing multiple selves, a concept we shall explore further in Chapter 8. This is the notion that multiplicity is not just to be found in 'other', but also in oneself.

There are two further points about this competence that are particularly pertinent to the twenty-first century. Firstly, that the challenge is not just handling a world that is multicultural in terms of its ethnicity, but also multidimensional in terms of its tasks and social demands (Haste, 2007). Secondly, that political and religious fundamentalism, still present in this century, stands opposed to notions of diversity and ambiguity (Haste, 2007).

Agency and responsibility

The agency and responsibility competence is central to a sense of being able to cope and to be able to problem solve when presented with multiple challenges. This competence feeds on prior experience of effectiveness and is reinforced by ways of narrating accounts of how individuals faced obstacles of various kinds and overcame them.

The 'agentic' individual is able to say to themselves I can do this or I can solve this problem. Haste argues that feeling thus requires experience of having an effect on one's environment, sometimes alone but usually with others (Haste, 2001).

The connection between agency and responsibility is most clearly spelt out by Haste in her 2001 chapter, where she outlines three different meanings of responsibility.

Responsibility 1 – Haste defines as duties and obligations to the community. These are the mores, the expectations and the rules as set by the community. Haste argues because of expectations, that agency does not usually extend far in this context. But the individual can decide not to fit into expectations and there may even be situations, for example of the whistle-blowing sort, where the individuals 'contravene normative pressures'.

Responsibility 2 – Haste defines as the sense of connection to others which generates care and concern. Accepting that people are inevitably intercon-nected, agency would be expressed in the effective negotiation of all those things which are involved in creating shared consensus and meaning including:

- interaction
- dialogue
- social processes.

Responsibility 3 – Haste defines as a sense of personal commitment to carry through one's value position into action and engagement. It is seen not only in the individual's autonomy but also in their interactions with others. In respon-sibility 3 the individual's driver is *internal* – they will take risks and compromise their own comfort to help others, with the sense that this is the only reasonable or right thing to do.

Finding and sustaining community

Haste's third competence of finding and sustaining community is played out through building social and interpersonal networks and relates to the capacity to find and sustain community links. Haste argues that through sharing infor-mation we connect to others and that this is the basic structure of any community (Haste, 2009). In the twenty-first century the capacity to maintain links electronically in the three overlapping domains of work, social and leisure is becoming increasingly important.

Part of this competence is defining *who is my community?* and involves answering the following questions:

- Who do I associate with?
- Who do I allow 'in'? (confidence, circle, etc.)
- Who do I allow close?
- How and where do I draw lines?

In a virtual world, the notion of maintaining boundaries is very important (Haste, 2007).

Managing emotion

Managing emotion is a competence that Haste justifies as striking the right balance between affect and reason and not privileging one over the other. There are those who are suspicious of the emotions but Haste argues that the important thing is to be able to differentiate how emotions can both validate and de-legitimize different kinds of experiences (Haste, 2009). This may suggest that we need to discern if a 'gut feeling' is legitimate or not.

Haste argues that over the past century in western culture we have seen a number of ways at looking at emotion and these still permeate thinking. Firstly, there has been the viewpoint that emotion disorganizes and distorts reason and in essence is 'not a trustworthy source of knowing' (Haste, 2007). Secondly, there has been the viewpoint that while reason is paramount, emotion has a functional role to energize cognition. Passion is still regarded as suspect, but 'competent' emotion directs one's affect to achieving the tasks set by one's cognition. Thirdly, there is another viewpoint that valorizes emotion over reason. This is a romantic outlook and is reflected in things like the search for a 'true' selfhood and 'authentic emotions' (Haste, 2001).

The breakthrough viewpoint for Haste is one which integrates emotion and cognition reflected in the neuroscience research of Antonio Damasio (see case study below) who established that individuals unable to exercise emotion are incapable of making effective reasoned judgements.

CASE STUDY – DAMASIO'S RESEARCH ON THE INTEGRATIVE SIGNIFICANCE OF EMOTION

Antonio Damasio argues that emotions are a crucial component of decision making and are at the heart of every decision that is made. Emotions, he argues, enable you to highlight things as good or bad. The 'lift' of emotion is a significant factor in swaying what we do. We conjure up these emotional states to guide us in one direction or another. Looking back on past experiences we remember not just factual data, which of course is very significant, but we also recall emotional data which we consider as well. Wisdom,

(Continued)

Managing technological change

Competence in managing technological change involves being open to exploring the potential of new technology and adaptively responding to the new technology's possibilities, particularly its impact on social practices. In the university environment this means embracing new ways of learning and of gathering and interacting with information.

Technological innovation has a way of changing social practice. An example that Haste provides is the advent of the mobile phone, where it has become, as she puts it, 'a prosthesis of the person' (Haste, 2001). As a consequence phoning a person overtook phoning a place.

The competence at issue with technological change is the ability to adapt to its implications (Haste, 2007) and to be able to respond both positively and creatively to the new opportunities that come with changes in social practices. It is also about ensuring that other valued practices are not lost. Haste underlines an 'integrative' dimension of competence that you don't hear elsewhere.

PROFESSIONALISM AND COMPETENCE

We have been stretched by considering Helen Haste's far-reaching framing of competencies, but as Haste herself acknowledges being competent at something implies being able to do something to a certain standard. If we fall short of the required standard we are familiar with the word incompetent.

Competences are bound up with professionalism. It is essential for employers to ensure their staff are able to do their work or to deliver a specific function to a particular standard. If not, this could even have legal implications for the employing organization.

A real-life example of a competency framework from a public sector organization is provided in Table 5.1. Firstly, let's note the areas of competence:

- effectiveness
- respect for others
- responsibility for actions
- customer focus
- information handling
- teamwork
- learning and continuous improvement
- communication
- planning and organization.

Secondly, the formatting of the framework is interesting because for each competence so called 'negative indicators' are listed. These indicate a falling short from the required standard. In addition, both expected and higher evidences of the competence are included. Taken together with the negative indicators this specifies degrees of performance for each competence where 'expected' indicates competence and 'higher' indicates excellence or exemplary performance. In getting the most out of people, the higher category of performance and its recognition are important.

The competence of customer focus exemplifies this approach and its definition along with the three degrees are listed in Table 5.1:

Table 5.1 Example competency framework

Customer focus: the ability to anticipate and respond to customer needs. Customers include everyone with whom an individual comes into contact, both inside and outside the organization.	
Negative indicators	'Not my problem'
	Fobs off customers/makes excuses
	Fails to respond to requests or leaves enquiries unattended
	Absolves responsibility
	Adopts 'take it or leave it' attitude
Expected	Is prepared to alter what is done to accommodate changing needs
	Deals with customer requirements effectively and in a positive manner
	Demonstrates active listening, takes an interest and checks understanding
	Demonstrates care and appreciation of the problems of others by providing individual support and consideration
	Accepts personal responsibility for ensuring customer service
	Seeks feedback to ensure that the service delivered is complete and has satisfied customer needs
	Always keeps the customer updated regarding work progress
	Answers emails and deals with calls promptly
	Recognizes own contribution to organization's goals

(Continued)

Table 5.1 (Continued)

Higher	Follows up to check and deliver additional needs
	Creates the opportunities for face-to-face meetings with customers to explain what is happening and resolve conflict
	Goes the extra mile and provides additional support to customers at personal inconvenience
	Anticipates customers' issues and needs in advance and takes positive action
	Encourages others to display understanding and commitment to the principles of customer care

Another real-life example of a competency framework, but this time of a senior manager, reveals a different profile of competencies and certainly a set which we might expect for senior management as follows:

- leadership
- teamworking
- staff development
- personal effectiveness
- communication
- reasoning and intellect
- business acumen
- managing change
- resource management.

Again, there isn't the space here to list all the ways in which each competency can be illustrated, so key words that capture the essence of each competency have been employed as an alternative. The important point to emphasize here is that this competency framework shows what is involved with the function of senior management and the range of competencies required to assume this responsibility.

Leadership – by example, vision, empowering, decision making, consistency, impartiality, motivational, continuous improvement, criteria for success, trustworthy, adaptable, accountability, clear rationale.

Teamworking – health and safety, fair, own limitations, resolves issues, handling conflict, individuals' contribution, expertise utilization, respects difference, committed to decisions, contributes to team, encourages participation, team focus, team performance.

Staff development – full potential, self-development, continual evaluation, constructive feedback, coaches and develops, developmental issues, learning through experience, developmental goals, recognized qualifications, training needs.

Personal effectiveness – difficult decisions, own competence, wins confidence, displays integrity, shows resilience, empowers others, positively influences, copes well, time management.

Communication – project representative, problem resolution, accurate writer, effective presenter, clear and concise, approachable and open, provides feedback, listens to others, handling information, consults with others.

Reasoning and intellect – creative and innovative, delivers goals, statistical information, balanced viewpoint, generates solutions, identifies problems, fair analysis, sound judgement.

Business acumen – ITC application, public service, projects improvements, front-line understanding, quality commitment, consultation procedures, decision impact, project commitment.

Managing change – coordinates initiatives, leads projects, identifies improvements, anticipates change, continual review, flexibility and confidence, influences staff, promotes change.

Resource management – control mechanisms, costed cases, risk identification, proactive management, value for money, security procedures, business efficiencies, effective budgeting, current and future priorities.

Guptara's core competencies

Prabhu Guptara writing in *Leadership and Management in the 21st Century* (2005) presents an alternative future perspective to Haste, one which is more functionalist in its perspective. Guptara argues that core competencies of the future will focus on three areas:

1 Excellence in marketing – where customer loyalty and retention will be uppermost.
2 Excellence in logistics – in the operation of 'intelligent' value chains.
3 Excellence in innovation – yielding new products and services.

Guptara says that the mega-corporations of the future will be best placed to obtain and exploit these excellences.

Matthew Taylor's empathic competency

Different again, Matthew Taylor writing in *Twenty-first-century Enlightenment* (2010) believes that empathic capacity will be a core competence for the future. This is part of Taylor's conviction that we shall need new ways of thinking about the world, which are better suited to the century ahead.

There are of course increased opportunities and indeed there is an increased need for this empathic universalism. Taylor argues, 'The opportunities for us to put ourselves in others' shoes have grown exponentially. Immigration, emigration, foreign travel, global culture and communication all provide us with reasons and opportunities to appreciate our similarities and respect our differences' (Taylor, 2010).

Taylor allies this to what he calls 'pro-social' behaviour, which has the capacity to strengthen society. It is a part of what David Halpern refers to as the hidden wealth of nations – all the ways of trusting, caring and cooperating (Halpern, 2010).

KEY CONCEPT – US AND THEM

David Berreby in his book *Us and Them: Understanding Your Tribal Mind* (2005) describes how each person operates with their own mind map to guide them in their daily contacts and interactions with other people. As human beings we simultaneously belong to a host of different human kinds and we are instinctively on the lookout for signs and symbols that indicate another person is part of 'our kind' – that is some common ground and a foundation for trust.

Berreby speaks of the 'suppleness of the mind' and its ability to very quickly assign or switch others between the categories of *usness* (those who evoke a 'we-feeling') and *themness* (those who evoke a 'they-feeling'). Empathy here could rest on almost anything, including a sense of common humanity. A bridge that unites you with another person could emerge from nowhere and be almost anything, like a shared sense of humour or attending the same university as a young adult or a mutual love of fishing. It doesn't need to be profound.

One of Berreby's points to underline is the significance of establishing trust or extending the circle of trust to encompass another, because this is central to the sense of usness. Trust is often assisted by a positive face-to-face encounter but it is still possible to achieve it without this. In either case people look out for any number of *signs* of connection.

Although the sense of usness can be broken, it is that state where another person 'is fit for the respectful exchanges of goods, services, information, and emotions that constitute life in a human community' (Berreby, 2005).

INDIVIDUALITY

Individuality is not just who you are, but what you do. It is something that is highly prized in the western world, reflecting a long tradition of what we might term the pursuit for self-actualization. There is much validity in this philosophy, however, we need to place alongside it another philosophy of working with others to realize visions and goals. There is a way of being both an individual and working well with others.

Let's return to our starting point. What is the substance or the essence of who you are as an individual? Well firstly, this is more than just the sum total of your characteristics and abilities. Secondly, even when you add to this your behaviours, i.e. what you do, it is plain to see that this doesn't encapsulate your whole individuality.

Your individuality is something profoundly plural and complex in as much as it reflects a whole host of things including your background, your family situation and history, your roots, your education, your life experiences, your friendships and so forth.

In the adult world it is relatively rare to meet people who are near fully actuated. When you meet someone who approximates this it is a noteworthy experience. There are a number of factors which hamper people being all they can be and bringing all of themselves to life's course with its multiple and continued personal interactions. The sense is that only a *measure* of our potential, and all the things we are and can be, is activated. Perhaps the following things explain this observation.

- Social conformity – doing what is expected socially and not venturing beyond this.
- Confidence – people not operating from a position of secure confidence in themselves and in their ability to handle a given situation.
- Fear – lack of confidence relates to fear, which actually takes many forms.
- Presence – people make different decisions about how to present themselves in a given situation. For example, how prominent to be, how to express themselves, how much of a lead to provide.
- Communication – people communicate in many different ways. Some are more fluent, verbose and assertive than others.

EMBODIMENT BOX – TOM RATH'S STRENGTHSFINDER

A powerful tool in self-definition is the StrengthsFinder 2.0 assessment to be found in Tom Rath's book, *Strengths Finder 2.0* (2007). Rath builds on Donald O. Clifton's and Gallup's work and the key observation by Peter Drucker that most people are wrong about what they think they are good at.

StrengthsFinder is in fact about defining and understanding one's key talents and the assessment identifies an individual's top five talents from a list of 34 themes. A talent here is understood as a 'natural way of thinking, feeling and behaving' (Rath, 2007). Rath argues that building on this natural endowment, knowledge and skills, along with practice, actually serves to amplify these talents.

Talents constitute the areas where an individual has the greatest potential to develop strengths, but according to Rath strengths are the result of talent multiplied by the investment of time and experience in practising and developing skills and building one's knowledge base.

(Continued)

(Continued)

The themes constitute a fascinating vocabulary for both articulating and appreciating the complexity of talents. These are listed below, along with a key notion of what the talent represents:

Achiever – a constant drive for achievement

Activator – 'you cannot not act'

Adaptability – flexible and productive where others buckle

Analytical – understanding patterns and connections

Arranger – conducting and seeking the perfect configuration

Belief – consistent to your firmly set values

Command – leading you to take charge

Communication – determined for your information to survive

Competition – rooted in comparison and coming out on top

Connectedness – knowing everything and everybody is connected

Consistency – upholding a consistent and balanced environment

Context – looking back for 'blueprints'

Deliberative – carefulness and vigilance for an unpredictable world

Developer – seeing the potential in others

Discipline – imposing structure on the world

Empathy – sensing the emotions of those all around

Focus – work out (even daily) where you are heading

Futuristic – a conjuror of visions for the future

Harmony – looking for areas of agreement and common ground

Ideation – 'fascinated by ideas'

Includer – stretches the circle wider

Individualization – intrigued by the individual qualities of each person

Input – a craving to know more

Intellection – characterized by intellectual activity

Learner – a great desire to learn

Maximizer – in pursuit of excellence

Positivity – optimistic and generous with praise

Relator – selective but very committed to relationships

Responsibility – taking psychological ownership for things committed to

Restorative – love solving problems and finding solutions

Self-assurance – great faith in own strengths

Significance – wanting to be significant in the eyes of others

Strategic – creating alternative ways to proceed

Woo – 'winning others over'

A relevant source on let's call it the possibility of actualizing as an individual and as a human being is John Wall's book, *Moral Creativity: Paul Ricoeur and the Poetics of Possibility* (2005).

Firstly, Wall argues that people have a propensity to deny what he calls their 'original creative capability' for several reasons:

- They cling to narrow or fixed worldviews (see Chapter 6) from the past.
- They acquiesce to systems of control in the present.
- They fail to engage with others in the formation of more human futures.

Secondly, while people have a perpetual possibility of bringing all of themselves to a situation or life in general, we also operate in a world where there is multiplicity, disorder, complexity and sadly even tragedy.

Thirdly, while recognizing the tension between our given (social) conditions and 'creative self-narration' (self-storying) it is possible for people to achieve the latter and to capture this way of expressing their true individuality.

Fourthly, Wall assigns Paul Ricoeur's term 'ipseity' to the self's ability to commit to certain projects and life plans, to overcome inevitable challenges here and in general to participate in forming and projecting a certain narrated (storied) identity – in other words, people achieving their individuality potential.

Finally, this is not an isolated task, but one which is achieved through relationship with others. Wall also speaks of the significance of what he terms inclusivity. This is about people overcoming their tendency to radically overlook others. It is a 'stretching apart' of former preconceptions and seeing the place of others in the formation of our true individuality.

EMPLOYABILITY FOCUS – SELF-CONFIDENCE

A key component in what can be described as 'turning up' in any interaction, or say in an interview, is confidence. It may be a reassurance to some, that lack of confidence in adults is widespread, meaning that many people are approaching situations and opportunities operating out of some sort of *deficit*, if only a *felt* deficit on their part. The other thing to highlight is that

(Continued)

(Continued)

confidence does not correlate with talent or gifting. Adults can have amazing talents and abilities and yet lack self-confidence.

But it is possible in your adult life to gain more confidence. Below are listed, some of the factors that can help us forward in this area.

Self-knowledge – to gain a greater understanding of oneself it is helpful to examine others. A considered examination of others will reveal that as human beings we are 'profiled'. There are some things that we do really well and other things that don't flow so easily. No one is different here. There are things for everyone where effectively you'd be taking them outside their comfort zone. An important part of gaining confidence is appreciating this profiled nature of being human and coming into a greater knowledge of your own profile.

Practice – as humans we learn through practice. Even riding a bike seems like a daunting experience when we begin. But balance almost magically arrives with practice. If we practise something we get better at it. Yes, there still is the factor of natural talent which means that we are disposed to some things more than others. We need to be prepared when learning or mastering something to put ourselves 'out there' and feel a little exposed as a result for a time or a season. These feelings of vulnerability do not last forever and it's the same for most people. Talent does not explain everything that people can do well. Often it's about practice.

Community – the best way to learn to do something and do something better is in the context of a supportive community. That's one reason why a healthy community of learning at university can be so significant. To do something better requires not just practice but also encouragement and feedback as to how we can improve. Even top tennis players have coaches to provide these things. The working environment is not so different, but the stakes are a little higher in that a certain competence is required. But a good manager, rather than a poor one, will be seeking to develop his or her people or team and again this can make for a positive community of learning.

Evaluation – this point relates to the others, but here the thing to emphasize is the importance of seeking feedback and evaluating your performance. For example, given an opportunity to see yourself giving a presentation that has been recorded is a way of gaining a fair perspective of your performance. Added to this it is important to listen to feedback that is given. Sometimes the attitude can be to contest this. It is helpful to consider, 'How might the person evaluating my performance have arrived at this observation?' This applies also to their encouragements and praise as well as their critique.

VALUES AND THE WORKPLACE

The remainder of the chapter is concerned with values and the workplace and consists of four very different elements and perspectives. The first focus on Martin Papapol (2006) is characteristic of an overtly political perspective, and like most political inputs you will instinctively respond to it. If it isn't your own point of view be careful not to dismiss the value of it. Papapol's critique of capitalism does at least reflect an important ability to stand at a distance from something one is usually imperceptibly a part of and consider how it works.

The second, Stuart Hart's (2007) framework, is ground breaking in its determination to strategize around the issue of sustainability. The quadrant presented shows how businesses can respond in a number of ways to the sustainability priority. It goes a long way beyond 'greening' as it is sometimes termed.

The third, the Leeds City Council case study, is illustrative of a bold attempt to put values right at the centre of a large organization responsible in some way for hundreds of thousands of people. It is interesting how an even higher bar is applied to senior managers and leaders and how the framework is reinforced through the appraisal system.

Finally, what it means to be an ethical practitioner in business is explored. This makes the important distinction between morality and ethics. In the twenty-first century it will be impossible to conduct business without the consideration of ethics. This reflects a growing ethical consciousness on the part of not only customers but all the stakeholders involved in business. This is not to suggest that abuses and exploitative practices will cease, however, business and professional credibility is increasingly bound up with an ethical approach.

MARTIN PAPAPOL'S *DIGITAL CAPITALISM*

> The need of a constantly expanding market for its products chases the bourgeoisie over the entire surface of the globe.

Martin Papapol's book, *Digital Capitalism: Towards a Manifesto for the New Left* (2006) begins with this extract from *The Communist Manifesto* (1848) by Karl Marx and Friedrich Engels. Papapol provides a critique of the current age (which he terms as digital capitalism) and his arguments are illustrative of a globally significant socialist worldview. These are summarized below:

- The former polar master–servant relation has mutated to the anonymous power of capital, who is the new employer.
- The proletariat are now so called *wage earners* and are no different from the *wage slaves* Marx spoke of.
- It is difficult to escape the necessity of having to present oneself to the market as a commodity whether one likes this or not.

- Management determines how labour (the wage earners) is organized, while wage earners must proceed as supervised.
- It is very easy to succumb to what Papapol describes as the 'mathematical cunning' and 'life-destroying' tendencies of digital capitalism.

The alternative, Papapol describes as 'self-formation' which is the creative 'task of planning and organising a dynamic structure of … living and as such a structure for one's life' (Papapol, 2006).

ETHICS BOX – HART'S SUSTAINABLE VALUE PORTFOLIO

Reading a book like *Capitalism at the Crossroads* by Stuart Hart could altogether change the way you look at business and the opportunity that businesses have to make a difference in what the foreword by Al Gore describes as 'the (new) age of sustainability' (Hart, 2007).

Hart proposes that businesses develop new technologies, new business models and new mental frames (related to worldviews) essential to the priority of sustainable development. He adds to this that he sees no inherent conflict between making the world a better place and achieving economic prosperity for all.

This is a bold attempt to cast a new vision for business and to throw off what is known as the 'great trade-off illusion' – that firms must sacrifice financial performance to meet societal obligations. It moves a business beyond looking at sustainable development as a matter of regulatory compliance to seeing it as a business strategy orientation and looking upon challenges to sustainability as opportunities.

At the heart of Hart's vision is his sustainable value portfolio consisting of four strategic areas as follows:

1 Clean technology strategy – this is radically centred on adopting a host of new technologies (e.g. nanotechnology, biomimicry and genomics to name but a few) to achieve great gains over the former, inherently less clean technologies.
2 Base of pyramid strategy – this is concerned with businesses re-orienting their vision to address unmet need at the base of the pyramid and make a difference in the areas associated with the failures of globalization, namely increases in population, poverty and inequity.
3 Pollution prevention strategy – this is about *doing more with less*, not just preventing pollution, but also achieving resource efficiency. In essence, controlling waste of all kinds.
4 Product stewardship strategy – this focuses on inviting the voices of stakeholders beyond the immediate operational control of a business. It would involve taking responsibility for a product's entire life cycle

(from beginning to end) and all the benefits of committed stakeholder engagement.

Because the adoption of these strategies is both complex and extremely challenging very few businesses will be able to successfully carry out activities in all four areas simultaneously. Hart suggests that businesses rate their capability in each of the areas on a scale that goes from the strategy being non-existent, through emerging and established, to finally being institutionalized. An unbalanced pattern across the four areas, for Hart, will spell missed opportunity and vulnerability.

CASE STUDY – LIVING OUR VALUES

Leeds City Council's *Our Values* is a behavioural framework intended to guide working practice with all stakeholders including communities, customers, partners, colleagues and teams.

There are five behaviours for all staff to apply to their professional practice that reflect the values of the organization and how well employees are living the values is incorporated into the appraisal system:

1 working as a team
2 being open, honest and trusted
3 treating people fairly
4 working with communities
5 spending money wisely.

For each of the five behaviours there are two sets of listed standards of behaviour, one for 'everyone' and one for 'managers and leaders'. The important thing to emphasize here is that the managers and leaders are expected to uphold two sets of standards – the standard applied to everyone and the standard applied to the responsibility of management and leadership.

Listed below are the standards for everyone to follow:

Working as a team for Leeds

- Keep up to date with important news and information.
- Take responsibility to help others.
- Have positive expectations of others and support them.
- Share your views, knowledge and ideas.
- Have a 'can do' attitude and learn from experience.

(Continued)

(Continued)

- Deliver work on time and take responsibility for your own workload.
- Seek feedback to drive improvements, to ensure others are satisfied.
- Work *with* others, rather than 'to' or 'for' them.

Being open, honest and trusted

- Do what I say I am going to do.
- Manage others' expectations and be realistic.
- Be patient and considerate, and listen to other people.
- Provide customer friendly information – jargon free and plain English.
- Be open to new ways of working.

Treating people fairly

- Appreciate everyone is different and respect the views and opinions of others – no 'one size fits all' approach.
- Recognize and value cultural differences.
- Understand individuals' communication and access needs.
- Appreciate the efforts of others and acknowledge a job well done.
- Be aware of language and cultural difference in all communications.

Working with communities

- Build knowledge of your customers, keep up to date/share information where appropriate.
- Proactively seek links and develop positive working relationships with community groups.
- Think about things from the point of view of others.

Spending money wisely

- Be flexible and support priorities.
- Before spending, ask 'what difference will this make?'
- Look for ways to improve processes and service delivery.
- Remember that it's not our money that we spend.

Particularly noteworthy here is perhaps the way that Leeds City Council has reinforced the importance of the behaviours by incorporating them in the appraisal system. It also articulates very accessibly some of the things we are highlighting in this book including the centrality of relating positively to difference of all kinds and what Helen Haste (2001) refers to as an 'agentic' approach to working.

Questions

1 Which of the five behaviours particularly stands out for you and why?
2 What about the multiple standards listed? Comment on them.
3 How do you think the framework for all employees might be improved?

THE ETHICAL PRACTITIONER

Why should a businessperson be concerned about operating as an ethical practitioner? We have provided a rationale consisting of six points here.

1 Ethics and professional practice – a good place to start is with the question as to whether ethics matter? If the study and consideration of ethics forms a part of the training of lawyers, accountants, doctors, nurses, the police, members of the armed forces, social workers and many other occupational areas (Vardy and Grosch, 1994), then we might reasonably conclude that ethics form an intrinsic part of professional training and practice. In all these occupations an understanding of ethics and the application of ethics are considered essential, so why should business and business management be different?

2 Ethical and moral agents – a businessperson whether they like it or not – or even if they are aware of it or not – unavoidably takes on the responsibility of acting as both ethical and moral agents. Since the two responsibilities are closely related it is important to distinguish between them. Morality is concerned with whether actions are right or wrong (Vardy and Grosch, 1994). Business people are unavoidably confronted by choices, decisions and ways of operating that have a moral dimension. They also inescapably act as ethical agents, in that business, like experience of other occupational areas, causes us to rationally reflect on human behaviour – not just the rights and wrongs, but also what is in the best interests of all concerned.

3 Carriers of theory – again whether aware of it or not, business people are carriers of ethical theory of all kinds. This reflects things like upbringing, family background, education and religious affiliation (Baelz, 1977). A study of or more exposure to ethical theory may help the business person to appreciate the ethical theories they subscribe to. They may also recognize their own way of ethical thinking in the theories outlined; and also the thinking of others. Since it is impossible to disconnect from our own ethical frame of reference when acting as ethical or moral agents, it is essential to become more aware of why we think the way we do.

4 Not always right – many things happen in business which make forming a judgement or making a good decision (with ethical implications) challenging tasks. Added to this, as Elford points out, we are living now in an age of widespread moral disagreement (Elford, 2000). This calls for both moral

seriousness and tolerance. Conversation with others, including those who see things very differently, becomes a part of the process of arriving at good or better decisions. Markham argues that we should welcome such pluralism (Markham, 2007).

5 Reinvention ethically – business people will find themselves confronted by new, difficult or controversial moral decisions (Gert, 2005). These will both prompt and necessitate deeper ethical reflection. Elford suggests that such decisions have the potential for great harm or great good (Elford, 2000). The raised stakes highlight the possibility (perhaps even adventure) of business people developing into ethical practitioners – of inventing and reinventing themselves as the latter. Business cannot be a value free zone. There are many and varied assumptions about what makes for a good business and a good business environment. Why should the business person be reticent to handle such complexities, or not rise to the challenges presented by giving due consideration to ethics?

6 Methodologically sure – finally, when handling ethical matters business people need to adopt and develop over time a trusted methodology. An understanding and consideration of ethical theory will support the development and application of a robust methodology. When confronted by any ethical issue, consideration must be given to which facts are relevant and which ones are not. Consulting different people with their different perspectives effectively increases the business practitioner's resource base. In good decision making, not all ethical conundrums or problems have unique correct solutions. This allows for creativity. Thankfully, ethical positions are provisional and subject to review and revision in the light of experience (Elford, 2000).

APPLIED PERSONAL DEVELOPMENT

Ethics is not the same as morality. With ethics it's not just a consideration of what is right and what is wrong, it's also the search for the good life or to be more accurate a life that would be good for all. This applies as much to business as any other area of society. As implied there is no way that all the people involved in these considerations will agree, which only adds to the ethical task.

In the same way that individuals have different values (in that they value different things), so do different businesses and this is very evident in the workplace. So where possible it is good to find employment in an organization that aligns with your own values. Values reflect all sorts of things including history, the nature of the business, its owners and, as we saw with Papapol, politics.

There is great potential for an individual not to actualize their talents. This could reflect limited opportunities or making some wrong turns and choices, but it is sometimes due to not identifying where their greatest potential lies. Sometimes it is due to lack of confidence and this is surprisingly prevalent in an adult population. The answer (in part) to all these shortfalls is a healthy community like the learning communities that can be found in universities. These can be and often are places of encouragement, exploration and discernment of your potential.

Universities are well placed to train students in the new ways of thinking that will prepare them for the contemporary and future worlds of business. A number of key words emerged from our overview of Helen Haste's and others research into competencies. There was the agentic individual. Increasingly we will hear the word empathy because of its bridge-building quality in a diverse world. Embracing difference in practical and creative ways will be increasingly important as will fruitfully handling emotions. The world is changing.

REFERENCES

Baelz, P. (1977) *Ethics and Belief*. London: Sheldon Press.

Berreby, D. (2005) *Us and Them: Understanding Your Tribal Mind*. London: Hutchinson.

Elford, R. J. (2000) *The Ethics of Uncertainty*. Oxford: Oneworld.

Gert, B. (2005) 'How common morality relates to business and the professions'. Available at: http://edepot.wur.nl/137690 (accessed 8 July 2013).

Guptara, P. (2005) 'Managers' lives, work, and careers in the twenty-first century', in C. L. Cooper (ed.), *Leadership and Management in the 21 Century*. Oxford: Oxford University Press.

Halpern, D. (2010) *The Hidden Wealth of Nations*. Polity Press.

Hart, S. L. (2007) *Capitalism at the Crossroads: Aligning Business, Earth, and Humanity*. Upper Saddle River: Wharton School Publishing.

Haste, H. (2009) 'What is "competence" and how should education incorporate new technology's tools to generate "competent" civic agents', *The Curriculum Journal*, 20 (3): 207–223.

Haste, H. (2007) 'Good thinking; the creative and competent mind', in A. Craft, H. Gardner and G. Claxton (eds), *Creativity Wisdom and Trusteeship*. Thousand Oaks: Sage.

Haste, H. (2001) 'Ambiguity, autonomy, and agency: psychological challenges to new competence', in D. S. Rychen and L. H. Salganik (eds), *Defining and Selecting Key Competencies*. Seattle: Hogrefe and Huber Publishers.

Leeds City Council. *Our Values*. Available at: www.transformingleeds.com/sections/about_the_org/our_values (accessed 24 October 2014).

Markham, I. S. (2007) *Do Morals Matter?* Oxford: Blackwell.

Papapol, M. (2006) *Digital Capitalism: Towards a Manifesto for the New Left*. Norderstedt: Books on Demand.

Rath, T. (2007) *Strengths Finder 2.0*. New York: Gallup Press.

Taylor, M. (2010) *Twenty-first-century Enlightenment*. London: Royal Society of Arts.

Vardy, P. and Grosch, P. (1994) *The Puzzle of Ethics*. London: Fount.

Wall, J. (2005) *Moral Creativity: Paul Ricoeur and the Poetics of Possibility*. New York: Oxford University Press.

6 GOING GLOBAL

● ● ● ● ● ● ● ● ● ● ● ● ● ●

A NOTE FROM THE AUTHOR

A generation ago you hardly ever heard the word *global* even mentioned. It was definitely there in the dictionary but it wasn't in the consciousness, that is the minds and thinking of most people. We might ask the question, what caused the change? Firstly, we moved from one age to another, a different period of world history, where different parts of the world were able to relate more freely and more easily with one another through what is known as globalization. This centres on an economic relationship and the development of trade and markets but it also has a political dimension through nation states seeking regional and international partners and resulting in greater integration, as seen for example in the European Union.

Secondly, we witnessed an economic and political restructuring of the world where the heightened rivalry of the United States with the former USSR expressed in the cold war came to an end and other significant players on the world stage like China and India emerged. Thirdly, there was an awakening in the consciousness of westerners not only to the emergence of the latter but also to Islam as a significant cultural entity as well as the so called 'global south'. The information revolution through startling advances in the world media contributed to this new consciousness.

This chapter is concerned with helping you as students to come to terms with the significance of the new global age and incorporates a helpful framework on becoming a global practitioner, expressed in skills, knowledge, awareness and values.

In Chapter 2 you will recall that we looked at modernism, postmodernism and late modernity. In this chapter we revisit this way of looking at stages of development but connect them with a concept known as worldview. This has a long history that originates in philosophy but it is an extremely useful way of explaining how different people have varying and contrasting takes on the same reality. Particularly in a global reality where all is heterogeneous we need to find informed and responsible ways of handling difference (or plurality), both personally and in our business organizations. Worldview studies equip us here but also suggest the direction in which the world is going. This also is enormously significant both personally and professionally.

Learning outcomes

When you have completed this chapter you will be able to:

- define different forms of global consciousness expressed at both individual and corporate levels including global responsibility
- outline the skills, knowledge, awareness and values involved in being a global practitioner
- relate ethics to the global age
- understand and apply the concept of worldview
- indicate and outline how worldviews are transforming.

GLOBALIZATION

Kosselleck (1985) perceptively observes that globalization is both a 'space of experience' as well as a 'horizon of expectation'. In other words, firstly it is experienced as an increasingly interconnected and interdependent world that through an onrush of advances in communication and transportation technology has shrunk both time and space. At the same time, secondly, it is the raising of consciousness of the world as a single place (Robertson, 1992) – as an entity *in itself*. In many respects this is a new geographical and political reality – an emerging and imagined community of postmodernity and a breaking out of modernity's statist view of the world, divided like a jigsaw into sovereign territories.

Relating to both aspects of globalization Creamer (1996) argues that it has sensitized many to a whole clutch of issues the world faces and created anxiety. From a business perspective alone this is an extremely relevant observation not only in respect of understanding the business environment, but also in terms of appreciating the business opportunities this presents for new products and services.

With the emergent global way of viewing the world has come a new terminology of how businesspeople and students should relate to the global. Below are some of the phrases we are increasingly hearing:

- global perspective
- global outlook
- global citizen
- global practitioner
- globally responsible leader
- global consciousness
- corporate global citizenship
- globally responsible organization.

GLOBAL PERSPECTIVE/OUTLOOK

For a businessperson or student to develop a global perspective or outlook this would be reflected in a number of ways:

- a critical appreciation of the concepts of globalization, sustainable development, global governance and global issues facing humanity in the twenty-first century
- understanding the role of business in relation to sustainable development and global issues
- self-awareness of global responsibility and a personal value system demonstrated in reflective practice and professional practice.

EMBODIMENT BOX – GLOBAL CITIZENSHIP

The fullest fleshing out of what being a 'global citizen' might entail is provided by Oxfam (1997) whose global citizen is someone who:

- is aware of the wider world and has a sense of their own role as a world citizen
- respects and values diversity
- has an understanding of how the world works economically, politically, socially, culturally, technologically and environmentally
- challenges social injustice
- participates in and contributes to the community at a range of levels from local to global
- is willing to make the world a more sustainable place
- takes responsibilities for their actions.

CORPORATE GLOBAL CITIZENSHIP

The World Economic Forum defines corporate global citizenship as 'improving the state of the world through business's engagement in partnerships that address key global societal challenges' (World Economic Forum, 2008). It argues that such citizenship is fundamentally in the self-interest of global corporations since their growth, prosperity and sustainability are all dependent on a stable global landscape. It adds that they have a responsibility of being engaged in society.

John Seitz (2008) lists the following things as global issues:

- wealth and poverty – and the uneven effects of globalization
- population – its explosive growth and prospects for supporting population growth
- food – how changes in climate, biotechnology, energy and the amount of arable land might affect food production
- energy – transition in energy sources and conserving energy
- the environment – pollution, deforestation, waste, resources depletion
- technology – both the developmental and destructive potential of technology
- alternative futures – looking for ways to transform our present type of development.

Anglia Ruskin University's (2010) global fitness framework perceptively adds a few more global issues:

- health – obesity, heart disease, hyper-tension, dementia
- over consumption
- role and effects of religion.

KEY CONCEPT – SUSTAINABLE DEVELOPMENT

The World Summit 2002 spoke of the three pillars of sustainable development:

1 economic development
2 social development
3 protection of the environment.

The Brundtland Commission (World Commission on Environment and Development, 1987) defined sustainable development as 'development which meets the needs of the present without compromising the ability of future generations to meet their own needs'. A shorthand of this is provided by an anonymous person who wrote, 'Please leave this planet as you would wish to find it'.

This led to what is known as the 'triple bottom line' construct in the field of corporate responsibility which has these three aspects: the economic, the social and the environmental.

GLOBALLY RESPONSIBLE LEADERSHIP

The Globally Responsible Leadership Initiative (GRLI) – co-founded and supported by the United Nations Global Compact and the European Foundation for Management Development (EFMD) – has a mission to act as a catalyst to develop a next generation of globally responsible leaders. In its *The Globally Responsible Leader: A Call for Action* it states, 'we need more responsible leadership to implement a more comprehensive model for sustainable development. This requires a profound change in individual mindsets and behaviours as well as overall corporate culture' (GRLI, 2008). The GRLI argues this will mean re-visiting three areas:

1 The raison d'être of the firm – defining progress around the core of entrepreneurial action and defined in terms of initiative, dynamism and innovation. Looking also beyond economics and profit growth to other forms of progress.
2 Leadership and ethical fitness – integrating ethics into the functioning of the firm and taking into account societal interdependence and global interconnectedness.
3 Responsible corporate statesmanship – embracing of new types of dialogue and anticipating new global regulations in collaboration with all stakeholders.

Mark Drewell's (2011) distinction between global responsibility and corporate social responsibility is useful here: 'Global responsibility is not corporate social responsibility. The two terms are not interchangeable. The former stands for engaging with the world's challenges head on, the latter for peer comparison in a broader system. Global responsibility begins with the question: "What kind of world do we want to build with the enormous resources we master?"'

EMPLOYABILITY FOCUS – THE GLOBALLY RESPONSIBLE ORGANIZATION

What are the sort of things we should be looking out for in an organization that seeks to be regarded as globally responsible?

- applies ethics in all matters and situations
- an ethical response to social issues
- environmentally, aiming for minimum impact and sustainability
- sources materials and handles labour responsibly
- comprehension of relevant cultural ethical codes
- equality in the workplace
- transparency applied to actions and accounting
- reflected in accountability for mistakes
- responsible for effects of products and actions on stakeholders.

THE GLOBAL PRACTITIONER

There are four interrelated aspects that one must embody to become a so called global practitioner:

- a certain *skills* set that will make for maximum employability in the global age
- specific *knowledge* of the global business environment
- critical *awareness* or consciousness permitting the handling of difference
- a *values* profile required to guide actions and behaviour.

Each of these will be examined in turn.

Global practitioner skills

Many of the key words that we might associate with global practitioner skills can be found in the Center for Creative Leadership's (CCL) research white paper, *10 Trends: A Study of Senior Executives' Views on the Future* (Criswell and Martin, 2007): communication, innovation, collaboration, relationship building and, of course, leadership. To these we'll add conversation and adaptation.

Communication

It would be difficult to overemphasize how important excellent communication skills are in the heterogeneous global arena. The diversity that confronts the individual or the business organization calls for a never-ending process of encoding and decoding our messages, which can be likened metaphorically to a bridge-building communication style and ability. The diversity calls for both interpretation and flexibility – being prepared to look for the appropriate way, the effective way to communicate with a specific person or group of people, and also being prepared to constantly adapt our approach. There is much to learn here.

CCL (Criswell and Martin, 2007) stress the importance of three things:

- the clarity/effectiveness of the message
- the frequency of communication
- utilizing a variety of collaborative technologies.

Jonathan Sacks emphasizes the significance of *conversation*, which is of course a higher-order communication skill. He speaks of the need for conversation that is, 'respectful, engaged, reciprocal, calling forth some of our greatest powers of empathy and understanding' (Sacks, 2002). The context we must remember here is not a comfortable and all forgiving homogeneity, but a 'new tribalism' that comes with globalization. Sacks adds that the global age has 'turned our world into a society of strangers'. It is far from an automatic process to make ourselves open to the stories of strangers, to find interconnectedness in the face of difference. Perhaps Sack's question here might be: does our conversation 'make space for *otherness*'?

Innovation

The CCL (Criswell and Martin, 2007) paper speaks of 'aiming for innovation' and strategies for building 'an innovation culture'. Of the latter they list the following:

- forming and relating ideas
- establishing task forces
- cross-functional innovation teams
- stage-gate processes (product development broken down into distinct stages).

Innovation skills are a difficult thing to pin down but are intrinsic to the search for maximizing human resources, particularly collaboratively.

Some light is provided here by borrowing some of the terminology of John Paul Lederach (2005). Here we might say innovation is bound up with:

- seeing at a deeper level
- breaking out into new territory and refusing to be bound by existing parameters
- imaginatively creating what does not presently exist
- adopting something closer to the artistic process of combining creativity, skill, serendipity and craftsmanship.

Taking up this latter point, innovation is all about creatively forming and connecting ideas. In this process effective incorporation of the latest technology can play a significant part.

Collaboration

What is immediately striking about the concept of collaboration is its plurality, rather than its individualism. This of course can be counter-cultural for many who have been trained to think in terms of individual attainment and performance. Like innovation, collaboration is another elusive term and CCL speak of it ranging from team development to interpersonal understanding as well as encompassing technology-driven skills (Criswell and Martin, 2007). They also make the important point that developing and encouraging a collaborative way of working is central to the task of leadership.

Lederach's thinking (2005) is very relevant here and highlights the connection between a collaborative approach and some of the other important skills or important building blocks needed by the global practitioner. Lederach speaks of four interrelated imperatives:

- the centrality of relationships
- respecting complexity and looking out for the unexpected (serendipity)
- providing space for creativity
- willingness to take risks.

Relationship building

This is a central skill and in an obvious way relates directly to good communication, collaborative working and leadership. In *The Home We Build Together: Recreating Society* (2007) Jonathan Sacks speaks of handling global plurality through integrative, not assimilative approaches – learning to live together by valuing our differences as well as our commonalities. This is about how to manage 'our separateness and togetherness, our differences and interdependencies' – something that is easily stated but is challenging in practice.

Adaptation

I have already referred to adaptation in the case of Erikson's thinking (Chapter 2). Here it is the best word for the skill of responding as positively and as well as one can to never ending and systemic change. The CCL paper speaks of it as an agility to respond to complex challenges and quotes the physicist Theodore Modis as arguing that the intensity of change will continue to increase at alarming levels (Criswell and Martin, 2007). The skill of adaptation also relates to an ability to handle information overload which is also a characteristic of the global age.

Leadership

We look at this subject in detail in Chapter 14. CCL underline the significance of a participative leadership style for the global age (Criswell and Martin, 2007).

Global practitioner knowledge

The global practitioner requires not only a certain skills set for the global age, but at the same time knowledge enabling them to comprehend this specific time in world history and its implications for the business environment.

An important place to start is Roland Robertson's observation that in recent years the very future of humanity and the world has been 'increasingly thematised via controversies' about the relationship between the species and the environment (Robertson, 1992). David W. Orr writing in *The Sustainability Revolution* (Edwards, 2005) speaks of this revolution as a response to a whole clutch of 'perils ahead' including 'rapid climate destabilization, species extinction, pollution, terrorism and ecological unravelling in its many forms, and the human, political and economic consequences'.

The listing of the issues alone highlights the need for an informed perspective on matters of such potential magnitude and significance. Intrinsic to this are two dimensions that are gaining almost universal ascent. Firstly, a *resource sensitivity* and optimization, originating from the keen sense of resources and capital being scarce (and consequently more precious/expensive). Secondly, a growing interest in *green business opportunities*, reflected in such things as green architecture, green engineering and green communities (Edwards, 2005).

Referring as we have to global responsibility, it would be responsible for global practitioners to have a good understanding and knowledge of the following four issues and how they relate to the businesses they are operating in:

1 Environmental stewardship, reflected in:

   ○ waste management
   ○ water management
   ○ energy conservation
   ○ climate consciousness
   ○ security of resources

2 poverty alleviation
3 working for peace
4 working against the denial of human rights.

ETHICS BOX – THE ETHICAL UNIVERSITY

Ronald Barnett (2009) describes the ethical university in six points. Universities are, he argues, inherently and inescapably ethical, but any organization or individual might be called the same if they set out to approximate the six points. You might say, 'ethics is as ethics does'. The ethical university:

1 Demonstrates concern for 'other' – which is reflected in their key activities. The very life of an organization adds value to the lives of those it makes contact with.
2 Is an ethically virtuous institution – it expresses virtue. All that is honourable and noble and good about humanity in its activity. Such virtue is not essentially about conforming to rules. Virtue overflows and flourishes over and above law.
3 Demonstrates ethical authenticity – this is not about achieving moral perfection. It is not sterile and ideal beyond the habitation of humanity. It is rather intentional in that it determines to live out its chosen virtues.
4 Operates in a contested field – there is always temptation to be something other than ethical. It is making decisions and operating, for example, to be more than purely market-driven.
5 Is super-saturated with values – its multiple stakeholders mean that value conflict is embedded in what it is and does. It is not singular but plural in its essential nature and identity. It must listen to all its voices.
6 Practises hospitality – it is tolerant of difference. It handles plurality. The stranger is welcomed. Discovering the same is unusual. It anticipates another perspective.

Global practitioner awareness

To the skills and knowledge needed by the so called global practitioner we now add awareness. This is encapsulated in Crispin Thurlow's term *'critical interculturality'* (Thurlow, 2004) which he says is all about 'the real struggle in respecting the dignity of difference'.

This is a struggle because, as Thurlow argues, interculturality inherently engages with 'dialectics, paradoxes and contradictions', and goes beyond the 'saccharine' and 'naïve' notions of harmony – what Alison Phipps (1999) terms 'intercultural magic' – that it is so easy to slip into. Thurlow speaks of this as a certain *e pluribus unum* – 'out of many, one' (Thurlow, 2004).

Difference, Thurlow argues, needs to be confronted by posing to oneself the difficult yet responsible question, 'What is it about *me* that makes this person seem strange?' This is a process of uncovering a set of what Thurlow refers to as 'privileged identifications', such things as patriarchy or Christian/white supremacy or heteronormativity.

DEVELOPMENT POINTER – ON STRANGENESS AND STRANGERS

We build here on Thurlow's (2004) question: 'What is it about me that makes this person seem strange?' Imagine somebody from a very different global background meeting you for the first time.

List five things, from their perspective, that they might find strange:

1

2

3

4

5

Think about how the 'strangeness' of strangers soon dissipates as you get to know them. What implications does this have for meeting others across boundaries and across cultures?

Global practitioner values

Shiel speaks of the need for a 'broader worldview' (Shiel, 2006). This encapsulates the values requirement to operate as a global practitioner, which is bound up with genuinely valuing plurality and out of this having the heart and the mind to deal with it.

A good place to start with introducing values is stated by Bordeaux école de management (2006) which speaks of helping its students to shape their personal and behavioural qualities to prepare them for the challenges of the future. These it asserts should conform to principles relating to:

- ethics
- respecting differences
- open-mindedness
- integrity.

This is a useful framework and we'll employ it here to flesh out in a little more detail what it means to possess global practitioner values.

Ethics

Ethics is the study of right and wrong and a search for the good life. Applied to business it explores how an organization can operate responsibly and contribute to the well-being of society. In a global context this is widened to global responsibility and operating for the good of all.

If we describe someone or an organization as ethical this suggests a 'high bar' of honour or principle. It is not commonplace and the implication is that it is easier to find unethical behaviour and practice. We might like to think of being ethical as upholding principles or being principle-minded. A number of these are listed in Table 6.1.

Table 6.1 Principles relating to being 'ethical'

Fiduciary principle	Acting in the best interest of the organization and its investors
Property principle	Respecting property and the rights of those who own it
Reliability principle	Keeping promises, agreements, contracts and other commitments
Transparency principle	Conducting business in a truthful and open manner
Dignity principle	Respecting the dignity of all people
Fairness principle	Dealing fairly with all parties
Citizenship principle	Acting as responsible members of the community
Responsiveness principle	Being responsive to the legitimate claims and concerns of others

Respecting differences

This is something we have referred to a number of times in this chapter, but respecting differences is also a value and is reflected in living and working alongside people whose lives don't look like ours.

Open-mindedness

This term could suggest and mean many things. It is helpful to contrast it with closed-mindedness which is associated with such things as intolerance, bigotry, unyielding attitudes, not listening, not caring, defensiveness and lack of education.

In the context of the global practitioner it accords with the new eclecticism that is a characteristic of the global age – that discovery that there are many ways to lead a life, even a good life. It perhaps also suggests that conforming to neo-liberalism, a dominant way of living and thinking, is not the only way.

Integrity

Such is the importance of integrity, this is our main focus in Chapter 8. Integrity is an incredibly broad and nuanced concept but overall when we speak of integrity we're signalling that something hangs or comes together. The contrast to this is a characteristic which splits off from the remainder and results in a fragmentation of sorts – something that takes away from the sense of the whole, or wholeness. Integrity is not moral perfection and that incorrect way of looking at it actually often 'hides' rather than integrates parts of us. Rather, it is handling plurality well – with honesty and seeking after wholeness and integration.

KEY CONCEPT – A GLOBAL ETHIC

The so called global ethic was significantly advanced by ground-breaking thinking from the Swiss theologian and theorist Hans Kung who in 1993 drafted the 'Declaration toward a global ethic' for the Council of the Parliament of the World's Religions. Under the Chairmanship of the former German Chancellor Helmut Schmidt the InterAction Council in 1996 adopted the declaration in its report, 'In search of global ethical standards'. We shall refer to the above as the King/Schmidt argument for a global ethic.

In essence this proposes that a new global ethic is needed for the new global order characterized as follows:

- minimal ethical standards to be accepted universally
- increased sense of common destiny
- increasing significance of supranational government and transnational companies alongside the state
- globalization of the world's challenging issues.

The new global ethic is founded on deeper 'obligations of conscience, love and humanity' and transcends the law, 'standing behind it and above it' (Kung, 1997). It constitutes an attempt to find a set of fundamental principles and values which could be held in common across all cultures and religions. What Kung would later describe as the 'golden rule of humanity' (Kung, 1997) suggested first, that every human should be treated humanely and second, that people should treat others as they wish others to treat them.

(Continued)

(Continued)

A global ethical consensus could only be moved forward with the support of all the major religions and through education, which occupied a crucial role in inculcating global ethical values.

Kung's 'golden rule' and his view of a global ethic has its critics. Richard Faulk claims it 'falls between two stools – either as an irrelevant piety or a utopian dream' (Faulk, 1999). If viewed in abstract terms they are too vague to have serious implications. If translated into action, Faulk says, they become too radical in relation to vested economic and political interests of the established order.

Relativists argue that moral values are different in every society and therefore any attempt to transform the consciousness of individuals through education would amount to a form of cultural imperialism.

Postmodernists point to the illusion of 'universal reason' and 'universal morality' founded upon a false view that the world is monocentric and rationally ordered – whereas in reality they argue it is polycentric and has no natural order.

Critics aside, the contribution of the Kung/Schmidt search for a global ethic is clearly important to stem significant global problems and injustices, as is the process of dialogue between cultures and religions as a route to a better future for many.

WORLDVIEW

Worldview is an extremely useful concept in navigating one's way around the global world and seeing one's own distinct way of life and thinking more clearly. It is derived from the German term *Weltanschauung* and can be defined simply as the way you think about life and the world. Peter Schwartz perceptively remarks, 'each of us responds not to the world, but to our *image* of the world' (Schwartz, 1991).

Alternatively, one could speak of worldviews as 'world ways' that are infused with values. In the following quote David Naugle highlights a historical human tendency to seek a unified way of both viewing and approaching the world: 'Theoretically the human mind is not satisfied with piecemeal knowledge, but seeks integrity in its understanding of reality. Worldviews are generated by the mind's aspiration to a unified comprehension of the universe, and answers to ultimate questions' (Naugle, 2002).

A vehicle that is used to select and unify our view of our life or the world and unconsciously gives away our values is the way we narrate or story life's experience. Even our histories do this in that they often reflect a particular perspective and struggle to represent all the voices involved in a particular history.

When it comes to classifying worldviews there are so to speak, many ways of cutting the cake. For example, we could speak meaningfully of a western worldview and contrast it with an Islamic worldview – the contrasting histories in their geographical aspect and different dominant religions creating different views of the world. Alternatively, we could look at a neo-liberal worldview and place this alongside a communist one. The worldview prevalent in specific countries is also a meaningful construct as are the worldviews that accompany different eras of history like a peasant or pre-modern worldview, a modern worldview and a postmodern worldview.

All these different ways of looking at the world approach the following 'worldview questions' in a contrasting way:

- Where are we?
- What are we?
- What's wrong?
- What's the solution?

And as stated above, the different worldviews would story the answers in contrasting ways.

The perceptive reader will immediately see that there are a number of influences at work shaping the worldviews that people hold – historical factors, related to these geographical factors, also political and religious ones and, of course, economic ones too. The implication is that the way of classifying worldviews is useful in highlighting specific patterns of thinking, however, in practice people, particularly in the global age, adopt something closer to a synthesis of different worldviews reflecting multiple and sometimes contrasting influences in their lives.

Lori Kanitz (2005) highlights that contemporary students of higher education possess this 'hodgepodge' of worldviews, which is a product of countless agents acting on them including such things as background, culture, peers, education and religion. Added to this are cultural influences including postmodernism, materialism, dualism and scientism.

Even accepting this observation that worldviews are combined, to something resembling a chowder of various elements, the concept remains a potent way of understanding plurality and diversity not only in ourselves, but in the countless people we encounter in our daily and business lives. Building on Thurlow's point, worldview helps us to appreciate the very real interpersonal and intercultural dynamic of strangeness: why I may appear strange in my ways and my outlook to others; and why others may appear strange to me. We are often the product of extremely different environments and even histories. The stranger remains strange until we know them a little more through conversation and the sharing of stories. Not only does this interaction permit a little more understanding of one another and our obvious differences, but it also helps us to see shared humanity and often unexpected things we share in common. We must all have had that experience where you think initially that you are not going to relate to someone because of your initial impression and then you discover in due course an emerging friendship that bears no relation to one's first encounter with them.

The classification of worldviews

A powerful resource in starting to classify worldviews is Paul Hiebert's book, *Transforming Worldviews: An Anthropological Understanding of How People Change* (2008).

Dovetailing with our analysis of modernity, postmodernity and late modernity in Chapter 2, Hiebert outlines worldviews that go with these ages, which he labels as follows:

- the modern worldview
- the postmodern worldview
- the post-postmodern or glocal worldview.

We will examine each of these in turn, but the usefulness of Hiebert's analysis is not just providing a time-line for explaining how the worldview has shifted in the western world, but helping us to understand and appreciate that other societies and people currently view the world through other – for example modernist – spectacles.

The modern worldview

A summary of Hiebert on the modern worldview is as follows:

- scientific progress and rationalization overcoming the arbitrariness of nature
- rule of the world through reason, science and government
- concern for this life and the emphasis on material abundance
- division of life into the spheres of public and private
- meaning and values based on self-realization
- territory as defining identity, e.g. people are 'Canadians', 'Germans'
- the state claims the ultimate loyalty of its citizens.

Table 6.2 Spheres of life in the modern worldview

Public	Private
Work	Home
Mechanistic order	Relational, organic order
Rationalized	Creative
Controlled emotions	Expressed emotions
Hierarchical control	Relational, equality
Production and profit	Consumption and entertainment
Science	Religion

We can perhaps see at the very least vestiges of the above in ourselves and in our own society, but Hiebert's modernist division of the spheres of life into the public and private is particularly prevalent in how many people still organize their lives.

The worldview of late modernity or postmodernity

Hiebert argues that postmodernity was ushered in by the collapse of the Enlightenment project with its belief in progress (Hiebert, 2008). A shift in worldview, he adds, rarely totally displaces the old worldview with the new one. Rather, the new 'incorporates many elements from the old but gives them new meaning within a new configuration' (Hiebert, 2008). His characterization of the worldview of late modernity or postmodernity is as follows:

- cultural and religious pluralism dominates views of otherness
- totalizing claims and overarching (meta)narratives are particularly suspect
- modernity said little about ethics and purpose
- postmodernity lives with anxiety and fear and calls for responsibility and imagination
- self is the centre of reality
- hyperconsumerism is the route to fulfilling ever-expanding needs and wants
- the myth of the coming apocalypse is prevalent.

The post-postmodern or glocal worldview

With the emergence of China and India along with Islam and the relative decline in western dominance (with its colonialism) Hiebert argues a 'new form of polycentered globalism has emerged' (Hiebert, 2008). The post-postmodern or glocal worldview, according to Hiebert, has the following characteristics:

- a resurgence in local and regional identities (through ethnic, cultural and religious conflict)
- the phenomenon of hybridity – development involving blending from a mix of influences
- the erosion of worldviews as 'coherent wholes characteristic of stable bodies of people' (Hiebert, 2008)
- glocalism raises profound moral questions, contrasting with modernity's focus on knowledge and postmodernity's focus on feelings.

On the latter characteristic, for example, the diverse and extremely complex migration patterns that have resulted from globalization has raised moral issues for economic and political migrants and their destination states/localities.

> Modernity itself has been characterised from the beginning by the paradox that the progress ideal, though touted as universal, has functioned as an ideological cover for certain less-than-universal interests. Modern ideals have served to legitimate patriarchal, European (and later American) violence against native peoples, blacks and other people of colour, women and nature itself. (Middleton and Walsh, 1995)

> It … slowly penetrates that globalization has a drawback; namely the growing divide between rich and poor. (Bakas, 2009)

> Any major new technology introduced into a society which is not by its nature just will exacerbate the gap between the rich and poor. (Guptara, 2002)

The above quotes from three different sources highlight a long history of first modernity and later globalization seemingly offering progress to all, but in practice delivering the fruit of progress very unevenly. It is important for the student who becomes global practitioner to be aware of the 'lumpy' nature of development and how it leaves certain people-groups, particularly the uneducated and unskilled, behind. This tendency for the train of progress to travel at high speed and leave people stranded contributes to the widespread sense of anxiety we have referred to, which manifests in politics and protests of all kinds on a global scale. At the same time certain groups are effectively disenfranchised by the pace of change and are not able, though many try, to make progress work for them. This might involve migration or traditional ways of life being displaced by industrial, commercial and technological development.

Middleton and Walsh's (1995) analysis of the uneven, and sometimes unjust, aspect of the continued 'progress myth' is as penetrative as any. Some of their most profound observations are summarized below:

- A bewildering cacophony resulted from all those who were voiceless under modernity articulating their claims in the postmodern situation.
- Waking from the nightmare of modernity we come to realize our part in what transpired and our complicity in its violence.
- The demise of modernity left a 'worldview gap' for many dispirited urban youth who expressed their sense of hopelessness in violent ways.
- Postmodernists highlighted the angst of the marginalized – of those who felt left out of the story.
- Many people still seek an alternative vision for the world engendering an economics of care and of enough, an ethos of listening and an environmental ethic of wise development.

A country-centric comparison of worldviews

Hiebert not only compares the worldviews of these different ages, but also provides a country-centric comparison of two of the globe's great economic powerhouses – comparing the worldview of the United States with that of India. Table 6.3 summarises Hiebert's analysis, and adds a comparison of the respective worldviews according to two overall themes: American equality versus Indian hierarchy; and American individualism versus Indian interdependence.

Table 6.3 A comparison of American and Indian worldviews (Hiebert, 2008)

American – Equality	Indian – Hierarchy
• All people are 'homo sapiens', therefore they are equals	• Hierarchy (expressed in caste) is both necessary and good
• Integration in the universe is based on homogeneity (not on diversity)	• Each person has a place in an order that encompasses spirits and the worlds of plants and animals
• The ideal society is one where all people have equal opportunities	• Values too are ranked
American – Individualism	**Indian – Interdependence**
• All people have rights to 'life, liberty, and the pursuit of happiness'	• Each caste with its unique function is essential for the whole society
• Communism, socialism and other economic systems stand in the way of freedom of the individual	• Each individual has tasks to fulfil within the family
• The self-made person fulfils the ideal of self-realization	• Diversity and cooperation are the ideals (not uniformity and competition)

Of course, it does not follow that every United States and Indian citizen will conform to the patterns of thinking outlined in Table 6.3, but it provides some useful broad brush strokes as to how people from different nation states might view the same reality very differently, because of contrasting assumptions and starting points. A western perspective might suggest we are free as individuals to work out what we think about certain matters and position ourselves as we please. Other societies would emphasize continuity with tradition and upholding ways of thinking and operating that may have been in place for generations.

Transforming worldviews

One might reasonably ask, 'How can worldviews be adjusted or even transformed?' This is a good question and one where the best answer comes from the Danish philosopher Søren Kierkegaard, whose thinking is expertly outlined by Patrick Gardiner (1988). Below is a summary of what we might term as 'Kierkegaard's method'.

- 'Life-views', as Kierkegaard called them, are pervasive (like attitudes) and cannot be dislodged by intellectual argument alone.
- To even recognize life-views (in oneself) demands an enlargement of self-awareness.
- This enlargement can be assisted by entering into a particular life-view eliciting its emotional foundations and practical implications including any limitations it imposes.
- At the same time, it is necessary to uncover how these elicitations diverge from those of alternative life-views.
- As a result of interior reflection and unclouded comprehension of particular life-views, people can choose to either remain the same or opt for fundamental change.

Gardiner highlights a number of things about Kierkegaard's thinking here. Firstly, that to begin with, people in the grip of a particular life-view are inclined to deceive themselves into supposing that there is no alternative. Secondly, that any illusion in their thinking can only be dismantled by this 'indirect' method or approach. And thirdly, that people need to be persuaded for *themselves* of a need to adjust their life-view.

KEY CONCEPT – THE ECOZOIC ERA

A revealing piece of writing entitled *Twelve Understandings Concerning the Ecozoic Era* by Thomas Berry (2009) expresses a prevalent and influential worldview in our contemporary time. We could term this an *ecozoic worldview* and its centres on a unified, interrelated and ecological view of the Earth and the meaning of life. Its 12 understandings are summarized below:

1 The unity of the universe. To see the universe as an interacting community, operating as a whole and as a communion of subjects, not a random collection of objects.
2 Modes of expression. To recognize that the universe expresses itself through communion (interrelatedness), differentiation (diversity), and subjectivity (self-organization).
3 Cosmogenesis. Seeing the universe as having developed and still developing through irreversible transformations – it is creative and emergent.
4 Earth. Looking upon it as a once only endowment.
5 The current dilemma. Regarding the health of the Earth community as resting on the decisions and actions of humans.

6 Transition to the ecozoic era. Recognizing the need to shift from the current technozoic perspective (seeing the Earth as resource) to an ecozoic perspective (making the well-being of the Earth community the primary concern).

7 The new story. Reflecting on the scientific story of the evolutionary development of the universe invites understanding of the meaning, value and role of humans.

8 Bioregionalism. Reorienting human activity to develop sustainable modes of living, build inclusive human communities, care for the rights of other species, and preserve the health of the Earth.

9 Ecological spirituality. Embracing ecological spirituality centring on the primal mystery and value of nature as a single sacred community.

10 Special contributors. Redefining concepts of value, meaning, fulfilment and norms of conduct with special contributions of women, indigenous people, science, and humanistic and religious traditions.

11 The Earth Charter. Setting out a set of values and principles to take the Earth towards the realization of the ecozoic era.

12 The great work. Bringing into being the ecozoic era involves everyone and requires the change of every aspect of human society.

Questions

1 What strikes you about this worldview? Do you support its perspectives?
2 Do you consider it utopian?
3 What are its implications for business?

APPLIED PERSONAL DEVELOPMENT

We commenced the chapter by looking at globalization – an economic and social force that has its blind followers and anarchistic critics. Table 6.4 summarises some of the arguments both for and against it.

The critical thinker needs to consider both perspectives and all the arguments. Globalization is here to stay and the great debate will rumble on. It is particularly pertinent to businesspeople who will find themselves, whether they like this or not, inextricably allied to the force. The same applies to us as consumers.

We have also investigated in this chapter a number of ways in which as businesspeople and individuals we can relate positively to all matters global. This should raise for us the following questions:

• What is my global perspective?
• Do I have a global outlook?

Table 6.4 Arguments for and against globalization

For	Against
Increasing integration of the world economy is favoured by multinational companies (MNCs) that account for 70 per cent of global trade	'Global capitalism' is regarded by its opponents as unjust and responsible for widening the gap between rich and poor
Macroeconomic stability and lowering of trade barriers producing sustained growth, it is argued, raises the real income of the poor – some formerly poor countries such as Taiwan, South Korea and Taiwan have seen spectacular growth	Naomi Klein is one of the most outspoken critics of globalization – in her book *No Logo* (2000) Klein argues that the concept of branding has turned citizens into consumers, reducing culture to a commodity form
Closing the door to globalization, supporters say, will hurt the poor – opposition is accused of self-interested protection of western jobs	Opponents argue for boycotting goods produced by MNCs produced by exploitative practices in developing countries

- Do I consider myself as a global citizen?
- Do I aspire to be a global practitioner?
- Will I be a globally responsible leader?
- What is the extent of my global consciousness?
- What is my view of corporate global citizenship?
- Will I attach myself to a globally responsible organization?

Following the book's emphasis on embodiment we put most flesh on what it might mean to become a so called global practitioner, which has four aspects:

- a certain *skills* set that will make for maximum employability in the global age
- specific *knowledge* of the global business environment
- critical *awareness* or consciousness permitting the handling of difference
- a *values* profile required to guide actions and behaviour.

For *any* person reviewing this profile and wanting to be a global practitioner this would raise a number of development aims and actions for their personal and professional development plan.

We have also made the case for global practitioners becoming conversant with the thinking and language of worldviews. This is a powerful way of looking at oneself, at other people (with their significant differences) and assisting collaboration in a diverse world – the world which, as businesspeople, is our business.

REFERENCES

Anglia Ruskin University (2010) 'Global leadership and global fitness framework'. Available at: www.heacademy.ac.uk/assets/bmaf/documents/publications/e-news/Global_Fitness_conference_call.pdf (accessed 20 June 2014).

Bakas, A. (2009) *World Megatrends: Towards the Renewal of Humanity*. Oxford: Infinite Ideas.

Barnett, R. (2009) 'The post-modern university: prospects of the ethical', in J. Strain, R. Barnett and P. Jarvis (eds), *Universities, Ethics and Professions: Debate and Scrutiny*. London: Routledge.

Berry, T. (2009) 'Twelve understandings concerning the ecozoic era', Center for Ecozoic Studies. Available at: www.ecozoicstudies.org/statements/twelve-under-standings-concerning-the-ecozoic-era (accessed 29 June 2013).

Bordeaux école de management (2006) *Global Responsibility: Progress Report 2003–2006*. Talence, Aquitaine.

Creamer, D. G. (1996) *Guides for the Journey*. Lanham: University Press of America.

Criswell, C. and Martin, A. (2007) *10 Trends: A Study of Senior Executives' Views on the Future*. CCL Research White Paper. Brussels: Center for Creative Leadership.

Drewell, M. (2011) 'On responsible leadership', *Global Responsibility: The GRLI Partner Magazine*, 5: 4.

Edwards, A. R. (2005) *The Sustainability Revolution: Portrait of a Paradigm Shift*. Gabriola Island: New Society Publishers.

Faulk, R. (1999) 'Hans Kung's crusade: framing a global ethic', *International Journal of Politics, Culture, and Society*, 13 (1): 63–81.

Gardiner, P. (1988) *Kierkegaard*. Oxford: Oxford University Press.

GRLI (2008) *The Globally Responsible Leader: A Call for Action*. Brussels: EFMD.

Guptara, P. (2002) 'Towards the right sort of globalization', Ridley Hall Foundation's conference on globalization, Cambridge, 21–23 June, 1–29.

Hiebert, P. G. (2008) *Transforming Worldviews: An Anthropological Understanding of How People Change*. Grand Rapids: Baker Academic.

Kanitz, L. (2005) 'Improving Christian worldview pedagogy: going beyond mere Christianity', *Christian Higher Education*, 4 (2): 99–108.

Klein, N. (2000) *No Logo*. London: Flamingo.

Kosselleck, R. (1985) *Futures Past: On the Semantics of Historical Time*. Boston: MIT Press.

Kung, H. (1997) *A Global Ethic for Global Politics and Economics*. London: SCM Press.

Lederach, J. P. (2005) *The Moral Imagination: The Art and Soul of Building Peace*. Oxford: Oxford University Press.

Middleton, J. R. and Walsh, B. J. (1995) *Truth Is Stranger Than It Used To Be: Biblical Faith in a Postmodern Age*. London: SPCK.

Naugle, D. K. (2002) *Worldview: The History of a Concept*. Grand Rapids: William B. Eerdmans.

Nederveen Pieterse, J. (2004) *Globalization and Culture: Global Melange*. Lanham: Rowman and Littlefield.

Oxfam (1997) *A Curriculum for Global Citizenship*. Oxford: Oxfam.

Phipps, A. (1999) 'Provisional homes and creative practice: languages, cultural studies and anthropology', in D. Killick and M. Parry (eds), *Promoting the Discipline: Marking Boundaries and Crossing Borders*. Leeds: Leeds Metropolitan University.

Robertson, R. (1992) *Globalization: Social Theory and Global Culture*. London: Sage.

Sacks, J. (2007) *The Home We Build Together: Recreating Society*. London: Continuum.

Sacks, J. (2002) *The Dignity of Difference: How To Avoid the Clash of Civilizations*. London: Continuum.

Schwartz, P. (1991) *The Art of the Long View: Scenario Planning – Protecting Your Company Against an Uncertain World*. London: Century Business.

Seitz, J. L. (2008) *Global Issues: An Introduction*. Malden: Blackwell Publishing.

Shiel, C. (2006) 'Developing the global citizen', *Academy Exchange*, 5, Winter: 18–20. Available at: www.heacademy.ac.uk/assets/documents/resources/publications/exchange/web0523_exchange_issue_5.pdf (accessed 20 June 2014).

Thurlow, C. (2004) 'Relating to our work, accounting for our selves: the autobiographical imperative in teaching about difference', *Language and Intercultural Communication*, 4 (4): 209–228.

World Commission on Environment and Development (1987) *Our Common Future* (The Brundtland Report). Oxford: Oxford University Press.

World Economic Forum (2008) '5 concepts of corporate engagement in society'. Available at: www.weforum.org/pdf/CGC/5ConceptsCorporateEngagement.pdf (accessed 20 June 2014).

PART II

SELF-AWARENESS AND DEVELOPMENT

7 SELF-DEVELOPMENT AND PROFILING

● ● ● ● ● ● ● ● ● ● ● ● ● ●

A NOTE FROM THE AUTHOR

This is the chapter I most wanted to write. It is full of ideas for how as adults we can develop. There are all manner of concepts, theories and models outlined here, any of which might provide a vital spark to ignite your imagination for self-development. Although I use the term *self-development* it is important to realize that our interactions and relationships with others are so central to any development we achieve or experience.

In the enneagram and Myers-Briggs I am presenting a couple of instruments that we may utilize to gain not only a greater self-knowledge, but also a greater knowledge of how others in significant and exciting ways are different from us. Reflective practice lies not only at the heart of professionalism but also is core to a greater consciousness of how we as individuals fit into a complex patchwork of people, organizations and wider social and even global forces. I present the German concept of *Bildung* to provide a vision for our formation as part of a wider human-wide formation. Finally I review a whole gallery of thinkers who from many different disciplines and backgrounds contribute key ideas to the issues of what is personal development and how it is achieved.

● ●

Learning outcomes

When you have completed this chapter you will be able to:

- describe the enneagram and Myers-Briggs
- start consciously to apply reflective practice
- define *Bildung* and understand its emphasis on personal formation
- select developmental inspirations from a number of sources
- comprehend the significance of other/s in our development

● ●

ENNEAGRAM

A test is always just one step in a process of getting to know oneself better, by discovering, as in a mirror, something new or different about oneself. (Ebert and Küstenmacher, 1992)

An enneagram is a nine-sided figure in a framework for understanding nine basic personality types, or 'enneatypes' as they are otherwise known. Key contributors to developing it in its current form have included Oscar Ichazo, Claudio Naranjo and Don Riso.

As is highlighted by the above quotation we need in self-development to avail ourselves of every good tool available in casting light on ourselves and others. There is much to learn about 'other' as it is termed, not only those with whom we share space and life, but also 'other' in ourselves – or put another way, coming into a better knowledge of who we truly are.

A good overview of the enneagram and a useful resource, in that it includes an 'enneagram test', is provided by Ebert and Küstenmacher's *Experiencing the Enneagram* (1992). The book enables one to identify which of the nine types is our so called 'home base' – a particular habitual orientation or what is sometimes referred to as a 'fixation'. As one considers the types it is important to bear in mind that all of them are present to some degree in every individual. In addition to our primary type there is a secondary type in the mix referred to as 'the wing'. The framework can be used to help people not only see themselves and others more clearly, but also to adjust ways of thinking and behaviour patterns developmentally. Ichazo and Naranjo (The Naranjo Institute, 2011) refer to the enneagram as being part of what is known as 'protoanalysis', meaning the beginning of analysing oneself and others, central to consciousness as well as personal development.

Although the Ebert and Küstenmacher book refers to Type One, Type Two, Type Three, etc., alternative labels are used in other sources. Table 7.1 shows how the nine types fall into three dimensions and how they coordinate in some measure to the better known Myers-Briggs classification built upon the thinking of Carl Jung.

Table 7.1 Enneagram types, triads and coordination with Jung

Enneagram Types	The Triad Types	Coordination with Jung
TYPE TWO	The Feeling Triad *Play the heart game*	Extroverted feeling type
TYPE THREE		
TYPE FOUR		Introverted intuitive type
TYPE FIVE	The Doing Triad *Head people*	Introverted thinking type
TYPE SIX		Introverted feeling type
TYPE SEVEN		Extroverted perceptive type
TYPE EIGHT	The Relationship Triad *The 'gut' types*	Extroverted intuitive type
TYPE NINE		Introverted perceptive type
TYPE ONE		Extroverted thinking type

Below are some pointers as to what characterizes the different enneagram types drawing on the observations of Richard Rohr (Ebert and Küstenmacher, 1992):

Type ONE – seek after perfection and self-perfection. Always hoping, and prone to disappointment and resulting anger, which is hidden. Self-image is as model human being. Need to discover their true feelings and stem irritated frustration before it becomes judgemental and resentful.

Type TWO – see themselves as love personified. Capable of much love and wonderful friendship, but subject to the expectation that if they love, they should have it in return. Can be highly manipulative, but interestingly also highly manipulable. Should look out for patterns of co-dependency.

Type THREE – the type that makes things happen. Pursue success for self-validation and love from others. Subject to the temptation to *appear* to be something rather than be something. Make an impression and just know how to impress. Must watch out for self-deception.

Type FOUR – marked by deep longing and the pursuit of beauty, particularly via the imagination and symbols. Are much drawn to both images and symbols and can be in love with their own deep sensitivity. Have the potential to see and elicit special qualities in others.

Type FIVE – seek fulfilment through intelligence and understanding. They have a tendency to distance themselves from others and give priority to their heads above their feelings. Have the potential to be great thinkers and philosophers but need to apply their knowledge in the service of others.

Type SIX – SIXes are what hold institutions and even the world together. Often conformist in an industrious and 'silent' manner. Can be looking for an authority they can trust because of lack of self-confidence and self-conviction. At their best, reliable and trustworthy friends.

Type SEVEN – like FIVEs and SIXes this type are head people. They are consummate 'planners' designed to maximize gain and minimize pain. They have a Peter Pan quality in that they look at life like children and avoid serious things and seek security in false joy.

Type EIGHT – big on presence, larger than life EIGHTs are filled with energy often in such a way that others find overbearing. Naturally combative, but with an inborn sense of justice, the key to this type is seeing the little boy or girl inside of them.

Type NINE – clear and transparent, straightforward and uncomplicated. Often liked, because they follow their impulses and energies. Addictive types who are often in search of some life-inducing stimulant. Also nice and peaceable, but are sometimes thought of as 'lazy'.

This section will have for many introduced them to the interesting concept of the enneagram. There is much wisdom in Dirk Meine's comment that 'the model aims at being an instrument in the service of self-knowledge', but Meine adds the caution that 'it might also seduce readers into reinforcing both old and new prejudices or lead them, through the enthusiasm it generates, to greatly over estimate its possible applications' (cited in Ebert and Küstenmacher, 1992). This equally applies to other personality frameworks used in the pursuit of self-knowledge and understanding others.

MYERS-BRIGGS

It's a must in personal and professional development to know about the Jungian derived Myers-Briggs personality type framework and an easy way to begin to both access it and understand it is to work out which of the 16 personality types one most closely identifies with. It is also a way of explaining how different people can be, in other words of appreciating the breadth of *other*. It also goes a long way to explaining what an extraordinary thing it can be to meet another person whose personality type is the same.

There are multiple sources of Myers-Briggs information and taster tests on the net but the latter should be differentiated from the bona fide MBTI (Myers-Briggs Test Indicator) questionnaire and results interpretation, which is conducted by an authorized MBTI practitioner. If the university or an organization offers this, be sure to commit to it. And like all such exercises the key is to be *authentic* in one's answers – and not try to second guess the device to look good. An authentic approach makes for accurate self-understanding and self-knowledge – and permits others to share this understanding and knowledge.

Table 7.2   The 16 MBTI types

ISTJ	ISFJ	INFJ	INTJ
ISTP	ISFP	INFP	INTP
ESTP	ESFP	ENFP	ENTP
ESTJ	ESFJ	ENFJ	ENTJ

At first sight the Myers-Briggs types 'labels' are simply baffling, but light comes with understanding what the letters stand for in code and the constituent four scales that determine one's posting within the framework.

Table 7.3   The Myers-Briggs Scales consisting of Carl Jung's eight functions

Introvert	Extrovert
Sensing	INtuitive
Thinking	Feeling
Judging	Perceiving

Critical to Myers-Briggs is accurately placing oneself on the above four scales representing continuums. For example, looking at the first Introvert/Extrovert scale you could either be an extreme, clear or borderline introvert or extrovert. Each of the terms is explained below, but the significance of the functions is highlighted beautifully by Jung's own words:

> In the struggle for existence and adaptation everyone instinctively uses his most developed function, which thus becomes the criterion of his habitual reactions. (Jung, 1933)

Introvert/extrovert – giving and getting energy

Looking first at the popularly known introvert and extrovert *functions*, as Jung called them, it is rare for people to make exclusive use of just one function. What happens instead is that one of the functions becomes the primary function and the other an inferior function (Stevens, 1994). This is important, because it denies the caricature of people regarding themselves as say 'out and out' extroverts without a hint of introversion (or the other way around).

Samuels et al. (1986) provide a penetrative definition of the two. Introverts are more excited or energized by the internal world, whereas extroverts direct their energies and get their energies from the external world. Fordham (1991) expresses the same using Jung's term *libido*. For the introvert the libido is concentrated on subjective factors, preferring reflection to activity. The extrovert in contrast directs their libido outwardly towards people and things, relationship with them and dependence on them. One type is not better than the other – they are just different ways of being.

Sensing/intuitive – gathering information

The sensing type takes everything as it comes to the senses. They pay sensory attention to the information they are gathering from what is going on around them. Fordham (1991) argues that a danger for this personality type lies in an over-valuation of the senses.

The intuitive type for Jung, gain a sense of where something is going and what the possibilities are, but without conscious proof or knowledge (Samuels et al., 1986). They are more attuned to grasping patterns and spotting connections between facts.

Thinking/feeling – making decisions

Thinking types make decisions and base their activities guided by their intellectual considerations, which classically includes objectively employing the well-known pros and cons approach. Feeling types in contrast use their feelings to make decisions. Samuels et al. suggest that Jung means something other than affect or emotion here. Rather they base their decisions on 'consideration of the value of something' (Samuels et al., 1986).

Judging/perceiving – handling the outer world

A fundamental difference between judging and perceiving types lies in the fact that so called Js like to have things decided (or you could say 'sorted' or organized). Ps in contrast, like things to remain loose and open-ended. The J is systematic whereas the P is flexible. A defining characteristic to look out for is also their contrasting attitude to *last-minute* pressure. The J doesn't like it and feels somewhat suffocated by it, whereas the P is creatively energized by it.

EMPLOYABILITY FOCUS – MYERS-BRIGGS' CAREER CHOICE

A superb resource on all matters Myers-Briggs is Isabel Briggs Myers' booklet *Introduction to Type* (2000). This includes a section on type and career choice. She underlines that while personality type is only one of a number of things (including skills and interests) to match to a career, nevertheless a career which enables a person to express and utilize their type preferences is likely to result in more satisfaction and engender more energy. This applies not only to the perhaps more obvious introversion/extroversion preference but all the four scales. A table in the booklet outlining combinations of Perception (S or N) and Judgement (T or F) suggests more satisfying career choices (with examples) as follows:

- ST: practical and analytical (banking, administration)
- SF: sympathetic and friendly (sales, support services)
- NF: insightful and enthusiastic (human resources, research)
- NT: logical and analytical (management, law)

The usefulness of Myers-Briggs again underlines the importance of taking any opportunity to correctly identify one's type by working with an accredited MBTI practitioner.

REFLECTIVE PRACTICE

Reflective practice is a large and significant area that could easily command a chapter of its own in personal and professional development. The term implies some level of detachment from oneself to critically appraise what happened in a given situation, how one handled it and even venturing to look into the whys of what happened.

Reflective practice occupies an important part of how for example, teachers, social workers and nurses are trained and developed. It is also a dimension of professionalism and has relevance in relation to business and management practice.

In this section we outline some of the theorists attached to reflective practice and a couple of models or methods of applying it. Reflective practice can in fact be applied to all aspects of life and experience, including the *student experience*. It is very likely to form an explicit or implicit part of your university study or assessment. This section will cast light on understanding its significance.

Donald Schön

Arguably the thinker most famously associated with reflective practice is Donald Schön. The full scope of his work is excellently summarized by Mark Smith (2001, 2011) but the following reflection-related terms are all quintessential Schön:

- *The Reflective Practitioner* – the title of Schön's (1983) well known book
- reflection-in-action
- reflection-on-action.

Reflection-in-action – often referred to as 'thinking on our feet', this involves:

- drawing on our experiences
- becoming cognizant of our feelings
- 'Attending to our theories in use' (Smith, 2001, 2011).

Reflection-on-action – which is done later, as it were, *after* the event and often includes:

- a process of writing up what happened or talking it through with a supervisor
- exploring why we acted so
- looking at what else was going on.

In both reflection-in-action and reflection-on-action Smith highlights that a certain consciousness of one's *repertoire* emerges – a dynamic collection of images, metaphors and theories that one is practically using, informing and guiding one's professional practice (Smith, 2001, 2011). Smith rightly adds that this consciousness feeds off space to reflect, both in the thick of the action and reflecting later on what happened.

FitzGerald and Chapman (2000) in their chapter on theories of reflection highlight the significance of Schön's thinking in understanding how professionals demonstrate an 'artistry of everyday practice', spontaneously drawing on embedded knowledge and theory. They add that Schön's particular contribution to reflection and reflective practice is his concentration on the individual's ability to address problems and develop skills associated with attaining certain standards of professional work or simply competence in practice.

Critical theorists

FitzGerald and Chapman, however, differentiate Schön's contribution from a group they call the critical theorists who enable the practitioner to both reflect on and understand the social world and the ways in which this broader context impinges on everyday practice. Famously, Freire in his groundbreaking book *Pedagogy of the Oppressed* (1972) describes so called *conscientization* as being like 'a dawning awareness' of how vying human interests and power structures effectively determine and perpetuate certain social situations.

For example, it is one thing understanding the social world by examining one's activity and the contribution it is making socially. Using what FitzGerald and Chapman describe as Freire's 'emancipatory' perspective permits another level of understanding, namely the effect that social forces have upon practitioners and their work. Conscientization permits the consideration of all manner of forces beyond the immediate situation and how they impinge on it – not only matters social, but matters political and historical as well. Theorists such as Marx and Freud facilitate this type of critical reflection: Marx because he permits insight into structural oppression; Freud because he raises for the individual the possibility of self-discovery and emancipation from repressive behaviours.

Chris Argyris

Another theorist to profile is Chris Argyris who interestingly, as Mark Smith points out, worked together with Donald Schön from their days together at Massachusetts Institute of Technology (Smith, 2001, 2011). Argyris highlights the critical point that practitioners (including managers) should be critically reflecting on how their *own* behaviour is contributing (often inadvertently) to an organization's issues or problems. To achieve this, the individual needs to abandon what he calls defensive reasoning (Argyris, 1991).

Defensiveness is also expressed in four values which Argyris argues underlie most people's embedded 'theories-in-use' as he terms it (see below).

1 They want to remain in control – human beings like to be in control and feel easily threatened and disempowered in situations where they are at the perceived mercy of others.
2 They seek to maximize winning and minimize losing – relating to that natural desire to want to do well and not badly.
3 They tend to suppress negative feelings – focusing on negativities and shortfalls. This may prevent people from seeing how their thinking has contributed to how something has worked out.
4 They consider that they are approaching a matter in a 'rational' manner – when they may be courting irrationality.

Smith also usefully highlights some of the terms and thinking that emerged from collaboration between Argyris and Schön as follows:

- *Theories-in-use* and *espoused theory* – it is important to differentiate between these two theories of action. The theories that are implicit in what practitioners do they termed theories-in-use, whereas the theories the same practitioners would want others to think they stand by they termed espoused theory (Smith, 2001, 2011). The distance or gap between the two also is important.
- *Single-loop* and *double-loop learning* – something always will go wrong for individuals and people working together in organizations. When the so called 'governing variables' of an individual or an organization (including given or chosen goals, values, plans and rules) are not questioned or challenged that is what Argyris and Schön termed single-loop learning. It often results in a change of strategy working within the same governing variables. In contrast where the variables themselves are critically appraised and are subject to alteration they termed this as double-loop learning.

METHODS OF REFLECTIVE PRACTICE

Quinn (2000) reviews three models of reflective practice as follows:

- Gibbs' reflective cycle
- Boud, Keogh and Walker's model
- John's model of structured reflection

Gibbs' reflective cycle is arguably the most utilized model here and consists of six cyclical stages as follows:

1 Description – describing what happened.
2 Feelings – defining feelings and thinking at the time.
3 Evaluation – evaluating what was good and bad about the experience.
4 Analysis – analysing the situation.
5 Conclusion – concluding what else could be done.
6 Action plan – planning for what to do next time.

A contrasting model is provided by Zeichner as highlighted by DeShon Hamlin (2004). Unlike the sequential models above, Zeichner identifies three *levels* of reflection as follows:

Level 1 – Technical

- the efficient application of professional knowledge.

Level 2 – Situational context

- places professional practice within its situational or institutional context
- asks for consideration of how context influences one's practice.

Level 3 – Ethical

- examines how professional practice is contributing to a just and humane society.

This model better gathers together the contributions of *all* the theorists as outlined in this section. Below is an outline of questions that employ Zeichner's three levels of reflection and can be applied to the student experience or professional practice:

Level 1 – Technical

- Describe how you are developing and applying the skills and qualities that go with a *professional* approach to [whatever]?

Level 2 – Situational context

- What is it like to operate as a student/worker/professional at [wherever]?
- How has your experience at [wherever] influenced your practice?

Level 3 – Ethical

- What are some of the ethical dilemmas you have faced as a [whatever]?
- What are the ethical and moral consequences of the way we operate as a [whatever]?

KEY CONCEPT – *BILDUNG*

A far reaching and at the same time elusive concept that is beginning to be heard in personal development circles is *Bildung*. This section will tease out why it should be gaining both attention and attraction.

Frederick Beiser probably gets closest to capturing in English the essence of the German term *Bildung* when he describes it as 'notoriously untranslatable' but adds that 'depending on the context, it can mean education, culture, and development'. He continues, 'it means literally "formation", implying the development of something potential, inchoate (meaning to cause to begin, bring out), and implicit into something actual, organised, and explicit' (Beiser, 2003). Peter Watson in *The German Genius* distils this further when he says of *Bildung* that it refers 'to the inner development of the individual, a process of fulfilment through education and knowledge' (Watson, 2010).

The radical application of *Bildung* is that it places personal development at the very *core* of learning rather than positioning it as a necessary *addition* to learning. The implication of this more strategic positioning is that it suggests that learning is for development of the person, not incidental to it. Not only *Bildung* but its application, as suggested, belongs to a Romantic *Weltanschauung* (worldview).

Suzanne Kirschner helps us trace how this Romantic emphasis embraced by German and English intellectuals (encompassing inner development and transformation of the person) was a response to the disappointment of all the hope invested in the French Revolution. Kirschner writes, 'The Revolution, which initially had Europe "thrilled with joy…" is quickly revealed to possess its own destructiveness and treachery' (Kirschner, 1996). The dashing of a moral and even spiritual hope invested in the Revolution is effectively re-directed from the public, political sphere to a more inward domain. The historian Carl Schorske argues that this prompted the birth of 'psychological man' as he might be called (Kirschner, 1996).

There are some famous names associated with such thinking including the ever influential Goethe and Samuel Coleridge. Watson highlights that Goethe often referred to his pursuit of *Bildung* and 'never lost his concern with the individual's responsibility for his own inner development' (Watson, 2010). Coleridge wrote of keeping alive the heart in the head and that there was no true knowledge without the inclusion of a spiritual and affective dimension (Kirschner, 1996).

To help us pin down what *Bildung* constitutes, an outline of its elements is provided below:

Sense and sensibility – the idea that the whole person is able to embody both human reason and what is referred to as sensibility, which incorporates 'the power to sense, feel, and desire' (Beiser, 2003). It is important to grasp here that both sense (reason) and sensibility are critical to formation and holism. Daniel Shannon, commenting on Hegel's *Phenomenology of Spirit*, speaks of a 'union between the heart and the mind' (Shannon, 2001).The implication is, however, that the senses must be re-awakened (Beiser, 2003).

Self-realization – this corresponds to a human yearning for completeness and is bound up with self-formation and even self-overcoming. It also involves development of consciousness and a progressive education of the self.

Reviving lost unity – a particularly Romantic notion of reviving a lost unity with ourselves, with nature, and with others (Beiser, 2003), not coincidentally constituting an *organic* whole. This is part and parcel of the aspiration to reverse a sense of alienation prompted by modernism (including estrangement from nature) and to, as Beiser puts it, 'reunify man with himself, nature and others, so that he would once again feel at home in his world' (Beiser, 2003).

The beautiful soul – Goethe and others spoke of 'the beautiful soul.' Again this was aspirational and constituted the culmination of self-development – an evident excellence of character enabling a person to approximate an ideal

(Continued)

work of art, forged through overcoming suffering and challenges of all kinds. The beautiful soul is realized at both the level of developing potentialities common to all individuals as well as those potentialities which are particular to the individual.

Freedom – freedom is central to *Bildung* – the notion that the individual commits themselves to their own self-development; that they freely choose a path that leads to the formation we have described. Love of all kinds, loving oneself, loving others and loving nature that one is allied to is a choice and a freedom.

A PERSONAL DEVELOPMENT GALLERY

Don Cupitt

Don Cupitt in *The World to Come* (1982) urges us to take on board two things in our thinking and personal development. Firstly, not to succumb to an illusory way of being and operating, which Cupitt argues amounts to a false consciousness. This effectively masks anxiety caused by disintegration all around and for older generations, the sense of mortality and facing the 'void', as Cupitt puts it. Development is facing up to this disintegration.

Secondly, the way to do this is to understand the 'new age', particularly as the west is experiencing it. We are living post Darwin, Freud, Nietzsche (we can therefore coin this *post DFN*) and the western world shall not be returning to the *supernaturalist* worldview that prevailed before the critical output of the above. However people might choose to think and operate, the new age is undeniably present in our world and thinking.

Cupitt's message is therefore understand the world, its thinking, its anxiety and don't embrace the illusory false consciousness that shuts out these things, and in a sense is therefore in denial of them.

Donald Winnicott

The famous paediatrician and psychoanalyst, Winnicott is perhaps best known for his notions of the True Self and the False Self.

The *True Self* for a whole manner of reasons is by no means an automatic thing for a person to operate in and reveal to all. Almost magpie like, it collects together experiences of aliveness and feeling real. Feeling real, Winnicott argues, is a way of existing as 'oneself' and a self one can retreat into for relaxation (Phillips, 2007).

The *False Self* hides the true self and is a measure of protection. It often complies with environmental demands. There is the possibility of becoming so dominated by playing the role of the false self that individuals may be completely at a loss when not playing its part. Sometimes also a person describes what is truly a part of themselves as 'false' because it is unacceptable (Phillips, 2007). Winnicott also refers to the so called 'transitional figure' who is somewhere between the True Self and the False Self.

The developmental implication of Winnicott's framework is for the individual to consider what they are effectively 'hiding' about themselves. The danger is of course that they can supress all manner of potentialities and creativity as well as other things they don't feel confident and able to show about themselves to others and the world.

It also raises the issue of what is acceptable and unacceptable compliance. It is professional in certain contexts to operate in a specific manner. At the same time, it may be possible and desirable to be both thoroughly professional and be one's true self, as is appropriate in the situation.

The False Self does cast a little more light on Cupitt's notion of false consciousness. Cupitt calls it 'illusory', Winnicott calls it 'false' in a masquerading sort of way.

John Macmurray

We might say the Scottish philosopher's key motifs are *friendship* and *action* and how these two things interrelate. Macmurray's view of the nature of human beings is not organic or mechanical, but personal. He wrote:

> The root of the error is the attempt to understand the field of the personal on a biological analogy, and so through organic categories ... We are not organisms, but persons. The nexus of relations which unites us in human society is not organic but personal. (cited in Creamer, 1996)

Adopting Macmurray's assumption would take us to a very different place in terms of both personal and organizational development.

At the core of Macmurray's thinking is a rejection of what is known as *mind–body dualism* – proposing instead the alternative idea that the two are intimately related or intended to function in unity. He viewed action by its very nature as including thinking. Doing contains thinking and these are not split modes of the self.

Macmurray also seeks to dismantle another kind of split – between the individual and *another* (shorthanded as 'you and I'). The contention here is that trapped on a desert island, if you were alone you could know what it meant to be human (and rational), but you couldn't possibly know what it meant to be a *person* until another human being arrived on the island and befriended you. As Creamer summarizes, 'The notion of person is only realized in relationship with at least one other human being' (Creamer, 1996).

Very wisely, Macmurray favours the term 'friendship' over 'love'. This perhaps takes us away from a certain unrealistic idealism contained in the notion that we can *love* all or a multitude. A better word is friendship because it is both more encompassing and more appropriate to what can be achieved with *many* and other. It can even be extended as being descriptive of a right relationship with the planet.

A profound characteristic of friendship is the freedom to be oneself or as Macmurray puts it, 'to be yourself *for* another person' (cited in Creamer, 1996, emphasis added). There is a power of what Macmurray terms mutuality, a shared and reciprocal freedom, present in friendship. A dynamic where one concludes, 'we need one another to be *ourselves*' (cited in Creamer, 1996, emphasis added).

Finally, to help us draw out the implications of Macmurray's thinking we have in Table 7.4 both radically adapted and revised a table that appears in Creamer's *Guides for the Journey* (1996). This acts as a way of comparing historical views of the self, reality, worldviews and primacy.

Table 7.4 Western philosophical development and its implications

	Premodern	Modern	Postmodern
Self as...	Substance	Organism	Person
Reality as...	Scientific	Ethical	Embodied
Worldview	Mechanical	Organic	Personal
Primacy of the...	Theoretical (Thinking)		Living

The most important things to take from this somewhat skeletal summary are the following observations:

1 The determination of the contemporary age and generation to place a life of action (and living) over theory.
2 A shift through time from a mechanical perspective on one's view of self and the world to an organic perspective, perhaps culminating in an emerging personal (or relational) perspective.
3 Consideration of the implications of an emphasis on embodiment, even over ethics? Perhaps the emergence of embodied ethics?

Bernard Lonergan

Another philosopher, the Canadian Bernard Lonergan, is regarded by some as one of the foremost thinkers of the twentieth century. He was an early critic of the destructive nature of modernity and its characteristic fragmentation. He argued that the important things were in people's minds and that modern culture was surging around us so as to present enormous challenges of being known, assimilated and transformed. A picture we could perhaps employ here is one of being caught up in swirling waters, which are by nature disorientating and constitute an anxiety provoking experience.

A key to Lonergan's thinking is what is termed 'self-appropriation'. We begin to understand what this involves in his own words:

> The individual *grows* in experience, understanding, judgement, and so comes to find out for himself that he has to decide for himself what to make of himself. (cited in Creamer, 1996, emphasis added)

This implies yet another navigational challenge.

Radically, Lonergan underlines the central importance of affectivity, i.e. feelings, in developing 'an internal compass'. It is *in* feelings, he argues, that possible values are first apprehended. Feelings are an essential constituent for Lonergan, who says that experience, understanding and judgement without feeling 'are paper-thin' (cited in Creamer, 1996).

The implication of Lonergan's thinking here is the authority he is attaching to what the individual feels. This is central to a sense of authenticity about taking a particular course of action and also highlights the negotiation of feelings involved in any meaningful decision.

Whereas Macmurray employed the term friendship, Lonergan does speak of love: operating in community; to create an ecological future; and an essential element of what he terms as 'historical consciousness'. Relationships characterized by mutual love and respect lead to transformation and the building of community, whereas those characterized by contempt, ignorance, exploitation and enmity tear it apart. Lonergan argues that concern for the future, a genuine 'heroic charity' also cannot be achieved without this same 'self-transcendence' – of 'we' consciousness substituting purely 'I' consciousness. Historical consciousness is the recognition that the world has changed and no longer clings to a world that no longer exists. One's worldview becomes infused with experience, understanding, judgement and love and is prepared to make the necessary changes 'appropriate to the emerging ecozoic age' (Creamer, 1996).

Nancy Schlossberg

Nancy Schlossberg's book *Overwhelmed: Coping with Life's Ups and Downs* (2008) is about facing and understanding transitions of all kinds. It's very easy to be overwhelmed by certain, even extremely common, transitions. With the most difficult transitions we may need some professional support – from say the university's counselling service – to help us navigate them. If in this section you relate to some of these challenges, it may be useful to purchase Schlossberg's book and use it as a resource. It is both practical and conceptually sound.

Very broadly *Overwhelmed* provides a summary of what transitions are; an extremely helpful framework of different types of transitions thus helping us to understand them; and finally outlines resources for facing them, or coming *through* them, if you like.

Schlossberg speaks of transitions unsettling us. A better word is possibly how they displace us, engendering a sense of feeling 'out of sync' (Schlossberg, 2008). Out of sorts, might even apply. Transitions, she says, can unsettle four things:

1 roles
2 relationships
3 routines
4 assumptions.

If it's a major transition all four will be shifted. Little wonder that they are disruptive.

Table 7.5 outlines Schlossberg's typology of transitions and provides examples that we can map our own transitions onto.

Table 7.5 Schlossberg's typology of transitions

Type of Transition	Example
Events: elected things that happen	moving, starting university, starting a new job
Non-events: 'Things we expect and hope for that somehow fail to happen'	
• Personal non-events	not doing as well at university as anticipated, not being in a great relationship
• Ripple non-events: the unfulfilled expectations of someone close to us, with the power to change personal roles, relationships, routines and assumptions	the loneliness of a divorced parent could ripple into their son's or their daughter's life
• Resultant non-events: these start with an event but lead to a non-event	rejection from law school and failing to fulfil a dream to become a lawyer
• Delayed events: an event that takes some time against expectation to materialize – can be non-events in the end	the hope that one is going to be a very successful/wealthy businessperson
Surprise transitions: the unexpected happening	having an accident, inheriting some money
Life on hold: the transition waiting to happen	waiting for Mr Right/Mrs Right, waiting to die
Sleepers: 'Start slow and creep up on us over time' – characteristically it's difficult to know when they started	putting on or losing weight, becoming bored with an important part of one's life, gradually falling in love
Countertransitions: multiple transitions or 'pileups' as Schlossberg refers to them, where one transition sets off another, related or unrelated transition, sometimes as a chain reaction. These countertransitions are felt cumulatively by the person experiencing them	graduating, moving to a new city to start a job and commence living with a girlfriend/boyfriend

Schlossberg proposes four resources to assist with navigating oneself through transitions:

1 Your situation – to gain an understanding of one's situation.
2 Your self – gaining a greater self-understanding including personality and outlook.
3 Your supports – sources of affirmation, assistance, even affection.
4 Your strategies – expanding one's repertoire of transition strategies.

Looking at the latter Schlossberg identifies three possible strategies for transitions:

1 Taking action to change or modify the transition – pragmatic responses such as developing a new plan, being more assertive, seeking advice and even if necessary taking legal action.
2 Changing the meaning of the transition – encompasses a whole range of options including: rearranging priorities, relabelling and reframing, developing rituals, using humour.
3 Managing reactions to stress – by doing such things as physical activity, playing, developing relaxation skills and adopting other ways of relieving and reducing stress.

Marcia Baxter Magolda

The term 'self-authorship' was coined by the psychologist Robert Kegan who observed a potential for individuals to generate their own beliefs, identity and social relations. Baxter Magolda has built a theory of self-authorship from this insight which may be summarized as follows:

- *Multidimensional self* – this involves learning about all the different types of people within oneself.
- *Holding environments* – Kegan's term for people's multiple life and work contexts including family, work and social cultures, which Magolda recognized can support or hinder personal growth.
- *Socialization* – becoming more aware of this as well as one's holding environments.
- *Internal authority* – constructing an internal self-authored perspective including beliefs, values and loyalties.
- *Extracting oneself* – from being oriented towards others' approval and from dependency on external authorities for beliefs, identities and social relations.
- *Casting off* – casting yourself into the great beyond. Something action and confidence based.
- *Construction* – actively constructing knowledge, identities and relationships.

Baxter Magolda identifies three dimensions at the centre of one's journey towards self-authorship:

1 *Epistemological growth* – this is knowing one's own assumptions and how they influence both our thinking and reasoning. It also involves 'accepting the limits, uncertainties, and dissolution of established beliefs' (Baxter Magolda et al., 2010). Baxter Magolda recognizes that epistemological convictions, i.e. what is in people's heads, significantly inform their sense of who they are and how they wish to construct relationships with others.
2 *An emerging sense of self* – this follows the stages of *dependency* (relying on others for this sense), growing *awareness* (the beginnings of building their own viewpoint) and *autonomy* (acting upon one's own ideas and beliefs). It is expressed in gaining confidence and a sense of presence.
3 *Choosing what relationships you want with others* – this is often something quite different from what others want of you or expect of you. It is to unhook from that sense of just trying to make others happy, or looking to them all the time for validation and approval.

Where these three dimensions are all working together Baxter Magolda's thinking suggests a person can find their 'internal voice'. One is then able to realign one's life choices with one's internal voice.

David Whyte

If drawn to things literary or poetic, you're sure to appreciate David Whyte's tour de force *The Heart Aroused* (2002) which invites us to place our imagination at the centre of our lives, our personal development and our organizations. Whyte argues that poetry's special gift is its dangerous truth allied with the part it can play in stirring our deeper unconscious life or as Whyte so appositely puts it:

> the task of a poet is to make the internal image appear whole in common speech.

There is an extraordinary chapter in the book entitled 'Coleridge and complexity', which would be worthy of being on every business student's reading list and connects '*work world*' as Whyte calls it with the thinking of the likes of Samuel Taylor Coleridge and John Keats. The imaginative businesswoman or businessman should always be on the lookout for making powerful connections between the world of work or the business world, and the wider world.

By way of a taster of Whyte's *The Heart Aroused* we have provided below an introduction to some the ideas he presents in the above chapter, particularly as they relate to personal development.

Imagination

There are a number of forces at work that can cause what Whyte refers to as our deeper unconscious lives to be suffocated by busyness, the cloning tendency of certain organizations and the tendency to sacrifice all on the altar of establishing ourselves in a career, an organization or a lifestyle. Whyte wants to alert us to these tendencies and expose the lie, where the individual says to themselves that they'll get back to some of the things they most wanted at some point. Whyte, quotes one of his extremely busy female contacts as writing:

Ten years ago ...

I turned my face for a moment

and it became my life.

This tendency to turn one's head is what concerns Whyte and particularly where it involves sacrificing the life of the imagination and more particularly what John Keats referred to as *the truth of the imagination*. Whyte's thinking is to encourage us and organizations not to negate this imagination, our soulfulness, but to recognize its huge potential to command a central and active role in our work lives.

Order and chaos

With some challenging writing, Whyte asks us to consider our attitude to chaos and even the very necessary part it plays in life and our development. Whyte tells us that Coleridge spoke of reconciling opposite or discordant qualities and this Whyte applies to reconciling the forces of order and chaos in our lives.

Many people (and organizations) both seek and strive for a kind of perfect *order*. This is an understandable search for stability and the quashing of anxieties in an uncertain world. Whyte's contention here is that this attitude can lead to *all* challenge – including the challenge of our imagination – being viewed as threat.

Whyte suggests that it is wrong to choose a 'phantom life', as he puts it, of seeking perfect order and argues instead of the need to hold together both order and chaos, expressed in a creative combination of rest and action. Living systems, he argues, have the characteristic of being robust and adaptable, whereas in evolutionary terms their 'settling down' or lack of verve is a sign of ill-health and danger.

Complexity

This leads on to Whyte's next major point about embracing a certain complexity. William Wordsworth refers to this as a 'dark invisible workmanship that reconciles discordant elements and makes them move in one society' (Wordsworth, cited in Whyte, 2002). Drawing also on the thinking of the physicist Steven Wolfram, Whyte also makes the point that complicated systems (like life itself) combine simplicity and complexity – that complexity arises out of the interaction of a great multitude of essentially simple components interacting simultaneously.

There is also wisdom to be taken from Whyte's citing David Wagoner's poem 'Lost' which contains the lines: '... Wherever you are is called *Here* / And you must treat it as a powerful stranger'. The powerful stranger present in our here and now is complexity and we must learn to live with it and pay attention to it – be 'clear eyed' about it, to use Prabhu Guptara's excellent phrase (Guptara, 1999).

So paying attention to complexity, we also bring into view 'our own interior images of desire' (Whyte, 2002). The two can live together and added to this we can pay attention to the world and the interior life of the organization we become a part of.

EMBODIMENT BOX – 'OUT'

Here we explore self-development and defining significances surrounding the word *out*. In Chapter 12 we examine the developmental significance of *outward* movement according to the famous psychoanalyst Erik Erikson.

branching out – independence, 'a golden opportunity', choice

moving out – leaving home, underestimating significance, control

left out – anxiety, forming new attachments, not being considered weird, fitting in

staying out – late nights, social scene

nights out – self-medicating, alcohol, sex, drugs, eating

sleeping out – protection

finding out – inquiry

coming out – sexuality, pain (powerful feelings), assertiveness

drawn out – in less of a hurry, protracted moratorium

starting out – rites of passage

blotting out – hiding self-doubt, low confidence and lack of direction

losing out – experiences of loss

APPLIED PERSONAL DEVELOPMENT

I hope you found something here to inspire. Personal development is both profoundly personal and social, so try not to think of it as being just an individual project.

If possible, embrace this notion of becoming more critically conscious of yourself and your practice. All of us are a work-in-progress, so look to cut yourself free from any defensive mentality towards change and challenge.

As I have attempted to show, the imagination and firing the imagination are significant. Explore ways to activate, appropriate and apply the imagination in both the professional and personal spheres of your life, doing this of course in consort with others. It can even be great fun.

And ethics is to look beyond yourself and see value there too – to look closely and carefully at others and learn from them. And learn difference, as if to acknowledge that your thinking, your way of being, is not the only way.

This will enable you to develop a greater consciousness for not only your own real needs (which are legitimate) but also the needs of others. Good businesses are built around satisfying *excellently* real human needs. You might even say that good business is an art.

REFERENCES

Argyris, C. (1991) 'Teaching smart people how to learn', *Harvard Business Review* 4 (2). Available at: www.ncsu.edu/park_scholarships/pdf/chris_argyris_learning.pdf (accessed 27 September 2013).

Baxter Magolda, M. B., Creamer, E. G. and Meszaros, P. S. (eds) (2010) *Development and Assessment of Self-authorship: Exploring the Concept Across Cultures*. Sterling, VA: Stylus Publishing.

Beiser, F. C. (2003) *The Romantic Imperative: The Concept of Early German Romanticism*. Cambridge, MA: Harvard University Press.

Briggs Myers, I. (2000) *Introduction to Type: A Guide to Understanding Your Results on the Myers-Briggs Type Indicator*. Oxford: OPP.

Creamer, D. G. (1996) *Guides for the Journey: John Macmurray Bernard Lonergan James Fowler*. Lanham: University Press of America.

Cupitt, D. (1982) *The World to Come*. London: SCM Press.

DeShon Hamlin, K. (2004) 'Beginning the journey: supporting reflection in early field experiences', *Reflective Practice*, 5 (2): 167–179.

Ebert, A. and Küstenmacher, M. (eds) (1992) *Experiencing the Enneagram*, trans. Peter Heinegg. New York: Crossroad Publishing.

FitzGerald, M. and Chapman, Y. (2000) 'Theories of reflection for learning', in S. Burns and C. Bulman (eds), *Reflective Practice in Nursing: The Growth of the Professional Practitioner*. Oxford: Blackwell Science.

Fordham, F. (1991) *An Introduction to Jung's Psychology*. London: Penguin.

Freire, P. (1972) *Pedagogy of the Oppressed*. Harmondsworth: Penguin.

Guptara, P. (1999) 'Life, work and careers in the 21st century'. Available at: guptara.net/prabhu_new/images/documents/ARTICLE_lwc (accessed 12 September 2013).

Jung, C. (1933) *Modern Man in Search of a Soul*. London: Routledge & Kegan.

Kirschner, S. R. (1996) *The Religious and Romantic Origins of Psychoanalysis: Individuation and Integration in Post-Freudian Theory*. Cambridge: Cambridge University Press.

The Naranjo Institute (2011) 'Dr Claudio Naranjo'. Available at: www.naranjoinstitute.org.uk/naranjo.html (accessed 24 October 2014)

Phillips, A. (2007) *Winnicott*. London: Penguin.

Quinn, F. M. (2000) *Principles and Practice of Nurse Education*. Cheltenham: Nelson Thornes.

Samuels, A., Shorter, B. and Plaut, F. (1986) *A Critical Dictionary of Jungian Analysis*. London: Routledge & Kegan Paul.

Schlossberg, N. K. (2008) *Overwhelmed: Coping with Life's Ups and Downs*. Lanham, MD: M. Evans.

Schön, D. (1983) *The Reflective Practitioner*. San Francisco: Basic Books Harper Collins.

Shannon, D. E. (ed.) (2001) *Hegel: Spirit – Chapter Six of Hegel's* Phenomenology of Spirit. Indianapolis: Hackett Publishing Company.

Smith, M. K. (2001, 2011) 'Donald Schön: learning, reflection and change', *Encyclopedia of informal education*. Available at: www.infed.org/thinkers/et-schon.htm (accessed 27 September 2013).

Stevens, A. (1994) *Jung*. Oxford: Oxford University Press.

Watson, P. (2010) *The German Genius: Europe's Third Renaissance, the Second Scientific Revolution and the Twentieth Century*. London: Simon & Schuster.

Whyte, D. (2002) *The Heart Aroused: Poetry and the Preservation of the Soul in Corporate America*. New York: Doubleday.

8

INTEGRITY MATTERS: THE INTEGRATED SELF AND ORGANIZATION

Learning outcomes

When you have completed this chapter you will be able to:

- comprehend the wide ranging ideas about what integrity is and consists of
- appreciate that integrity is bound up with overcoming and prevailing, not posturing and pretending

(Continued)

- explain what is meant by the terms teleopathy, the living contradiction and the dialogical self
- understand the perspectives of integrity involving owning up to struggle, embracing multiplicity and handling difference
- reflect on how the system can work against personal and organizational integrity.

INTEGRITY AND BOWIE'S MORAL CLIMATE

A great starting point for an overview of integrity, as it has been traditionally thought of, is Norman Bowie's introduction to it in *The Oxford Handbook of Business Ethics* (2010), which deals with both the individual with integrity and the organization with integrity. For Bowie, integrity is the equivalence of being ethical and moral, where a moral way of operating 'requires that one consider the impact of one's actions on others'. He adds to this that an organization with integrity is an 'organization with a certain sort of moral climate' and that this is expressed in its actions and commitment to moral principle. The latter could also be said of an individual with integrity.

This takes us in the direction of integrity as being *embodied*, because in an organization a moral climate is not just expressed through, say, allegiance to ethical commitments (set out in a code of ethics), but is embodied in the character of the organization's staff and evident in the organization's way of life (including routines and structures) and ways of rewarding and disciplining.

Integrity can also be thought of as *dependability* – related to steadfastness expressed in good time keeping, working faithfully beyond the sight of management, loyalty to the organization and other members of staff. Most profoundly perhaps it is demonstrated in supporting rather than effectively undermining an organization's progress.

At the same time acting with integrity is something achieved through *contention* – an individual exhibits good character 'in the face of adversity or temptation' and an organization 'when it is true to its goals of purposes, especially when there are obstacles impeding them or temptation to deviate from them' (Bowie, 2010).

Integrity for Bowie might also amount to the ability of *owning up* to a failing or deficiency. This is expressed when he says, 'individuals with integrity are individuals who accept responsibility for any negative consequences caused by their actions'.

Integrity is bound up with living out and expressing one's values. Profoundly we express our values through actions, but also through our words. Integrity expresses a certain quality of wholeness or completeness – and the whole or complete person not only has values, but expresses them. Where we stand in terms of having values and expressing them has ethical implications.

In terms of expressing integrity there are four broad groups of people:

- The *understated* – these are people with developed values that are falling short in expressing and articulating them. They remain silent when they should speak up about their values. They fail to 'speak to power' perhaps through lack of courage, hesitancy and fear of compromising self-interest. The values might be there, but they're not 'out there'. This falling short of dialogical engagement could have serious ethical implications. The person of integrity is able and willing to speak up.
- The *espousers* – these are people where the tendency is for them to espouse certain values, but not be as committed to them as their words suggest. It may be fashionable to state an allegiance to certain values, which may be considered the thing that one has to do to gain favour within a group of people or an organization. It is plain to see that this is also a matter of integrity and espousers are effectively 'running the gauntlet' and could be subject to exposure at some point. A hollow 'espouser' of a certain principle may in the end mean that a certain principle will not be practically and effectively applied.
- The *heralds* – this is the desired position to achieve in terms of expressing one's values and demonstrating integrity. Such a person acts as a herald of a valued principle and at the appropriate and telling time is able to express and articulate this principle. It doesn't have to be done in a triumphal way as the term may suggest. The thought here is closer to the notion of the herald being and bringing good news.
- The *silent* – it is a sobering thought that people could occupy this position. These are those who effectively have few values to bring to a situation or organization. Their values offering might be underdeveloped, and little by way of expressing or articulating values is presented. To be silent thus is not a position of integrity.

Questions

1 Which position is closest to your own?
2 What do you think would help you to operate more as a herald?
3 Think about organizational cultures and how they effectively encourage certain positions? Site examples.

In the world of business ethics it is important to understand the differentiation between Friedmanite and Freemanite viewpoints. The first relates to the famous monetarist economist Milton Friedman (1912–2006). The second relates to R. Edward Freeman (1951–), also an American, but a philosopher and stakeholder theorist.

Friedman argued that managers' responsibility consists in providing financial returns to the owners. According to Bowie this is the prevalent viewpoint taught in US business schools. Returning to the notion of creating a moral climate in an organization, a Freemanite viewpoint factors in the interests of the various corporate stakeholders and thinks business should be a value-creating institution. Bowie endorses Freeman's thinking and argues that 'stakeholder theory provides the *basic* moral framework for organisational integrity' (Bowie, 2010, emphasis added).

He adds that an organization should operate as a moral community and not be confined to a set of economic relationships and proposes seven substantive moral principles in harmony with those who wish to work within Kant's ethical theory as follows:

1 When making any decision consider the interests of all the affected stakeholders.
2 Policies and rules that are implemented represent all those affected by them.
3 All decisions do not reflect the interests of one stakeholder taking priority over the interests of all other stakeholders.
4 When a situation arises where it appears that the interests of one group of stakeholders must be sacrificed for the interests of another, the decision is not based solely on the basis that one group is larger than the other.
5 The principle that a person is never treated merely as a means to an end is adhered to.
6 Every profit-making organization also has an imperfect duty of benefit to society.
7 Procedures are established to ensure that stakeholder relations are governed by rules of justice.

CASE STUDY – JOHNSON & JOHNSON CREDO

Below are a number of key excerpts from each of the four sections of the Johnson & Johnson credo:

We believe our first responsibility is to the doctors, nurses and patients, to mothers and fathers and all others who use our products and services …

Our suppliers and distributors must have an opportunity to make a fair profit …

We are responsible to our employees, the men and women who work with us throughout the world …

We must provide competent management, and their actions must be just and ethical …

We are responsible to the communities in which we live and work and to the world community as well.

We must be good citizens – support good works and charities and bear our fair share of taxes …

Our final responsibility is to our stockholders …

When we operate according to these principles, the stockholders should realize a fair return.

Regarding a code of ethics, Bowie very wisely argues, that by themselves these codes are 'not a good indicator of an organization's commitment to ethics' and returns to his theme that to be effective a code needs to be part of a broader moral climate. If the latter is absent, the code will amount to no more than 'window dressing'. Bowie's good sense is also expressed when he refers to them as, 'useful as general guides' (Bowie, 2010). The visibility as well as the authority of the code is important. Johnson & Johnson's credo he argues is 'a living, pervasive and enforced document' that actually contributes to organizational integrity.

Professional ethics can all too easily, Bowie adds, be based on 'transcendent ethics'. This, we might argue, causes it to take on the feel of the rule of the 'higher path' or 'higher way'. Bowie suggests instead that ethics needs to be grounded instead in a recognition of our humanity as revealed by psychology, sociology and economics.

EMPLOYABILITY FOCUS – EMPLOYERS SEEKING INTEGRITY

Employers will often state that they are seeking for their employees to have integrity. However, it is worth stopping and reflecting on what they might have in mind in stipulating this. Below are some of the things that this is likely to mean for employers:

- *Honesty* – there is a strong association with most people that integrity is bound up with honesty. Other adjectives we might group together here include decency, well mannered, upright and dependable. In the workplace

(Continued)

(Continued)

this attitude of integrity is much sought after, reflected in an honest attitude to company time and resources, fulfilling one's word and promises and treating others with the utmost respect. The person of integrity, for example, would not 'throw a sicky' (as it is expressed) because they wanted the day off to attend to other matters.

- *Consistency* – a large part of being an employee is maintaining the sense that one is a representative of the company or organization. In other words, when acting on behalf of the organization, how it is viewed by various stakeholders including customers and neighbours is often down to the individual employee's behaviour and conduct. In football, this is reflected in the phrase that you are 'wearing the shirt' and an employing organization very reasonably attaches professional expectations to how you conduct yourself on behalf of the organization. This extends to what you would say about the organization and fellow employees in private and social circles.

- *Symmetry* – this is a similar notion to consistency but focuses on the professional alignment between the values of the organization and the values of the individual employee. From an employer's perspective the strong preference would be to employ people who 'fit' the values and culture of the organization, both those stated and those that are not stated, but nevertheless evident and present. We might say that where alignment exists there is a certain symmetry or 'mirroring' – and this is also an aspect of the integrity an employer seeks.

- *Reliability* – a significant aspect of professionalism and integrity as far as the employer is concerned is the characteristic of reliability. This is reflected in many ways, the importance of which only becomes truly evident where it does not exist in an individual employee. It might begin with being on time, for work and for meetings and other commitments. It might be expressed in going the extra mile, where this is needed, on behalf of the customer and the organization. We speak of 'give and take'. A good employment situation is one where there is sufficient goodwill for there to be reciprocal give and take between the employer and the employee. So by reliability as expressing integrity, this doesn't imply an exploitative posture and relationship from the employer to the employee.

Questions

1 Can you think of anything else an employer might have in mind when it is stated that they want integrity in their employees?

2 Integrity might be said to consist of 'what happens when nobody is looking'. Discuss?

3 Have you experience of working where integrity was not reciprocal, but one way?

A theory that fits this sense of groundedness is Kenneth Goodpaster's thinking on *teleopathy*, derived from combining the Greek roots for 'goal' and 'disease' and outlined in his book, *Conscience and Corporate Culture* (2007). In essence teleopathy is the unbalanced pursuit of purpose, in either individuals or organizations. In its most extreme form it involves a suspension of ethical awareness in the decision-making process.

This accords with a view that integrity is about retaining balance and perspective and Goodpaster argues the principle components of teleopathy are:

- *fixation* – or singleness of purpose under stress
- *rationalization* – or self-serving justification, leading to
- *detachment* – a kind of moral schizophrenia or ethical double-standard.

Teleopathy involves voluntarily shutting one's eyes to aspects of moral responsibility and wandering into a moral 'blind spot'. This leads onto the idea that integrity is bound up with consciousness and that you can't have integrity, unless you open up your consciousness. Greater consciousness we might argue would invite more information, more complexity and ask more questions. It effectively dismantles an over-simplistic way of looking at the world and life. The more one invites more information and listens to more voices of those that are effectively stakeholders in any decision, the more concrete as an entity, the more organic in its reality, integrity becomes.

KEY CONCEPT – THE LIVING CONTRADICTION

The inevitable gap between our actions (our practice) and our rhetoric (what we say we stand for, that is our values) Jack Whitehead (1980) refers to as a 'living contradiction'. This is an encouragement for all practitioners who are seeking to 'practise what they preach' and align behaviour with what they want to stand for. Whitehead's take on this is that consciousness of this gap alerts the reflective practitioner of the developmental need to close it. Note that it is referred to as a contradiction and not hypocrisy.

Hypocrisy is rather when we pretend to have certain beliefs and values – a form of deceit, sometimes referred to as 'window dressing'. The conscientious person or professional will seek to mind the gap and attempt to live a life that is true to what they believe. This attitude is also about seeking to live out one's values more fully. This way, apparent contradictions can therefore be integrated or brought back into alignment – an exciting angle on integrity.

Moira Laidlaw (2008) makes a distinction between the internal and external living contradictions as follows:

(Continued)

(Continued)

- the *internal* living contradiction – the gap in the individual
- the *external* living contradiction – the gap between what one wants to do and what the social/institutional/hegemonic/political conditions support.

Laidlaw's application of Whitehead's theory suggests that the systems we are a part of or subject to can work against us achieving integrity.

Robinson and Dowson (2012) have also built on the Whitehead theory and specified the following implications of the living contradiction, particularly in relation to integrity:

1 The gap is never resolutely closed.
2 Therefore there is an ongoing state of irresolution.
3 Integrity involves integrating such contradictions.
4 The gap is minded through dialogue with others.
5 Others help us to integrate contradictions.
6 The solution is therefore not a concept, but is personal (in other words, you cannot practise by yourself).

On examination, these are far reaching implications and amount to a very different way of looking at and achieving integrity.

ERIKSON ON INTEGRITY

A section on the developmental psychologist Erik Erikson's view of integrity is provided here to broaden our conception of what integrity encompasses and illustrate its enormous significance for the individual and the individual taking their place alongside others in wider society. At the very least it provides a different perspective on the notion of integrity as it is often understood and referred to.

For Erikson, integrity is a key element of identity development and communicates overall the sense of life coming together for the individual as distinct from its counterpart, the *despair* of a life that doesn't deliver this sense of purpose and fulfilment. Central to achieving or experiencing integrity is accepting life for what it is, with its multiple challenges and complications, yet integrating these turbulences into an outlook where the individual can say with some self-dignity that they are *content* with how their life is unfolding or has unfolded (Capps, 2004). This is something far more positive, more rewarding, than a fatalistic resignation of how life has turned out. In his book *Childhood and Society*, Erikson suggests it is 'a state of peace and serenity' (Erikson, 1963), which creatively and significantly ties integrity much closer to a sense of well-being.

As introduced in Chapter 2, Erikson posited a life stages theory to explain how individuals – that is, children and then adults – develop across their lifespan. Adults, according to Erikson, can and will change for the better if they navigate well the transitions that they will inevitably face. These transitions, which Erikson referred to as 'crises', are virtually continuous, but inspirationally with the individual adapting rather than maladapting to these multiple challenges, the individuals acquire virtues or vital strengths.

In Erikson's theory one crisis, most associated *though not exclusively so* with late adulthood, is the battle for integrity – where integrity is the adaptive response and despair the maladaptive tendency. If integrity prevails then the vital strength of wisdom is added.

Erikson's biographer Lawrence Friedman has cast further light on how Erikson viewed and interpreted integrity, which is summarized in Table 8.1.

Table 8.1 Eriksonian aspects of integrity – adapted from Friedman (2000), with the addition of explanatory notes

Luminous	transmitting and communicating clarity
Active	with a sense of movement
Central	being ever present rather than peripheral
Whole	rather than fragmented
Coherent	rather than incoherent
Continuous	and connected, as distinct from scattered
Generative	giving of oneself to others and the next generation
Inclusive	receiving and embracing
Aware	awareness rather than numbness
Indivisible	as distinct from being divided
Chosen	a sense of being selected, not bypassed
Safely bounded	having boundaries, as distinct from being overrun

Another inspirational dimension of Erikson's theory is his dynamic view of identity (Schwartz, 2001). This is refreshing news for the individual who is offered throughout their adult life the opportunity to not only positively develop their identity, but also develop integrity.

Furthermore an exciting article by Schachter (2005) suggests how Erikson's theory can best fit with the postmodern western context we introduced in Chapter 2. Schachter's argument can be summarized as follows:

- Erikson shows how the social, cultural and environmental context we inherit and interact with are all bound up with our identity development.
- Such is the constant and insecure flux as experienced in the contemporary social context that anxious adults are afraid to ask Erikson's questions: 'Who am I?' and 'How do I fit into an adult world?' It makes for a certain paralysis in acquiring a sense of direction, progress and purpose.

- Erikson's theory attaches greater significance to community than the postmodern context – with its idealization of the individualized self – is delivering.
- A centralizing and harmonious identity is near impossible in the postmodern context where the notion of fluid and multiple selves is closer to reality.
- Erikson argued for a configuration or holding together of these multiple identifications.
- Schachter suggests integrity in the postmodern context be conceptualized as something closer to an 'inclusiveness, retaining identity elements in a loose confederate structure' (Schachter, 2005).
- In summary, integrity becomes a matter of extending inclusivity to diffuse multiple identifications rather than holding them together in some relationship or organizing structure as Erikson proposed.

MULTIPLE IDENTIFICATIONS AND DIALOGICAL SELF THEORY

Regarding multiple identifications, this simply means identifying with many things that are not necessarily related. A couple of frameworks will make this point abundantly clear.

Firstly, we see this illustrated in the different domains the individual occupies. Adams et al. (1989) proposed a framework consisting of four ideological domains (politics, religion, occupation and philosophical lifestyle) and four interpersonal domains (friendships, dating, sex roles and recreation). Looking across these eight domains the individual has multiple identifications. What, for example, is the relationship between adopting a certain political position and one's dating relationships?

Peter Raggatt's (2012) life history constituents framework also points to the individual's multiple and varied identifications. His research participants are asked to list 24 constituents including six significant people, six life events, eight objects and four aspects of body image (liked and disliked body parts).

Using these frameworks, we remind ourselves here that integrity is how all these identifications and constituents are somehow organized together (Erikson) or simply *included* in an attitude of inclusivity (Schachter).

Dialogical self theory as presented by Hermans and Gieser (2012) is useful here and casts more light on the relationship between multiple identifications, particularly in the postmodern contemporary context.

William James at the close of the nineteenth century observed that people and things in an individual's environment, as far as they are felt as 'mine' in some way *belong* to the self. Examples might include: my mother, my car, my cat, my enemy and my nose. This paved the way, Hermans and Gieser argue, for later theoretical developments recognizing 'oppositions to and negotiations with the *other-in-the-self*'.

Dialogical self theory understands the other-in-the-self as constituting a multiplicity or polyphony of voices, each needing to be heard in a dialogical sense, rather than silenced, denied or suppressed.

A globalizing society has presented and created opportunities for innovation of the self, expressed in greater plurality and multiple sites for self-engagement (Raggatt, 2012) – even hybrid combinations of identifications. Hermans and Gieser suggest that globalization is not just a reality outside the individual, but also a constituent of a dialogical self.

They conclude that in the modern model of the self this dialogue can be centring and unifying, whereas in postmodernity, dialogue can also be decentring. This suggests that integrity isn't necessarily bound up with bringing things together, but may be about embracing multiplicity, within ourselves.

INTEGRITY AND IDENTITY

More light is cast on this notion of integrity as a form of inclusivity by Richard Ned Lebow in his book *The Politics and Ethics of Identity* (2012). Firstly, Lebow argues that the notion of remaking ourselves is a western notion originating with Romantic philosophy and Rousseau. Secondly, he argues that a unitary, consistent and essentially stable identity is an illusion and puts forward instead that our identities are multiple, discontinuous and shifting.

He describes modernism as 'totalizing' and people being 'induced' to stay within assigned unitary statuses by suppressing and hiding divided and diverse identities. They may even deny contradictory identity components by appearing to commit themselves fully to one affiliation. In some sense, this tendency is masked by how people only show part of themselves to others and others having no recourse to another person's reflections about themselves.

Accepting Lebow's argument, integrity becomes a rather different idea from one we may be accustomed to. Instead of presenting ourselves as unitary and seamless, integrity may be closer to accepting before the world our multiple, dispersed and even fragmented (*zerstreut*) self-identifications. To get to such a position of integrity would for Lebow involve the 'psychologically unsettling' state of accommodating 'other' in oneself. For Lebow, this is close to what Benhabib (1986) describes as 'the capacity of the subject to let itself go'.

Drawing out the implications of Lebow's thinking for integrity, these are as follows:

- Instead of thinking of integrity as somehow holding it all together or bringing it all together into some coalescing unity we might think instead of integrity as accepting our dispersed and forever fragmentary identifications.
- In the case of the latter this is closer to authenticity and does not involve the typical suppression and denial of diversity (or 'other') within oneself.
- It also takes the individual towards experiencing integrity as resolution – as accepting one's diversity and not warring against it.
- Lebow underlines that 'multiple selves are not necessarily incoherent selves' but they are far from *seamless* (my word), or presenting as such.

- If individuals can 'renounce the fiction of consistent and stable identities' then perhaps organizations can too.
- The payback of not devoting so much time and energy to forms of denial and unitary 'false' perfection might be considerable for both the individual and the organization.

EMBODIMENT BOX– WHAT INTEGRITY IS NOT

Building on Brown's notion of integrity being virtue not vice we might usefully reflect on what integrity is not. Cox et al.'s (2005) list of characteristics that undermine integrity reminds us of the kind of things that stand in integrity's way and explanations have been added to clarify some of these splendid but stretching terms:

Capriciousness – full of conceits. Fanciful and whimsical. An unpredicted and unwelcome overflowing.

Wantonness – associated with carelessness and wastefulness. Idle extravagance.

Triviality – of trifling character. Of paltry substance.

Disintegration – conveying the idea of something coming apart and fragmenting. Perhaps the disintegration or crumbling of a principle subject to attrition or pressure.

Weakness of will – a will that falls or soon withers away.

Self-deception – deceiving oneself and inviting self-delusion.

Self-ignorance – lack of self-awareness and associated with blind spots.

Mendacity – habitual lying or deceiving. Dwelling essentially in falsehood rather than the truth.

Hypocrisy – associated with pretence and sham. Projecting a false image of virtue or goodness contrary to true character.

Indifference – goes with apathy and unconcern. Critically involves an absence of care or feeling.

CORPORATE INTEGRITY

An excellent book by Marvin T. Brown *Corporate Integrity: Rethinking Organisational Ethics and Leadership* (2005) is a must reference for anyone interested in thinking about what organizations having integrity look like.

Brown argues that corporate integrity will pop up everywhere across an organization and will be evident in how it attempts to respond ethically in five dimensions of its corporate life:

1 the cultural
2 the interpersonal
3 the organizational
4 the civic
5 the environmental.

We shall examine in turn these five dimensions of corporate integrity below.

First, let us examine Brown's foundational thinking on integrity, summarized as follows:

- He views integrity as *wholeness*, but critically he argues that this wholeness is evident in the quality of the organization's relationships and underlines what Srivasta and Barrett (1988) refer to as 'the wholeness of the interaction'.
- Critically he identifies integrity as being bound up with trust. He astutely remarks, 'if people have integrity, then we can usually trust them'. In the face of high-profile corporate scandals this is a much sought after virtue.
- Integrity is also expressed, Brown argues, in alignment between what one says and what one does.
- Inclusion is also a dimension of integrity as the organization seeks to include different interests and the interests of different stakeholders.
- And refreshingly, he reminds us that integrity is virtue, not vice. This suggests that integrity has some shining quality about it and is praiseworthy.

EMBODIMENT BOX – BRENKERT (2010) ON WHISTLE-BLOWING AND INTEGRITY

There are many and varied definitions of whistle-blowing according to George Brenkert (2010) but they generally include the following characteristics:

- An individual has access that permits knowledge of inside, confidential or private information.
- This individual reports something they consider to be illegal, immoral or contrary to the values of the organization.
- The matter is reported either internally or externally to person(s), not in the direct line of reporting, considered capable either directly or indirectly of stopping the wrongdoing.
- The wrongdoing is sufficiently serious to merit this action.
- The wrongdoing affects the public interest, though not necessarily immediately or directly.

Whistle-blowing, adds Brenkert, is normally justified on three grounds:

(Continued)

(Continued)

1 The *harm theory* – people and systems within an organization are cited as causing harm, sometimes bodily harm or death.
2 The *complicity theory* – the justification rests for the whistle-blower upon their complicity in wrongdoing prompting the sense that they are doing something morally wrong.
3 The *good reasons theory* – this is where whistle-blowers sound the alarm to spotlight neglect or abuses that they consider threaten the public interest.

Brenkert adds his own integrity theory of whistle-blowing which has at its core what he refers to as a principle of positional responsibility (PPR). This principle, Brenkert says, morally obliges people who have special knowledge of wrongdoing by virtue of their position to report it.

A person of integrity for Brenkert is someone who will defend their 'values and norms even when doing so is inconvenient or difficult' (Brenkert, 2010). They are prepared to remain faithful to these values and norms even in the face of adversity and temptation. Their decision to blow the whistle highlights anchoring beliefs and principles. Not to do so would be to compromise these, as well as PPR.

Looking at the five dimensions, Brenkert teases out what integrity looks like in each dimension by highlighting the challenges it seeks to meet:

1 In the *cultural*, the key is being open to differences and disagreements.
2 In the *interpersonal*, the challenge is to view the quality of relationships in the organization as being paramount, expressed in an outlook of interdependency rather than separation.
3 In the *organizational*, in essence we are seeking consistency or alignment between organizational purpose and conduct, something easily said but challenging in practice.
4 In the *civic*, the organization with integrity exhibits a *cooperative* relationship with private and government agencies. It views itself as a member of wider civil society.
5 In the *environmental*, the link is made between the fate and future of the organization and the fate and future of the earth.

Being something that most people believe they have, it is easier to claim integrity and speak about it than it is to have integrity and to practise it. For Brown the key strategy in achieving cultural integrity is dialogue, which is bound up, he argues, in openness.

To support this Brown outlines Barnett Pearce's (1989) typology of communicative practices, where there are four types as follows:

1 *Monocultural communication* – such patterns of communication can often be seen in traditional cultures 'where no one seriously questions the community's basic beliefs' (Brown, 2005) Their stories are seen as sacred and true – and are not questioned. The monocultural dimension is reflected in the fact that they do not see others as being *different* from themselves. The past is significant and is used to interpret right actions in the present.

2 *Ethnocentric communication* – this is similar to monocultural communication in that ethnocentric communicators do not question their own norms and assumptions, but differs from it in their treatment of others who are regarded, to use Pearce's (1989) phrase, as 'non-natives'. This amounts to viewing others as not only different, but inferior.

3 *Modernistic communication* – a fundamental break was achieved from the above two types of communication with the advent of modernistic communication particularly with regard to the attitude towards their inherited stories, myths and rituals – what Pearce refers to as the 'treatment of resources'. Modernistic communicators reflecting discovery of the world, and to a certain extent a sense of controlling it, are open to all manner of new experiences along with other customs and beliefs.

4 *Cosmopolitan communication* – the departure from the three other types of communication is that cosmopolitan communication gives primacy to coordination rather than coherence. Belief is suspended and stories from all sources are welcomed with a view to seeking and finding mystery (about the human condition), which for the cosmopolitan is always more than any *one* source can provide.

Brown challenges us to look at our own communication practice and organizational communication practice in the light of the above typology. He also goes on to argue that in a pluralistic society, where we are continually faced by cultural diversity, adopting the cosmopolitan pattern of communication expresses the most integrity, in that if integrity is about wholeness in interaction, this communication style recognizes and takes seriously all parts of a whole (Brown, 2005).

Brown uses this foundation to build his theory that the practice of dialogue, integral to a cosmopolitan approach to communication, constitutes the way of integrity. Next, drawing on the thinking of the Jewish theologian Martin Buber, he casts dialogue as being essentially about what is created in the sphere of the 'between' (Buber, 2002) when 'individuals turn toward one another, and acknowledge each other's presence' (Brown, 2005).

The possibilities of dialogue, Brown lists as follows:

- *Seeing others as different* – and hearing others as a distinct voice.
- *Asking questions of inquiry* – in the sense of revealing that you don't know the answer.
- *Acknowledging another's resources* – honouring experiences, talents and skills one doesn't have.
- *Exploring the unknown* – to learn more about a topic or subject.

- *Developing thought* – moving into what constitutes 'un-thought' territory.
- *Gaining self-understanding* – seeing ourselves in the communication we have co-created.

INTEGRITY AND THE SYSTEM

A thought provoking notion highlighted by Cox et al. (2005) in their article on integrity is to what extent are social and political conditions inimical, i.e. unfriendly or adverse to a life of integrity? Here, *social* would encompass family, business and religion and *political*, political structures and processes. The article rightly highlights that integrity is often thought of as being a private or personal matter with a focus very much on an individual person or for that matter even an individual organization.

Instead, what if the way of integrity is very much supported or countered by one's family and friends, or the organizations one is attached to, or even the overall system which the individual encounters on a daily basis? Here the article raises the challenging question of, 'Are political and social conditions in contemporary liberal democracies conducive both to acquiring the self-understanding necessary for integrity and, more generally, to … acting with integrity?'

This suggests that the acquisition of integrity and its furtherance are very much a question of *nurture*, not only (one's) nature. This does explain what a profound effect being a part of a business school that seeks to support and further the development of business leaders having integrity can have.

The article adds that social and cultural structures present in contemporary society can be inimical to the acquisition and development of integrity in all sorts of small-scale ways, as follows:

- If professional life calls us to highlight positives and cover up negatives that in reality are an intrinsic part of, say, a product offering, there are many instances where we might be steered to manipulate and bluff the truth.
- Selling oneself and promoting the company can pander to a disingenuous approach that lacks integrity.
- Again, the construction of certain standards, codes and company mission statements can be motivated from a desire for appearance, rather than relating necessarily to substance.

ETHICS BOX – INTEGRITY AND THE PRESERVATION OF THE SOUL

The poet David Whyte, author of *The Heart Aroused: Poetry and Preservation of the Soul in Corporate America* (2002), speaks of this as though it is a real and present danger when he says, 'to preserve our deeper desires amid the pressures of the modern corporation is to preserve our souls for the greater life we had in mind when we first took the job' (Whyte, 2002).

This accords with Goodpaster's words when he speaks of integrity as, 'a kind of wholeness or balance that refuses to truncate or close off the qualities of the heart – that refuses to anesthetise our humanity in the face of what can sometimes be strong temptations to do so' (Goodpaster, 2007).

The picture emerging here is one of wrestling to keep our heart or soul intact in the travail of working for a living with all its potential compromises. The famous political scientist Francis Fukuyama shows the same sensitivities in his book *The End of History and the Last Man* (1992). The thing to keep one's eye on in contemporary liberal democracies is the tendency to pursue 'material gain rather than glory' (Fukuyama, 1992), by which Fukuyama means something closer to honour. Drawing on Nietzsche, he sounds the warning of 'a society of bourgeois who aspired to nothing more than their own comfortable self-preservation.'

INTEGRITY AND THE RESOLUTION OF CONFLICT

Another key idea introduced by Cox et al. (2005) is the notion of integrity resolving self-conflict. It is easy when introducing the notion of self-conflict to think first of desire (which takes us to the realm of sexual ethics), but as Cox et al. point out, conflict ranges over:

- commitments
- principles
- values
- wishes.

Frankfurt (1987) suggests that integrity is about coming through to a position of wholeheartedness and asserting one's values in the face of possible inconsistency. This implies a settling of inevitable self-conflict. The weakness perhaps of this way of thinking about integrity is that true wholeheartedness is not just about finding one's principles and making the right decision, but also about stilling the inner conflict. The latter constitutes a wholehearted peace.

This model of seeing integrity not as the automatic assertion of principle but overcoming inner conflict to do the right thing and feel right again in oneself, is a profound way of looking at integrity.

A similar idea is expressed by Jonathan Sacks in his book *The Home We Build Together: Recreating Society* (2007). Sacks introduces the following ways of operating, all of which cast light on the notion of integrity overcoming difficulty and conflict, both potential and actual:

- *Integration without assimilation* – this is about treating something 'other' or diverse with dignity and respect but without trying to change it or make it conform to one's obvious allegiances. Integration communicates here the sense of acceptance, as does not applying pressures associated with assimilation. As Sacks writes, 'integrated diversity values the dignity of difference' (Sacks, 2007).
- *What we build* – a key for Sacks is building something together, because it is in doing something positive together (in a team) and committing to a project that in some sense furthers society so that difference can be integrated. To build in this sense switches the focus for Sacks from rights to responsibilities, from claims to contributions (Sacks, 2007).
- *Side-by-side* – there is something profoundly different about the posture and positioning of building side-by-side rather than remaining face-to-face. Integrity permits this important change of attitude, perspective and positioning.
- *Mystical dialogue* – Sacks helpfully draws a distinction between what he describes as dialogue in the Platonic sense of a collaborative search for truth and dialogue as a human encounter, at its most intense and non-judgemental. Drawing on Buber, Sacks argues what can happen in the encounter is that 'all else falls away' and the two people meet and are fully open to the other. 'What happens when two selves *truly* meet is dialogue' (Sacks, 2007, emphasis added). It has the quality of an unscripted encounter and to genuinely meet in *das Zwischenmenschliche* is true, even mystical dialogue. As Sacks summarizes, 'neither attempts to change the other, but both are changed by the very act of reaching out'.
- *Redrawn boundaries* – where this type of dialogue occurs there is the potential to see redrawn boundaries, so those and that which constitutes *difference* are no longer, as it were, across the table, but instead are found alongside. Sacks says in summary, 'what broke the wall of estrangement and inter-group hostility was simply the necessity of working together to solve a shared problem'.

Incorporating Sacks' thinking we can spell out the implications for integrity, as follows.

- A dignity of difference seeks to integrate, not assimilate.
- Working together, side-by-side to build something and solve a problem is the way of integrity.
- In such situations an unexpected dialogue can transform former perspectives.
- And can culminate in a moving of boundaries and shared positioning.

DEVELOPMENT POINTER – THE LIVING CONTRADICTION AND ME

The pointer from *the living contradiction* is centred on training oneself to be more aware of the gap between how things turn out and what one had intended – a bit like when you personally suffer a surprising sporting defeat. There could be a hundred and one reasons why you fell short of your own standard – anything from having an off-day to feeling worn down. Integrity isn't *never* falling short. Integrity is realizing – owning up to the fact – that you let yourself (and others) down and wanting to take steps to do better next time.

1 If people can fail and still have integrity does that change the way you view the word?
2 How would *you* define integrity?
3 Have you got it?
4 Look out for it, not its opposite, in others. Where have you noticed it in others and how would you follow their example?

APPLIED PERSONAL DEVELOPMENT

We have probably come a long way in this chapter to checking the glib idea that virtually everybody has integrity, which possibly at first sight is due to the fact that most people equate it with honesty and decency.

We have noted what may be in an employer's mind when they say they want their employees to have integrity. Although this call usually reflects a fairly straightforward understanding of integrity, it is both a reasonable and a laudable request. We examined what integrity was not, and can see that it remains a 'high bar' in that it is not cleared without thinking or trying.

A range of concepts and ideas about integrity introduced to us this notion that integrity involves a certain struggle – of prevailing where you might not prevail, overcoming obstacles and difficulties where good people and good organizations mess up. The notion of the living contradiction raises the issue that integrity is about facing one's failure or the possibility of failing and determining to do better.

Integrity in our social context of late modernity is morphing into something quite different from how integrity has hitherto been viewed – making it closer to moral authenticity than moral perfection. The postmodern realities of plurality (both within and without) and difference call for this new understanding of integrity. Drawing on Erikson's thinking we can conclude that it is closer to making peace with oneself and extending peace to others than seeking to occupy some moral high ground above reproach of any kind.

Integrity that looks like the former rather than the latter will also be subject to contestation of all kinds. The individual or the individual organization *may* find themselves without support from others and the system in pursuing this version of integrity. It demands much moral courage and the abandonment of a way of being that seeks to present oneself or one's organization as excellent in every possible way, rather than human.

REFERENCES

Adams, G. R., Bennion, L. D. and Huh, K. (1989) 'Extended objective measure of ego identity status: a reference manual'. Unpublished manuscript, Logan: Utah State University.

Benhabib, S. (1986) *Critique, Norm and Utopia: A Study of the Foundations of Critical Theory*. New York: Columbia University Press.

Bowie, N. E. (2010) 'Organisational integrity and moral climates', in G. C. Brenkert and T. L. Beauchamp (eds), *The Oxford Handbook of Business Ethics*. Oxford: Oxford University Press.

Brenkert, G. G. (2010) 'Whistle-blowing, moral integrity, and organisational ethics', in G. C. Brenkert and T. L. Beauchamp (eds), *The Oxford Handbook of Business Ethics*. Oxford: Oxford University Press.

Brown, M. T. (2005) *Corporate Integrity: Rethinking Organisational Ethics and Leadership*. Cambridge: Cambridge University Press.

Buber, M. I. (2002) *Between Man and Man*, trans. R. Gregor-Smith. London: Routledge.

Capps, D. (2004) 'The decades of life: relocating Erikson's stages', *Pastoral Psychology*, 53 (1):3–32.

Cox, D., La Caze, M. and Levine, M. (2005) 'Integrity', *Stanford Encyclopedia of Philosophy*. Available at: http://plato.stanford.edu/entries/integrity (accessed 29 August 2013).

Erikson, E. (1963) *Childhood and Society*. New York: W. W. Norton & Co.

Frankfurt, H. (1987) 'Identification and wholeheartedness', in F. Schoeman (ed.), *Responsibility, Character and Emotions: New Essays in Moral Psychology*. New York: Cambridge University Press.

Friedman, L. J. (2000) *Identity's Architect: A Biography of Erik H. Erikson*. Cambridge MA, Harvard University Press.

Fukuyama, F. (1992) *The End of History and the Last Man*. London: Penguin.

Goodpaster, K. E. (2007) *Conscience and Corporate Culture*. Malden, MA: Blackwell.

Hermans, H. J. M. and Gieser, T. (2012) (eds) 'History, main tenets and core concepts of dialogical self theory', in H. J. M. Hermans and T. Gieser (eds), *Handbook of Dialogical Self Theory*. Cambridge: Cambridge University Press.

Johnson & Johnson. *Our Credo*. Available at: www.jnj.com/sites/default/files/pdf/jnj_ourcredo_english_us_8.5x11_cmyk.pdf (accessed 24 October 2014).

Laidlaw, M. (2008) 'Living educational theorising: how I developed a more democratic educational practice'. Available at: www.spanglefish.com/moiralaidlawshomepage/index.asp?pageid=118264 (accessed 20 August 2013).

Lebow, R. N. (2012) *The Politics and Ethics of Identity: In Search of Ourselves*. Cambridge: Cambridge University Press.

Pearce, W. B. (1989) *Communication and the Human Condition*. Carbondale and Edwardville: Southern Illinois University Press.

Raggatt, P. T. F. (2012) 'Positioning in the dialogical self: recent advances in theory construction', in H. J. M. Hermans and T. Gieser (eds), *Handbook of Dialogical Self Theory*. Cambridge: Cambridge University Press.

Robinson, S. and Dowson, P. (2012) *Business Ethics in Practice*. London: CIPD.

Sacks, J. (2007) *The Home We Build Together: Recreating Society*. London: Continuum.

Schachter, E. P. (2005) 'Erikson meets the postmodern: can classic identity theory rise to the challenge', *Identity: An International Journal of Theory and Research*, 5 (2): 137–160.

Schwartz, S. J. (2001) 'The evolution of Eriksonian and neo-Eriksonian identity theory and research: a review and integration', *Identity: An International Journal of Theory and Research*, 1 (1): 7–58.

Srivasta, S. and Barrett, F. J. (1988) 'Foundations for executive integrity: dialogue, diversity, development', in S. Srivasta (ed.), *Executive Integrity: The Search for High Human Values in Organisational Life*. San Francisco: Jossey-Bass.

Whitehead, J. (1980) 'The observation of a living contradiction', paper to BERA Annual Conference, Cardiff University, 4 September.

Whyte, D. (2002) *The Heart Aroused: Poetry and Preservation of the Soul in Corporate America*. New York: Doubleday.

9 CAREER AND LIFE PLANNING

● ● ● ● ● ● ● ● ● ● ● ● ● ● ●

A NOTE FROM THE AUTHOR

A good study skill is to start with researching the key words of an essay or assignment title. Always have an excellent dictionary to hand. This will also enhance your word power and your spelling, both of which are important elements of being skilled in communication.

The Word Detective (2009) website has an interesting piece on the derivation of the word career and its sister word careen, the latter meaning to lean over or tilt. We are familiar with 'career' meaning 'profession or course of employment or activity'. The Word Detective adds that the root of 'career' is the Latin 'carrus' meaning a wheeled vehicle. This conjures up an image of a chariot and many of you will have already spotted it is the source of the word 'car'.

A Middle French derivative of 'carrus' was 'carrière' which means 'racecourse' and the web piece adds that when the noun first appeared in English it meant 'racetrack'. This links to the idea of career meaning to rush at full speed. But it also led to it meaning 'course of life'.

All these nuances are relevant in a chapter on career and life planning, which I have put together because in reality they are inseparable. A career is often a big part of a person's life and a person's life sometimes amounts to their career. The chapter examines how to bring some planning or design to our career and our life.

Grace Jantzen's groundbreaking book *Foundations of Violence* (2004) traces western roots to the Greco substrata with its epic tales including the *Iliad* and the *Odyssey*. This book goes a long way to explain how westerners are inclined to the metaphor of *journey* with all its adventure, choice points, challenges and perils.

With this in mind, I have put together an original combination of theories and resources to assist you with your own career and life journeys, including:

- 'matchmaking' and its importance in our choice of career and direction
- appropriately, the model of career anchors by Edgar Schein

- the exciting *constructivist* (all will be explained) theoretical contribution of Mark Savickas
- the notion of creating our own story
- and listening out to the stories of others as a life and career resource
- of balancing the input and output sides of our lives
- and the ethical questions posed by the life of the Man of Steel, Andrew Carnegie.

Learning outcomes

When you have completed this chapter you will be able to:

- comprehend the significance of story in our lives and careers
- gain a sense of the kind of career that would align with who you are
- understand what Savickas means by self-concept
- assess the input and output balance of your life
- story your way forward in the direction of 'flourishing'.

TRANSITION

Edgar Schein's (1978) metaphor for career development is a journey from mountain range to mountain range separated by flat valleys. Traversing a mountain range signifies recurring transitions, with the peaks representing *choice points* where people must decide which way to head. A (pastured) valley on the other hand is a more settled, routinely functioning career chapter.

This *Lord of the Rings*-esque way of looking at careers involving times of transition and more settled times is a picture we can apply to both career and life planning – the expectation of seasons of relative security and times of insecurity.

According to Schein many people come to feel they have 'ruined' their careers or have failed or fallen behind in some sense. This can relate to past choices, Schein's so called 'choice points'. These feelings of regret and longing apply to career and aspects of life in general.

Another sense that people have is of a gap, Schein argues, between what people had in mind or hoped for and how things turn out. The dream versus reality dynamic is something also to look out for in career and life management.

Many people are in search of meaning for their careers. For others, they might express this as a sense of vocation. The desire to want to make a difference is commonplace. For many reasons, finding a career that fits these heartfelt or soulful aspirations is by no means an automatic process.

Life will inevitably include many transitions. Even coming to study at university is a life transition in itself. It is perhaps helpful to be more conscious of the fact that it is a transitional time for others too.

Beyond university there are further transitions. Becoming more comfortable in the face of uncertainties and insecurities is an important and needed life skill. It also highlights the importance of making good decisions in relation to our working lives and our lives beyond work.

CAREER PLANNING

Hopson and Hugh argue that the aim of career education, or a careers component in one's journey of learning and work experience, is for each person to discover their work–life purpose, sometimes referred as vocation, through a blending of employed and non-employed work (Hopson and Hugh, 1973).

Career planning process

There are eight accepted steps to the career planning process as follows:

1 Awareness of need to make career decision.
2 Studying your environment.
3 Self-study.
4 Generating occupational alternatives.
5 Information gathering on occupational prospects.
6 Making a decision or ranking your prospects.
7 Implementing career decision through training and job search methods.
8 Using feedback to evaluate a decision.

Personal growth is intrinsic to the above process.

Accurate self-knowledge and self-esteem underpinning the whole career planning process is a product of personal growth. Remember the key here is operating out of an accurate self-estimation, avoiding the twin dangers of underestimation (reducing oneself) and overestimation (inflating oneself).

Self-enlargement through personal growth permits a healthy attitude to critical (containing constructive) feedback. The individual needs to know what they are doing right and where they are falling short/down. Facing this information assertively is a measure of personal growth and allows the individual to better locate a helpful path forward.

Life and work experience doesn't always yield personal growth, however, ironically perhaps all life's experiences have a potential to do so, if approached with reflection (including self-examination) and maturity, both marks of personal growth. In other words, personal growth begets more personal growth, a kind of snowball effect.

CAREER THEORY – JOHN HOLLAND

A good place to start with career planning is with John Holland's theory of careers and this is expertly outlined in Robert Lock's book, *Taking Charge of Your Career Direction: Career Planning Guide* (2000). There are some first principles in career planning which fit well with completing a profiling tool like Holland's.

Appeal to the imagination – a career decision or venture starts with an idea. Yes, it needs to be realistic, but capturing the imagination should be there in the mix of one's attitude to a certain choice of career direction.

'Matchmaker matchmaker' – some career paths will suit the individuals, 'fit' them if you like, better than others. Voltaire once said, 'the best is the enemy of the good'. Alternatively, you will have also heard, 'the good is the enemy of the best'. In our career planning we need to be searching and making endeavours to find at the very least a 'good fit'.

Profile building – building a self-profile, constituting a critically accurate view of oneself, is the product of years of self-study, discerning strengths and weaknesses, likes and dislikes, successes and limitations. Inevitably a profile emerges from such self-study and reflection.

About benchmarking – observing others closely is a way not only to appreciate that we need one another's complementary and contrasting skills and abilities, but also to reach a greater understanding as individuals of what we are like and what we can do.

Reciprocity – where there is 'fit' the first principle of reciprocity kicks in. This is the notion that your compatibility with a certain career area will not only suit you, but you will also suit the employment opportunity, from an employer's perspective potentially activating a win/win 'rollerball' dynamic.

These principles accord with the Holland theory, which asks the individual to rank (from the most dominant to the least dominant) the following six personality types, resulting in one of 720 possible profiling combinations:

- **Realistic** – technical and mechanical, practical and realistic, e.g. mechanical engineer.
- **Investigative** – scientific and theoretical, analytical and rational, e.g. scientific researcher.
- **Artistic** – self-expressive and literary, creative and idealistic, e.g. interior designer.
- **Social** – cooperative and people-centred, humanitarian and caring, e.g. teaching.
- **Enterprising** – persuasive and managerial, assertive and energetic, e.g. marketing manager.
- **Conventional** – structured and orderly, efficient and systematic, e.g. accountant.

So if the above was your order you would be coded as a R I A S E C. You could equally be a C E S A I R, or any other of the multiple combinations.

Applying our first principles to the Holland theory, the following questions might arise:

- Which of the six types do you most and least relate to? For imagination, think about the words which for you personally have the most energy attached to them.
- Thinking of the best and the good, which is the closest to what you've always wanted to do? Can you select a second (back-up plan) and a third option?
- Which types most accord and least accord with your profile of strengths and weaknesses, likes and dislikes, etc., that have emerged from life and working experiences?
- Try and think of somebody who embodies the types from your network of family and friends. Who are you the closest to, and the least like in terms of your talents and interests?
- In which of the areas can you imagine yourself thriving and your contribution and enthusiasm being most appreciated?

1

2

3

4

5

Once you have placed your six personality types in order of their congruence to you, consult Gottfredson and Holland's (1996) *Dictionary of Holland Occupational Codes* to generate occupational prospects.

The Holland theory, Lock argues, accords with the notion that career choices are an expression of personality (Lock, 2000). He adds to this that vocational stereotypes, meaning the ideas that people have about different occupational options – including the status and community roles of such occupations – have some validity.

CAREER ANCHORS – EDGAR SCHEIN

Edgar Schein developed the idea of career anchors to help the individual more accurately define what it is they are actually seeking from a career. Not surprisingly this varies. Schein argued, 'A person's career anchor is the evolving self-concept of what one is good at, what one's needs and motives are, and what values govern one's work related choices' (Schein, 1990).

Schein's aim was to create a typology that would help the individual to develop this kind of self-insight and decipher their priorities. The identification of an individual's career anchor is enabled through the completion of a self-diagnostic exercise. These might be formally completed as part of employer learning and development programmes or accessed informally via the internet.

TF – technical and functional competence

- committed to a work-life of specialization
- can devalue the concerns of the general manager
- would leave an organization if not able to express their expertise
- will accept management position that permits continuation of expertise.

GM – general managerial competence

- regard knowing several functional areas as a must
- view specialization as a trap
- drawn to combination of analysing, supervising, influencing, leading and controlling
- aspire to a position of leadership where decisions make a real difference.

AU – autonomy/independence

- an overriding desire to do things their own way
- not wanting to be constrained by an organization
- a high value attached to maximum freedom and autonomy
- may enjoy choosing their own work hours.

SE – security/stability

- those attracted to what Schein terms the 'golden handcuffs' (Schein, 1990)
- a package of guaranteed work, benefits and pension offer
- drawn to stable organizations offering long-term employment.

EC – entrepreneurial creativity

- to create or build a product or service that is an extension of the person
- inevitably expressed in starting own enterprise sooner or later
- 'Obsessed with the need to create' (Schein, 1990).

SV – sense of service

- centred on service to others
- the career expresses commitment to an important cause
- may involve a sense of seeing others change as a result.

CH – pure challenge

- a sense they can conquer all (anything or anybody)
- bound up with winning or winning over
- enjoy overcoming 'impossible' challenges.

LS – lifestyle

- desiring a career that integrates with a chosen lifestyle
- family needs are often a major consideration here
- sometimes this relates to personal growth/well-being needs.

CAREER COUNSELLING – MARK SAVICKAS

Mark Savickas locates his career thinking in the midst of the *flux* we are experiencing. He labels himself as a 'constructivist' (the explanation of which lies below in the useful Savickasesque glossary) and the content of his theory is profoundly reassuring for adults facing all manner of challenges in search of (and transitioning towards) employment opportunities that might accord with the individual's self-concept.

To grasp the richness and relevance of Savickas' thinking we have structured this section in four parts as follows:

1 Hallmarks of postmodern turbulence – places Savickas' theory in the postmodern context we are experiencing. This expresses how Savickas sees this context and teases out its implications.
2 Career construction theory – outlines the theory as it is introduced in his book *Career Counseling* (2011).
3 A Savickasesque glossary – summarizes some of the perhaps unfamiliar terms and concepts associated with his thinking as presented in the above book.
4 A Savickas self-concept exercise – which represents something Savickas presented to practitioners at the International Career Studies Symposium (2010) in a session entitled 'Life Design'.

Hallmarks of postmodern turbulence

- distress – more specifically anxiety and frustrated anger
- recurrent transitions
- including frequent dislocations from employment assignments
- disrupted sense of self
- demand for flexible employability – supported by lifelong learning
- self-management – of career, along with self-navigation.

Career construction theory

- Career practitioners assist adults to construct a career story – a way of linking small stories, of narrating a large story and defining the next episode.
- Individuals take possession of their lives – only they can *narrate* how they see themselves and what they want to do.
- Self-awareness and self-knowledge lies at the heart of this self-construction – and narrating a story is assisted by language.
- An individual can flourish in a community an occupation provides.
- Although the individual narrates the story, he or she does not author it alone – this is a collaborative activity, with a more individualistic emphasis in western societies.
- Identifying and articulating a theme delivers a sense of integration for the individual – in how they see themselves and explain themselves to others.
- Career construction is part of a wider identity narration – fixing the flaw in one area empowers the individual to overcome adversity in another.

A Savickasesque glossary

Table 9.1 A Savickasesque glossary

Biographicity – a core concept for Savickas, from Alheit (1995). A process by which individuals 'integrate new and sometimes puzzling experiences into their biographies' (Savickas, 2011)

Constructivist practitioners – careers practitioners and others who alternatively steer towards constructivism, which holds that human knowledge is a construction, 'built from the cognitive processes … and embodied interactions with the world of material objects, others and the self' (Polkinghorne, 1992)

Golden theme – a controlling *idea* implicit in a plot. Has the potential to 'articulate a purposive attitude towards life and states the idea that the life serves' (Savickas, 2011). Savickas believes there is both an explicit plot and a theme forming two perspectives on a narrative identity

Identity capital – in Savickas' view produced by biographicity and identity work. Essentially encompasses individuals knowing, liking and using their own story

Inner journey – the implicit theme is a kind of 'emotional odyssey' as Savickas (2011) puts it. The implicit theme concerns the inner journey and relates to the individual's 'central conflict' including associated needs and longings

Micronarrative – the small stories gathered in narrative processing of identity

Macronarrative – the micronarratives are integrated to construct a large story or macronarrative. The latter 'explains our self to our self … and explains our self to our people' (Savickas, 2011). Savickas sourced the terms micronarrative and macronarrative from Neimeyer and Buchanan-Arvay (2004)

Narrative identity – McAdams and Olson (2010) defined this as 'an internalized and evolving life story that a person begins to develop in late adolescence to provide life with meaning and purpose'

Objective career – the sequence of roles an individual occupies from school to retirement. As it were, *chronicled* in a CV

Outer journey – the explicit plot is told and concerns the so called outer journey including events, turning points, life-defining moments and so forth

(Continued)

Table 9.1   (Continued)

Positivist practitioners – careers practitioners and others who steer towards positivism, which rejects any claims to knowledge not grounded in scientific investigation, and regards religious and metaphysical thinking as antiquated (Law, 2007)

Story line – the individual is enabled to see dislocations and interruptions as transitions and plots a story line bridging (sometimes difficult) discontinuities

Subjective career – emerges from the cognitive and imaginative process of constructing a story about one's working life

A Savickas self-concept exercise

In the lead up to his self-concept exercise Savickas made the following points:

- Career is about self-construction.
- Culture provides us with inspirational identity fragments.
- Career amounts to implementation of one's self-concept.
- A story is created to make you feel more complete.
- A strength comes from solving a problem.
- Strengths become social contributions.

EMBODIMENT BOX – DEVELOPING A SELF-CONCEPT

Who do you admire?

How are you like them?

How are you different from them?

Who would you like to pattern your life after?

Identify three role models:

List ten of their characteristics:

You now have a self-concept.

What is your all-time favourite story?

In what ways are you living this script?

What is your favourite saying? (See note at end of chapter.)

DOTS AND BEYOND

A well-known career planning model is called DOTS and was developed in its classic form by Bill Law and Tony Watts in the late 1970s and updated in 1999. Elements of the DOTS model are summarized in Table 9.2.

In planning and developing a career, the model suggested that people needed to know the following:

- the career *opportunities* available to them
- how to navigate their way – making career *decisions* – to where they want to be
- understanding the job market, how to apply for jobs, and handling the *transition* involved
- gaining greater *self*-awareness of their skills, strengths and knowledge.

Table 9.2 Elements of the classic DOTS model and its later version

classic DOTS	Opportunity	decision	transition	self
	'Where am I?'	'What will I do?'	'How will I cope?'	'Who am I?'
later version	career exploration		career management	self-development

The important point to grasp here is that this was presented as a lifelong process for all adults.

As is outlined in Bill Law's (2001) NICEC Briefing Paper, his new DOTS model extended the earlier versions with two further dimensions as shown in Table 9.3:

Table 9.3 Added dimensions in Law's new DOTS model

Classic (first) dimension	Coverage	What people need to know
Two further dimensions	Processes	How knowledge is processed
	Influences	Allowing for emotional and social pressures

The two new dimensions allow for:

- How adults process knowledge before action, including the processes of sensing, sifting, focusing and understanding (see Law, 2001).
- Psychological realities and (often limiting) self-beliefs. Law (2001) has said, 'the great enemy of career development is stereotyping'.

LIFE PLANNING

We can look at life planning in a number of ways. Three ways are explored here:

1 as balance
2 as story
3 as flourishing.

As balance

Work–life balance

Don Browning (2006) argues that we naturally pursue the so called 'goods of life'. These include such things as food, health, pleasure, wealth, companionship and safety. We discover, however, that it is extremely difficult to have all the goods of life at the same time and that the goods effectively compete with one another for time and commitment. Added to this, Browning comments, the efforts of others to secure these goods conflict with our own. The eminent philosopher Paul Ricoeur speaks of these conflicting goods of life producing various forms of violence (i.e. harm) to the person and in wider society (Browning, 2006). At the root of much anxiety in western society is perhaps this elusive desire to clutch hold of and securely protect a whole collection of these goods we have come to expect. Browning concludes that these conflicting goods present us with difficult choices.

The dynamic cycle

We might describe Frank Lake's (1966) dynamic cycle as a conceptual framework for thinking about the issue of balance in one's life. It is called the dynamic cycle because it involves movement – the inflow (or input) of what Lake terms *acceptance* and *sustenance* and the outflow (or output) of *sense of significance* and *achievement*. Table 9.4 offers an explanation of what these terms mean.

Table 9.4   Frank Lake's dynamic cycle

INPUT	*Acceptance*	Personhood requires loving relationships and sources of acceptance
	Sustenance	Relationships also have the potential to supply people with what they need
OUTPUT	*Sense of significance*	The above phases make for a sense of personal value and well-being
	Achievement	Also, the 'achievement of some work or skill or service that is personally and socially meaningful' (Christian, 1991)

Lake's dynamic cycle contributes a number of considerations regarding the notion of 'balance' in our lives:

Input before output – in hectic contemporary lifestyles the reminder that input must come before output is key.

Relational priority – all four aspects of Lake's cycle have a relational dimension and the significance of the relational on the input side of the cycle is particularly noticeable.

Personal application – further personal application of the dynamic cycle might be achieved by critically asking oneself the following questions:

- *Acceptance* – what are the relational sources of true and abiding acceptance in my life?
- *Sustenance* – other than relational input what are the other things I need in my life to sustain a sense of well-being, e.g. health and fitness?
- *Sense of significance* – what things in my life express and output a sense of significance?
- *Achievement* – what achievements can I point to that add to my life and the life of others?

Organizational application – an organization can apply the cycle's principles by asking its employees the following questions:

- *Acceptance* – how accepted do you feel here?
- *Sustenance* – in what ways does the organization sustain your well-being as a person?
- *Sense of significance* – is your status at work broadly commensurate with your gifts, and abilities? If not, why not?
- *Achievement* – if you didn't return to work, what meaningful activity might disappear with you?

As story

Sartre argued, 'a man is always a teller of stories, he lives surrounded by his own stories and those of other people; he sees everything that happens to him in terms of these stories' (Sartre, 1964).

There are several things we can draw out of this sentence by Jean-Paul Sartre:

- We all tell stories.
- We have the potential to listen to and learn from other people's stories.
- Stories are a means of understanding ourselves, others and the world we live in.

Caroline Ramsey's (2005) narrative learning cycle casts light on how the narrating of our stories initiates a cycle of learning and development that culminates in action plans and action. It is divided into four stages as shown in Tale 9.5.

Table 9.5 Ramsey's narrative learning cycle

Stage 1 – Narrating my story	I narrate (tell) my story. The act of telling my story is what may be termed as a constructive process. Something is created or brought into being in the act of telling that did not exist before. This of course raises the issue of clarity and relevance of the story I am narrating
Stage 2 – Exploring other stories	I listen to the stories of others. I realize that others have stories to tell from which I can learn. We need, as Jonathan Sacks puts it, to 'make ourselves open to their stories' (Sacks, 2002)

(Continued)

Table 9.5 (Continued)

Stage 3 – Re-narrating	Through telling my story and hearing other stories I am able to see my new story in a new light. I am therefore able now to re-narrate (or re-tell) my story
Stage 4 – Social performance	I turn my re-narrated story into action. For Ramsey (2005) this is a social performance, in that my actions invite both response and supplement, but they also contribute to what emerges from ongoing relating

So adding to what we took from Sartre, Ramsey's cycle has added:

- Stories are re-narrated as a result of the sharing of stories.
- Action plans and actions flow out of the re-narrated stories.

Relating to the latter point, Vanhoozer (1990) maintains that courses of action are always narrative in nature. This suggests that we narrate ourselves forward. This makes our life and career planning a creative process encompassing the activation of the imagination. This is not something individualistic but, as Ramsey has showed us, is bound up with working and living alongside others and hearing their stories.

The following A to Z on narrative illustrates the scope and nature of story and the telling of stories in our life and in our culture. This scope and nature is far more profound than just the childhood experience of listening to a tale being read to us from a book, say by a teacher. Narratives of various sorts, shapes and sizes fill our consciousness and more. Our minds are a bricolage of the memories, key and other moments, the places we've been, the faces we've seen, songs, films, scenes seen on television and computer screens. These images are all 'storied' (connected to story and often configured as story) and any one of them could be retrieved and translated into words or telling by what Wengraf (2001) labels as a SQUIN (a single question aimed at inducing narrative), i.e. by asking someone a simple question that begins with words like, 'Tell me your story of how…'

This accords with Bruner's point as selected by Uwe Flick (2006):

> When someone tells you his life (story) … it is always a cognitive achievement rather than a through the clear-crystal recital of something univocally given. In the end, it is a *narrative achievement*. There is no such thing psychologically as 'life itself'. At very least, it is a selective achievement of memory recall; beyond that, recounting one's life is an interpretive feat. (emphasis added)

A to Z on narrative

There is a lot we could say about the significance of narrative. Given this, we have summarized many aspects of narrative thinking and terminology in Table 9.6 below.

Table 9.6 An A to Z on narrative

A for Approach	The *narrative approach* is based on the idea that people 'construct and reconstruct their lives continuously in order to give meaning to life-events and to integrate new experiences' (Schroots and Assink, 2005)
B for Beginning …	A story has a beginning, middle and end. Rankin (2002) places this centrally to the definition of story as follows: 'a synthesizing of heterogeneous elements; a synthesis in which a beginning, middle and end are construed, where each element and each stage contributes to the whole'
C for Constructed	Narratives constitute an arrangement of elements – actions, events, characters, experiences and situations (Rankin, 2002). Alheit (2002) argues stories do not happen in the real world but, rather are constructed in our minds
D for Dialogue	For Ramsey (2005) the sharing of narrative offers great dialogical potential 'for hearing alternative voices and so enabling a more communal reflection on events that could be considered relevant to future joint action'
E for Explore	Narratives enable us to explore all manner of things about ourselves and our world. Narratives function like a 'mirror' – reflecting and reproducing 'that which already is' (Parris, 2002)
F for Fictive	Ricoeur's view is that narrative is 'fictive', meaning that it is subject to the imagination through interpretation. Alheit (2002) explores the gap between a narrative's truth and fiction when he says that there is a structural similarity between things happening for people in the 'real world' and what is relayed in their narratives
G for Grabbed	An interesting way to look at people is to ask, 'what's the story that has grabbed them?' It could of course be closer to the fact that the story has in some way actually mugged them
H for History	Histories and stories are two major forms of narratives (Vanhoozer, 1990). Jovchelovitch and Bauer (2000) make the point that personal stories are expressive of larger societal and historical contexts
I for Identification	Jenni Russell (2012) contends that we want to hear other people's stories because we are hungry to understand our own. We want, she says, 'to know how others handle conflicts in their lives because we want to manage ours'
J for J. R. R. Tolkien	A pioneer in the area of rehabilitating the imagination, Tolkien spoke of the capacity of story to awaken desire (Helms, 1974)
K for KDPs	Stories can be analysed for what McCormack and Milne (2003) term as *knowledge disclosure points* (KDPs). These take the form of the following: critical incidents, turning points, decisions, judgements, problem resolutions and learning events
L for Living	Vanhoozer (1990) suggests narratives create and display the myriad ways that we can live
M for Meaning making	We share stories to search out what is meaningful. Sacks (2002) says we are 'the meaning-seeking animal'. Added to this, we reflect on our past and try to render it a meaningful whole (Stiver, 2001)
N for Numinous	A force which is 'urgent, active, compelling and alive'. Or as also penned by Rudolf Otto, 'something that captivates and transports him with a strange ravishment, rising often to the pitch of dizzy intoxication' (1958)

(Continued)

Table 9.6 (Continued)

O for Odyssey	*The Odyssey* by Homer was described by T. E. Lawrence (1992) as the 'first novel of Europe'. It is one of the most influential books ever written and tells a ten-year story of Odysseus' wanderings after the fall of Troy. Like many stories it has acted in some capacity as a guiding narrative, constituting some 'model' for others to follow or reference
P for Plot	Aristotle observed that the function of plot was to organize a multiplicity of incidents into a story
Q for Q-sort	The California Q-sort is a set of 100 descriptive statements designed to provide a comprehensive view of personality (Clausen and Jones, 1998). The selection of the most characteristic statements the individual identifies with has the applied usage of facilitating the generation of stories for each card. Alternatively the individual could relay a story (with a plot), encompassing a few of the cards
R for Rival narratives	Smith (2009) says that over the past 200 years the west has seen a struggle between a number of major rival narratives: American experiment; militant Islamic resurgence; Christian metanarrative; capitalist prosperity; progressive socialism; and scientific enlightenment
S for Self-concept	Weiten et al. (2012) define this as 'your mental-picture of yourself' and add that it is a collection of self-perceptions. It is particularly influenced by the responses of others in our lives
T for Turning point	Turning points, Colton et al. (2006) say, are those pivotal moments when 'something changes, for the better or for the worse'. They may be accompanied by a difficult choice and arrive at a time of crisis or conflict. When hearing a story we listen out for turning points
U for Unify	Alheit (2002) observes that we use stories to unify our identity
V for Vivid	Ellenwood (2006) suggests we need stories that are vivid and vexing. The best biographies often possess these qualities
W for Worlds	A successful story-maker or teller creates another world, a heterocosm (Helms, 1974). In addition, narratives constitute possible ways of doing things, possible worlds (Vanhoozer, 1990)
X for X-Men	… or any other contemporary narrative that has some significance for the individual. See our discussion on a self-concept drawing on Mark Savickas (2011)
Y for Yahweh	Andricopoulos (2008) speaks of the culture of ancient Greece being 'replaced' by the Judaeo-Christian culture and then by capitalist culture. Each age comes with its own set of stories. So called *meta-narratives* are when one story or set of stories is employed to dominate and control others, including smaller stories. Postmodernity is marked by a rejection of meta-narratives
Z for Zeus	Zeus has been selected here to exemplify the category of mythology in our telling of stories. Myth relates to what is felt or considered to be 'true'. In instances where we know that it is pure fiction, it is used to examine and illuminate complexity and subjects that cannot be approached 'head on'

EMPLOYABILITY FOCUS – THE APPLICATION AS STORY

One can very easily see how a job application is what one might term a 'narrative construct'. Not only has the applicant often in some way 'storied'

themselves on some level as getting the job and relating it to their life story, it also asks the applicant to 'story' themselves at a number of critical points.

- *The application form* – very clearly this calls for the applicant to story their life to date and by implication requires the applicant to story how what they offer coincides with what the employer is looking for. It is very common for CVs to effectively overlook important details that are integral to what the applicant is offering – that should, as it were, be a part of the applicant's story of who they are and what they can offer.
- *The covering letter* – this like the application form relays information and is integral to the job application, but it often tells some sort of story and certainly underlines the 'match' characteristics that the employer seeks. It implicitly requires the applicant to answer the question, 'Why should we consider your application for this post or vacancy?' The applicant briefly summarizes their case to be selected and this effectively is a story.
- *The interview* – each interview question will require 'hard' information that the interviewer can formally record, but the answers to all the questions together effectively tell a story. Looking at individual questions and answers, the common question, 'Why do you want to work here?' requires a storied answer.

A couple of things to underline here. When we speak of telling a story, we don't mean making something up that is not true, or even the notion of 'spinning a yarn' as it is known. Added to this it is important also to highlight that in talking about the telling of one's story we are not suggesting prolonged answers at the interview or inappropriately extended letters and application entries.

Below are some final points about how to think of a job application as sharing one's story:

- Is your story both clear and inspirational?
- What is interesting about your story?
- How does or how could your story coincide with the story of the organization or the story of what the organization is seeking in this appointment?
- If you cannot imagine (or story yourself) as fulfilling the role, then your application is not likely to be attractive to a potential employer.

KEY CONCEPT – TELLING (NOT JUST TALKING) STORIES

An invaluable resource is Shawn Callahan's (2013) story telling input on the website *Anecdote*. Callahan provides a number of key principles in the telling of stories, as follows:

(Continued)

(Continued)

- *In it to win it* – Callahan says, 'you only get the benefits of storytelling if you're telling a story'.
- *Telling (not just talking) stories* – there are many who are, as Callahan puts it, 'merely talking about stories but not telling any'.
- *Listening out for stories* – spotting a story, Callahan argues is, 'the key to effective story-work'.

Here's how Callahan says we spot a story:

1 It starts with a time or place marker, sometimes a character.
2 There is a discernible plot – a series of connected events.
3 It includes people talking (dialogue) and doing things.
4 The storyteller is sharing something you want to hear – something that will raise your eyebrows, as Callahan remarks.

Callahan's following points illustrate how we might journey from good to great in our storytelling:

- A story should ably describe what happened.
- A good story is one that helps you clearly see what happened.
- A great story, Callahan says, 'helps you feel what happened'.

We can attach Callahan's principles of storytelling to a number of helpful questions for eliciting stories as outlined in Stephanie Colton et al.'s (2006) *Story Guide* produced for the Swiss Agency for Development and Cooperation:

'Tell me about a time when ...' / 'Tell me about a moment when ...'

- You faced a dilemma or a dilemma in your project.
- You or your team experienced a significant turning point.
- You dealt with a real crisis on a project. What happened before, during and after it?
- You felt really proud to be part of something.
- You took a real risk and it paid off or didn't pay off.
- You were really inspired by what was going on around you.
- You encountered an obstacle and overcame it.
- You saw one of your organization's values really brought to life/being acted out.
- Your partnerships were working really well.
- You saw positive changes happen as a result of your work.

'O what a story'

Andrew Carnegie was born in Dunfermline, Scotland's ancient capital, on 25 November 1835. His was a humble background, the son of William Carnegie, a damask linen weaver, and Margaret Carnegie. The depression of the 'hungry forties' led the family to emigrate to Allegheny City, Pennsylvania in 1848. At 13 Andrew started work as a bobbin-boy in a cotton factory.

In 1850 Andrew switched to a post as a telegraph messenger boy in Pittsburg telegraph office. Soon after, Colonel James Anderson announced that he was going to open his private library of 4,000 volumes to 'working boys' in Pittsburg. Andrew by virtue of the fact he didn't work with his 'hands' didn't qualify and wrote a letter to the Pittsburg Dispatch arguing that he was still a working boy.

The Colonel was so impressed by Carnegie's appeal that he shifted the criteria. It was James Anderson's generosity that formed the inspiration later for Carnegie to devout a substantial part of his fortune to gifting towns and cities in more than a dozen countries with as many as 2,811 libraries.

The young Carnegie visited Anderson's library every Saturday.

By 1853 Carnegie had become clerk and telegraph operator for Thomas A. Scott, assistant superintendent of the Pennsylvania Railroad Company. Two years later Scott asked his young adult clerk if he could find five hundred dollars to invest in the Adams Express stock. This was the first of a number of enterprising initiatives Carnegie would take on his journey to become one of the world's foremost ironmasters.

In 1901 Andrew Carnegie sold the Carnegie Steel Company (as a major part of what became the United States Steel Group) and gave the rest of his days to the causes of education and world peace. His recently published book *The Gospel of Wealth* (1900) argued that 'the man who dies rich dies disgraced'. He accordingly distributed the vast majority of his £60 million share of the sale.

In the British Isles he is best known for his 660 libraries. He is less known for being a member of the Peace Society of Great Britain and becoming in 1907 the first President of the Peace Society of New York. He gave £1.5 million for the establishment of The Palace of Peace at The Hague and was one of the first to talk of a 'league of nations'.

It shattered Carnegie when the Great War (as it is called) broke out in 1914. He died soon after the end of the first global war in Lenox, Massachusetts on 11 August 1919.

EMBODIMENT BOX – THE EUDAEMON INDIVIDUAL

Richard Kraut (1979) speaks of the 'eudaemon individual'. This relates to Aristotle's term eudaemonia sometimes incorrectly interpreted as 'happiness'. Kraut suggests that 'well-being' and 'flourishing' are much closer to its meaning for Aristotle.

Kraut's article in *The Philosophical Review* highlights how Aristotle would characterize the eudaemon individual.

- fully developed and exercises the virtues
- has a strong desire for life
- directs desires to worthwhile goals
- realizes life's potential
- fulfils the function of a human being
- only a eudaemon life is well lived.

T. R. Irwin (1975) differentiates between Aristotle's virtues of character and intellectual virtues. The former are the result of habituation and are learned through practice, whereas the latter result from teaching about ethics. For Aristotle intellectual virtues 'do not determine a man's ends'.

A. C. Grayling (2000) presents eudaemonia as flourishing and 'living richly'. He rightly highlights Aristotle's conception of a eudaemonic person as the 'megalopsychos' (or 'great-souled' individual). This implies a life that has thriving and expansive qualities about it. Grayling remarks, 'the goal of ethical life is multiple in character, involving respect and concern for others, and a duty to improve oneself and to use one's gifts for the sake not only of others but also of the quality of one's own experience' (Grayling, 2000).

APPLIED PERSONAL DEVELOPMENT

Remember in applied personal development we essentially ask the question, 'So what?' In other words, what are the personal and professional implications of some of the things we have examined in the above chapter?

Looking firstly at life and career as journey it is important to appreciate that every life will contain a mixture of adventures and struggles, great surprises and difficulties. Appreciating this will give a sense of perspective. At the same time, it is good to remember that it is only our life – it doesn't belong to anyone else. This has important implications for taking responsibility for our own lives. Using the story perspective we have introduced in this chapter would prompt the message that it is your life to story.

This has important implications for the whole matching process, that is finding a career in life that matches what essentially you are looking for. We need here a positive yet robust self-knowledge and self-appreciation, avoiding the twin dangers of lack of self-belief and a somewhat deluded over-estimation of ourselves. Approaching Holland's model and Schein's anchors with honesty and criticality will enable you to move forward with a realistic positivity.

The key to all the content on story, both the theoretical thinking of Mark Savickas and also Caroline Ramsey's narrative cycle, is understanding the importance of the imagination and creativity in the whole process of storying one's life forward. At the same time, there is an important message here about listening out for other people's stories. These provide not just inspiration and learning, but equip us in understanding the breadth of not only ourselves but also those who work and live alongside us in a postmodern contemporary society. Such things are important not just for career and life planning, but also in the general operation of business.

Andrew Carnegie's story showed how a series of some canny decisions led to his extraordinary success and how he decided to give his fortune back to ordinary people through supporting the causes of education and peace. It also shows that Carnegie could have made very different decisions in his professional and personal life. That's what I've been trying to highlight about the responsibility we have to make our own stories. In Carnegie's case he took note of the example and story of his senior, Colonel James Anderson, and the rest as they say is history.

NOTE ON SAVICKAS SELF-CONCEPT EXERCISE

What is your favourite saying?

Savickas says, 'This is the best advice to you right now'.

REFERENCES

Alheit, P. (1995) 'Biographical learning: theoretical outline, challenges, and contradictions of a new approach in adult education', in P. Alheit, A. Bron-Wojciechowska, E. Brugger and P. Dominicé (eds), *The Biographical Approach in European Adult Education*. Vienna: Verband Wiener Volksbildung.

Alheit, P. (2002) 'Stories and structures: historical time and narrative'. ESREA Life History and Biography Research Network Conference, Geneva, 7–9 March.

Andricopoulos, Y. (2008) *The Greek Inheritance: Ancient Greek Wisdom for the Digital Age*. Exeter: Imprint Academic.

Browning, D. (2006) *Christian Ethics and the Moral Psychologies*. Grand Rapids, Michigan: Eerdmans

Callahan, S. (2013) 'How to spot an oral story', *Anecdote*, 13 October. Available at: www.anecdote.com/blog (accessed 15 October 2013).

Christian, C. (1991) *In the Spirit of Truth: A Reader in the Work of Frank Lake*. London: Darton, Longman and Todd.

Clausen, J. A. and Jones, C. J. (1998) 'Predicting personality stability across the life span: the role of competence and work and family commitments', *Journal of Adult Development*, 5 (2): 73–83.

Colton, S., Ward, V. and Brutschin, J. (2006) *Story Guide: Building Bridges Using Narrative Techniques*. Berne: Swiss Agency for Development and Cooperation.

Ellenwood, S. (2006) 'Revisiting character education: from McGuffey to narratives', *Journal of Education*, 187 (3): 21–43.

Flick, U. (2006) *An Introduction to Qualitative Research*. London: Sage.

Gottfredson, G. D. and Holland, J. L. (1996) *Dictionary of Holland Occupational Codes*. Odessa, FL: Psychological Assessment Resources.

Grayling, A. C. (2000) 'No reason for Charles to get married; we're obsessed with his happiness, and our own', *Independent on Sunday*, 11 June.

Helms, R. (1974) *Tolkien's World*. London: Thames & Hudson.

Hopson, B. and Hugh, P. (1973) *Exercises in Personal and Career Development*. Cambridge: CRAC.

Irwin, T. H. (1975) 'Aristotle on reason, desire, and virtue', *The Journal of Philosophy*: 567–578.

Jantzen, G. M. (2004) *Foundations of Violence*. London: Routledge.

Jovchelovitch, S. and Bauer, M. W. (2000) 'Narrative interviewing', in M. W. Bauer and G. Gaskell (eds), *Qualitative Researching with Text, Image and Sound*. London: Sage.

Kraut, R. (1979) 'Two conceptions of happiness', *The Philosophical Review*, 88 (2): 167–197.

Lake, F. (1966) *Clinical Theology: A Theological and Psychiatric Basis to Clinical Pastoral Care*. London: Darton, Longman and Todd.

Law, B. (2001) 'New DOTS: Career learning for the contemporary world', NICEC Briefing. Available at: www.hihohiho.com/memory/cafnewdots.pdf (accessed 15 October 2013).

Law, S. (2007) *Philosophy*. London: DK.

Lawrence, T. E. (1992) *The Odyssey of Homer* (trans.). Ware: Wordsworth Classics.

Lock, R. D. (2000) *Taking Charge of Your Career Direction: Career Planning Guide, Book 1*. Belmont, CA: Wadsworth/Thomson Learning.

McAdams, D. P. and Olson, B. D. (2010) 'Personality development: continuity and change over the life course', *Annual Review of Psychology*, 61: 517–542.

McCormack, C. and Milne, P. (2003) 'Stories create space for understanding organisational change', *Qualitative Research Journal*, 3 (2): 46–59.

Neimeyer, R. A. and Buchanan-Arvay, M. (2004) 'Performing the self: therapeutic enactment and the narrative integration of traumatic loss', in H. Hermans and G. DiMaggio (eds), *The Dialogical Self in Psychotherapy*. New York: Brunner-Routledge.

Otto, R. (1958) *The Idea of the Holy*. Oxford: Oxford University Press.

Parris, D. P. (2002) 'Imitating the parables: allegory, narrative and the role of mimesis', *Journal for the Study of the New Testament*, 25 (33): 33–53.

Polkinghorne, D. E. (1992) 'Postmodern epistemology of practice', in S. Kvale (ed.), *Psychology and Postmodernism*. London: Sage.

Ramsey, C. (2005) 'Narrating development: professional practice emerging within stories', *Action Research*, 3 (3): 279–296.

Rankin, J. (2002) 'What is narrative? Ricoeur, Bakhtin, and process approaches', *Concrescence: The Australian Journal of Process Thought*, 3: 1–12.

Russell, J. (2012) 'Brit lit recoils from the way we live now', *Sunday Times*, 1 January.

Sacks, J. (2002) *The Dignity of Difference: How to Avoid the Clash of Civilizations*. London: Continuum.

Sartre, J. (1964) *Nausea*, trans. Lloyd Alexander. New York: New Directions Publishing.

Savickas, M. L. (2011) *Career Counseling*. Washington, DC: American Psychological Association.

Schein, E. H. (1978) *Career Dynamics: Matching Individual and Organisational Needs*. Reading, MA: Addison-Wesley Publishing.

Schein, E. H. (1990) 'Career anchors and job/role planning: the links between career pathing and career development'. Available at: http://dspace.mit.edu/bitstream/handle/1721.1/2315/SWP-3192-22603401.pdf (accessed 21 June 2014).

Schroots, J. J. F. and Assink, M. H. J. (2005) 'Portraits of life: patterns of events over the lifespan', *Journal of Adult Development*, 12 (4), December.

Smith, C. (2009) *Moral Believing Animals*. Oxford: Oxford University Press.

Stiver, D. R. (2001) *Theology After Ricoeur: New Directions in Hermeneutical Theology*. Louisville: Westminster John Knox Press.

Vanhoozer, K. J. (1990) *Biblical Narrative in the Philosophy of Paul Ricoeur*. Cambridge: Cambridge University Press.

Weiten, W., Dunn, D. S. and Hammer, E. Y. (2012) *Psychology Applied to Modern Life: Adjustments in the 21st Century*. Belmont, CA: Wadsworth.

Wengraf, T. (2001) *Qualitative Research*. London: Sage.

Word Detective, The (2009) 'Careen/Career: you're doing it wrong'. Available at: www.word-detective.com/2009/08/careen-career/ (accessed 18 October 2013).

10 THE NUTS AND BOLTS OF CAREER COMMUNICATION

● ● ● ● ● ● ● ● ● ● ● ● ● ● ●

A NOTE FROM THE AUTHOR

There isn't anything intrinsically complicated about applying for a job, but it does call for an extremely challenging consistency. I'll unpack what I mean shortly, but it's obviously not an easy process, otherwise good candidates would be matched up with suitable jobs without a long wait or multiple job applications. Like a lot of things, consistency comes with practice and the more jobs you apply for, provided you don't get disheartened, the more fluent you can become with the communication involved in a job application.

The communication skills called for in the process constitute a 'high bar' of performance as you are usually required to:

- produce an accurate and appealing CV
- match this and your application form carefully to the job description and person specification
- perform at an interview, answering all the questions and handling well the pressure of the situation in the way you conduct yourself
- give a presentation, a common feature of the process
- attend what is known as an assessment centre, again increasingly favoured by employers, involving group work and interpersonal skills as well as interviews and a presentation.

Anyone can see from the bullet points above that there is nothing easy about securing a sought after job. Maintaining my point that it is not complicated, my intention in this chapter is to break the process down into its component parts – hence the title the 'nuts and bolts' of career communication. Added to this, however, it is vital to see how its parts need to integrate. The job applicant should try to present across the whole process a smooth and integrated (as distinct from disjointed and fragmented) 'story' of who they are and how they suitably match the opportunity.

Many of you will enjoy a night out at the cinema. When you select a particular film, you're the one who is, as it were, in the driving seat. This in a number of respects reflects the same principles that the members of a selection panel use to shortlist and appoint a person to a job. The parallel will become clear from the following questions:

- Why did you choose a particular film? And what caused it to stand apart from the others on offer?
- What influence did the main headlines in how the film was presented have on your choice? And what were the film's clear selling points?
- In what ways did the poster or advert or report capture your imagination? And give you what you were looking for?
- In some way you identified yourself with the film. You said, 'I want to go to that film'. How does this matching process work?

Because a job application is essentially a presentation of yourself, you could describe it as a performance. Indeed some even think of it as a kind of game, hence the phrase 'playing the game', which is something some people do rather well. However you view it, try to see yourself and what you're presenting, both on paper and in person, from the selector's perspective.

Learning outcomes

When you have completed this chapter you will be able to:

- appreciate the significance of producing a well-integrated application
- recount a number of strategies to quell inevitable nerves
- work towards presenting the story of what you offer
- sharpen your sense of what makes a good presentation
- understand what to expect at an assessment centre
- know how to contribute in group work.

THE KEY PRINCIPLES

Viewing the application process as a whole from producing a CV to meeting potential employers in an interview or assessment centre, there are a number of key principles to keep in mind.

- Practice – the adage is true, 'practise makes perfect'. No one commences the job application process as the finished item. Even extremely talented and instantly appealing candidates, from an employer's perspective, need practice to 'lift their game'. This should provide some reassurance to those who are conscious of a confidence deficit. When you gain the experience of attending an assessment centre, the discerning candidate can observe that everybody has something to be working on in terms of how well they communicate, across the span of the job application experience and process.

- Learn from the experience that went before – which leads us to the next point, which is that no job application experience is wasted, not for the applicant who is also a reflective practitioner. The model here is close to a sports coaching model. Every game or event experience, if reflected upon, can yield a rich return of learning – areas where you did well, to be repeated; and pointers for improvement arising from things you don't want to repeat. So the principle here is simply, learn from experience and you will improve.

- Learn from other life experiences – interestingly, so many of life's experiences can feed into the job application process. It takes more than simply rehearsals and former performances to produce an accomplished actor. The latter is able to integrate so many aspects of themselves and their experiences with the particular performance in question. Work hard, therefore, to do likewise by bringing your personality and developed characteristics and your total self to the process.

- Matching – for those familiar with the dating, sometimes called mating, game, it works in a similar fashion. The best dates and most fulfilling relationships are where there is a good match. The irony here can be that if the candidate, like the person dating, doesn't communicate who they are; and what truly they have to offer, the next person will.

- 'Turning up' – which leads us on to the next principle which, again, is not complicated but certainly is not an automatic practice: expressing your true abilities and potential in the application process. Does the CV truly reflect the candidate? Has the candidate done themselves justice in the application pro-forma? Was the candidate interviewed the same person as got up that morning? Was the person not only professional but also 'real' in their presentation?

- Nerves can suffocate your personality – sadly nerves can suppress creativity and stop the performance from flowing. A certain degree of fear, some might call it respect for the process and consciousness of the gravity of the event (say an interview), is needed. But too much fear is counter-productive and counter-creative. For those who struggle here, the point must be underlined that, like learning to swim, time in the waters of the whole job application process will chase away those perfectly normal fears and apprehensions.

- Telling your story – obviously not your whole story, but the story of yourself that is relevant to the job in question. The reason we use the term 'story' is that this suggests the integration and structuring of a diversity of key themes, facts and information. A storying of oneself permits the employer to gain a full picture of the applicant and to connect one relevant piece of information with the next. A young adult (with less adult years) has a greater opportunity to craft a smooth and integrated story. There is an art to bringing together a full presenting of yourself that is relevant, authentic, interesting, integrated and structured.

- Research – that is, study, underlies the application process. It is vital to closely study the job being offered, the key documents here being the job description and the person profile. Added to this it is essential to research the organization, including even members of staff that you would be working with. This latter dimension of researching the employer and relevant managers via the internet is not difficult. Networking is also relevant here, perhaps knowing somebody who works in the organization. The key here is developing an enquiring mind, a bit like a journalist, to do your 'homework' on the job, the organization, relevant staff and other industry-relevant contextual information.

EMBODIMENT BOX – 'TURNING UP'

Below are ten aspects of what it means when we speak of someone turning up, and for each aspect we compare this with an embodiment suggesting the opposite.

- engaged – disengaged
- best foot – back foot
- flowing personality – 'switched off' personality
- want it – ambivalent
- presented – unpresented
- tailored – untailored
- aimed – directionless
- positive – negative
- confident – anxious
- enthusiastic – unstirred
- momentum – static.

THE JOB

Beware of being what I term 'emotionally monogamous' when looking and applying for jobs. This is a tendency some people have to over-invest themselves in pursuing specific jobs and it is usually reflected in people not applying for enough jobs to give themselves a better chance in seeking employment. The more you emotionally commit to a specific opportunity to the exclusion of other opportunities, the greater the likelihood of disappointment if the job is ultimately not secured. In a highly competitive job market, therefore, you need to be seeking out multiple opportunities and completing multiple job applications, on an ongoing basis. Multiplications of applications is the key here.

This is not to suggest that every application should be rattled off without concerted care and attention. Rather it is to underline that the job application process for most people is closer to a marathon than a sprint, requiring 'mental discipline' as well as careful and consistent effort.

There are multiple sources of jobs and depending on your personal circumstances, it is obviously a great advantage if you are prepared to look at a number of geographical destinations. In a globalizing world international job experience is an exciting, albeit often challenging option. If you have a second or third language it is always useful to maximize the development and application of this employability asset.

It is good to remember that in finding and furthering job opportunities, networking is as significant as the internet. These two dimensions, the personal and the internet platform for advertised posts, are not an either or, both should be embraced. Perhaps think of them as two hands. On the one hand, it is important to regularly trawl the internet for arising new openings as advertised on leading sites. On the other hand, you should constantly recall the very human dimension of maximizing the contact opportunity, both with people whom you know who can assist in all sorts of ways, and by opting to build personal bridges in the whole application process.

THE ARCHITECTURE

The written application, the cover letter and the CV are obviously all written communications. It is fair to say that the onus, therefore, in securing a place on the short-list primarily lies in your ability to present yourself in writing.

Unlike oral communication, employed in an interview, a presentation or at an assessment centre, written communications call for exacting standards. Paper, albeit electronically transmitted, is not forgiving of errors, be they spelling mistakes, typos or grammatically deficient sentences and paragraphs. If these 'showpieces' are flawed, the next candidate's will be perfect. The stakes are high and the losses (of rejected applications) considerable.

As critical as it is, exacting accuracy is not the only consideration here. Another is making your case to be shortlisted by the employer. Think of it like the courtroom. On the one hand, those judging your presentation can be persuaded. On the other hand, your case can be thrown out.

We are familiar with the phrase, 'more haste, less speed'. Applying this to the above written communications that make up the application process prior to shortlisting, watch out for being too hasty to 'fill in' boxes on the pro-forma, rattling off a well-used CV and giving only cursory attention to the cover note.

All these communications provide an opportunity to 'flow' with a well-worded case, each item integrating with and reinforcing the next – 'speedy' in the sense of being easy to read and succinct, rather than heavily concentrated and over-laboured. Think of them as what we'll term, 'Written Comms 1, 2, 3'.

1 The application form's design suggests the quantity of information the employer is seeking. Read the questions carefully, providing only information which supports your case to be shortlisted. Think quality, not quantity. Think persuasion, not falsity.
2 The CV is 'tailored' for every job application and should not exceed two sides of A4. It will be reviewed in literally seconds and anything that causes the reader difficulty will mean that it drops into the second or third pile.
3 The employer, likewise does not have time to figuratively wade through a wordy cover letter. In addition, a letter which says 'nothing', only following the formality of pointing to the other attachments or enclosures also can be viewed as a waste of time. At the very least, it is easy for it to constitute a wasted opportunity.

The tables below constitute a number of additional starting resources relating to the written dimension of the job application.

Spelling

We all make spelling mistakes, but an application going to an employer with needless errors discredits the applicant and can give the impression that they have rushed it. Sometimes it can speak of a casual attitude to an important opportunity. In summary, spelling mistakes do not do the applicant any favours at all. So when producing a CV, completing a pro-forma and composing a cover letter, be sure to check it over, at least twice. It is always a good idea to ask someone to fulfil an editorial function, obviously someone who is accustomed to reading formal documents with an ability to spot mis-spelt words.

Table 10.1 Twenty-five commonly mis-spelt words

Accommodate	Committee	Extremely	Maintenance	Psychology
Addresses	Completely	Fulfil	Necessary	Recommended
All right	Conscientious	Immediately	Occasional	Separate
Benefited	Consistent	Independent	Omitted	Successfully
Colleagues	Definite	Lose	Privilege	Unnecessary

While it is true that the spell check facility that comes with MS Word eliminates needless spelling mistakes, it is no substitute for careful proofreading. You have to be particularly vigilant with on-line job applications where there is no spell check. Remember too, that spell check doesn't spot missing words, the use of an incorrect word and a number of common grammatical mistakes.

Action orientation

Employers are always on the lookout for people with positive energy, who will work hard, get things done, meet deadlines and possessing a 'can do' attitude. Their search for the action-oriented is expressed in the phrase that employers are often looking for candidates who can 'hit the ground running'. In one respect this is a big ask, but in a competitive job market, it is not hard for employers to expect such levels of energy and commitment.

Review Table 10.2, which lists 25 skills expressed as verbs. These constitute a selection of words a job applicant can use in written sentences to highlight former experiences that demonstrate skills development, and at the same time communicate the kind of dynamism employers seek.

Table 10.2 Twenty-five skills as verbs

Achieving	Establishing	Influencing	Motivating	Producing
Communicating	Generating	Initiating	Operating	Promoting
Completing	Guiding	Integrating	Originating	Resolving
Coordinating	Implementing	Leading	Overseeing	Responding
Developing	Improving	Managing	Planning	Undertaking

Well worded

Table 10.3 highlights common grammatical mistakes found in written communications. Obviously, the way something is worded is just as significant as how it is spelt. The aim is to produce written communications that are grammatically correct and a pleasure to read. Mistakes here always interrupt the flow of how something is worded and remember, the final pair of eyes to read the written pieces constituting your job application can hold the key to your future.

Table 10.3 Ten common mistakes when writing

I wonder what **its** origin is?	**It's** a beautiful day, i.e. it is a beautiful day
Her professional **practice** is most impressive	He has to **practise** the violin for hours
'**There** you see, you can do it'	**Their** way has always been to welcome visitors
'**You're** so right about that'	'It's now **your** turn'
An elephant, not **a** giraffe	**A** sparrow hawk and **an** eagle
When standing alone **I** should be a capital	Where **it** comes with another letter **it** can be small
It's a shame when you just out a word	**miss** out a word
Remember **color** in the United States	is **colour** in the United Kingdom

It is extremely easy to write extremely long sentences using too many words where it would make more sense to use less words and divide what you want to say into a couple of sentences	Conversely, sometimes, it's overdone. Sentences are short. This stops flow. Remind you of anything? A text message?
The other thing to watch out for is paragraph length	These too can be too long or too short.

In summary, the tables above are a reminder that even an experienced writer will commonly make mistakes:

- Common spelling mistakes relate to writer oversights and spelling 'blind spots', i.e. those words one has an ongoing tendency to mis-spell.
- Writing can always be improved for flow and interest as well as accuracy and grammatical correctness. The list of skills as verbs provides the job applicant with words that not only convey a certain dynamism but reinforce that the applicant is multi-skilled. Try incorporating these into applications.
- Table 10.3 listing ten common mistakes which emerge even from experience of writing. Yes, these sorts of mistakes will be reduced with practice, but it is surprising how even an experienced writer will commonly 'overlook' some of these things, especially when in a hurry.

EMPLOYABILITY FOCUS – A CASE FOR A PD FILE/PORTFOLIO

You will have heard of the saying that applying for a job is a full time job in itself. There is much truth to this statement. For most people the job application process involves multiple applications over a sustained period of time. Because job applications cannot be 'rushed off' but should be the product of careful and detailed thought it is important to use the time available for job applications efficiently.

One way of doing this is to collate a permanent store of the detailed information that is repeated with every application, including educational and job related dates. Of course, all this can be held electronically in an e-portfolio format. At the same time many people find it helpful to have hard copies to hand of certain documents that can also be referred to when completing the next application.

This principle applies not only to what we might term as administrative particulars like dates and grades pertaining to educational and employment histories, but also paragraphs and forms of words that have been crafted for former applications, which work rather well. The applicant does not want to have to, so to speak, reinvent the wheel for every new job application.

So this concludes the case for having a PD portfolio and e-portfolio. It is important to add that it is extremely helpful to approach each application with a positive outlook – particularly in relation to what one can personally offer to a given job opening. Having a PD file permits the applicant to remind themselves and 'rehearse' all they have to meet the job specification.

THE CV

Students who are applying for jobs need to be aware that considerable developed resources and assistance is freely and readily available from university careers services and university libraries. Our intention here is to point students in the direction of what is waiting for them to utilize. This applies very much to the production of template CVs that are tailored appropriately for every job application.

Careers services invariably offer CV workshops and clinics that enable the student to connect with the expertise and experience of careers staff. In addition to this, careers services usually offer free booklets of how to produce both professional and appropriate CVs, and through secured appointments staff will often walk students through such resources. It is tempting to think that one can proceed here alone. This is a mistaken notion.

The CV word search in Table 10.4 contains two sets of possible responses to an employer reviewing an applicant's CV. Ask yourself (and perhaps others checking your CV) whether the former positive impressions and responses are triggered, or the latter less favourable ones emerge.

Table 10.4 Contrasting responses to CVs

Favourable		Unfavourable	
professional	crisp	yeah yeah yeah	sloppy
clear	wow	boring	cocky
impressive	'yes'	dull	colourless
intelligent	personality	'next'	'no'
character	sound	overstatement	understated
creative	interesting	full on	intense
attractive	colourful	stuffy	clashing
matching	flow	odd	difficult
coordinated	attention to detail	limp	weak
harmonious	easy	uninviting	unwanted
inviting	wanted	over the top	vacant
fit	more	doubt	risky
rich	humanity	overwhelming	less
integrity	stands out	poor	forgettable
focused	strong	unfocused	serious
culture	individuality	tame	superior
smile	relate	unaware	no way
edge	aware	mad	loopy
refreshing	authentic	eccentric	comedian

Favourable		Unfavourable	
cool	presented	rebel	childish
want	honesty	anger	resentful
responsible	mature	problem	insecure
good head	finished	prove	unprofessional
complete	whole	inauthentic	lazy
dependable	reliable	don't want	broken
added value	extras	baggage	basic
team player	range	unsettling	oddball
span	credentials	loner	contradictory
credible	enthusiastic	conflicted	passionless
upbeat			

It would be helpful to underline here a number of general principles that apply to the production of an effective CV, particularly in the context of submitting one as part of the job application process.

- It should always be targeted – tailored for each job application and possibility.
- Its content should inform – with the reader being able to quickly identify credentials and relevant experiences.
- It should be persuasive – remembering that a CV essentially promotes the person it presents.
- It should have a dynamism – reflecting achievements and active skills.
- It should be succinct and to the point.

THE COVERING LETTER

Similarly, there are a number of general principles that apply to the production of a covering letter, which should be seen as a supporting item and not as a cursory formality. The covering letter should:

- where possible, be addressed to a named individual
- be a positive communication from start to finish
- include key details like address and the job title
- like the CV, be succinct and to the point
- cover why one is interested by the job
- underline key points about what one can offer.

Again, career service resources and library books available in all university and public libraries present useful templates and alternative formats.

A key point to remember is that whether one is a student or already in full time employment, one is always building on former experiences of completing written applications, whether for previous jobs or in the case of students and graduates, applications to universities. Mark Stewart's book, *Peterson's Perfect Personal Statements* (2004), in this context is a reminder of all the learning gained through a successful university application. The message here is that success can be repeated. Stewart's ten do's and don'ts for writing personal statement are instructive in principle to the written aspects of a job application.

Do:

1 strive for depth, developing a couple of themes, ideas and experiences
2 look to present what sets you apart from others
3 highlight what makes you 'tick'
4 be yourself – not the 'ideal' applicant
5 seek to express some creativity
6 include what attracts you to the opportunity
7 be affirmative about yourself
8 evaluate rather than merely recount experiences
9 seek others' help in proofreading
10 utilize an appropriate typeface.

Don't:

1 simply repeat information found elsewhere in your application
2 complain about previous experiences
3 come across as a fanatic or extreme in your personal views
4 state money as being central to your motivation
5 use your minority status to 'appeal' for special favour
6 flatter the organization
7 miss opportunities by slipping into hackneyed introductions and conclusions
8 be gimmicky
9 submit additional materials if not requested
10 get the name of the contact, department or organization wrong.

THE INTERVIEW

The first principle of a good interview is quelling nerves. For most candidates, nervousness and anxiety surround this critical element of the application process. Such fears are perfectly normal and the interviewers both know and understand this. On the other hand, nerves need to be counteracted to ensure as good a performance as is possible. There are a number of simple things you can do to put yourself at ease.

- *Shortlisted!* – it is good to remind yourself of the achievement of being shortlisted. For Lees this suggests that the selectors believe you have the credentials and strengths to do the job (Lees, 2013). In terms of gaining confidence such successes need to be celebrated.
- *Location* – prepare for the interview by doing homework on where the interview will be taking place. Work out, in detail, how to get there, using public transport and so forth, and how much time to allow for the journey to arrive in good time for the scheduled interview. If you don't do this, it simply adds to the anxiety on the day.
- *Dress* – diffuse anxiety also by wearing the appropriate clothes. Get at least one and preferably two second opinions as to the suitability of our choice of clothes for a particular organization. In an increasingly image-conscious world even your choice of colours is important. The right choice and colour of footwear is an example. It is good to stand out from the rest, but not inappropriately. And remember to match a characterful choice of clothes with one's personality. Image without this will only take you so far.
- *Preparation* – if you haven't prepared as much or as well as you could have done this will 'nag' at most candidates and again increase a sense of anxiety. Which is yet another good reason to be thoroughly prepared for the interview.

In-tray exercises and tests

Interviews are often preceded by exercises and tests of various kinds. You are usually told in the letter of invitation to attend an interview that there will be these additional assessments. So called in-tray exercises vary in nature, but allow the interviewing organization to assess certain abilities and aptitudes without having to cover these in the interview questions. They often incorporate a measure of pressure, often some time pressure, but this is usually not unreasonable. Don't panic when confronted by such an exercise. It is important to 'gather yourself' and focus around producing something you are satisfied with in the given time constraint.

Pre-interview tests also come in a number of shapes and sizes. This could be a:

- *Psychometric test* – here don't try to 'second guess' or 'rumble' what the employing organization is looking for. Just answer the questions truthfully and with integrity. Remember, there are no right and wrong answers in a psychometric test.
- *Personality test* – the same applies with a personality test, so it is futile to set out to impress a potential employer with a supposed personality or psychometric profile. It could be that the organization wants a specific sort of personality to fit into an existing team.

- *Ability test* – these can be to do with mental agility or testing how somebody reacts to pressure. What ability test you would sit would depend upon the job on offer.

Interview formats

There are three main variations of interview formats:

1 *One-to-one interviews* are more common in small organizations and businesses. This format certainly does tone down the formality of the occasion and can even move towards it feeling more like a conversation than an interview. Here it is relevant to quote John Lees' (2013) point, than so called 'partial interviews' happen all the time, with business contacts taking opportunities to explore possibilities with potential employees.
2 *Sequential interviews* simply means where there is one interview after another. This can retain the one-to-one format. It simply reflects a preference for this way of operating the process, favoured by certain organizations.
3 *Panel interviews* are increasingly favoured, particularly in the context of scrutinized and regulated HRM processes. They inevitably have a more formal feel than one-to-ones and tend to be viewed as more frightening or challenging by job applicants. In a panel there is usually one person who acts as chair. They lead the interview process, but will introduce other members of the panel. It is customary for each person present on the panel to ask questions in turn. Answers, in a regulated interview, are marked and the candidate with the highest interview mark emerges.

ETHICS BOX – PRESENTING THE TRUE SELF

How would you view a politician whose pitch seemed essentially to be saying, 'I can be anything you want me to be – I just want the opportunity'. 'Hmm', you think, 'what do you really stand for?' This relates to the principle of integrity that we have particularly set out to explore in this book. Our human reaction to this kind of posturing would probably be two-fold. Firstly, we might consider the politician as disingenuous (or a 'fake'), which is not a quality that would draw us. Secondly, we might also think that the person sounds a little desperate. Ironically, the politician in question in their dynamic with us would have given too much power away. It doesn't speak of their dignity nor, related to that, their integrity, which is closest to a form of completeness or wholeness amounting to being 'the real deal', as it is termed.

So there is learning for us here in how we present ourselves to others and particularly to those we would naturally seek to impress. We have utilized the heading presenting the true self because this captures two genuine notions. The first is the notion of it being a 'presentation'. A job application is an integrated and multi-faceted presentation of oneself. Here we are 'framing' ourselves or 'storying' ourselves in a way that our audience can comprehend and in a way that is fit for purpose, i.e. a job application. Not all aspects of who we are can be relevant to the job application so we are presenting a 'bounded' self. Secondly, we are seeking at the same time to present a true self. It is easy here to veer, depending on our personality, to either understating or overstating our true selves. The former don't 'turn up' to use our phrase employed in this chapter. The latter run the great risk of their pitch sounding insincere or hollow.

So set out to both present and be your true self. If you have selected a job opportunity that matches who you are, then it's a question of faithfully presenting all you have to offer – understatement and overstatement doesn't do this.

First impressions

We could coin it the Clinton principle. The former President of the United States was taught by his mother to give everybody his best attention when he met them for the first time. To apply this to all people, irrespective of their economic and social standing, is of course also a democratic principle. John Lees underlines the importance of the first 30 seconds of an interview in his words below. All it may be helpful to add here is to think first:

sit completely still, look straight ahead and await the first question. (Lees, 2013)

Remember an authentic interview is still a performance, so from the beginning of an interview it is important that you project a demeanour of confidence and 'togetherness', while remaining calm under pressure. Lees adds that this will quickly influence the interviewers to look upon a candidate as 'capable of growing into the job' rather than 'probably lacking the experience' (Lees, 2013).

You will have heard it said not to fold your arms. In terms of body language this indicates a certain defensiveness and is a give-away that the candidate is not relaxed. Table 10.5 lists some classic do's and don'ts of interview body language.

Table 10.5 Do's and don'ts of interview body language

Do	Don't
• smile and look content	• smile incessantly
• sit comfortably	• shuffle and move around
• look at the interviewer(s)	• look around the room

(Continued)

Table 10.5 (Continued)

Do	Don't
• adopt a positive posture	• appeal to the interviewer(s) through nerves
• speak clearly and crisply	• mumble or speak out 'umm'
• make it obvious you've finished your answer	• use long and laboured answers
• give the interviewers equal eye time	• grimace in the face of a difficult question
• be respectful and honouring	• overdo movement and use of the hands
• use accessible words	• use bad language
• remain calm and relaxed throughout	• be defensive or get annoyed

Using a kitchen-based analogy, avoid the twin traps of undercooking and over-cooking. In other words, depending on your personality there is a tendency for most people not to emerge at an interview. Others on the other hand, can overdo it in the following ways:

- over-disclosing
- over-communicating
- over-selling
- over-powering
- over-reacting, by being defensive and so forth

DEVELOPMENT POINTER – *STRICTLY COME DANCING*: BODY LANGUAGE AND INTERVIEW PRACTICE

An interview is a miniature of where you are up to in terms of what your body language suggests to those you are meeting. In the same way as some people are 'naturals' when it comes to dancing, socially some people seem to know just how to handle meeting others. But everybody can improve their performance with some practice. Below are some pointers for how to do better at your next interview, focusing around body language training.

First impressions – smile, but not in a false or crazy or fixed way. The heat is on but try not to 'shut down' in any way. If you do you are unlikely to be able to raise your game. Be positive and determined to present who you are and what you have to offer.

Eye contact – don't stare! Wide eyes indicate unease. Wandering eyes are also off-putting. Your eyes should ideally match your positivity. Confidence and respect and attentiveness are seen in the eyes.

Posture – an interview panel is not a firing squad. Loosen up, but not to the extent of slouching. You can be too cool as well as uncool. Legs apart can look unseemly. At the same time you don't want to look like a golf ball sat ready on a tee. Posture should indicate 'I'm ready' and confident to have this conversation.

Dress – it would be too late at the interview to realize that you got this aspect of body language wrong. You don't want to be thinking to yourself 'I don't feel comfortable (now)'. There is a way of dressing which leads the interviewer naturally to your face. You shouldn't be wearing shoes that, positively or negatively, the interviewer can't take their eyes off.

Proximity – respecting another's zone isn't a significant issue in this kind of social meeting. Still, the handshake should not be served cold or limp. On the other hand a grip can be too tight and too long. Think of the hand-shake as being symbolic of one's friendliness and the need to be neither distant nor overfamiliar.

Others – no powerful aftershave or perfume. Check laces and zips. Breath should be fresh. Watch out for the speed you're speaking. Ignore distractions (like their shoes) and avoid nervous laughter and snorting.

Preparation, preparation, preparation

Many interviews are won and lost in relation to the key dimension of preparation. Preparation isn't everything when it comes to an interview, because there is also the performance at the actual interview, but performance is often determined by preparation. We have structured below a number of elements where it is vital to spend time preparing for an interview. Think of these things as giving you a chance to be, as John Lees puts it so well, 'the best version of yourself you can muster on the day' (Lees, 2013).

The story wars

A big part of presenting well at an interview centres on what we've termed the story wars – that is, the interviewee's strategy for how they will story themselves at an interview. The word story here is not intended to be associated with telling fiction, but rather how the interviewee will craft and structure their story through the interview process.

Here we have re-labelled John Lees' two story elements as the micro and macro stories, to outline the two levels at which an interviewee must prepare to story themselves:

The *micro stories* – what are the small stories that the interviewee should be looking to share at the interview? Each of these stories should be 'short enough to be remembered, but long enough to be worth hearing' (Lees, 2013).

The *macro story* – this is what Lees refers to as the 'big picture' (Lees, 2013). This is what the small stories add up to and the interviewee should be able to summarize into three or four bullet points what they must try to convey about themselves.

Homework

Preparing for interview questions is not unlike anticipating exam questions. Studying the job description and person specification and combining this with some research on the organization will enable the interviewee to work out the sort of questions that are likely to be asked. Lees takes this further by positing that 'somewhere in the interviewer's mind will be that half dozen things that really matter' (Lees, 2013). Our suggestion here is that interviewees go into an interview having given time and thought to both the likely questions and the employing organization's priorities as indicated through careful analysis and even network research.

Questions to ask

Usually at the end of an interview, the interviewee is asked whether they have any questions. The correct response here is not to politely decline the opportunity provided. Neither is it a good idea to possibly convey through the questions asked that the interviewee is not convinced by the job. The suggestion here is that the interviewee prepares two or three genuine questions arising from their careful research, that will not sound negative, suspicious or 'hollow' (suggesting they're not genuine questions). Furthermore, this is not the time to discuss the money.

THE ASSESSMENT CENTRE

An assessment centre is a selection process often utilized by blue-chip organizations to assess a number of prospective employees together over a more extended period than the traditional interview process permits.

This section adopts a fly-by approach to what for many adults is an unknown experience. Considering that some interviews include presentations we might have examined the latter sooner, however, an assessment centre is extremely likely to include a presentation of some nature and therefore the supporting information on presentations immediately follows the overview of assessment centres.

Preliminaries

At the outset it is important to highlight that if many applicants feel reticent about interviews then assessment centres and their programmes, often including presentations, fill most applicants with fear. How can these understandable anxieties be tackled?

Firstly, it is perhaps helpful to get to the root of one's concern – to try as it were to deconstruct why one is anxious about the prospect of an assessment centre. The unknown, especially when the stakes are high, classically jangle people's nerves, and some mystique typically surrounds what the assessment centre will consist of. This is combined with uncertainty as to how one will fair in this assessment environment including meeting other candidates, which for many raises feelings associated with vulnerability.

Secondly, it is important to keep in mind the following. I'anson (2012) reminds us that it is a level playing field for all candidates. In other words, one person's uncertainty is not that different from the next person's – everybody is in the same boat together. Continuing with this metaphor remember that over the time of the assessment centre, typically a full day but sometimes extended, there are going to be some surprises along the course of the programme. Everybody is facing these challenges.

Thirdly, it is good to remember that although an assessment centre is essentially competitive – this adding to the pressure of the day or couple of days – as can be observed in television programmes like *The Apprentice*, working well with others and making the most of the collective nature of the assessment centre experience are intrinsic to one's performance over the time of assessment. If you can get past understandable reticence to enjoying being in the boat together with other people then this could amount to a win-win.

Fourthly, the programme includes multiple elements which add up to a penetrative and comprehensive assessment. It is good to keep in mind here that this structure is designed to act as a matching process or, as I'anson (2012) puts it, 'about fitting round pegs in round holes'. The implication is that the assessment centre is simply about selecting the right person for a particular job. The right candidate does not emerge through perspiration and pleasing behaviours. In view of this it is essential that candidates 'let go' of style-cramping fears and all manner of thought processes that lead only to their 'shutting down', not emerging.

Content

The right hand column of Table 10.6 lists the sort of content that you may expect at an assessment centre. The key thing to remember here is that every component and even every aspect of the assessment centre experience matters. Maun's (2012) comment that the assessors are seeking a continuous picture of each candidate gets to the nub of why employers opt for this form of process. This means everything is open to interpretation, even an informal chat over coffee with one of the assessors.

In view of this it is important not to 'hide', even if this is your perfectly understandable initial instinct when under pressure. Below are listed some of the moments when candidates classically hide:

- when meeting the assessors
- when meeting the other candidates
- at meal times and coffee
- in down-time
- in group work.

The left hand column of Table 10.6 is a reminder of the list of key competencies that the assessors typically look for candidates to demonstrate at the assessment centre. It is useful to think about how these relate to the programme items. For example, on the matter of time management this is very simply expressed in being on time for all the programmed activities. Again, if asked to give a five minute presentation, don't go over the time stipulated.

Table 10.6 Relating the demonstration of key competencies to typical assessment centre activities

Looking out for key competencies	Typical content of assessment centres
Adaptability	Introductions
Ability to establish rapport	Presentations – focusing on communication skills
Communication skills	Psychometric tests – be true to who you are
Thinking skills	Ability tests
Time management – ability to work and perform under pressure	Interviews – asked a series of critical incident questions
Assertiveness – not about being bullish	Group work – forced leadership (Maun, 2012: 254)
Energy – enthusiasm	'In-tray' exercises
The assessment of soft skills	Informal interaction over meals (if residential the social dimension enlarges)

Group work

Group work typically involves four to six candidates. The activities involving group work are usually divided into preparation time and delivery of a stated objective. An assessor will often sit in on the preparation to observe and assess interactions. Here again, it's important to underline that assessors are always on the look-out for good teamworking skills. This encompasses how a given candidate relates to others and importantly also how others respond to them.

We have listed below a number of tried and tested tips for group work:

- Don't try too hard – put your best foot forward but try to be your normal self.
- Set out to work with, not to alienate, others – don't allow a competitive spirit to leak into becoming or appearing brash and defensive.
- Sit centrally, not on the 'edge' – remembering the point above about not hiding.

- Volunteer for key roles – choose roles that will suit you and will cause you to shine. This can itself be a fairly competitive process. Try not to appear either too eager or reticent to take up different roles.
- Avoid horns and halo – as Maun (2012) puts it – the stereotyping of others into unrealistic extremes.
- Display a democratic attitude to others – teamwork is also demonstrated by bringing others in, encouraging others without being patronizing.

Philip Burnard, in his book *Learning Human Skills* (2002), presents an insightful list of typical group processes as follows:

- Pairing – where two group members are talking to each other, not the group.
- Projection – where group members don't take responsibility but blame others.
- Scapegoating – where hostilities and frustrations are directed at one person.
- Shutting down – where a group member withdraws from participation in the group.
- Rescuing – where one member of the group takes it upon themselves to defend another group member.
- Flight – this takes a number of forms including avoidance, intellectualizing, changing the subject and flippancy.

One can easily see from Burnard's list the group behaviours to avoid.

Assessors are usually seeking what might be described as a well-rounded individual with the following characteristics:

- a bit of an all rounder
- a person who initiates
- someone who listens carefully
- not necessarily one of the louder types
- a team player
- confident
- inclusive of others.

Presentations

In one sense every presentation completed at university and in job application experiences serves the next one. Improvements come with practice but also through processes that provide feedback and encourage reflection on presentations. It is particularly valuable if you ever get the opportunity, sometimes made available at university, to see a filmed recording of your presentation. 'Disproportional' fear is often attached to this component of the selection process. This often simply reflects lack of presentation experiences, combined with the heightened sense of importance in performing well in this significant part of the application process.

Rebecca Corfield (2010) suggests there are ten reasons why employers incorporate a presentation as part of the selection process, all of which are instructive to reflect on:

1 to test the candidate's knowledge of particular aspects of the job description
2 to cover an area they might have alternatively assessed in the interview
3 to reveal more about the candidate's views and personality
4 to see if the candidate can handle and stick to the brief
5 to assess the candidate's communication skills
6 to demonstrate the preparation and professionalism of the candidate
7 to see how the candidate performs under pressure
8 sometimes, to see how the candidate deals with a presentation on the day
9 to ascertain how persuasive and interesting the candidate can be
10 to assess how the candidate interacts with the audience and handles questions.

Below we have summarized the signs of a good speaker. These are things to aim for and, in due course, seek as far as possible to perfect through multiple presentation experiences.

Authority – was command evident in the candidate?

So what – was there something for the listeners to take away or apply?

Clarity – was the presentation crisp and well-structured?

Relaxed – did the candidate look at ease?

Enthusiasm – did the candidate display energy and passion?

Performer – how did the presentation go as a performance?

Knowledge – did the candidate know what they were talking about?

Human – did the candidate turn up as a human being?

Edge – did the candidate demonstrate some 'bite' or conviction?

CASE STUDY – PRINCIPLES FROM ANY PRESENTATION

Start with any presentation you have done at university. How did you feel? There's probably some indicator there of how you'll feel at an interview. You probably experienced a range and mixture of feelings: some anxiety that it would come together, or go to plan; perhaps a tad exposed and vulnerable in front of your peers. At the same time, you may have been excited about the opportunity to share your work and perhaps something of yourself. As you'll recall, some things go well, other things not so well. That is an indicator of your profile as a communicator, but you can improve everything with a positive attitude combined with practice.

Reflection on assessment experience

Whatever the outcome of the highly competitive process of applying for a job it is important – because it involves such a significant investment of time, energy and, for most people, emotions – to reflect on what went before. This is equally as important if you get the job as it is if you didn't get it. In a fluid job market the next application is never that far away.

Where possible, build on every experience by gaining feedback. Sometimes you have to pursue employers for this, but if short-listed it is usually given if requested. It is easy to convince yourself in the context of not getting a job that the last thing the employer wants to hear is 'Why not?' Even a nugget of information can be of value in the context of your next application.

APPLIED PERSONAL DEVELOPMENT

We started the chapter by saying that job applications are not complicated but nevertheless call for exacting and high standards of communication. You will have noticed as we went on to deconstruct the job application process, from the application pro-forma to assessment centres, how a number of key words popped up again and again. The following half-dozen have special significance:

- integrated
- group
- matching
- practice
- presentation
- story.

Integration highlights the importance of it all coming together, of the distinctive elements not simply being repetitions of what went before. Application processes invariably involve groups – often a panel of interviewers and sometimes exercises involving working with other candidates. This simply reflects the significance of groups in the workplace. Selectors are assessing whether applicants match the person specification and performance they are looking for. Practice enables applicants to grow in confidence and stature. These factors permit matching to show. All presentations have the quality of being a show. This doesn't suggest they should be disingenuous to be professional. The strong candidate, often the chosen one, is the person who is able to tell the story of how they match what the selectors are seeking. This consists in relaying smaller stories evidencing desired skills and characteristics.

REFERENCES

Burnard, P. (2002) *Learning Human Skills: An Experiential and Reflective Guide for Nurses and Health Care Professionals*. Oxford: Butterworth-Heinemann.

Corfield, R. (2010) *Knockout Job Interview: How to Present with Confidence, Beat the Competition and Impress Your Way into a Top Job*. London: Kogan Page.

I'anson, J. (2012) *You're Hired! Total Job Search 2013*. Richmond: Trotman Publishing.

Lees, J. (2013) *Just the Job: Smart and Fast Strategies to Get the Perfect Job*. Harlow: Pearson Education.

Maun, R. (2012) *Job Hunting 3.0: Secrets and Skills to Sell Yourself Effectively in the Modern Age*. London: Marshall Cavendish Business.

Stewart, M. A. (2004) *Peterson's Perfect Personal Statements*. Lawrenceville, NJ: Thomson Peterson's.

FURTHER READING

Eggert, M. (1992) *The Perfect CV: All You Need to Get It Right First Time*. London: Century Business.

Howie, G. (1968) *Aristotle on Education*. London: Collier Macmillan.

Rogers, H. (2010) *Guide to Writing a CV and Conducting a Successful Interview the Easyway*. Brighton: Easyway Guides.

Yate, M. J. (2008) *Great Answers to Tough Interview Questions*. London: Kogan Page.

11 VOLUNTEERING AND INTERNSHIPS

● ● ● ● ● ● ● ● ● ● ● ● ● ●

A NOTE FROM THE AUTHOR

If you are wanting to volunteer or do an internship, don't let anything stop you from doing so. There is probably no such thing as a 'wasted' placement, such is the power of the placement to show you something about yourself, or organizations or the wider world. Such an opportunity will help you to figure out what you want, what you want for your future and what realities hold sway in the workplace.

If you are not inclined to volunteering and internships I would like to persuade you to think again. In a competitive job market such experiences add to what you can offer an employer. The more you look into the possibilities of a useful placement the greater the chance of you securing one which you will look back on as constituting a good use of your time.

Below I have listed some of the immediate benefits of volunteering and internships. It is likely that any placement experience will yield a number of these things:

Work experience – employers are always on the lookout for people with work experience and interesting life experience. Added to this it will increase your confidence as you encounter 'other' in some way and come through the placement with the experience behind you.

New skills – in the placement it is likely you will be introduced to something new to you. Many aspects of it might transpire to be the unknown or the unfamiliar. This may constitute an opportunity to learn new skills and ways of operating.

Organizational/business insight – every organization is in some way unique and at the same time has certain things in common with every other organization, for example, in the way that both you and your placement organization are managed. This will provide you with insights into the world of business and organizations in general.

(Continued)

(Continued)

Network contact – a placement could result in a job or a referee who is happy to support future job applications. You will meet new people and these contacts may be significant or useful in some way.

Personal awareness – you will learn a lot of things about yourself. It may underline things that you are good at and show you other areas that need more development and work. It will cast some light on your future, showing you perhaps what you are not suited to as much as what you are.

Other insights – it is impossible to list all the things that may emerge from the placement, but the more open you are to learning from the experience the more insights that will emerge.

Learning outcomes

When you have completed this chapter you will be able to:

- clarify your objectives for undertaking a volunteering placement
- define what is a cooperant and state its implication for student volunteering
- explain what is a social entrepreneur and a voluntourist
- outline Sweitzer and King's (2014) four stages of an internship
- state the six characteristics of high impact learning
- understand how reflective practice fits with volunteering and an internship.

VOLUNTEERING

It may be tempting to think that all volunteering options are worthy of one's time and commitment. Unfortunately, this is not the case and there is a world of difference between a well-organized and strategically thought through placement and one which is neither of these. Seek a placement with a reputable organization and make enquiries about the organization and management of the placement programme.

Broadly speaking there are two types of formal volunteering options on offer. The first of these would identify themselves as belonging to a development branch of volunteering referred to as volunteering for development (or V4D). The second type operate with a different ethos from the first type and might be termed as 'gapping' organizations. As the name suggests these are commercially oriented operators aimed at gap year students.

Volunteering England define volunteering as 'any activity that involves spending time, unpaid, doing something that aims to benefit the environment or someone (individuals or groups) other than, or in addition to, close relatives' (Volunteering England). This definition encompasses informal as well as formal volunteering activity such as community participation.

Practicalities

When arranging a volunteering placement an important practicality is appreciating that the relationship is tripartite and involves the volunteer, the sending organization and the host organization. One can see from just listing the three parties involved (and sometimes there's a fourth with the university) that there is much scope for a mismatch of expectations or coordination issues. This again highlights the importance of working with reputable organizations using channels and projects that have been sufficiently tested.

ASET's good practice for placement guides (www.asetonline.org) are a useful resource and remind the student and all the parties involved in the volunteering relationship what a placement should look like and the sorts of things that particularly the student is wanting to achieve from a placement. One's health and safety is obviously paramount and again this highlights the need for care when selecting a placement.

CASE STUDY – THE THIRD SECTOR

Holdsworth and Quinn (2010) highlight the growing significance of the third (or non-profit) sector, which they also observe is a sector that has undergone considerable professionalization in recent years. This means that it not only offers increasingly credible volunteering placements, but also employment opportunities.

A good resource on all matters relating to the third sector is *Understanding the Social Economy and the Third Sector* by Bridge et al. (2009). Labelling and defining the third sector is a task in itself and the book describes how the third sector encompasses an extremely wide range of organizations having an economic impact but not belonging to either the public or private sectors of the economy. The US use of the term is essentially not at variance with its European use. The book quotes Gunn (2004) as suggesting that it 'consists of private organizations that act in the economic arena but that exist to provide specific goods and services to their member or constituents'. Gunn adds that they are not about enriching their owners and some are about doing social good.

(Continued)

(Continued)

Bridge et al. (2009) provide an indicative list of third sector activities, a selection of which is provided below to illustrate the sector's breadth: chambers of commerce, charities, cooperatives, credit unions, enterprise agencies, independent schools, mutuals, political parties, social housing schemes, sports clubs, foundations, golf clubs, housing associations, trades unions, youth clubs.

Their book also contains a useful chapter on the term social capital, which has great significance particularly in the third sector. The famous political scientist Robert Putman (2007) defined social capital as 'the networks, norms and trust that enable participants to act together to effectively pursue shared objectives'. In view of the fact that many policy makers consider social capital as being a prerequisite for economic growth and regeneration this explains why governments will provide various forms of support for social capital at individual, community and national levels. A good example at each of these levels respectively is: greater support for families and parenting, promoting institutions that foster community, and service learning in schools.

The authors rightly present the concept of social capital as only one of a number of different and necessary types of capital needed, supporting the view that social capital is no substitute for 'the provision of hard economic resources such as jobs, cash, skills and opportunity' (Bridge et al., 2009). The DFID (UK Department for International Development) model (DFID, 1999) illustrates this:

- Social capital – encompassing networks and connectedness, membership of more formalized groups and relationships of trust, reciprocity and exchanges.
- Human capital – the skills, knowledge, ability to labour and good health enabling people to pursue a livelihood.
- Natural capital – the wide variation of natural resources required for living and production.
- Physical capital – the basic infrastructure and producer goods needed to support livelihoods.
- Financial capital – the money resources needed for people to achieve their livelihood objectives.

Objectives

Below are listed some of the possible objectives for the student undertaking a volunteering placement employing terms that are used professionally. When researching the sending and host organizations the student should, depending on what they are wanting, look out for these things in their internet and company literature searches and when speaking to the above organizations and placement officers/careers departments involved. A good source of information is also speaking to current/past placement students.

- Capacity building – an opportunity to develop and exercise specific skills and competencies. Which skills and competencies does the placement information highlight?
- Personal development – this is something over and above skills and competency acquisition and development. It is bound up with the enlargement of the person, of gaining more confidence and the development of characteristics. What does the sending/host organization state about these more transformative possibilities?

KEY CONCEPT – COOPERANTS

Volunteers are often surprised to discover that far from the host group or organization being the beneficiary of one's time and commitment, the benefit of volunteering is more often mutual and that often the volunteer is the net beneficiary of the placement.

Recognizing this, the Canadian agency CUSO International speaks of 'cooperants' rather than volunteers. This is a term which indicates that the relationship is more two-way than one might have anticipated. It also counters that often subtle notion underlying the colonial north–south dynamic of 'cultural and economic superiority' (Rockliffe, 2005).

- Business development – every placement is an opportunity to learn about business, its excellences and where and how it falls short of excellence. Also to learn about and from its operators (including leaders and managers).
- Cross-cultural skills/learning – in a global age this dimension of a volunteering placement should be much sought after. Not only do you learn about specific cultures and their ways but the skills of experiencing and handling such differences can be transferred in your working and personal life.
- Global perspective – especially where the volunteering placement is overseas but not necessarily so, the global perspective it provides is worthy of being an objective in itself.
- Contribution to sustainable development – that is, in the host countries. A good question to ask critically is does the volunteering and the volunteering

placement, being a part of a volunteering project, add value, or not? And what tangibly is that value?

- Public relations between countries – it is easy to overlook this objective but the politics and public relations of representing one's country is somewhere present in a volunteering placement. The student is not only 'remembered' for their individuality, but also for what they (often unknowingly) represent. Some placements make much of this dimension in enhancing international relations and global understanding.

ETHICS BOX – VOLUNTOURISM

Voluntourism is the term used to refer to volunteer tourism which involves volunteers from developed countries travelling on tourist visas to the less developed world to work as volunteers. As the term suggests, the pursuit in some way combines volunteering with holidaying and sometimes travelling. Volunteer activity typically involves the restoration of certain environments or alleviating, in some way, the poverty or need of a particular community or group.

A well-written working paper by Daldeniz and Hampton (2010) draws out the distinction between VOLUNtourists and volunTOURISTS, reflecting a different balance of volunteer motivation and also examines the typical impacts (both positive and negative) of the two types of voluntourism.

Researching first the motivations, it is clear that in both types of voluntourism volunteer motives are inevitably mixed, with a dominance of factors that are inevitably self-interested. In the case of VOLUNtourists there is often a component of seeking to do something useful.

Moving on to impacts, with both types of voluntourism the researchers found cultural tensions between volunteers and hosts emerging from 'typical tourist behaviour' including excessive alcohol consumption, partying and sexual activity. The tensions heightened when, as the researchers highlight, local friends joined the social activity and imitated volunteer behaviour (Daldeniz and Hampton, 2010). Positive local impacts were more evident in VOLUNtourists than volunTOURISTS.

This raises a number of ethical considerations:

- Is it OK for western volunteers to relax in western ways when volunteering in the global south?
- Is voluntourism where there is little moral engagement or rationale achieving anything for global south host communities and groups?
- Is it right to effectively buy an experience to enhance one's CV?

If the placement forms part of your university assessment you may be required to produce a self-reflexive biography or reflective blog. Alternative names include reflective diary and reflective learning log. Don't be intimidated by the titles – the key is reading and understanding the assessment instructions.

In all cases the biography is a way to demonstrate or evidence that the student has achieved certain learning outcomes, which will vary somewhat from university course to course.

This said, there are a number of principles of assessing such pieces of work and these are outlined below for consideration.

Firstly, remember that it is the quality of your learning and not the quality of the placement that is being assessed. This means that even if a placement is a disappointment or contrary to high expectations, much can be taken from it as a learning experience.

Secondly, learning can usually be achieved (and is sometimes assessed) in three areas:

1 There is self-learning. This can be focused on skills acquisition and development, but it can also extend beyond skills. Professionalism, for example, combines skills with characteristics and personal ethics.
2 There is learning from 'other'. This can be what we learn from other people and it is often useful to reflect critically (that is both positively and negatively) on another person's practice. 'Other' also encompasses what you learn from going into an organization. Again, critical reflection on such experiences may form part of the assessment.
3 There is what we might term 'meta-learning' (relating to the concept of meta-awareness). Evident in an experience of this nature is learning bound up with matters which overarch the former two areas of learning. This type of learning might involve reflections on matters political or economic or cultural or ideological, all played out in some way in the placement experience. For example, the student might be struck by how globalization is reflected in the project their volunteering is allied to. Be sure to check what your assessors are particularly seeking.

Thirdly, if your assessment includes this kind of biography or log, the best way to go about completing one is by regularly making notes and writing reflections daily. If not, key thoughts and details will be lost and the task of collating (later) observations and learning will become arduous.

Fourthly, there are different levels of reflection as illustrated by Bain et al.'s (1999) labels, listed below, to which are added summarizing explanatory notes. The aim is to achieve the highest level of reflection:

(Continued)

(Continued)

- Level 1 Reporting the matter – the assessor might term such reflection as 'descriptive', and minimal learning on the part of the student is evident.
- Level 2 Responding to the matter – there is a reaction in the reflection, and some felt response is apparent, but overall little learning is evident.
- Level 3 Relating to the matter – at this level the student is beginning to properly relate to their experiences, connecting them to their knowledge and past experiences. Some understanding is evident in their learning.
- Level 4 Reasoning about the matter – there is an explanatory, even analytical quality about the reflection and the student is moving towards deep understanding in their learning.
- Level 5 Reconstructing (restructuring) the matter – the reflection is high level and original thinking. Learning has gone so far as to be internalized.

Fifthly, a good word to keep in front of yourself at all times when on a placement is engagement, because the assessor always looks out for this. In other words, to what degree has the student engaged with all they have experienced on their placement. Where the student is asked to reflect on ethics or any ethical issue the assessor is looking for the student's moral engagement, that is their consideration of what is right and wrong for all the parties or people involved.

KEY CONCEPT – A SOCIAL ENTREPRENEUR

An entrepreneur, according to Bolton and Thompson (2003), is a person who 'habitually creates and innovates to build something of recognised value around perceived opportunities'. A social entrepreneur is someone who applies this skill or talent to solving social problems. Their business, argues Martin Clark (2009), becomes part of the solution. If we measure the conventional entrepreneur's success primarily by profitability, Clark adds, the social entrepreneur is working towards two bottom lines: profitability and social output.

There are over 55,000 social enterprises in the UK alone comprising a mix of cooperative businesses, housing associations, development trusts, community enterprises and social firms (Clark, 2009). The raison d'être of such organizations is effecting social benefit – of targeting a segment of people who are neglected, marginalized or suffering and applying the organization's expertise, creativity and action to turning around the fortunes of the target group and helping to address their issues in society at large (Osberg and Martin, 2007).

Clark identifies seven types of social entrepreneur:

1 The social business entrepreneur – someone who finds a market-based solution and a sustainable (profit making) business model with the aim of achieving a social good.
2 The citizen business entrepreneur – where social entrepreneurs work through creating new institutions and adapting existing ones rather than through social businesses. Social change is achieved through a range of activities from community projects to campaigns.
3 The public sector business entrepreneur – known as 'civic entrepreneurs', they are social entrepreneurs found in public institutions. They look for entrepreneurial solutions to issues under the public sector's umbrella of responsibilities.
4 The corporate social intrapreneur – as the name suggests, a social entrepreneur who effects change from inside a corporate environment. Clark suggests that they often start out as employees who try to get issues of social concern higher up the company's agenda.
5 The environmental social entrepreneur – where the social entrepreneur is dedicated to promoting adoption of environmentally sustainable behaviour in their organization and beyond it.
6 The new philanthropist social entrepreneur – a new breed of rich men and women who set up foundations and organizations to put their fortunes to good use.
7 The latent social entrepreneur – this is the person who is on the way to becoming a social entrepreneur. Social entrepreneurship is a different way of looking at business, social need and the world. Something causes the latent social entrepreneur to dedicate their skills, energies, flair and business acumen to a social end.

INTERNSHIPS

An excellent single resource on internships is Sweitzer and King's book, *The Successful Internship* (2014). That's what every student committing themselves to an internship would naturally want. But as the following focus on internships will show, drawing on the thinking of the above authors, this is not something that will happen even easily, never mind automatically. An internship is a partnership of sorts and to work well requires some key things from both parties as well as good communication between employer and student.

What is an internship?

Sweitzer and King describe an internship as 'an intensive field experience, and often a critical component of many academic programmes' (2014, emphasis added). The highlighting of its intensity, both its timetabling in a student's life and its accompanying challenges, prepares us for the content and spirit of their guidance. They do add that the intensity increases in the case of a graded as distinct from a voluntary (or optional) internship, but if the student is looking to an internship as a potential employer the stakes will always be heightened, whether it's a grade or a job, or the natural desire to impress.

The following employability box goes a long way to outlining why we might want to incorporate or secure an internship and why we might view it as a self-development and employability asset.

EMPLOYABILITY FOCUS – THE ASSET OF AN INTERNSHIP

It is helpful to keep before us a number of factors that make doing an internship a great idea from an employability perspective.

Applying knowledge – making an immediate bridge between things that one has learned in the lecture theatre or classroom and exploring how this knowledge translates in the field.

Theory and practice – a dimension of applying knowledge is understanding how theory is relevant or is used in the workplace. The gap between teaching content and practice is an important matter to get to grips with.

Problem solving – a large part of an internship is problem solving, but in a different context from university.

Adaptation to change – the related concept of adaptation applies here. It can sometimes feel like 'sink or swim' but as the section will show there are ways of avoiding unnecessary exposure.

Transformative potential – an internship has great potential to transform the outlook of a student and can deliver greater self-confidence and an optimistic outlook for future possibilities.

Learning professionalism – this is an on-going matter for all employees and involves years of learning. Sweitzer and King (2014) make the point that each profession has an implicit contract, involving ethical and moral obligations, to wider society – which is also a journey of becoming a more responsible and contributing member of society.

Managing the emotions – the strains of the workplace and its distinctly adult context arrive in many forms. These must be managed.

A very human experience

We have coined the phrase 'a very human experience' to frame our understanding of the nature of an internship. Using academic vocabulary we might alternatively speak of the affective dimension of an internship – how it makes the student feel. Rationality is paramount but looking at matters cerebrally alone is not how adults function. The head and the heart are both assets and both require a lifetime of training to function healthily. So we can hardly expect an early experience of work that really matters to the student to be without challenge or learning. If we expect some turbulence then we might feel somewhat comforted if and when it arrives.

We will shortly outline Sweitzer and King's 'map' of the four stages, from a student perspective, that make up an internship experience, but before coming to this navigational tool it is worth underlining some of the likely affective content of an internship:

- Anxiousness and concerns are normal, a bit like when starting at university, regardless of how conscious (or reminded) one is of such feelings.
- It helps to appreciate that others before oneself have felt this way and that any other intern will be experiencing the same underlying feelings.
- Dissonance is a word we can use to describe the gap between what one expects and what happens – and the distance between what a theory suggested and what one is experiencing. Examining such dissonance is an important part of the reflective dimension of one's internship and may well form part of the assessment process.
- In addition to the internship, meanwhile life goes on – what might be referred to as life's context. The student may still be in a relationship, have a social and family life, have other responsibilities and concerns. The internship somehow enters the 'existing mix' of a student's life and although there may well be some restructuring to allow for it, one can see immediately that this involves some adjustment and challenge.
- Finally, stuff happens with an internship, things that are not unusual in the workplace, and these things will impact one emotionally as well as requiring the concentration of one's mind and thought processes. Below are some of the things that could impact the intern: issues the whole organization is facing; pressures in a specific department or unit; supervisory (management) and support issues; issues requiring greater clarity from an intern's perspective; office politics; health and safety concerns.

Internship stages

Central to Sweitzer and King's guidance on internships is their stage model consisting of four stages and the on-going possibility of 'disillusionment' as they term it. Interns journey through the stages at different rates of speed and emotional intensity. Each stage has its own obstacles to overcome and its own opportunities for new learning.

If the intern is aware of these different stages it may assist her or him in navigating the internship both as a whole and multifaceted experience.

Table 11.1 Sweitzer and King's internship stage model

Stage 1 **Anticipation**	Sweitzer and King refer to this as the 'what if' stage where the lead up to the internship creates a sense of anticipation but also uncertainty and a degree of anxiety, all perfectly normal and to be expected. The intern naturally wants to get off to a good start which will be as much the responsibility of the employer as the intern. Critical tasks include clarifying the role and purpose and developing key relationships.
Stage 2 **Exploration**	This stage is about finding one's feet and moving towards competence, which doesn't come immediately and automatically. Intrinsic to settling into a role is understanding how it works. In this stage the gap between one's expectations and the reality of the internship becomes evident. Sweitzer and King state it is important here to remember as challenges emerge, 'the only way around is through'.
Stage 3 **Competence**	There is a measure of relief when the intern comes through to this stage. The feel good factor increases and the sense of being a part of the organization rather than an outsider arrives. Something to watch out in the competence stage, however, is the pressure that comes with trying to meet commitments both in and outside the internship.
Stage 4 **Culmination**	As its name suggests this stage comes towards the end of the internship and can engender a variety of feelings. The intern might be relieved about completing the internship, proud about what they've achieved and even a little sad about moving on. Sweitzer and King suggest that if the internship has involved some disappointments or concerns it is very challenging for the intern to express these proportionally and assertively, i.e. in the right way. Perhaps it is good to watch out for blame and to forget the internship is a very human experience.
Throughout **Disillusionment**	At one time in Sweitzer and King's stage model disillusionment was a stage in itself. Later, however, they thought it was more accurate to speak of the possibility of the intern slipping into disillusionment at any stage of the process. The term is bound up with the intern disengaging with the internship. A conscientious or hopeful attitude on the part of the intern can switch to their feeling demotivated and disillusioned. To counter this possibility *high impact* practices (as outlined below) are what the employer and the intern should aim for.

Ensuring a high impact internship

High impact learning is only achieved for students according to George Kuh (2008) through practices exhibiting all the following characteristics:

- daily decisions
- quality feedback
- application opportunities
- reflection opportunities
- relationship building
- overcoming obstacles and remaining engaged.

We have elected to employ Kuh's framework to organize specific guidance in these areas provided by Sweitzer and King and bring these together under the heading of ensuring a high-impact internship, which we would hope is the aim of both the intern and the employer. A primary application of Kuh's individual characteristics is contained in each of the following headings.

Daily decisions – stemming from purposeful tasks

For tasks to be purposeful the intern needs to be sure of her or his roles and responsibilities. This characteristic being securely in place or not, will reflect how well organized or thought through the employer has been in providing the internship opportunity. Also of significance here is the intern's working relationship with the site supervisor.

The intern should be able to say, 'I know and understand what is expected of me':

- my role, purpose and goals have been clarified
- I am clear about these
- they are spelt out in documentation
- my on-site supervisor has walked me through them
- I can access my site supervisor daily for any clarification I need.

Quality feedback – must include this

Effective feedback, according to Sweitzer and King, is:

- specific, not vague
- concrete, not general
- descriptive, rather than interpretive
- best delivered using an 'I' not 'you' statement
- checked for understanding from the receiver.

Adding to this, we've all been in situations where we get some feedback and we're disappointed with it, perhaps because we've tried hard or felt that we'd put our heart and soul into a venture or a project. When we find ourselves in this situation it is good to remember that it is best to fully process the feedback once we've got over the initial jolt of disappointment. This is where the adage to 'sleep' on things involving emotions is helpful. Once we have distanced ourselves from the moment, we can begin to unravel the feedback that we've been given. A good place to start is with the question, 'what is true about the feedback I've received?' A coaching perspective here is also helpful. See the experienced or senior person who has given you the feedback as fulfilling the role of a sports coach. We need to be capable of critically appraising and taking on board assessments of our performance. As professionals none of us are, so to speak, 'the complete item'. There is learning in the capability to listen and hear.

Application opportunities – to be able to apply learning

An exciting dimension of an internship is being able to relate our university learning to the working context. Sweitzer and King speak of this as integrating theory and practice which essentially explores how 'classroom' theory and knowledge translate into useful and guiding input for the internship and the workplace in general. They add that this process can be troubling because 'you may find that your theories don't seem to work'.

This is all part and parcel of transforming, they argue, theoretical reasoning to practical reasoning. Theory and knowledge inform practice. Another way of looking at this is to reflect on the fact that all practitioners are drawing upon an often undefined body of theory and knowledge. We test our learning in the theatre of life including the workplace. Professionally we discover what works and is helpful. No piece of learning is wasted if it in some way contributes to or informs our practice. But our learning continues in the workplace and we learn much from others who are drawing upon quite different learning and life experiences with their embedded theories, both of the formal and informal variety.

Reflection opportunities – and achieving reflective dialogue

We introduced reflective practice as an aspect of professionalism in Chapter 7. Here we examine how reflection forms part of the mix of characteristics that makes for a high impact internship.

There are some students who struggle to grasp why reflection occupies a central place in the internship experience and typically forms part of the assessment when an internship is graded. Interns may be required to keep a journal or to submit reflective pieces of writing as part of an internship portfolio.

The capturing of our reflections forms a record of the very human experience which is an internship. Reflections describe the journey that an intern commits themselves to when they join an organization for a determined period of time. It maps:

- an intern's personal journey, learning and growth, specifying learning and growth points and including challenges faced and further self-discoveries
- an intern's observations of 'other', what they have learned through observing others and what they are learning about organizations
- an intern's reflections on ethical issues that arise, issues of professionalism and issues of responsibility.

Good reflective observations and writing demonstrate gains in awareness. Gains in personal awareness, gains in the awareness of 'other' and gains in what is sometimes termed 'meta-awareness', which coincides with greater ethical consciousness.

Sweitzer and King helpfully focus much attention on seeing oneself more clearly. On:

- recognizing our reaction patterns
- discerning our dysfunction (everyone has them)
- spotting our family default behaviour and attitudes
- seeing ourselves in conflict mode
- appreciating our own cultural profiles.

Reviewing this section it becomes obvious that there is no shortage of subject matter to write about in a reflective journal – the possibilities are endless and do of course reflect the individuality of the intern. We have added the following ten questions the intern can ask themselves at the end of every working day:

1 What stands out about what happened today and how did it make you feel?
2 What did you notice or hear today that is noteworthy?
3 What change, however slight, do you detect in yourself?
4 What are your thoughts about the internship site?
5 How does anything you are experiencing relate to your career or future?
6 What are you learning about yourself – your skills, strengths and character?
7 How are you fairing in your role and what are its implications?
8 What added value are you providing by virtue of your work and presence?
9 What are your thoughts about others who work with you and what's the learning here?
10 If you could start the day again, what would you do differently and why?

DEVELOPMENT POINTER – EBENEZER'S SOCIAL CAPITAL AND PUSHING PAST HUMBUG

We all know the story of Ebenezer Scrooge from Charles Dickens' 1843 novel *A Christmas Carol*. There are broadly two types of wealth – financial wealth and a wealth in friendships.

It would be unusual (except on Facebook) to count our friends and unlike a bank balance friendship is a difficult thing to measure. Still, there is a way of looking after our relationships and even prospering in this area of our life.

There is also much truth in the saying, 'It's not what you know, but who you know'. Out of this a number of development pointers arise:

- Who knows you? Are you visible or miserable?
- Ebenezer came to his senses and turned over a new leaf in his appreciation of people. It isn't complicated, valuing others and relationships.
- Don't overlook the significance of others as you move onto your next placement or career experience.

Relationship building – with key co-workers

Sweitzer and King regard the relational aspect of an internship as a make or break factor. Co-workers occupy the world of the internship and to experience positive and healthily functioning professional relationships is a world apart from encountering unsatisfactory and dysfunctional ones. However, it is good to remember that the intern has responsibility here also. Certain interactions and attitudes will either feed a working relationship or undermine it. We return again to that notion of an internship being a very human experience.

A critical dimension of the internship is engaging with others and remaining engaged with them – seeing others as sources of learning and support – and not falling into the temptation to disengage from co-workers. An important aspect of learning the most from others and having the most positive relationship possible with them is not judging people harshly because they don't share the same characteristics or background. This takes us to the sixth high-impact internship characteristic, which involves a determined and 'open' attitude to achieve engagement with others through overcoming reticence associated with encountering 'other'.

The following questions focus the internship's all-important people issues:

1 Am I trying here?
2 Am I trying too hard?
3 Am I trying to be liked?
4 How can I work at being appreciated and respected instead?
5 Is this person a possible mentor or role model?
6 What am I learning from person X?
7 What is the staff turnover in this department/organization?
8 How good is the atmosphere irrespective of me?
9 What sort of person seems to be most appreciated by the organization?
10 Who is a source of support and makes a difference to me here?

Overcoming obstacles and remaining engaged

We have included below an embodiment box listing some of the competencies needed to navigate the relational and community dimensions of an internship, which are at the same time competencies that are particularly valuable in the contemporary context of late modernity (introduced in Chapter 2). This is why we have described them as new competencies. The internship, like university, provides another opportunity to exercise and develop these competencies.

EMBODIMENT BOX – NEW COMPETENCIES AND THE INTERNSHIP

Below are listed a number of competencies that not only might be appreciated by co-workers in the internship but also the organization itself. In addition these so called new competencies are ones to develop for the future.

- flexibility
- receptivity
- sensitivity

- open-mindedness
- cultural competence
- understanding the human context of the work
- in search of 'new knowledge.'

Sweitzer and King describe cultural competence as 'being able to work and communicate effectively with people from a range of cultural backgrounds' (Sweitzer and King, 2014). This encompasses a disposition of being open to diversity. Adding to this, the notion of being flexible, receptive, sensitive and open-minded suggests someone characteristically more sponge-like than unyielding, someone able to move and respond, rather than being 'fixed' and inanimate.

Sweitzer and King speak of 'discovering new knowledge by exploring authentic questions and problems' emerging from new learning experiences. All these things point to the intern's ability to adapt successfully to the new environment they find themselves in.

An important part of adaptation is respecting the differences to be found in a new community. Here's a list of things to look for in others and in a community:

- core values
- sources of pride
- clothing (what does it suggest/communicate)
- conversation topics
- attitude to education
- communication style
- political loyalty
- attitude to work.

Spotting core values   People value a great range of things and what they value often reflects their individuality as well, typically things like a person's background, upbringing, education and employment experience.

A list of some of Sweitzer and King's headings (which we've rearranged in alphabetical order) will help us get started here. We've added a question for each heading to clarify its usefulness in identifying values.

- Autonomy – does the person have an individualistic or collectivist outlook?
- Family – what is the person's attitude to family?
- Hygiene – how does the way the person presents themselves reflect their values?
- Religion – how does the person's religion correspond to their values?
- Sexuality – what are their views about sexuality (perhaps expressed in their conversation)?
- Work – what significance does the person attach to work?

In addition to identifying, i.e. listing, people's values, we can go further in understanding them by looking out for the things that people direct a disproportional amount of their resources (both time resources and other resources) to supporting or sustaining the things they value. For example, if the person is a Vegan their value will be animal welfare or animal rights. They express this value structurally in their lives by choosing this way of living above convenience.

A person's value might be reflected in the charities and organizations the person would be most inclined to support or volunteer for. You could ask someone if they were running a sponsored marathon, which charity's shirt would they be most proud to wear?

A successful internship

Every internship has the potential to be a rich learning experience. In addition to this, obviously it is much better if the outcome is a win-win for both the intern and the organization. This concentrated overview of internships has highlighted that this is the intern's responsibility as well as the organization providing the internship opportunity. Because the internship is what we described as a very human experience, it has also highlighted that it will involve challenges of all kinds and that the intern will pass through stages on the journey to completing the internship.

Kuh's (2008) six high impact learning characteristics applied to internships showed something of this mutuality of responsibility held by both the organization and the intern in making the internship a successful experience. We've added here a couple of coaching items: one on sources of empowerment for the intern and a final item on what the so called engaged intern looks like. Both lists constitute what employers want and are looking for in prospective employees.

EMBODIMENT BOX – SOURCES OF EMPOWERMENT

By sources of empowerment we mean qualities, outlooks or ways of operating that will ensure the vitality and endurance needed to remain engaged in the internship and overcome its expected challenges (Sweitzer and King, 2014). Interestingly, these are some of the very things most prized by employers and would if cultivated and developed add to the intern's employability.

Sweitzer and King offer a good set of questions to ask about all the sources of empowerment, as follows:

- How do you currently embody this source of empowerment?
- What could you do practically to enhance the demonstration of this source of empowerment in the internship?

- (In due course) has anyone commented positively on you demonstrating this quality or outlook?

You could even ask for help or progress tracking (therefore providing accountability) from your supervisor with any of the following six sources of empowerment:

1 Positivity – storying yourself and your daily actions and encounters positively. Adopting a positive and optimistic outlook rather than a negative and self-defeating/dispiriting one.
2 Perspective – looking at something again perhaps in a different light or from a different angle, particularly being aware of the human tendency to overlook certain positives, referred to sometimes as 'blind spots'.
3 Discussion – being open and able to explore an issue through discussion, especially where the subject matter involves one's own performance, is a sought after ability. Here a person demonstrates they can apply criticality, even to themselves.
4 Humour – never underestimate the gift and validity of humour. It does of course need to be appropriate, but a peppering of humour in one's practice enhances professional relationships and often diffuses difficulty and awkwardness.
5 Language – the causal loop between the language used, its engendering of feelings and, finally, behaviour. Change the language and the outcome of behaviour changes in the end too.
6 Mindfulness – giving a matter more of ourselves, more of our concentration of energies, even greater consciousness.

One can easily see how an intern adopting the six sources of empowerment would amount to a different proposition altogether from the same intern operating on a deficit of these qualities, outlooks or ways of operating. We bring this section to a close with a list of 20 things we might associate with an engaged, in contrast to a disengaged, intern (see Table 11.2). It is self-evident that an employer would value the practices listed.

Table 11.2 The engaged intern – 20 signs 'it's working'

The engaged intern:
1   Takes **responsibility** for their performance and learning
2   Demonstrates **respect** for others' expertise and experience
3   Wants to **be successful** in what they do
4   Welcomes **new tasks** and responsibilities

(Continued)

Table 11.2   (Continued)

5	Demonstrates inquiry – **asks questions** and seeks clarification
6	Demonstrates **self-motivation** and self-discipline
7	Approaches tasks **professionally** and with humility when called for
8	Demonstrates **assertiveness** rather than aggression or passive aggression
9	**Self-motivated** to complete tasks and projects
10	Demonstrates **intellectual curiosity**
11	Demonstrates the ability to give **an account** of their performance
12	Able to solve problems with a **'can do'** attitude
13	Demonstrates a sense of **personal agency**
14	Able to **self-initiate** tasks and directions when called to
15	Does not 'buckle' or **give up** easily when faced by challenges
16	Demonstrates the ability to **connect** different sources of knowledge
17	Sees themselves as a **lifelong learner**
18	Demonstrates an enthusiasm for upholding the **quality** of their work
19	Able to work **independently** – able to focus without distraction
20	Able to work **collaboratively** – contributes in team

APPLIED PERSONAL DEVELOPMENT

You have heard the expression 'thinking outside the box'. This particularly applies to the opportunities presented by doing a volunteering placement or an internship. In an extremely competitive job market the student is looking out for something that might differentiate them from the next strong candidate or applicant – something that might give them a little more 'edge', not only in the mind of the employer, but also in the mindset of the student applicant herself or himself. The right sort of confidence, a founded confidence, is based upon having faced new and challenging experiences and situations and coming through them – meeting the challenge if you like.

Volunteering and completing an internship are not easy options and you will recall that I coined the term 'a very human experience' in presenting the latter. Of the former I introduced you to the term cooperant, which kind of contains a promise that far from the stereotype of one's volunteering centring around helping others, in the end the net beneficiary is usually the volunteer themselves.

Let's close this chapter by saying a little more about how volunteering and completing an internship constitute thinking, indeed venturing, outside the box. Firstly, it will probably not be the most convenient of options for you to pursue. This relates to the fact that in the end it has to fit in with the rest of your life – your studies, your social life and even the geography of your life. It will likely involve travelling perhaps to another city and even another country.

Another sense in which volunteering or an internship is outside the box, is that it will involve a high component of being taken beyond one's comfort zone. Both these experiences involve venturing into an unknown, meeting a completely different set of people and finding oneself fulfilling responsibilities the likes of which one has not experienced before. You can perhaps see why, when assessing a student's learning from these experiences, their reflective journey is so significant. Here the student herself or himself articulates all the things they are learning about themselves, about fulfilling a role that might be new to them and about how the experience in some way challenges or changes their perspective about social, economic, political and ethical realities, or if you like meta-realities, they are confronted by.

A good manager or leader is conversant with three dimensions of human experience and the importance of:

- self-knowledge
- knowledge of other
- knowledge of controlling and complex overarching systems of economics, politics and thinking.

Perhaps a better word than knowledge might be consciousness. A volunteering placement or internship will certainly expand the student's consciousness.

If you do volunteer or become an intern try to keep this in mind. Don't put the entire focus on your own performance. Instead, place alongside this your own learning.

- What does the experience tell you about yourself?
- What are you learning from others and about organizations?
- What are you learning about business and wider realities?

REFERENCES

Bain, J. D., Ballantyne, R., Packer, J. and Mills, C. (1999) 'Using journal writing to enhance student teacher's reflectivity during field experience placements', *Teachers and Teaching: Theory and Practice*, 5 (1): 51–73.

Bolton, B. and Thompson, J. (2003) *The Entrepreneur in Focus: Achieve Your Potential*. London: Thomson.

Bridge, S., Murtagh, B. and O'Neill, K. (2009) *Understanding the Social Economy and the Third Sector*. Basingstoke: Palgrave Macmillan.

Clark, M. (2009) *The Social Entrepreneur Revolution: Doing Good by Making Money, Making Money by Doing Good*. London: Marshall Cavendish.

CUSO International 'The path of/the cooperating(e) – voluntary'. Available at: http://cusointernational.org/fr/Volontaire/l-experience-du-cooperant-volontaire (accessed 7 August 2013).

Daldeniz, B. and Hampton, M. P. (2010) 'Charity-based voluntourism versus lifestyle voluntourism: evidence from Nicaragua and Malaysia'. Working paper No. 211.

Canterbury: Kent Business School. Available at: http://kar.kent.ac.uk/26302/1/ VOLUNtourists_vs_volunTOURISTS_Daldeniz__Hampton__2__Web.pdf (accessed 10 August 2013).

DFID (1999) *Sustainable Development Guidance Sheets*. London: DFID.

Gunn, C. (2004) *Third Sector Development: Making Up for the Market*. Ithaca, NY: Cornell University.

Holdsworth, C. and Quinn, J. (2010) 'Student volunteering in English higher education', *Studies in Higher Education*, 35 (1): 113–127.

Kuh, G. D. (2008) *High-Impact Educational Practices: What They Are, Who Has Access, and Why They Matter*. Washington DC: Association of American Colleges and Universities.

Osberg, S. and Martin, R. (2007) 'Social entrepreneurship: the case for definition', *Stanford Social Innovation Review*, Spring.

Putman, R. (2007) 'E pluribus unum: diversity and community in the twenty-first century', The 2006 Johan Skytte Prize Lecture, *Scandinavian Political Studies*, 30 (2): 137–174.

Rockliffe, B. (2005) 'International volunteering and evolving paradigm', *Voluntary Action*, 7 (2): 35–44.

Sweitzer, H. F. and King, M. A. (2014) *The Successful Internship: Personal, Professional, and Civic Development in Experiential Learning*. Belmont, CA: Brooks/Cole Cengage Learning.

Volunteering England, 'What is volunteering', Available at: www.volunteering.org. uk/iwanttovolunteer/what-is-volunteering (accessed 6 August 2013).

PART III

THE RESPONSIBLE PRACTITIONER

12 FREUD & SONS: A VOCABULARY FOR UNDERSTANDING PSYCHOSOCIAL DEVELOPMENT

● ● ● ● ● ● ● ● ● ● ● ● ● ●

A NOTE FROM THE AUTHOR

Being what is referred to as an 'Eriksonian' and having spent many years researching Erik Erikson (1902–1994), when I originally planned this book I had intended to devote a chapter to outlining and applying his developmental thinking. There is still space for me to present many of Erikson's key ideas, however, on reflection it seemed more valuable to place his theory alongside those of some of his contemporaries, all of which are included in this chapter, who were significantly influenced by Sigmund Freud (1856–1939).

Freud is often referred to as the 'father of psychoanalysis' and one of the key thinkers of the last century, both moving on and shaping thinking in the west. My rationale for providing an overview of Freud and those who built on his thinking, titled here as 'Freud & Sons', is that Freud and those who followed him provide a *vocabulary* that can be usefully employed in not only self-understanding (and self-development), but also the understanding of 'other', and of western society.

We owe much to Freud in helping us to comprehend the psychological complexity of human beings (Hurding, 1985). Our complexity reflects a number of important realities, as follows:

- that there is more to all of us than is immediately apparent and professionally revealed
- that our potential can be both enhanced or thwarted by our complexity
- that understanding ourselves and 'other' involves getting to grips with this complexity.

Another reason for my including this chapter is that it illustrates the principle of – in the pursuit of criticality – overcoming trigger reactions to people,

(Continued)

(Continued)

subjects and ways of thinking we may not have had an opportunity to consider in detail. Freud is popularly associated with an eschewed over-emphasis on sexuality. Psychoanalysis, on the other hand, is often thought of as only applying to those with mental health issues. Both perspectives are dismissive in spirit and would cause these onlookers to miss important insights provided by both Freud and the field of psychoanalysis, both of which are extremely relevant to all people.

Added to this, many regard matters psychological as unfamiliar or inaccessible. So a secondary purpose in presenting this Freudian and post-Freudian body of theory is to encourage an open, rather than a prejudiced or dismissive, attitude to alternative ways of thinking. This is extremely important as we will increasingly encounter in close proximity people who look at things and life in a different way from us.

Learning outcomes

When you have completed this chapter you will be able to:

- gain a vocabulary to articulate developmental opportunities and challenges
- understand Freudian thinking and theorists that followed him
- grasp what is meant by unconscious ego defences
- identify projection at work in oneself and others
- respect the notion of a subjective viewpoint or experience
- see personal development as an intergenerational process.

PRELIMINARY TERMS

Psychology – the scientific study of the mind and behaviour (Snowden, 2010a).

Psychiatry – Trethowan and Sims (1983) state this 'comprises the recognition, prevention, diagnosis and treatment of illnesses of which the principal manifestations are mental'.

Psychoanalysis – Roy Lee (1948) suggests psychoanalysis will always be associated with Freud, whose pioneering role in the field far outstrips that of any other psychoanalyst who followed after him. It began as a method of treating certain kinds of mental disorders (Lee, 1948) but has developed into a discipline which seeks to help all manner of people, as Josef Breuer put it, 'transform neurotic misery into common unhappiness' (and perhaps something even better) by supporting a process whereby motivation is expressed directly, rather than going off sideways into symptoms (Malcolm, 1982).

Psychosocial – Hetty Zock observes that in his early work Erikson substituted the term 'psychosocial development' for 'ego development' because he wanted to emphasize that ego development always takes place in a social context (Zock, 2004). Erikson referred to his life-cycle model (see below) as an 'integrated psychosocial phenomenon' (Erikson, 1964) and spoke of its stage-specific tasks as 'psychosocial tasks' or 'psychosocial issues' (Zock, 2004).

Hysteria – 'Hysterical symptoms are a return of repressed memories in a different form' (Samuels et al., 1986). Thorley and Stern (1979) highlight the so called 'gain' that those exhibiting hysteria seem to derive from hysterical behaviours, which are sometimes 'bizarre'. Hysteria, they add, is associated with high levels of anxiety, often in response to stress.

Neurosis – What Carl Jung ably described as a state of 'inner contradiction' or not quite being at one with yourself (Sharp, 1998). Sharp suggests it results from adaptation that has failed (Sharp, 1998). Erik Erikson in turn described it as 'inner two-facedness' (Erikson, 1958). Everybody to some extent is subject to neurotic anxieties, however, neurosis needs to be differentiated from *psychosis* which is a more serious and disabling mental disorder requiring medical input.

WAIN'S WORLD THAT WAS

A book which places Freud in his historical context and helps highlight the significance of his thinking in western culture is Martin Wain's (1998) *Freud's Answer: The Social Origins of Our Psychoanalytic Century*. Wain sets the scene by describing the relative continuity of what he terms the *gemeinschaft* world, a world that existed from the beginning of history to 1800 and gave its inhabitants an automatic and stable sense of identity (Wain, 1998).

Wain argues that the old world was effectively 'murdered' by the industrial and French revolutions and an old order, consisting of three institutions – the church, the nobility and the family – was dismantled (Wain, 1998). In the 1880s Europe, he says, entered a social crisis consisting of upheaval strangely combined with excitement. There was the birthing of what he terms a pleasure principle, a 'philosophy of pleasure, born of freedom, self-interest and competition' (Wain, 1998).

The new values that emerged at this time included not only pleasure, but money, advancement and struggle. The neurologist Jean-Martin Charcot (1825–1893) took an early interest in a malady then called hysteria and was one of the first to demonstrate a relationship between psychology and physiology. In 1885 one of his students was Sigmund Freud. Wain summarizes, 'into this atmosphere of hysteria and crisis stepped the Freudians with their message of healing' (Wain, 1998).

FREUD

The Freudian corpus

Roger Hurding (1985) defines Freud's 'primary elements' as being fourfold:

1 *A scientific determinism* – everything that happens, including every human event, act and decision, is pre-determined by what went before.
2 *Emphasis on the unconscious mind* – Freud differentiated between the conscious and unconscious mind, the latter constituting a deeper layer of the mind which may never reach consciousness.
3 *A driven sexuality* – understanding human behaviour as directed towards certain ends by powerful instincts, emphasizing particularly the primacy of sexuality and the presence of libidinal expression in early childhood (Wertlieb, 2004).
4 *A developmental approach to personality* – reflected in Freud's stage theory.

For the student who wants to acquaint themselves with the full thinking of Freud the list of references and further reading provide a number of useful resources. Our concern in this chapter, however, focuses on introducing the vocabulary of Freud and the so called *Freudians*.

The significance of childhood

Freud discovered how the impressions and experiences of early childhood played an unexpectedly significant part, he argued, in human development. He both recognized and conceptualized the centrality of first the mother figure and then the father figure in a child's psyche and added to this the contention, as summarized by Erich Fromm, that 'every child is what the parents have made of it' (Fromm, 1994). This, of course suggests that the way to understand a person is to appreciate the content of their childhood and that every adult is aware of childhood experiences of being loved or neglected, or even both. Freud's theorizing here permitted the possibility of childhood trauma on many levels and the space for young people and adults to uncover such trauma.

A degree of controversy has always surrounded Freud's view that the human being, even a child, legitimately has sexual and relational needs relating to both their physicality and their desire for intimate relationships. The sense of dependence that infants have on their mothers (or caretakers) amounts to something visceral and is centred on attachment. Horan helpfully adds, 'when Freud claims that young children desire their mothers or want to sexually possess them, he is using the term "sexual" in the broadest descriptive sense, to represent the total energy a child possesses' (Horan, 2008).

The unconscious

It is difficult to imagine viewing the world without Freud's ground-breaking theory of the unconscious – the source of all our desires and activity, effectively 'hidden' from our consciousness (Horan, 2008). Rudnytsky (1991) reminds us here that emotions can be repressed and yet continue unconsciously.

Clark comments that Freud believed he had 'discovered the subterranean motives of conduct' (Clark, 1980). The Freudian method centres on managing into consciousness (Fromm, 1994) drives that have been repressed and frustrated, often owing to their being unacceptable to the conscious image individuals have of themselves (Horan, 2008).

In 1923 Freud in his book *The Ego and the Id* proposed a new dynamic model of the mind. He added to the simple division of the mind into conscious and unconscious, three different but overlapping aspects of the way we think, to cast light on 'the apparent battle that goes on between different levels of consciousness' (Snowden, 2010a). We may already have heard of the 'id', 'ego' and 'super ego', but the words Freud originally used can be translated as 'the it', 'the I' and 'the Over-I', which are, as Ruth Snowden puts it, 'perhaps rather more self-explanatory'.

> The id ('the it') – is the primitive unconscious part of the way we think, that we are born with and is concerned with 'inherited, instinctive impulses' (Snowden, 2010a). Much of the id has to be suppressed in order to fit in with society.
>
> The ego ('the I') – is the part of the way we think that is practical and rational and reacts to external reality. It is what the person thinks of the self (or the I) and is protected by a whole system of unconscious ego defences.
>
> The superego ('the Over-I') – is the part of the way we think that oversees and monitors behaviour. One aspect of the superego is what we call the conscience but Snowden argues it incorporates the teachings of the past and social rules (Snowden, 2010a). Freud viewed large parts of both the superego and the ego as normally unconscious.

The ego defences

The ego defences, what Freud labelled as 'defence mechanisms', include a number of unconscious strategies. Jahoda (1977) argues repression is in Freud's thinking the dominating defence but we will outline here other strategies Freud identified, including projection, denial, rationalization and sublimation. Jahoda adds the important point that ego defences are employed not only in illness but also in health in support of the synthesizing function of the ego in dealing with anxiety arising from internal and external challenges that beset the individual (Jahoda, 1977).

Repression

An urging force of the id, ego or superego which produces anxiety may be nullified or restrained by a checking force called repression. There are two kinds of repression: primal repression and repression proper. The former are innately determined barriers which, as Hall (1979) describes them, 'are responsible for keeping a large part of the contents of the id permanently unconscious'. These include strong taboos that are kept out of awareness. Repression proper forces a dangerous or unpleasant memory, idea or perception out of consciousness. Although employed by everyone to some extent as necessary for normal personality development the so called 'repressed' are those who depend on this defence to the exclusion of other ways of adjusting to threats.

Projection

Calvin Hall in his examination of Freud describes projection as a very prevalent defence mechanism. In large part, he argues, projection arises from not taking responsibility for one's behaviour from an early age, but instead attributing one's own feelings and motives to the external world (Hall, 1979).

Samuels et al. (1986) argue that projection may be viewed as either normal or pathological (caused by physical or mental illness) and as a defence against fear. The 'target' for one's baggage of emotions, often beyond one's will or ability to systemize or fully comprehend, is a person or object external to oneself. Negative feelings and sometimes unacceptable parts of one's personality including taboo urges are 'projected' onto another person or a group. The problematic emotions are therefore displaced, and the person projecting encounters some measure of relief.

On the other hand, projection is not just negative. Another person, group or thing can become the 'carrier' of all that is good, true and valuable to an individual as they project onto others more positive and desirable elements. Here with this positive personification, the person or object external to oneself can effectively be given in all probability more 'credit' than they are due, expressed in an idealization of sorts.

ETHICS BOX – DEBUNKING PROJECTION

Carl Jung viewed projection on the part of an individual as 'an ineradicable tendency to get rid of everything he does not know and does not want to know about himself' (Jung, 1958). Seen in this light, one can see how projection might easily lead to injustices of all kinds.

In the field of analytical psychology, emphasis is placed on projection constituting a means by which the unconscious aspect of one's personality is revealed to ego-consciousness, an uncovering that is of value. Carl Jung articulated a five stage process (Samuels et al., 1986) whereby that which is projected can ultimately be recollected and reintegrated by the 'projector' in question.

- In stage 1, the person is convinced that what they see in the other is reality.
- In stage 2, the person gradually becomes aware of a 'gap' between their projection and the other as they 'really' are. The two are no longer synonymous.
- In stage 3, some kind of assessment or judgement is attached to this difference thereby specifying the difference now recognized.
- In stage 4, the person concludes that the projection was illusory or plainly erroneous. Cupitt would probably term this as an abandonment of 'false consciousness' (Cupitt, 1982).
- In stage 5, the person undertakes their own search for the sources and origin of the projection. This may have both personal and collective origin. Janet Malcolm (1982) argues that the purpose of such psychoanalysis is not to comprehend the nature of reality, but to acquaint the person with herself or himself. 'Nothing we say or do or think', Malcolm writes, 'is ever purely rational or irrational, purely real or transferential. It is always a mixture' (Malcolm, 1982).

Malcolm hints at what could be seen as a 'romantic' dimension to this often bewildering mixture of perceptions and associated behaviours where both the 'heroic' and 'tragic' can be clearly seen at work. Rand and Torok (1997) penetratingly speak of psychotherapy as having the potential to restore in people, 'the life of desire that has been crushed under the oppressive weight of decades of self-censorship or internalized parental and societal prohibitions'. Seen in this light, psychoanalysis is also a good 'preparation for understanding other people'.

CASE STUDY – PROJECTION AND FALLING IN LOVE

An obvious example of projection is falling in love (Berry, 2000). That is not to suggest that when this happens the realization that you are projecting is of any use in tempering your enthusiasm. This is a way of easily comprehending what Freud's concept of projection is all about. Depending on your personality, to a large extent it is not just that the other person is worthy of

(Continued)

Transference

Projection is often popularly confused with transference. Freud identified the latter as a process by which analysands (people undergoing psychoanalysis) displaced on to their analysts feelings based on their experiences of earlier figures in their lives. Janet Malcolm rather neatly captures the phenomenon of transference in her interpretation that it's 'how we all invent each other according to early blueprints' (Malcolm, 1982).

Denial

Denial works in a similar way to repression, but is characterized by the refusal to accept the reality of a situation (Snowden, 2010a). It has popularly entered into everyday discourse when we speak of people being 'in denial'. Seen as an ego defence people have an ability to deny matters they do not wish to admit. Snowden adds the closely related defence mechanism of denial in fantasy, where undesirable reality is transformed, often by children, into something individuals can cope with.

Rationalization

Here an individual finds an acceptable excuse to cover up something that is unacceptable to the ego – another so called 'ego defence'. This can encompass lying one's way out of a situation to avoid taking responsibility and feeling guilty.

Sublimation

This is an unconscious process, which Freud largely associated with transferring sexual drive (the libido) into 'non-sexual, socially acceptable or safe activity' (Snowden, 2010a) including, for example, creativity of all kinds. Today, it more often refers to the transformation of the emotions in general.

Freud's libido theory, Wertlieb (2004) argues, is a far reaching but controversial dimension to Freud's thinking. In 1923 Freud described libido as 'the dynamic manifestation of sexuality', however, in time he came to broaden the notion of libido to include sensual as well as sexual aspects to life (Wertlieb, 2004).

CARL JUNG

At one time, Freud regarded Carl Gustav Jung (1875–1961) as his 'theoretical heir' (Robbins, 2000), however, in 1913 Jung broke away from

Freud and founded a system of psychology that become known as *analytical psychology*. Jung differed from Freud on a number of important points and the following headings highlight a few quintessentially, so called *Jungian* terms and concepts.

Collective unconscious

Robbins (2000) argues that Jung thought that he had discovered evidence for a collective unconscious shared by all human beings, characterized by the inclusion of so called *archetypes* (see below). As Ruth Snowden stories it, 'Jung began to wonder whether it was possible that alongside all the information collected from [people's] own everyday lives, people also carried archaic residues', fragments of 'inherited impressions and imagery, stored in myth-like form' (Snowden, 2010b). As highlighted by Burt Hopkins, the unconscious included not only contents that were once conscious, but stored contents incapable of *ever* becoming fully conscious (Hopkins, 2004).

Archetypes

Ruth Berry (2000) states that Jung's discovery included that the human mind seemed to produce 'universally recognizable symbols and imagery' and in due course he called such imagery an archetype. The word archetype is a fusion of two Greek words – 'arche' meaning first and 'type' meaning imprint or pattern. According to Snowden (2010b), Jung viewed archetypes as being like deposits of frequently repeated human experiences. Archetypes help people to comprehend and come to terms with common experiences such as birth and death, change and transformation, growth and development, success and failure. Archetypes, Jung said, are accompanied by an atmosphere of the numinous (Berry, 2000), which can alternatively be described as carrying a 'strong potentially overpowering charge of energy which is difficult to resist' (Samuels et al., 1986). Davis highlights that for Jung, dreams and myths are constellations of archetypal images. This makes myths, like dreams, *happen* to human beings (Davis, 2003).

Anima and animus

Samuels et al. (1986) define anima and animus respectively as 'the inner figure of woman held by a man and the figure of man at work in a woman's psyche'. For Jung, anima/animus were significant archetypes and have been historically represented in many forms including Aphrodite, Athena, Beatrice/Apollo, Alexander the Great, Romeo. Berry highlights that passionate attractions and falling in love occur with anima/animus projection (Berry, 2000).

The persona and the shadow

A couple of well-known Jungian terms are *the persona* and *the shadow*. The persona is like a 'mask' which the person presents to the world, whereas the shadow holds parts of the self which the person does not want to, or feel able to, be freely identified with. The latter may be associated with guilt or shame and as a defence mechanism against this, the person might project fault onto others. At the same time the shadow can contain positive content such as characteristics the person has lost touch with or hopes that have been thwarted. So called 'shadow recovery' involves facing up to the contents of the shadow and re-integrating its reality within the conscious part of the personality.

Individuation

We close this section on Jungian terms with perhaps his most hopeful, for many his most inspiring concept of individuation. Christopher speaks of the process by which the person becomes more of him or herself (Christopher, 2000) whereas Sharp defines individuation as 'the development of the individual personality to its full potential' (Sharp, 1998). Samuels et al. astutely add here the notions of a human becoming whole, both 'indivisible and distinct from other people' (Samuels et al., 1986). As adults, this underlines the significance of psychological, as well as physical maturity.

Strictly speaking it's a term that dates back to Gerard Dorn in the sixteenth century and was also employed by the philosopher Schopenhauer, but Jung was the first to apply the principle to psychology. It would be easy at first glance to associate individuation with a kind of extreme individualism, but as Jung himself said, 'individuation does not shut out from the world, but gathers the world to oneself' (Samuels et al., 1986). In considering the self-realization of great artists against Jung's ultimate of individuation, Samuels et al. speak of how Mozart, van Gogh and Gaugin individuated in so far as they perfected their talents and amalgamated these with their personalities. However, they add that they probably did not achieve individuation in terms of personal completeness and relationships. They conclude that it would make a difference in society if people commit to the 'arduous journey' of individuation of both kinds (Samuels et al., 1986).

EMPLOYABILITY FOCUS – OCCUPATIONAL INDIVIDUATION

Carl Jung's notion of individuation – actually achieving something approximating all that we could (or is it should?) be – is extremely inspirational. Many people would aspire to individuate in all sorts of dimensions of their lives and the prospect of occupational individuation drives many people forward in giving of themselves to their careers, developing themselves through pursuing higher education and studying to gain professional qualifications, not to mention their taking on increased responsibilities in the workplace and switching jobs, towns and careers in the search of finding something better, something that better fits them.

Below are a few pointers around occupational individuation framed as a series of questions.

1 What associations or objects energize or inspire you? These could range from animals to libraries, accounting to clothing. Look around your dwelling or examine your bookshelves for clues.
2 Do you have a sense of vocation for anything or any group of people? In life overall, try to express rather than repress this. You may be able to express this occupationally.
3 As the first paragraph suggested few people end up doing something they are really individuated by without working hard towards this end, involving effort, sacrifice and risk. What would you be prepared to do, give up or risk to achieve an occupational goal?
4 Beware idealization. Do you have a tendency to idealize the things and notions that capture your imagination?

MELANIE KLEIN

Melanie Klein (1882–1960) was born in Vienna into what a biographer, Phyllis Grosskurth, presents as an entangled and neurotic family situation (Grosskurth, 1986). She discovered the writing of Freud in her twenties and saw herself as a follower: 'I'm a Freudian', she once declared, 'but not an Anna Freudian!' (Grosskurth, 1986). She entered psychoanalysis with Sandor Ferenczi in Budapest and with his encouragement began to work in what was then an undeveloped field: psychoanalysis with children (Gomez, 1997).

For anybody who wants to look in more detail at the personal background and theories of Melanie Klein, Lavinia Gomez's chapter on her in the book *An Introduction to Object Relations* (1997), is recommended. Gomez contends that Klein's difficult upbringing and subsequent marriage produced something akin to a 'continuing state of mourning through much of her life' (Gomez, 1997). She adds, however, that Klein was able to use her pain to theorize the complex presence of loss, guilt, loneliness, envy and a sense of persecution, present in human beings, in Klein's thinking, from earliest infancy (Gomez, 1997).

Revealed in play

Central to Klein's contribution to the field of psychoanalysis is one of her most important innovations, Klein's psychoanalytical play technique, where she maintained that even before children could express themselves verbally their emotions could be observed by watching them at play. Gomez highlights how working with Klein, each child's toys were kept in a dedicated (and lockable) drawer in the consulting room (Gomez, 1997). This was the child's space too, with no one apart from the analyst having access to it.

Subjective experience

Another innovative dimension of Klein's approach is expressed in the significance she attached to what we might term subjective experience, amounting to envisaging the person (of any age) as Gomez puts it, 'a subjective agent within the subjective world of relationship, conflict and change'. She adds, 'The outer world is experienced through the medium of the inner world'. Departing from Freud, Klein viewed instinctual impulses not as physiological drives, but as hopes, fears and wishes, all experienced in bodily terms (Gomez, 1997).

Splitting

Bateman and Holmes say that it was following Klein that contemporary psychoanalysts adopted the term 'splitting' to refer to a division of an object into 'good' and 'bad' (Bateman and Holmes, 1995). Along with denial and projection Klein identified splitting as one of a number of ego defences to manage the fundamental anxiety felt by human beings (Gomez, 1997). This conflict that is regarded as intrinsic to the person, is of course quintessentially Freudian (Gomez, 1997).

Good defence?

As highlighted by Bateman and Holmes (1995) Klein's followers have gone on to consider defence mechanisms not just as transient psychological processes, but psychological configurations that coalesce into rigid and inflexible systems, what O'Shaughnessy thinks of as defence organizations (O'Shaughnessy, 1981). Bateman and Holmes add that psychoanalysis recognizes now that defences can be maladaptive, immature, neurotic or even psychotic. At the same time, there are defences that are associated with development and maturity, such as the use of humour, used appropriately (Bateman and Holmes, 1995).

ERIK ERIKSON

Like Carl Jung, essentially Erik Erikson (1902–1994) comes after Freud and was much influenced by him, and particularly through Erikson's close association with Freud's arguably greatest disciple, his daughter Anna Freud (1895–1982).

But also like Carl, Erik was able both to build on learning from Freud and carve his own path as one would expect from yet another significant theorist.

Erik Erikson's thinking is unique in its wide ranging applicability to personal and professional development at the level of the individual, the organization and the wider global context. An overview of a number of Erikson's key terms and concepts below will cast light on the particular life stage, experienced by young adults, which popularly coincides with a first experience of studying and living at university. His principle of adaptation explains how individuals and organizations progress in that familiar 'two steps forward one step back' fashion so associated with the opportunity and challenge of life. Much of Erikson's thinking is devoted to suggesting how people and generations can work together to effect positive change – to progress projects of all kinds, both personal and professional, that would founder without cooperation.

Stages of life

Erik Erikson is perhaps best known for his stage theory of human development. In *Childhood and Society* (Erikson, 1950) he presented eight stages of psychosocial development to complement Freud's stage theory of psychosexual development. An important thing to grasp at the outset when looking at Erikson's stage theory is that it is not an individualistic model, neither does the individual pass from stage to stage in a constant, uninterrupted and linear fashion (Robinson and Dowson, 2012). It is Lawrence Friedman (2000) who helpfully highlights that progression through the life cycle is an inter-generational process, where people in one stage assist those in others.

According to Erikson, each stage centres on a 'crisis' as it is termed, the navigation of which results in a personality outcome. Adaptation to the stage's challenge or crisis results in the creation of specific virtues. Alternatively, maladaptation to the challenge will result in the virtue's negative counterpart. Healthy development associated with adaptation is a responsibility shared by the generations (Robinson and Dowson, 2012) and virtues emerge as Erikson puts it, through the 'interplay of successive and overlapping generations, living together in organised settings' (Erikson, 1964).

This 'living together' consists of more than incidental proximity. Rather, the individual's life stages are 'cogwheeling' (see below), as Erikson described it, with the stages of others. The individual, therefore, moves through the life cycle as they move others – a process Erikson labelled as an 'integrated psychosocial phenomenon' (Erikson, 1964).

Identity crisis

Erikson's infamous term 'identity crisis' is often popularly applied to men in midlife as depicted in movies like *American Beauty*. In actual fact there is not one but, according to Erikson, a number of 'crises' that develop naturally and inevitably throughout the life cycle. Successful navigation of these crises, with the help of others, can result in relative happiness. However they also have potential for discontent and neurosis (Notable Names Database, 2014).

Many young adults reading this can remember something of what Erikson refers to as the adolescent identity crisis. This is often a turbulent time of rapid physical growth and hormonal change combined with the assumption of responsibilities, leading the teenager in the direction of adult responsibilities (Sugarman, 2001). Erikson describes the identity crisis of this stage as centring on what he terms 'identity versus role confusion'. The battle for identity definition, a sense of continuity and sameness, focuses around all manner of questions, as captured by Richard Stevens (1983):

- Who are they?
- What kinds of relationship should they pursue?
- How should they dress, behave, react?
- What new boundaries are they to draw up for themselves?

These are not easy decisions and the potential for confusion resulting from experimentation and navigating the new and unknown is the danger. The resolution to this crisis lies in developing a defined personality and also understanding how this fits together with the social reality they are confronted by (Sugarman, 2001).

The next life stage, labelled as young adulthood by Erikson, commences around 18–20 years and centres on the mutual search for a shared identity (Stevens, 1983). In the life-cycle model this plays out in a tussle between what Erikson terms 'intimacy versus isolation'. Ironically, the hard fought for separate identity, pursued in adolescence, is in some sense put at risk in the pursuit of intimacy and the fusing of one's life with another's (Sugarman, 2001). Intimacy of course encompasses sexual intimacy, but for Erikson it is much more than this (Stevens, 1983). The 'counterpoise' of intimacy is as expressed by Richard Stevens, isolation and fear, of another encroaching on the essence of one's identity. This can lead to what is termed 'distantiation' (Stevens, 1983).

An important point to highlight here is that, like Carl Jung and Sigmund Freud, Erik Erikson was no cold theorist. His theory emerges from personal experience and Erikson as much as anybody experienced travail in being exposed to a plethora of personal challenges that must have played out in Erikson's journey from being a teenager to young adult and beyond. Challenges included:

- not knowing his biological father
- being ethnically both Jewish and a Dane growing up in pre-war (World War II) Germany
- struggling to readily find or define his vocational identity, or as Erikson would put it, the main executive of his identity (Erikson, 1958).

The essence of the young adulthood stage of Erikson's life cycle is captured by Kit Welchman (2000) who identifies from a close study of Erikson's writing three themes young adults contend with:

1 The experience of what Erikson called 'adult duty' – everything bound up with entering the adult order.
2 The 'competitive encounter' so characteristic of this life stage, played out in the securing of relationships and jobs.
3 The significance of matters sexual, and how young adults navigate their way in moving towards something more stable in this sphere.

Forward-outward-upward

Erikson's obituary published by the *New York Times* on 13 May 1994 speaks of him as the 'Psychoanalyst who reshaped views of human growth' (*New York Times*, 2010). Erikson's thinking, focusing on the great potential for people to develop, including as adults, can be examined through the framework of *forward-outward-upward* into which we can slot a number of Erikson's ground-breaking terms and concepts, as shown in Table 12.1.

Table 12.1 Erikson's concepts organized into forward-outward-upward thinking

Forward	Outward	Upward
• Epigenesis	• Generativity	• The ethical orientation
• Leeway	• Cogwheeling	• Pseudo-species mentality
• Virtue		• The great personality

The forward dimension of personal growth is reflected in how an individual has ample opportunity, despite the 'two steps forward one step back' flavour of life for so many, to keep on growing through the life cycle. Erikson's theory views the potential for transformation in adulthood positively.

Epigenetic principle – development, Erikson argued, happens according to an epigenetic principle. This principle suggests that we develop through an unfolding of our personalities across the lifespan, which Erikson divided into eight stages. There is a great optimism about Erikson's theories of development and Erikson effectively championed the wonderful potential for people, using his words, to be 'reborn, renovated, regenerated' (Erikson, 1958), even as adults.

Leeway – this was Erikson's term for the freedom of people to be their true selves and to grant such freedom to others (Hoare, 2002). Leeway for Erikson conveyed a freedom that could be observed in childlikeness and play, associated with notions of originality, creativity and abandon. Related to leeway Erikson spoke also of *actuality* and *mutuality*.

Actuality – this is Erikson's term for the releasing of one's own and another's ability to participate effectively. His term *mutuality* is where people mutually inspire one another to actively engage their selves, strengths and abilities.

Virtue – central to Erikson's forward looking thinking is the idea that out of inevitable struggles across the lifespan, potent or vital strengths (virtues) might emerge. Human development is not an automatic, nor for that matter easy, process but rather for Erikson development emerges from contestation, where the adaptation to challenge, assisted by others, yields important developmental gains including the virtues of love, wisdom and care.

Personal growth expressed outwardly conveys the idea of how we grow in relation to the social world. In Erikson's thinking there is little or no scope for human beings growing and thriving in isolation. His theory pushes against tendencies to view growth in an individualistic sense, which Erikson would think of as closer to an unhealthy self-absorption.

Generativity – 'Generativity … demands that, having decided what we care about, and what and whom we care for, we stake out what and whom we must and can take care of' (Erikson, 1980). Erikson's concept of generativity underlined the instinctual power of human beings to care, extending to whatever they generate, leave behind, create or produce (Erikson, 1964). It is expressed, therefore, not only in the care parents give to their children, but also caring for one's works and ideas and whatever one leaves to the next generation. Carol Hoare highlights that for Erikson the developmental pinnacle for each adult was their being a caring, generative person (Hoare, 2002).

Cogwheeling – Erikson's term cogwheeling conveys something of how he saw health and development being a product of the generations present in society working together and interliving together. An individual's life stages cogwheel with the stages of others, Erikson argued, moving them forward as they move others. Erikson added that this was an integrated psychosocial phenomenon (Erikson, 1964). Friedman (2000) highlights how Erikson viewed this process as one of mutual dependency.

When we speak of personal growth in an upward direction, this conveys a number of ideas present or implicit in Erikson's thinking including:

- striving towards a higher morality
- developing in the face of infinity
- realization of human potential.

The ethical orientation – although Erikson suggested that human conscience remains partially infantile throughout life (Erikson, 1963), through what he termed as the 'ethicality' of everyday experiences (Erikson, 1969) people had the potential to develop from being ideologically minded, to becoming moralistic, to ultimately becoming ethical in their outlook and practice. This was what Erikson referred to as our 'ethical potential' (Erikson, 1970). The latter was encapsulated in Erikson's rephrasing the Christian so called golden rule, but conforming it to his understanding of the significance of intergenerational mutuality as follows: 'it is best to do to another what will strengthen you even as it will strengthen him – that is, what will develop his best potentials even as it develops your own' (Erikson, 1964).

Pseudo-species mentality – operating ethically involved for Erikson breaking away from archaic fear (Erikson, 1959) and fear of radical otherness (Erikson, 1975). Erikson spoke of the oppressive nature of what he termed a 'pseudo-species mentality', how many groups (religions, ideologies, tribes and so forth) 'provide their members with a firm sense of God-given identity – and a sense of immortality' each behaving 'as if they were separate species created at the beginning of time by supernatural intent' (Erikson, 1966). Erikson here proposed a new ethics based upon more inclusive identities (Evans, 1967) and a greater consciousness of what any generation owes to every other one (Roazen, 1976).

The great personality paradigm – through his study of the history transforming great personalities such as Martin Luther, Gandhi, Jefferson and Martin Luther King, Erikson highlighted the multiple linkages between individual and society. These figures were not only influenced by their own eras – they also monumentally struggled to transform their historical situations, simultaneously as they remade themselves. Erikson saw this as 'lifting' their individual struggles to the level of those felt by the many in wider society; and trying to solve for all what they could not solve for themselves alone (Lifton, 1974).

EMBODIMENT BOX – PRESENCE

There cannot be anything more powerful to encounter than presence. Think about that perhaps handful of people who have truly captured your imagination, by simply walking into the room? And when they open their mouths to speak the charisma doesn't dissipate. What can account for this level of magnetism, this power of personality?

In a contemporary world which both honours and pursues celebrity status it must have something to do with the notion of a performance. There must be some dimension of their presentation of themselves which is, so to speak, deliberate and relating to a training of how to present oneself in a particular light, that works for others.

At the same time the word charisma is derived from a Greek notion of gift or freely given. The power of presence sometimes has this quality too. That the person is particularly and peculiarly gifted or akin to a gift to others.

Perhaps a third sense of presence centres around something which is closer to maturity or wholeness or even them embodying love. The shadow side of this is possibly expressed in somebody whose essence, their very bodily presence, is close to something menacing or not to be trifled with.

(Continued)

In the context of meeting people for the first time, presenting ourselves to others and giving ourselves as full human beings to others in social situations, this concept of our having and developing presence is extremely relevant. You've heard the phrase 'he hasn't got it'. What is the 'it' factor here? And is the 'it' factor something you are interested in developing?

APPLIED PERSONAL DEVELOPMENT

It is likely that reading this chapter has stretched you. While terms associated with psychoanalysis are both revealing and useful the concepts that underlie them are sometimes difficult. In learning, that doesn't mean we should not persevere. My hunch here is that one or two terms or concepts will have been particularly useful for you, because they may have gone some way to helping you better understand a situation or a challenge you have faced or someone close to you has faced. If something particularly has emerged I'd encourage you to read around this matter using the list of references and further reading at the end of this chapter. If what it has highlighted personally troubles you in some way, can I underline the resource of the counselling service at your university.

Appreciating our own complexity and the complexity of others is not only central to our own development but it is a matter of lifelong learning. Sometimes this is expressed as understanding 'other' in ourselves as well as discovering 'other' in those we share life and the world with. Freud helped us all forward in this task, if only by raising the question of what is at work in us and others that we are not presently conscious of.

Which of the four psychoanalytical theorists most captured your imagination? Was it Freud with his notion of gaining a better understanding of one's total self, one's undiscovered self and the significance of one's earliest years? Was it Jung whose focus through the collective unconscious highlighted the significance of history with its archetypal characters? Or perhaps it was Melanie Klein, just one of the many women who have contributed to the thinking presented in this chapter and who particularly highlighted the significance of our subjective perceptions. Or finally, perhaps Erikson's life stages helped you to plot where you are in your life journey and where you are placed with respect to becoming a generative and ethical adult. Perhaps he reminds us all in the west not to lose sight of the significance of all the generations working together and the need to embrace inclusive identities.

The following questions enable us to convert this investigation of Freudian and post-Freudian theory and theorists into defining personal development goals.

- Are you aware of potentialities or parts of yourself that you have not explored, perhaps through lack of confidence or lack of opportunity?

- Given the defensive nature of one's ego, is there anything you are highly protective of that might be halting your own personal development?
- Objective reality is important, but the manager is constantly contending with the reality of subjective perspectives and experiences. In the area of the subjective what is it that you need to gain a better appreciation of?
- How can you cogwheel more effectively with others? Perhaps opening yourself up to working with others across the generations? Perhaps learning with those who at one time you may have overlooked?

REFERENCES

Bateman, A. and Holmes, J. (1995) *Introduction to Psychoanalysis: Contemporary Theory and Practice*. Hove: Routledge.

Berry, R. (2000) *Jung: A Beginner's Guide*. Abingdon: Bookpoint.

Christopher, E. (2000) 'Gender issues: anima and animus', in E. Christopher and Solomon, H. McFarland (eds), *Jungian Thought in the Modern World*. London: Free Association Books.

Clark, R. W. (1980) *Freud: The Man and the Cause*. London: Jonathan Cape.

Cupitt, D. (1982) *The World to Come*. London: SCM Press.

Davis, C. T. (2003) 'Archetypes as defined by Carl Jung'. Available at: www.cathedralcatholic.org/faculty-resources/65/1/Jung's%20Archetypes.pdf (accessed 6 February 2014).

Erikson, E. H. (1980) 'Work and love in adulthood', in N. Smelser and E. H. Erikson (eds), *Themes of Work and Love in Adulthood*. London: Grant Mcintyre.

Erikson, E. H. (1975) *Life History and Historical Moment*. New York: W. W. Norton & Co.

Erikson, E. H. (1970) 'Reflections on the dissent of contemporary youth', *Daedalus*, XCIX (Winter).

Erikson, E. H. (1969) *Gandhi's Truth: On the Origins of Militant Nonviolence*. New York: W. W. Norton & Co

Erikson, E. H. (1966) 'The ontogeny of ritualization', in R. Loewenstein, L. Newman, M. Schur and A. Solnit (eds), *Psychoanalysis – A General Psychology: Essays in Honour of Heinz Hartmann*. New York: International Universities Press.

Erikson, E.H.(1964) *Insight and Responsibility: Lectures on the Ethical Implications of Psychoanalytical Insight*. New York: W.W. Norton & Co.

Erikson, E. H. (1963) *Childhood and Society*. Harmondsworth: Penguin.

Erikson, E. H. (1959) *Identity and the Life Cycle: Selected Papers, with a Historical Introduction by David Rapaport*. New York: International Universities Press.

Erikson, E. H. (1958) *Young Man Luther*. London: Faber and Faber.

Erikson, E. H. (1950) *Childhood and Society*. Harmondsworth: Penguin.

Evans, R. I. (1967) *Dialogue with Erik Erikson*. New York: Harper.

Freud, S. (1923) *The Ego and the Id*. London: The Hogarth Press

Friedman, L. J. (2000) *Identity's Architect: A Biography of Erik Erikson*. Cambridge, MA: Harvard University Press.

Fromm, E. (1994) *The Art of Listening*. London: Constable & Company.

Gomez, L. (1997) *An Introduction to Object Relations*. London: Free Association Books.

Grosskurth, P. (1986) *Melanie Klein: Her World and Her Work*. London: Hodder and Stoughton.

Hall, C. S. (1979) *A Primer of Freudian Psychology*. New York: New American Library.

Hoare, C. H. (2002) *Erikson on Development in Adulthood: New Insights from the Unpublished Papers*. Oxford: Oxford University Press.

Hopkins, B. (2004) 'Analytical psychology', in W. E. Craighead and C. B. Nemeroff (eds), *The Concise Corsins Encyclopedia of Psychology and Behavioural Science*. Hoboken, NJ: John Wiley & Sons.

Horan, C. (2008) 'Psychoanalysis and philosophy', *Philosophy Now*, July/August: 10–13.

Hurding, R. F. (1985) *Roots and Shoots: A Guide to Counselling and Psychotherapy*. London: Hodder and Stoughton.

Jahoda, M. (1977) *Freud and the Dilemmas of Psychology*. New York: Hogarth Press.

Jung, C. G. (1958) *The Undiscovered Self*, trans. R. F. C. Hull. London: Routledge & Kegan Paul.

Lee, R. S. (1948) *Freud and Christianity*. Harmondsworth: Penguin.

Lifton, R. J. (1974) 'On psychohistory', in R. J. Lifton and E. Olsen (eds), *Explorations in Psychohistory: The Wellfleet Papers*. New York: Simon & Schuster.

Malcolm, J. (1982) *Psychoanalysis: The Impossible Profession*. London: Pan Books.

New York Times (2010) 'Obituary: Erik Erikson, 91, psychoanalyst who reshaped views of human growth dies'. Available at: www.nytimes.com/learning/general/onthisday/bday/0615.html (accessed 8 February 2014).

Notable Names Database (2014) Erik Erikson. Soylent Communications. Available at: www.nndb.com/people/151/000097857/ (accessed 8 February 2014).

O'Shaughnessy, E. (1981) 'A clinical study of a defensive organisation', *International Journal of Psychoanalysis*, 62: 359–369.

Rand, N. and Torok, M. (1997) *Questions for Freud: The Secret History of Psychoanalysis*. Harvard: President and Fellows of Harvard College.

Roazen, P. (1976) *Erik H. Erikson: The Power and Limits of a Vision*. New York: The Free Press.

Robbins, B. D. (2000) 'Carl Gustav Jung'. Available at: http://mythosandlogos.com/Jung.html (accessed 10 January 2014).

Robinson, S. and Dowson, P. (2012) *Business Ethics in Practice*. London: Chartered Institute of Personnel and Development.

Rudnytsky, P. L. (1991) *The Riddle of Freud: Jewish Influences on his Theory of Female Sexuality*. London: Estelle Roith.

Samuels, A., Shorter, B. and Plaut, F. (1986) *A Critical Dictionary of Jungian Analysis*. London: Routledge & Kegan Paul.

Sharp, D. (1998) *Jungian Psychology Unplugged*. Toronto: Inner City Books.

Snowden, R. (2010a) *Freud: The Key Ideas*. Abingdon: Bookpoint.

Snowden, R. (2010b) *Jung: The Key Ideas*. Abingdon: Bookpoint.

Stevens, R. (1983) *Erik Erikson: An Introduction*. Milton Keynes: Open University Press.

Sugarman, L. (2001) *Life-span Development: Frameworks, Accounts and Strategies*. Hove: Psychology Press.

Thorley, A. and Stern, R. (1979) 'Neurosis and personality disorder', in P. Hill, R. Murray and A. Thorley (eds), *Essentials of Postgraduate Psychiatry*. New York: Grune and Stratton.

Trethowan, W. and Sims, A. C. P. (1983) *Psychiatry*. London: Baillière Tindall.

Wain, M. (1998) *Freud's Answer: The Social Origins of Our Psychoanalytic Century*. Chicago: Ivan R. Dee

Welchman, K. (2000) *Erik Erikson: His Life, Work and Significance*. Buckingham: Open University Press.

Wertlieb, D. L. (2004) 'Libido', in W. E. Craighead and C. B. Nemeroff (eds), *The Concise Corsins Encyclopedia of Psychology and Behavioural Science*. Hoboken, NJ: John Wiley & Sons.

Zock, H. (2004) *A Psychology of Ultimate Concern: Erik H. Erikson's Contribution to the Psychology of Religion*. Amsterdam: Rodopi.

FURTHER READING

Brome, V. (1984) *Freud and His Disciples: The Struggle for Supremacy*. London: Caliban Publications.

Conn, W. E. (1977) 'Erik Erikson: the ethical orientation, conscience and the golden rule', *The Journal of Religious Education*, 5 (2): 249–266.

Cybulska, E. (2008) 'On Freud's unconscious debt to Schopenhauer and Nietzsche', *Philosophy Now*, July/August: 13–16.

Edmundson, M. (2007) *The Death of Sigmund Freud: Fascism, Psychoanalysis and the Rise of Fundamentalism*. London: Bloomsbury.

Erikson, E. H. (1969) *Gandhi's Truth: On the Origins of Nonviolence*. New York: W. W. Norton & Co.

Kahr, B. (2013) *Life Lessons from Freud*. London: Pan Macmillan.

Kvale, S. (1992) *Psychology and Postmodernism*. London: Sage.

Lechte, J. (1994) *Fifty Key Contemporary Thinkers: From Structuralism to Postmodernity*. London: Routledge.

Mitchell, J. (1990) *Psychoanalysis and Feminism*. London: Penguin Books.

Rank, O. (1932) *Art and Artist: Creative Urge and Personality Development*. New York: W. W. Norton & Co.

van der Post, L. (1976) *Jung and the Story of Our Time*. Harmondsworth: Penguin.

13 RESPONSIBLE BUSINESS PRACTICE

A NOTE FROM THE AUTHOR

What is the link between personal development and responsible business practice? This might be something that you haven't thought about before. I commence this chapter by generating a list of reasons that might motivate people to want to develop, and follow on from this in listing why people also might aspire to develop as responsible business practitioners.

First, why develop?

- to be all you can be
- to be proud of yourself and of what you have achieved
- to be effective in business
- to be successful (to do well) in business, however you define that
- to relate positively and healthily towards other people
- to take you towards what you want, sometimes called empowerment
- to give you options
- to move forward, in the right direction
- to become strong and express strength
- to cooperate with how life is wanting to teach us.

Secondly, why responsible?

- to achieve integrity
- to make a difference (see embodiment box below)
- to be a help and an inspiration to others
- to contribute to community building
- to develop others
- to create something of substance and worth
- to do something to be proud of
- to be professional
- to do the right thing
- to push beyond self-centredness.

This chapter paints a number of pictures to consider. Firstly, it shows us what a responsible organization looks like, which in turn helps us to identify a responsible organization according to a number of characteristics. Secondly, it takes three business functions – marketing, accounting and human resource management – and presents how these functions look when occupied by responsible practitioners. These portraits also in one sense act as mirrors, for you to hold up and see yourself in. Which of the portraits is most like you, or which portrait is closest to how you want to look, or to be?

I selected the chapter title, responsible business practice, because it neatly applies to both organizations and to individuals. Try to think of responsible business practice as a scale and not either/or, i.e. think of how responsible a business or business professional is and not whether such and such are responsible or irresponsible. What's their responsibility profile and how can they develop further in responsible practice?

Learning outcomes

When you have completed this chapter you will be able to:

- see the connection between personal development and responsible business practice
- define what is meant by a responsible business
- comprehend different levels of being responsible as a practitioner
- summarize the responsibility issues for each of the three major business functions
- list pointers for your own personal and professional development.

PRELIMINARY TERMS

Organization – there are a variety of types of organizations, including: private firms and corporations, governments, non-governmental organizations, international organizations, armed forces, charities, not-for-profit organizations, partnerships, cooperatives and universities. Business and management principles apply to all organizations, some might say increasingly so. Scarce and strategic resources need to be carefully and deliberately managed.

Corporate responsibility or CR – usually framed around the so called 'triple bottom line' with its financial, social and environmental components. Sometimes referred to as 'people, planet, profit', this framework connects corporate responsibility to sustainability. A responsible organization might even be referred to as a 'triple bottom enterprise'. Robinson and Dowson (2012) have extended this to the quadruple bottom line, adding meaning and purpose – a clear sense of what the organization stands for – into the CR mix.

Responsible practice – this is how responsibility, or gathering together the multiple bottom lines, is seen in organizational or professional practice. Some responsible practices are compulsory under the law – others are at the discretion of the organization. To excel in this, organizations and practitioners need to be able to reflect on their practice and be genuinely self-critical. It is enhanced by accountability, that is being held to give an account, preferably to a respected authority whether a body or an individual.

QUADRUPLE BOTTOM LINE RESPONSIBILITY

There is no such thing as a responsibility-free business action or decision. Our world is pregnant with consequence and meaning, and this also envelops business activity. So we might meaningfully be able to speak of business activity as having both positive and negative financial, environmental, social and existential impact.

Impact experienced in these different ways is outlined below. Here we capture the essence of the type of impact and bullet point a number of key considerations for each category (or bottom line).

Economic impact

When we speak of business survival the first and primary consideration is profitability. This permits a business to produce goods and services, provide employment, pay taxes and facilitate community growth. Without financial performance all the above are threatened. Financial responsibility is therefore paramount. There are responsible and irresponsible ways of making good profits. The following list highlights a number of important financial matters, which will inevitably have an economic impact:

- sticking to budget
- responsible spending (financial self-control)
- responsible borrowing
- accounting for costs over the life cycle of a product
- socially responsible investment
- corruption prevention
- CSR information disclosure.

Environmental impact

This is perhaps the highest profile of the impact areas at the present moment in time. When we speak in terms of sustainability the first thing most people think of are so called 'green' issues. Consciousness of this environmental impact has grown enormously in the post-war period. It has become a priority as well as fashionable for corporations to consider their 'environmental footprint'. Added to this environmental performance is an important aspect of an employer brand. Many people do not want to be associated with an environmentally irresponsible business organization. A list of environmental issues and impacts is as follows:

- minimizing negative impact on the environment
- minimizing energy use, achieved through setting targets for energy consumption
- measured waste generation
- greenhouse gas emissions
- disposal of harmful materials
- checking unnecessary travel – includes green commuting
- depletion of natural resources
- clean production.

Social impact

The issue of social impact being a hard area to measure might be bound up with the idea that corporations have not historically been held accountable for the social impact of their operations. The fact that people don't immediately connect social responsibility with business means that business has been able to side step responsibility in this area. The following list of social considerations highlight the very real impact business can have in the social sphere. Like the other bottom lines it is important to remain positive about the opportunity for good in each of the spheres:

- working for social change
- fair trade
- labour standards of international suppliers
- human health (including mental-health) costs
- human rights – a rights-based approach
- gender equality
- SA 8000 social accountability expressed as a standard.

Existential impact

In using the term existential in this context we are highlighting how business contributes meaning or a sense of purpose, or alternatively undermines and erodes these. This dimension is often acutely felt by employees who might speak of being a part of a meaningful enterprise taking themselves and others (including consumers) in the direction of the pursuit of the good life. In contrast they might report a sense of meaninglessness and genuinely struggle to see a good purpose in their work and in what the organization is achieving. We've listed below a number of issues that impact an organization's fulfilling of its potential to add to meaning and purpose:

- emphasis on offering good or services that add meaning and purpose to the consumer
- community enhancing initiatives and developments in the workplace
- canteen/refectory enhancements including design, menus and other benefits to the employee
- teambuilding ethos and people development
- selection and oversight of management to develop community, team and employer sense of worth
- meaning and purpose being central leadership and governance concerns
- adoption of a sustainable development ethos that achieves meaning and purpose.

KEY CONCEPT – THE RESPONSIBLE BUSINESS ORGANIZATION

A helpful way to approach the notion of business responsibility is to think of it as being connected to how an individual is responsible. There is a tendency to put onto business an unrealistically exacting standard for business organizations to achieve – what we might term total, i.e. absolute, responsibility. We wouldn't ask the same of even the most noble individual and yet, businesses are led by and are comprised of ordinary as distinct from extraordinary human beings. Why should we expect businesses to be any different or any better than the most responsible of individuals? This is not negating the pursuit of excellence. Rather it is suggesting that discovering a responsibility profile is as likely in a business organization as it is in a businessman or businesswoman.

Below we are suggesting how to arrive at what we might term a responsibility profile for a business organization, consisting of ten areas for analysis, even self-examination, on the part of businesses:

1 Responsible from top to bottom – looking across the breadth and depth of the organization what are its areas of strength and weak spots in terms of it exercising responsibility? Which functions of the business are ahead of others here? Are there any particularly vulnerable aspects to the business in terms of responsibility standards, even legal standards?

2 Responsible by design – do systems and strategies integrate, indeed prompt and encourage responsible practice? Does what transpires in the course of ordinary business activity accordingly fall short of responsibility standards?

3 Responsible in word – what is the logos (Greek for word) of the organization, reflected in published and promoted codes and reporting;

constantly spoken (and reinforced) messages about how the business operates; and how the organization's product or service is presented to the customer? Is the organizational logos responsible?

4 Responsible in deed – do the deeds of the organization, its actions and strenuous endeavours, match its responsible rhetoric? Can we say of the organization that it is responsible in word and deed? Perhaps the organization is ahead in the area of deeds and needs to develop a matching logos to reflect what it is achieving in terms of its responsibility? This accords with the idea that criticality applied to the matter of business responsibility does not have to be inquisitorial.

5 Responsible indeed – where can the organization or the organizational function or department point to where it has achieved a level of responsibility worth celebrating? It is important here that areas of responsibility are measured quantitatively and via key performance indicators.

6 ROI responsible – ROI denoting return on investment, how can the organization relate and trace its responsibility practices to their impact on the bottom line?

7 Environmentally responsible – in view of the business organization's scale and nature, how is it achieving environmental responsibility? For example, how is it performing (statistically) in terms of recycling and waste disposal?

8 Socially responsible – in relation to a growing consciousness of a business organization's connectivity with all manner of stakeholders, both internal and external to the organization, how can the business both measure and report on its performance in this area?

9 Responsible in purpose – is the organization's purpose clear? Is it stated or is it implicit? And is it responsible?

10 Responsible on purpose – to what extent is responsibility an organizational priority? Does it have responsibility targets? How often is the word responsibility and its associated terms heard, for example, ethics and the triple bottom line? By the board, senior management, middle managers and others?

RESPONSIBLE CORPORATE VALUES

Responsibility is usually associated with the adoption, articulation, expression and furtherance of values. We are familiar with the notion of 'walking the talk' which implies that the aim, an aspect of integrity, is to close the gap between what we say we stand for and how we live our lives or operate in practice.

Learning is about recognizing the inevitability of this gap. Some are quick to accuse individuals and organizations of hypocrisy when the gap becomes apparent or, more seriously, is exposed. We need to respond to one another with care here. Central to people development and an organization developing along responsible lines, is the creation of a learning environment where people and businesses develop the criticality and consciousness to identify these so called 'gaps' for themselves and the moral imagination to desire to close them, thus aligning stated principles with practice.

Table 13.1 below outlines a number of possible corporate values. The key here is getting inside or 'behind' the words to consider the implications of truly adopting and living these values. This is a community or collective task. The individual is supported in this process by others. Corporate values cannot be treated as an add-on to sound 'good' to others (including customers), or even ourselves. They should be seen as being integral to all the organization does and what the organization stands for.

Table 13.1 Responsible corporate values

Consciousness	It would be surprising to find consciousness per se listed as a corporate value. Corporations will often speak, however, of being environmentally conscious. Consciousness is bound up with being aware and with this awareness comes responsibility. This in turn is allied to so called corporate conscience.
Honesty	We have all heard the phrase 'as honest as the day is long'. Many people view honesty as a basic human value and seemingly a simple corporate value to claim. In a world of marketing 'front' and 'smoke and mirrors' (i.e. manipulative) behaviour, encountering honesty might be considered as remarkable or counter-intuitive.
Transparency	The metaphor that comes to mind when speaking of transparency is an 'open book' and showing one's workings. This contrasts with hidden practices and information. Leaders and managers have a significant responsibility in making sure the organization is transparent. It is a key way of operating in dialogical relationships.
Equity	As a corporate value being equitable or having equity is a claim to being fair. Internally, this might be reflected in decision-making processes being fair or being considered fair by all those affected. Externally it might be seen in the corporation's attitude to issues of social justice.
Community	A community value involves respect for the family and the corporation's neighbourhood and having practices which benefit these groups. It is also reflected in the corporation's partnerships.
Dependability	Dependability or an alternative word which communicates surety and integrity (being true to what people associate with you or expect from you) is bound up with consistency. The consumer places their trust and invests a certain loyalty in the corporation's name.
Equality	The corporate value of equality is a shorthand for the organization upholding and furthering equal rights. Equal opportunities is a well-known and used phrase and equality for women is not a completed agenda. The law upholds matters of equality but the scope for going beyond the law in this area is searching in terms of corporate attitudes.
Freedom	Again, this value is likely to be labelled in different ways, invariably involving creativity. The value of freedom encompasses the discovery and celebration of the joy of living. It is also often associated with self-expression, self-help and taking responsibility for oneself.

In summary let's resist the temptation to list or tick off corporate values as if these noble principles are trifling things – to effectively underestimate their significance and value when found in organizations or seen in an organization's people and practice.

RESPONSIBLE MARKETING

What does responsible marketing look like? Laczniak and Murphy's (2006) basic perspective set constitutes a comprehensive description. Consisting of seven basic perspectives (BPs), marketers can examine themselves, their motivations and their practice, in the light of these.

- BP1 following a 'people first' dictum
- BP2 exceeding the law in behavioural standard
- BP3 examining the process of how marketing decisions are made
- BP4 cultivating higher moral imagination in managers and employees
- BP5 articulating and embracing a core set of ethical principles
- BP6 embracing the stakeholder concept
- BP7 delineating an ethical analysis/decision-making protocol.

Laczniak and Murphy (2006) suggest that the basic perspective set operates best as an integrative whole, the idea here being that all these perspectives constitute important dimensions of what it means to be a responsible marketer. Table 13.2 summarizes the essence of each BP.

Table 13.2   Laczniak and Murphy's seven basic perspectives explained

---

BP1 following a 'people first' dictum

- being of service to people
- creating perceived and real social benefit
- marketing decisions not disadvantaging society

BP2 exceeding the law in behavioural standard

- ethics implies assuming more duties than covered by law
- law lags behind public opinion (what the public want)
- associated with so called stakeholder theory

BP3 examining the process of how marketing decisions are made

- differentiating the intent, from the means, from the outcome of a marketing action
- looking at side effects of marketing actions

BP4 cultivating higher moral imagination in managers and employees

- ethical and moral sensitivity varies
- to instil an improved ethical reasoning capacity
- illustrated by a typology of manager moral development (see Table 13.3)

(Continued)

Table 13.2 (Continued)

BP5 articulating and embracing a core set of ethical principles

- offers five ethical precepts for consideration including: non-malfeasance, non-deception, protecting vulnerable market segments, distributive justice, and stewardship (see Table 13.4)

BP6 embracing the stakeholder concept

- intrinsic to a long-term habit of ethical behaviour
- aligned with protecting brand equity
- internalizes moral sensitivity about multipronged influences

BP7 delineating an ethical analysis/decision-making protocol

- supported by ethical training opportunities
- enshrined in the seven steps of moral reasoning

Laczniak and Murphy's framework raises a number of key questions for marketers, including:

- What might reveal, according to Laczniak and Murphy, that we're treating consumers, not as people, but only as objects, or as a means to some business end? This relates to BP1, which puts people first.
- How might we map or profile ethical and moral sensitivity in marketing managers and others? Here we present Laczniak and Murphy's useful four level model, relating to BP4, which focuses on the cultivation of a higher moral imagination.
- Where might we start in terms of articulating, adopting or developing a number of key ethical precepts? This relates to BP5, which is all about embracing a core set of ethical principles.

People, not things

Responsible marketing treats consumers as people, not things. Resisting objectifying people (regarding them as objects), which links to dehumanizing them, can be reflected in a number of practices, highlighted by Laczniak and Murphy.

- High pressure selling tactics – these can exploit less resistant, less confident consumers, and annoy others.
- Coercion in the channel distribution – for example, using significant economic leverage to squeeze price concessions and make unreasonable demands.
- Over-the-top psychological approaches – this might include, for example, the psychological suggestion that a product or an offer might soon be gone.
- The sexual exploitation of women – in advertising, for example. Used to manipulate consumers and prey on their desires.
- Price gouging in times of product shortage or customer exposure – that is, pricing goods or services at a much higher level than is reasonable or fair to them.

Homo economicus, or economic human, views people as rational human beings. Traditional economic models suggest that Homo economicus will attempt to maximize their utility, in terms of both monetary and non-monetary gains.

Behavioural economists and neuroeconomists suggest that the Homo economicus conception doesn't allow for decision making and consumer behaviour that is clearly not centred in so called rationality but views people as more complex, more 'human', following impulses and steering relating to their psychology and what are termed their metaphors.

THE PRINCIPLED BUSINESS PRACTITIONER

How can we understand, or map, the variation to be found in marketing practices in terms of their reflecting moral and ethical sensitivity and consciousness? Laczniak and Murphy present a four-level model based upon Kohlberg's thinking on moral development. This suggests how individuals might progress or slip back in terms of their level of responsibility practice and thinking. Four types of practitioners emerge corresponding to the four levels, as shown in Table 13.3:

Table 13.3   Laczniak and Murphy's Kohlbergian four level model

Egoistic

- personal moral resolve is immature
- practitioners on this level mostly respond to rewards and punishments
- so called business 'crooks' are often egoistic (Laczniak and Murphy, 2006)

Legalistic

- overtly espouse law as their guide
- have a law-equals-morality approach
- view business strategy as a game – they operate within the rules of the game

Moral strivers

- capable of considering and applying stakeholder claims
- demonstrate empathy-for-others (Laczniak and Murphy, 2006)
- still heavily dependent on company rules and policies
- seek to do the ethical thing

Principled

- foresee the impacts of their decisions
- can incorporate stakeholder claims
- apply prevailing ethical norms and applicable law

The model is helpful in highlighting how people operate on different levels of moral and ethical consciousness and through time how they can also grow and develop in their exercise of ethical practice. The limitation of the model is that it may suggest that the practitioner operates all the time on a certain plane, when in reality a person's practice may have a more 'patchy' characteristic. In other words, they may operate on more than one level. Laczniak and Murphy (2006) highlight the possibility of practitioners slipping back in terms of practice to a lower level, perhaps due to specific pressures coming to bear on them.

EMBODIMENT BOX – MAKING A DIFFERENCE

It is refreshing to hear business practitioners and other people speak positively in terms of wanting to make a difference. Here we unpack what this might mean for those who express this sentiment. Professional practice is about giving structure to a sentiment – converting a wish and a value into a way of operating and into action, pushing beyond it perhaps only amounting to a vague idea. Making a difference can mean:

- to positively contribute to community
- to demonstrate strength of character
- to venture beyond self-centredness and self-interestedness
- to make a difference to others and have a positive significance for others
- to be adult as a human being, strong enough to care for others
- to add value to the world
- to take others forward, not back
- to express nobility, integrity, care, stature
- to help others make a difference too and work with others to achieve change.

The bullet points suggest how 'making a difference' might be directed. It is often expressed in communal activity and contributes to community building and enhancement. Erik Erikson (1964) suggests as human beings that we are a 'teaching species' – we learn from one another and most effectively when all the generations are contributing to this learning. Making a difference implicitly involves encouraging or activating this educating and learning aspect of what it means to be human. We learn from one another and together. It takes us in the direction of being all we can be … together.

Professional practice, either being a part of a recognized professional body or seeking to achieve a certain standard of behaviour at work, helps the practitioner in reaching a higher plane. Being around others and working with them can help or hinder this kind of progress. Some people may act as inspirational models of behaviour and stir others forward by way of example – 'show others the way', we might say. Added to this, ethical advancement expressed concretely and practically in specific practice is assisted by working together in team.

Articulating core values

Laczniak and Murphy (2006) present four core values they see as being clearly applicable to the field of marketing. Our researchers, however, are clear in pointing out that the four they propose are not the four, but a four, underlining that core values are adopted by free choice and that the choice extends beyond the four they present, as shown in Table 13.4.

Table 13.4 Laczniak and Murphy's four core values explained

Non-malfeasance

- to never knowingly do harm to others through marketing decisions and strategies
- accords with applying product safety standards and measures

Non-deception

- never intentionally mislead or unfairly manipulate consumers
- building trust through trading relationships

Protecting vulnerable market segments

- includes children, the elderly, those more vulnerable mentally, and the economically disadvantaged
- stems from extending dignity to all people

Distributive justice

- not adding to the disadvantage of the least well off segments in the market
- does marketing practice contribute in some way to an existing economic or social divide?

Reflecting on Laczniak and Murphy's approach here, a couple of important principles emerge.

Imposition versus choice – organizations often unwittingly impose values on employees. This betrays a very parental attitude on the part of the organization and profoundly doesn't accord with regarding and treating staff as mature adults.

Ill-defined versus articulated – there is value in not only knowing what one stands for, but also in being able to articulate this. The articulation of chosen values reinforces ownership of them. For example, if we take building trusting trading relationships (belonging according to Laczniak and Murphy to the core value of non-deception), it is helpful for a practitioner to be able to say that this is what they are looking for and why it is important to them. This identification and articulation of a core value increases everyone's consciousness of it – the practitioners themselves and those in a trading relationship with them. This also increases accountability, which is central to ethical development. Through both owning and stating a value the practitioner is inviting both self-accountability and accountability to those people who the practitioner is in an accountable relationship with.

Neuromarketing

We have all had experience of passing a bakery shop and smelling the wonderful aroma of fresh bread. Of course it acts as an inducement, or is it a trigger, to purchase something freshly baked. But what of the practice of a bakery deliberately diverting the aroma into the street, where people are walking by? Is this manipulation or just smart trading? What is the difference between this and a fruit seller artistically arranging the produce, or even a piece of effective advertising that captures one's attention and imagination?

The so called neuromarketeers recognize that the consumer is more than Homo economicus and responds in a profound, if not very human way to not just sights, but body experiences of all manner, including sounds and smells and touch. As early as 1978 Gendlin spoke of the 'felt sense' of an experience, evoking not only a physical sensation or feeling, but one that also incorporates emotional and cognitive content (Gendlin, 1978).

Natasha Singer's *New York Times* article, 'Making ads that whisper to the brain' (2010), is an excellent introduction to the world of neuromarketing and raises the question as to whether those who set out to comprehend, then map, then sell to people's brain activity surrounding consumption, might be accused of so called brandwashing. This term is an amalgam of branding and brainwashing and raises the concern, felt by some, that such knowledge of the consumer might be used in such a way that is not in the consumer's best interests or the best interests of wider society.

Reflecting on this, it seems that the converse might also be true. Neuromarketing might be closer to brainwatching as we'll coin it – understanding the complexity and detail of what human beings truly want – to make buying decisions that relate to their core motives and true feelings. Tanja Schneider's (2011) review is helpful here in that neuromarketing is presented as employing revelatory techniques that conjure up an image of the consumer as a subconsciously steered figure, who is not always aware of why they are drawn into making certain consumer choices.

A key foundational technique in neuromarketing was developed by Zaltman and is known as ZMET (Zaltman metaphor elicitation technique). This constitutes a way of mapping how consumers actually think their way to pressing the 'buy button'. According to Zaltman such consumer thinking is bound up with metaphors as he describes them (Chaney, 2010), which are mental representations triggered by aesthetic and sensorimotor promptings. According to Hirschman (2007) metaphors are carriers of human meaning and brands attach themselves to these metaphors.

What if the consumer is more than Homo economicus, but closer to a being with feelings and desires, that also thinks. Joseph Turrow, quoted by Singer (2010), argues 'there has always been a holy grail in advertising to try and reach people in a hypodermic way'. This isn't by any means, in and of itself, irresponsible marketing.

In a crowded marketplace where consumers encounter sight overload particularly, neuromarketing could be a smart way to appeal to the core of what consumers are really looking for.

RESPONSIBLE ACCOUNTING

Irresponsible accounting is an oxymoron. It would be the equivalent of incorrect mathematics or perhaps closer to teaching a way of doing mathematics not based upon accuracy and that overlooked miscalculations, both of which would have serious implications. Ever since business trade has involved the use of money to buy and sell goods and services, the ideal of responsible accounting has never been far away. The trader, for example, has always wanted to accurately count takings.

At the same time, however, wherever money is exchanged, there are corruptions of all kinds. Business and accounting can be subject to human greed and avarice. There are a hundred reasons why accounts might be incorrect or inaccurate. It is in the interests of some that accounts are falsified or 'presented' in a certain way, sometimes to effectively mislead others.

This is the fascinating in-built tension at the very core of the world of accounting and the accountant – to strive for accuracy and also be wise to human manipulation and weakness, in the exchanges of monies intrinsic to doing business. Competitive pressures only sharpen the necessity for responsible accounting.

For all of accounting's evolved complexity over the centuries, accounting is one of those words that tells us a great deal of what is central to it as both a business function and as a profession. It is easy to work out from this what might be considered responsible and irresponsible accounting.

- It involves counting – accountants count money, hence we refer to them as 'money men' (a term which of course encompasses women). This has taken on greater sophistication over time.
- It suggests taking everything into account – the full length and breadth of the resources of a business, expressed numerically, in financial terms.
- It includes giving an account – presenting calculations and workings, to business owners, senior management, the government, investors and shareholders.
- It also requires an account – from those handling monies, from budget holders and those proposing and planning business developments and acquisitions.

From his study of the history of financial accounting in Finland, Virtanen (2009) identifies five accounting themes which he presents as developing consecutively over time. These cast light on the evolving scope and significance of accounting as an important and integral part of business. Table 13.5 outlines Virtanen's five themes, indicating what characterizes them and adding each theme's implication in terms of the notion of responsible accounting.

Table 13.5 Virtanen's five accounting themes with responsibility watchword and implications

Theme	Summary description	Responsibility *watchword* and implications
1. **Entrepreneurship theme**	• Accounting as writing down in accordance with certain rules • Accounting as providing a current viewpoint of the financial position of a business • Accounting to monitor debts and receivables and balancing these	• *Accuracy* • Is the accounting in order or sloppy? • Who is performing the function of accounting? • Is the delegated responsibility being performed faithfully? • Does the owner or bookkeeper have sufficient expertise to perform the accounting?
2. **Academic theme**	• Accounting as involving a formal education and training • Accounting as a functional specialism within business • Accounting as being recognized as have strategic significance	• *Education* • Has this ensured a standard of accounting performance and expertise? • Is the accountant performing a vital strategic role? • How is the accountant handling their significance and authority?
3. **Governance control theme**	• Accounting as conforming to governmental accounting and taxation rules	• *Rules* • Is the accountant following the rules? • Is accounting practice legal but unjust? • Is accounting party to a business practice which doesn't benefit society?
4. **Professional theme**	• Accounting as subject to the ways of professional accounting • Accounting as performing an audit function • Accounting as following a professional code of ethics	• *Detachment* • Is the accountant operating as a professional? • Is the accountant making ethical disclosure recommendations? • Is the accountant practically following professional codes?
5. **Financial market theme**	• Accounting as producing and presenting data for shareholders and potential investors	• *Presentation* • Is the presentation accurate or misleading? • Does it meet the needs of investors?

Table 13.5 reveals how accounting developed, from the records kept by traders to a presentation of whole businesses for international investors. It highlights an evolution of information needs for a widening sphere of stakeholders. In the beginning the trader-owners were the sole lords of accounting. There are now many lords of accounting, including accountants themselves, which have developed into a professional category of management, senior management, leaders and consultants.

From Virtanen's history we developed a number of responsibility watchwords for accountants and accounting practice:

- accuracy
- education
- rules
- detachment
- presentation.

It will be clear to the reader what are the strategic implications of accounting achieving responsible practice. A falling short here produces inequities of all kinds. Irresponsible accounting, reflected in all manner of slips and deceptions (see Table 13.6), is indeed an oxymoron.

Table 13.6   Slips and deceptions – ten types of irresponsible accounting

1	**Sloppy accounting**	variously caused and motivated
2	**Inaccurate accounting**	can involve error or be deliberate
3	**Falsified accounting**	involving hiding, failing to disclose information
4	**Incomplete accounting**	where accounting information is lost, again sometimes deliberately
5	**Ill-advised accounting**	accountants who are not advising correctly and professionally
6	**Self-serving/interested accounting**	failing to serve clients and acting in their own interest
7	**'Narrow' accounting**	accountants that don't esteem our functions and specialisms
8	**'Pocketed' accounting**	accountants who operate, so to speak, in the pockets of those who reward them
9	**Power accounting**	accountants motivated by power
10	**Number accounting**	accountants who have no regard for people

RESPONSIBLE HRM

HRM according to Greenwood (2002), 'involves the effective management of people to achieve organisational goals'. Classically, it divides into two broad and contrasting approaches known as 'hard' HRM and 'soft' HRM. These are outlined in Table 13.7, but as Truss et al. (1997) highlight, the two approaches are based on opposing views of human nature, resulting in two different managerial control strategies.

Table 13.7 Contrasting hard and soft approaches to HRM

	Hard HRM	Soft HRM
Focus	resource	people
View of employee	instrumental	having intrinsic value
Management approach	tight (low-trust) strategic control	loose (high-trust) control through commitment
Training	skills-focused	for development

Greenwood (2002) adds that in practice it is often difficult to distinguish the hard and soft approaches to HRM, whereas Truss et al. (1997) suggest that neither hard nor soft approaches accurately represent what is actually happening within organizations and that the key to understanding an organization is to appreciate the difference between what an organization says it stands for and what it actually does or practises.

The content of HRM, the stuff of the HRM function if you like, is summarized in Table 13.8. The responsibility pointers as we've termed them are aspects of responsibility associated with each role that HRM fulfils. For example, taking HRM's L&D (learning and development) role, organizations will vary as to how or how well they will develop their people. Opportunities for learning and development vary enormously from one employer to the next (feeding directly into the issue of employer brand as it is known). Opportunities might consist of various training programmes through to access to formal and professional education as an implicit component of personal and professional development.

Table 13.8 HRM's typical roles and their associated responsibility pointers

HRM Role	Responsibility Pointers
Recruitment and selection	• accessing employees • selecting them fairly (equal opportunities)
Health, safety and well-being	• encompasses employee support • supporting the health of the worker • working environment
Job design and performance	• so called 'job fit' • the mouse's wheel (job design) • appraisal function
Rewarding and motivating employees	• employee benefits • a just wage
Learning and development	• developing people • providing opportunity • providing access to further, higher and professional education

HRM Role	Responsibility Pointers
Equal opportunities	• protecting against bullying, discrimination, harassment • selection and promotion
Disciplinary function	• a needed corrective in an organization – to keep it on track • fair discipline
Industrial relations and disputes	• advisory role with senior management • solving disputes of all kinds • preventative approach

Robinson and Dowson in *Business Ethics in Practice* (2012) detail a number of typical HRM-related ethical issues. These include:

- remuneration
- the working environment
- employee rights and discrimination
- harassment and bullying
- whistleblowing.

ETHICS BOX – THE ISSUE OF GENDER

We are first human beings and second have a gender. Most of the ethical issues surrounding gender in one way or another involve people losing sight of this common humanity. We have chosen to approach this focus on gender-related issues by looking at it through outlining a number of key terms.

Harassment – sexual harassment involves unwanted advances of a sexual nature. This not only encompasses inappropriate touching, but also flirtation, staring and making unwanted remarks. In an organization such behaviour might be reported such that it becomes a matter for HRM to deal with.

Power differential – sexual harassment can result from people misusing their seniority, exploiting the vulnerability of a younger employee. It is not unheard of for senior people to expect sexual favours in return for promotions and the like.

Patriarchal attitudes – the 'rule of the fathers', which might be reflected in gender imbalances in an organization's management, senior leadership and governing body.

(Continued)

(Continued)

> *Gender stereotyping* – this involves having specific, often narrow, notions of what is associated with a gender. For example, it might be expressed in an organization frowning on men with long hair.
>
> *Sexual exploitation* – advertising and brand development can involve this. This can relate to how an advertising model is presented. The other side of this coin is how the consumer's propensities in the area are being exploited too.

Ethics are part of the territory wherever human beings live and work together. Personal development encompasses not only how we personally respond to all manner of ethical dilemmas but how we conduct ourselves in the face of injustices of all kinds. Employees become employed managers and leaders and find themselves in positions in organizations where they can directly influence what we might term the responsibility architecture in their organization. To step up to the plate here involves personal and professional development.

Appreciating that a responsible way of operating is far removed from being something one grows into 'automatically' and without reflective practice (see Chapter 7) is illustrated by Geoffrey Hunt's (2000) article on whistleblowing, where Hunt effectively draws a distinction between 'telling' the world and doing the same in a responsible manner, as follows:

- making sure that your facts are right
- appreciating the overall seriousness of the object of concern
- having exhausted internal channels
- refraining from exaggeration and distortion
- avoiding hurt to innocent parties
- putting aside any inclination to personalize or act vindictively
- choosing the proper time
- disclosing to the most appropriate party.

The points above penetratingly highlight the high bar that is responsible practice, requiring significant personal and professional development reflected in such things as care, attention to detail, right motive, protecting others and exercising courage.

EMPLOYABILITY FOCUS – DEVELOPING A MORAL IMAGINATION

It is rarely, if ever, explicitly stipulated, but employing organizations would implicitly value what Lederach, in his book *The Moral Imagination* (2005), calls peacebuilding. Here, Lederach presents the essence of peacebuilding as founded on four disciplines, each of which helps to develop the moral imagination. We have outlined these four disciples below, drawing out their value also in terms of employability.

Relationships – Robinson and Dowson (2012) summarize Lederach's emphasis on the centrality of relationships by stating that 'peacebuilding requires that people be able to envisage their interconnectedness, mutuality and shared responsibility'. Breaking out of a narrow individualistic outlook and striving for relational enrichment reaps benefit for everyone in the employing organization.

Paradoxical curiosity – the practice of paradoxical curiosity rests on respecting complexity. Lederach proposes a certain scepticism of our initial perceptions of others and the development of the capacity to learn from the unexpected (serendipity). The ability to look beyond appearances and suspend judgement in our interactions in the workplace and beyond constitutes a profound employability skill or capacity.

Creativity – Lederach speaks of the provision of space for the creative act (Lederach, 2005). Organizations can provide this space, but the individual can also create it. We wilfully determine to be creative and out of creativity new ways of operating and thinking emerge. Remember the creative human action is one that moves beyond what exists and produces something new and unexpected. This refreshes interactions and organizations.

Risk – 'reaching out' involves the willingness to risk, without any guarantee of success or safety. It has been likened as a step into the unknown.

Hilary Ha-ping Yung's research (1997) explores how challenging it can be to be professionally responsible in the face of bureaucratic role conceptions. In the case of student nurses working in Hong Kong, it suggests that a primary loyalty to humanitarian patient care was challenged by a highly bureaucratic environment which also decreased the professional orientation of the nurses, who experienced what the researcher described as a 'reality shock'.

Ha-ping Yung documents how getting through the workload efficiently involved struggling to serve patient needs. This raises the important issue of job design and challenges the idea that professionals have the time and space to apply critical thinking skills in contexts of high-pressure, highly bureaucratic and systemized job roles. Nurses found themselves in a situation where they had little power and authority to make free ethical choices.

Employee engagement

I'm not a human resource; I'm a human being. (in Jacobs, 2013)

David MacLeod and Nita Clarke's timely thinking on what in HRM circles is known as employee engagement seeks to promote the humanity in human resources.

The UK government emphasizes the need to promote a well and healthy workforce (Greasley and Edwards, 2014). For MacLeod and Clarke (in Jacobs, 2013) this means employee engagement consisting of promoting positive 'enablers' and overcoming potential barriers for organizational engagement.

Failures in this area can be related to:

- lack of senior management support
- need for practical support and advice
- poor line management
- cynicism of employees.

MacLeod and Clarke's four enablers are as follows:

1 Strategic narrative – this centres on effectively communicating the organization's story and inviting employees to see their place in it. Without a sense of ownership here engagement will be held back (Chamberlain, 2012).
2 Engaging managers – as many as 70 per cent of employees are neutral about their bosses or don't trust them (Jacobs, 2013). MacLeod and Clarke suggest here that the way forward is for organizations to engage their managers, who in turn can contribute to the engagement of all employees.
3 Employee voice – employees must feel that their managers and bosses are listening to them (Chamberlain, 2012). This involves management and leadership in going beyond establishing what employees are feeling, to asking 'Why?'
4 Organizational integrity – values, so to speak 'on the wall' (Chamberlain, 2012) can easily differ from how colleagues and bosses are actually operating, which leads to distrust and cynicism. MacLeod and Clarke suggest that an organization's values need to be reflected in day-to-day behaviours.

Story, trust, voice, integrity. At first sight some would say this is the 'warm and fuzzy' content one would expect from HRM. However, as Brown and Reilly (2013) highlight the outcomes of increased employee engagement are significant for any organization:

- increased job performance
- reduced lateness
- decreased turnover/intention to leave
- increased altruism
- increased conscientiousness.

APPLIED PERSONAL DEVELOPMENT

In this chapter we highlighted the link between personal development and responsible business practice. We suggested that personal development implicitly involves taking responsibility: for one's own life; in our treatment of others; and in how we contribute to issues facing the whole world. An underlying theme here was breaking out of self-centredness, alternatively referred to as self-absorption.

We set out in this chapter to present pictures of what responsibility looks like. We started with what characterizes the responsible business organization and then turned to considering responsible marketing, responsible accounting and responsible HRM. These notions are relevant for anyone having an association with business and with business professionals, but they are key in terms of our career journeys.

What sort of organization are we going to give, in terms of our time and energies, a large portion of our lives to working in? The responsibility record and responsibility profile of an employing organization could have great significance for us as individuals. The organization will either develop us and develop us as responsible practitioners or thwart our potential. We presented this notion that organizations are like people on a larger scale in that an organization too has the potential to develop (or even slip back) in terms of its ethical consciousness and practice.

Internal power play, bickering and silo thinking mean that business functions as well as departments and individual staff members often don't esteem one another as they should and such disunities waste much time and resources in organizations. Our hope is that looking at the functions of marketing, accounting and HRM has highlighted the critical importance of each of these areas. The challenges that each function faces, in terms of responsible practice, are fascinating. I'd ask you here, which of the functions captured your imagination and why? There may be a clue there as to your career direction, or indeed how you might develop as a responsible practitioner if you are already operating in one of these functions.

We finish this chapter by taking a specific issue from each of these three functions and converting it into a personal development pointer:

- Thinking about the four types of practitioner – egoistic, legalistic, moral striver and principled – what type of practitioner do you want to be? Remember the significance of others in this matter.
- Turning to our five watchwords – accuracy, education, rules, detachment and presentation. These are aspects of professionalism that highlight the high bar which true professionalism constitutes. Does the notion of developing into a true professional inspire you? Think about the kind of organization that might support your professional development.
- Finally, so called hard and soft approaches to management tell us a great deal about the challenging realities of corporate life. What issues do these contrasting approaches raise for you as perhaps a future manager or your current experience of being managed or of management?

REFERENCES

Brown, D. and Reilly, P. (2013) 'Reward and engagement – the new realities', *Compensation and Benefits Review*, 45: 145–157.

Chamberlain, L. (2012) 'Four key enablers to employee engagement', *Personnel Today*, 27 January. Available at: www.personneltoday.com/hr/four-key-enablers-to-employee-engagement/ (accessed 28 March 2014).

Chaney, D. (2010) 'Analysing mental representations: the contribution of cognitive maps', *Recherche et Applications en Marketing* (English edition), 25: 93–115.

Erikson, E. H. (1964) *Insight and Responsibility: Lectures on the Ethical Implications of Psychoanalytical Insight*. New York: W. W. Norton & Co.

Gendlin, E. (1978) *Focusing*. New York: Bantam Books.

Greasley, K. and Edwards, P. (2014) 'When do health and well-being interventions work? Managerial commitment and context', *Economic and Industrial Democracy*, 4 March: 1–23.

Greenwood, M. R. (2002) 'Ethics and HRM: a review and conceptual analysis', *Journal of Business Ethics*, 36: 261–278.

Ha-ping Yung, H. (1997) 'The relationship between role conception and ethical behaviour of student nurses in Hong Kong', *Nursing Ethics*, 4: 99–113.

Hirschman, E. (2007) 'Metaphor in the marketplace', *Marketing Theory*, 7: 227–248.

Hunt, G. (2000) 'Whistleblowing, accountability and ethical accounting', *AVMA Medical & Legal Journal*, 6: 115–116.

Jacobs, K. (2013) 'Engagement special: David MacLeod and Nita Clarke on engage for success', *HR Magazine*, 5 April. Available at: www.hrmagazine.co.uk/hr/features/1076832/engagement-special-david-macleod-nita-clarke-engage-success (accessed 27 March 2014).

Laczniak, G. R. and Murphy, P. E. (2006) 'Normative perspectives for ethically and socially responsible marketing', *Journal of Macromarketing*, 26: 154–177.

Lederach, J. P. (2005) *The Moral Imagination: The Art and Soul of Building Peace*. Oxford: Oxford University Press.

Robinson, S. and Dowson, P. (2012) *Business Ethics in Practice*. London: CIPD.

Schneider, T. (2011) 'Book review: Ernest Dichter and motivation research: new perspectives on the making of post-war consumer culture', *History of Human Sciences*, 24: 180–184.

Singer, N. (2010) 'Making ads that whisper to the brain', *New York Times*, 13 November. Available at: www.nytimes.com/2010/11/14/business/14stream.html?_r=0 (accessed 14 March 2014).

Truss, C., Gratton, L., Hope-Hailey, V., McGovern, P. and Stiles, P. (1997) 'Soft and hard models of human resource management: a reappraisal', *Journal of Management Studies*, 34 (1): 53–73.

Virtanen, A. (2009) 'Revealing financial accounting in Finland under five historical themes', *Accounting History*, 14: 357–379.

14 RESPONSIBLE LEADERSHIP AND GOVERNANCE

● ● ● ● ● ● ● ● ● ● ● ● ● ●

A NOTE FROM THE AUTHOR

Today's leaders must do business with their heads up, sensing and interpreting the evolving world around them, sensitive to the needs and priorities of others inside and outside their business, to make new connections and brilliant compromises, and have the ability to see the new opportunities as they emerge. (Fisk, 2010)

So begins Peter Fisk in what he has to offer on the subject of inspiring leadership. I'd like to commence this chapter by bullet-pointing some of this sentence's core elements and ideas:

- sensing, or sensitive, to 'other' – to see
- interpreting, what's happening inside and outside the organization
- embracing the new and what's emerging
- making connections, even through compromises.

Inspiring leadership according to Fisk is also about followship as he terms it. To stir followers, to capture their imagination, with content that inspires them to break out of mediocrity, to move and go see.

We are all followers, but we can become leaders too. My purpose in this chapter is to reveal what it means to be a responsible leader and particularly one in this new age in which we find ourselves, an age where we are seeking as businesses to connect profit, to people, to planet, to purpose.

Leadership is often confused with management. I hope to differentiate them here. It's also important when focusing on leadership not to overlook the function and responsibility of governance in an organization. I describe those who govern as gatekeepers of all manner of responsibility measures and attitudes.

Learning outcomes

When you have completed this chapter you will be able to:

- clearly differentiate between leadership and management
- outline the major theories of leadership
- define how you might develop as a responsible leader
- identify models of governance including the King model
- comprehend the significance of different types of business related codes.

KEY CONCEPT – LEADERSHIP OR MANAGEMENT?

The two are often confused. Roger Gill in *Theory and Practice of Leadership* (2006) has endeavoured to clarify how we might differentiate leadership from management.

'Management is about path following, leadership is path finding.'

'Management is about controlling and problem solving; leadership is about motivating and inspiring.'

'Both managers and leaders are needed: for clarity of goals and direction, managers need leaders. For the indispensable help in reaching goals, leaders need managers.'

Consider the three quotations: in reverse order, there is no question that they need one another. It should never be a case of leaders versus managers, although this happens. Functionally leaders are expected to originate and define direction. Also functionally, managers report to leaders.

Confusion arises when we start to speak of what leadership and management are about for a number of reasons. Managers do provide leadership, and leaders have invariably managed their way into their leadership position. The second quotation isn't suggesting that managers cannot motivate and inspire their teams. Perhaps we're returning here to emphasize that functionally the two roles differ.

The first quote suggests the leader is a pathfinder, for the organization as a whole. This is not the brief of the manager, who is expected to follow the lead provided, but in countless contexts not in a slavish, uncreative or unintelligent way.

Overall, when considering the distinction between leadership and management we must be careful not to emphasize the significance of one function, at the expense of the other.

Fisk underlines that management is focused around 'getting things done' while leaders 'engage and energise people in a higher purpose, an inspiring vision, in seeing what is possible' (Fisk, 2010). In a nutshell, he comes closest to articulating how managers and leaders best integrate functionally.

However, beyond clearly appreciating the difference between the functional responsibilities of leaders and managers, confusion arises here because of the popular use of the terms, as is highlighted by the examples below:

- The word 'manager' is often connected with football management. Here we might think of greats such as Alex Ferguson, Pep Guardiola, Jose Mourinho and Rinus Michels. There is no doubt that these managers are also significant leaders and that 'football management', as it is referred to, calls also for leadership skills.
- Particularly in the context of customer dissatisfaction we would ask to see 'the manager'. Imagine here being in a hotel, or restaurant, or a store. We might say, 'Who's in charge here?' In these contexts the manager is regarded as 'the number one'. Unless our issue is not attended to, there is no regard as to whether organizationally there might be someone above them in terms of ownership or leadership.
- The title 'managing director' is also subject to this kind of 'open-ended' understanding. The job involves both management and leadership. Their attention to detail is paramount and at the same time in terms of responsibility and accountability to them as employees, so to speak, the buck stops here.

WHAT IS LEADERSHIP?

We commenced the chapter with Fisk's take on leadership in our contemporary global world. Robinson and Smith argue that leadership, particularly as applied to business, is a contested concept and underline that there is much debate about even how leadership is defined. Added to this, is their important observation that varied viewpoints emerge from different leadership contexts (Robinson and Smith, 2014).

Our intention below is to provide an overview of a number of views of leadership, highlighting what each theory contributes to the emerging picture of what is a leader and teasing out their implicit relevance in our age of responsibility, as it is sometimes termed.

Before we do this it is helpful to remind ourselves of Covey's framework of meta-, macro- and micro-leadership as presented in his book, *Principle Centred*

Leadership (Covey, 2009). This suggests not only that leadership is multi-faceted in its nature and scope, but also that it is multi-levelled or, put another way, operates on many levels, where leadership is needed for organizations (whether private, or public sector, or non-governmental) to effectively function.

Meta-leadership:

- o encompasses the much referred to notion of vision casting or setting vision
- o places great responsibility on leaders, entrusted with directing the organization's journey
- o there is much at stake, making meta-leadership a duty of care.

Macro-leadership:

- o focuses on strategy, organization and process to achieve the vision both defined and articulated by leaders
- o is bound up with targets and measurability.

Micro-leadership:

- o is centred on relationships
- o focuses on how power is used, misused or abused – in its impact on people
- o attends to enabling change in an organization.

It would be easy to look at the three levels and think of them as being hierarchical. But examination of their content reveals that all these aspects of leadership are important. Neglect of any one of their associated responsibilities could have serious consequences.

LEADERSHIP THEORIES

Trait theory

The notion of leaders having distinguishing traits is a commonly held view of leadership. A whole spectrum of traits are associated with leaders including drive and energy, clear-headedness, a sense of security in assuming responsibility, maturity and the aura of authority. As Robinson and Smith (2014) highlight, trait theory is bound up with two readily discernible perspectives. Firstly, what is termed as a 'functionalist' approach to leadership – suggesting that a set of traits enable leadership functions to be achieved. Secondly, the 'great man' myth – the idea that certain innate capacities are only offered by exceptional individuals constituting an elite group, which casts light on why in a competitive market place they can command a high price.

Trait theories are particularly prevalent in the United States and the UK and reflect their time of development and ascendency pre-dating the challenging fluidity of the postmodern globalizing context. Furthermore, they don't emphasize ethical identity or meaning, as highlighted by Ciulla (2004), as being central to leadership. Significantly, they are not associated with the opportunities and challenges of multiculturalism or global interdependence.

The legacy of the trait theory is perhaps that it led to an overemphasis on leadership being about having or exercising certain skills. The skills profile of a leader does not in itself result in good leadership. The 'great man' myth also has what amounts to an inherent limitation. Many would-be leaders and leaders are somehow 'great' in their own estimation, or capture the imaginations of people for a variety of reasons, including control and manipulation. Again, these kinds of greatness don't in themselves mean the leader can lead.

KEY CONCEPT – THE POST ENRON PHENOMENON

As highlighted by Campbell and Kitson, it is fair to speak of a post Enron phenomenon (Campbell and Kitson, 2008). We might reasonably apply this to many matters including:

- the possibility of leadership failure
- the exposure of unethical business practices
- even loss of faith in the capitalist system.

For a detailed outline and analysis of the Enron case we direct the reader to Robinson and Smith's book *Co-charismatic Leadership* (2014). We have summarized below their significant insights, particularly in relation to the Enron case exemplifying the danger and consequences of leadership failure.

The fall of Enron in 2001 has gained almost mythical status as has the name Skilling, the then CEO of Enron, as an exemplar of fallen, if not bizarre, (male) power abuse. At one point the seventh largest company in the United States and reaching a valuation of $70 billion Enron possibly constitutes the all-time most infamous case of corporate failure due to unethical practice, precipitated by the uncovering of fraudulent 'special purpose entities', that is, limited companies created by Enron to hide the debts of the organization. As we shall see, the fraud and failure was due to dubious, ultimately abusive, leadership practices exemplified most pertinently by at one point Skilling's *Star Wars* imagery of himself as Darth Vader, with his traders as storm troopers (Schwartz, 2002).

Drawing on Sherman (2002), Robinson and Smith highlight how the Enron experience conforms to leadership abuses found typically in the cult dynamics associated with new religious movements, namely:

- a charismatic leader, at the centre of the organization pitching himself (usually male) as the source of truth

(Continued)

(Continued)

- an overarching emotionally based vision, both driving and inspiring the organization's members
- a culture characterized by conformity and fear.

We note particularly here how in Enron, 'leadership could not be subject to question or criticism' (Robinson and Smith, 2014).

Ironically the leadership of Enron, as is well known, focused on developing a good and trustworthy image for the corporation, reinforced by a code of ethics, known as RICE (respect, integrity, communication, excellence). The code, as Robinson and Smith highlight, was used as an integral part of a wider series of narratives and ritualistic devices (Robinson and Smith, 2014), which convinced investors, workers, even journalists and academia of the credibility of Enron.

They add that employees actually considered themselves 'special' to be identified with Enron and belonging to a 'special organisation' (Robinson and Smith, 2014). This was reinforced by an appraisal system that kept everyone on their toes and heightened the anxiety of remaining 'in' and at the centre of the organization's myth.

As Robinson and Smith (2014) highlight, awareness of Enron's wider business environment, and the capacity to respond to it, was not valued by the organization. The image of employees being at war with those outside the organization was reinforced and a sense of responsibility to life beyond Enron was lost.

Transactional and transformational leadership

James Burns in his book *Leadership* as early as 1978 differentiated between transactional and transformational leadership. Transactional leadership is centred on targets and places value on processes enabling consensus above any notion of core values and organizational purpose.

Transformational leadership on the other hand constitutes what it, as it were, says on the tin. The transformational leader enables, even empowers, the organization to change and respond to change. For Burns, a hallmark of such a leader is their ability to both access and process a wider set of data encompassing different perspectives and resulting in better leadership decisions (Robinson and Smith, 2014).

Burns (1978) says that the transformational leader should:

- expand the followers' understanding and profile of needs
- transform the followers' view of self-interest
- increase the confidence of the followers

- elevate the expectations of followers
- enable a fuller appreciation of the leader's intended outcomes
- enable behavioural change
- motivate followers to higher levels of personal achievement.

Robinson and Dowson (2012) argue that at the heart of transformational leadership the leader is 'enabling the members of the group to develop moral maturity'.

Servant leadership

ETHICS BOX – THE SERVANT LEADER

At first sight the notion of a servant leader appears as a misnomer. As Robinson and Dowson's treatment of this category of leadership highlights, it is essentially about putting the needs of those who are being led first – ahead of the organization or even the customer (Robinson and Dowson, 2012). This only adds to the sense of it appearing remarkably radical or even unrealistic. Laub (2004) defines six core behaviours of servant leadership as follows:

1 valuing people
2 developing people
3 building community
4 displaying authenticity
5 providing leadership
6 sharing leadership.

The response to this profile might be something along the lines of, well we certainly wouldn't want to be led without such values. If we add to this Greenleaf's ten core characteristics of a servant leader, perhaps we are persuaded that there is great value in looking more closely at this model of leadership (Greenleaf, 1977):

1 listening
2 empathy
3 healing
4 awareness
5 persuasion
6 conceptualization (the capacity to develop a vision)
7 foresight (the capacity to understand and learn from the past, and apply these lessons to the present and future)

(Continued)

(Continued)

8   stewardship
9   commitment to the growth of the people
10 building community.

Robinson and Dowson underline that as important as the concept of service is, an overemphasis of this and care to the exclusion of concern for self and with organizational sustainability can lead to an ethics that is polarized and imbalanced (Robinson and Dowson, 2012). It may be relevant to add here when speaking of responsibility that we are in search of something which doesn't so much drip goodness (which may be unrealistic), but which drips humanity, or approximating the best way things can be. This may be another way of looking at what Fisk (2010) called a brilliant compromise.

The great value of the servant leader model as suggested by Ciulla (2004) is that it essentially reconfigures the relationship and power between leader and follower (Ciulla, 2004). Laub astutely adds that the self-interested characteristic of the leader becomes of secondary importance to the good of those they lead (Laub, 2004).

Relational leadership

There are many people in search of models of leadership based around relational and holistic considerations. Bass (2005) even goes so far as to suggest that interaction between people is the key dimension of leadership. Robinson and Smith (2014) pitch this around the leader's ability, in a complex world, 'to facilitate an on-going exploration through dialogue', involving all the stakeholders. No small task indeed. They cite Alimo-Metcalfe and Alban-Metcalfe's (2005) research which forms the basis of the following embodiment box.

EMBODIMENT BOX – THE RELATIONAL LEADER

Consider the profile below emerging from research with leaders in the UK's Health Care Trusts:

- valuing individuals – developing others with an inclusive approach
- networking and connecting – both inside and beyond the organization
- enabling and delegating – a key to empowering others
- integrity and openness – we might summarize as 'honesty + +'

- remaining accessible – symbolizing sensitivity to the needs of others
- being decisive – being able to take risks when considered necessary.

Valuing others, connecting with them, enabling them, being open, being accessible, being decisive. Practicing relational leadership constitutes a high bar in exercising personal and leadership skills.

- Can you imagine yourself providing this kind of leadership?
- What aspects of this profile would stretch you and why?

Complexity theory leadership

This theory of leadership suggests that complexity (or chaos) as it is encountered should be embraced enabling participants, in the fight for survival, to adapt. It involves a 'letting go' of the will to tightly control and seek instead to influence. Robinson and Smith (2014) suggest it is allied to the so called Ulysses myth, an underlying narrative in the west, where uncertainty is a given and the hero in everyone is drawn out through the adventure and challenge.

Eco-leadership theory

Part of the strength of this theory of leadership is its contemporary relevancy. Simon Western's (2008) eco-leadership has four aspects:

1 connectivity – accepting that the global social and physical environments are interdependent
2 systemic ethics – reflected in the pursuit of sustainability and the common good
3 leadership spirit – paying attention to such things as encouraging creativity, imagination, community and friendship
4 organizational belonging – applying belonging concurrently to many relationships and focusing on self and group worth.

Theories of leadership – conclusion

Trait, transactional, transformational, servant, relational, complexity theory, eco-leadership – even the sequence of descriptions echo something of the developmental journey of Ulysses. All the theories have usefulness in capturing aspects of what it means to lead.

The notion of responsible leadership implies an increase in maturity and reflexivity. There is a sense, highlighted by Robinson and Smith, of how transformational, servant and relational leadership theories trump what came before them, particularly in their being value-centred as they put it (Robinson and Smith, 2014). Added to this the latter two theories bring us right up to date, suggesting that responsible leadership is concerned also with adaptation to emergent global realities based on principles that are here to stay, even if we find ourselves still in Ulysses' sea of challenging indifferences and threatening meaninglessness.

EMBODIMENT BOX – AM I A LEADER?

Simple. Look around. Is there anybody following? It could of course be that you have not started to lead. Leadership is about carrying in your very person, something which on some scale captivates others. The notion of captivation has been carefully selected. Strangely, or is it sadly, one is able to captivate others with fear, but the kind of leadership we are promoting here is certainly something closer to respect and the best kind of captivation is one based on inspiration – where followership happens because people are free to follow, because they see in you or me something which they want to invest in. The leader finds that their followership want to give their attention, their time, even their life. The leader has somehow inspired their 'backing' them so.

Here are a few questions which help you to figure out whether you are a leader:

1 Think about who you follow? Do you have that effect on others?
2 Remember scale. Leadership happens on all sorts of levels. In what situations do other people invariably follow you?
3 Think about the relationship between leadership and confidence. In what contexts do you find yourself confident to lead?
4 Recall the great leaders. Those ones that inspire you. In what ways are you like them? Try not to be delusional about this. Think in what ways have I been like them and found others at least interested in what I'm doing or saying?
5 Try experimenting. Sharing your ideas, providing a lead, doing something in a different sort of a way. Then on reflection, asking did it make any difference to anyone? Did anyone follow you? Was anyone inspired? Did it connect with what anyone desired? Were they stirred to express approval? Did anyone say 'yeah'? Did they smile when you spoke out, in a good way?
6 Is your life progressive? In what ways are you ahead of the game? Where are you heading and is that where others would want to go? To use Peter Fisk's term, where is your head up (Fisk, 2010)? Where are you head and shoulders inspiringly above others? Does anybody know what's in your head – what you're thinking about, or what you stand for? And if your head has dropped, why should anyone follow?

RESPONSIBLE SELF-LEADERSHIP

Brown and Fields (2011) contribute an important notion to any examination of leadership, namely self-leadership. This section outlines a number of their key terms which not only expand our understanding of all that is involved in leadership, but also permit us to explore further the often implicit issue of 'Am I a leader?' or the more advanced question of 'How am I to develop as a leader?'

> *Internal locus of control* – Brown and Fields define this as 'the extent to which an individual believes they have control over the events and situations in their lives'. At first sight, this not only names a certain trait we associate with leaders but it also profoundly links to the existential considerations surrounding self-leadership as raised (see below) by Lips-Wiersma and Mills (2014). As Brown and Fields suggest, a person with a greater internal locus of control tends to believe that what results or happens is a consequence of their own efforts and decisions.

> *Internals and externals* – an internal is a person who believes that they have control over their own destiny. In contrast, an external is a person who believes 'outcomes are determined by factors or people outside their control' (Brown and Fields, 2011). So in the context of self-leadership, internals look to their own behaviour, whereas the focus for externals usually centres on luck or fate or the actions of others.

> *Self-regulation and self-efficacy* – if self-leadership fruitfully focuses on considering and directing one's own behaviour then the mechanisms that Brown and Fields label as self-regulation and self-efficacy have significance here. This suggests that self-leadership is bound up with submitting to one's own regulations, rather than looking to others to provide this. Self-efficacy is about breaking free from the approval of others, which for many people is metaphorically attached, like a drip.

Implications – responsible self-leadership

We could summarize self-leadership with the phrase, 'ultimately it's down to me'. It is healthy for the person to control their own destiny, to fashion themselves rather than be fashioned by others in terms of behaviour, to self-regulate and self-approve. We could alternatively present this as taking personal responsibility.

But the implication of our employing the term responsible self-leadership is to highlight that all these dimensions of self-leadership can be gathered up and directed to a responsible end – to control one's own destiny but with others in view; to fashion oneself to be useful to others as well as oneself; to self-regulate responsible behaviour and self-approve when one has acted responsibly.

Applying the research of Lips-Wiersma and Mills (2014) suggests how existentialist thinking might inform our search for both finding meaningful work and making secured work more meaningful. In both it is important to counter the tendency for individuals to lose a sense of self through becoming subject to certain instrumental pressures.

The research of Lips-Wiersma and Mills might prompt us to ask a series of penetrating and revealing questions:

- How are you working towards finding employment truly reflecting who you are?
- To what extent do you view yourself as an 'inevitable victim of circumstance'?
- What adjustments might enable you to find meaningful work, or work meaningful?
- Have you in any respect drifted away from what you want?

A number of themes these questions highlight are particularly relevant in the contemporary context of the struggle to find employment that suits the individual, or to capture (or re-capture) a sense of work being meaningful:

- *Connectedness* – the possibilities created through connecting with others: realizing common struggles; acting as resource to one another; knowing each other beyond instrumentally being part of an organization function.
- *Autonomy and independence* – avoiding 'being in others' as Sartre (1957) warned against – being the pawns and visions of others, rather than being our authentic selves (Lips-Wiersma and Mills, 2014).
- *Decision responsibility* – accepting that we are the ultimate arbiters of our decisions (Lips-Wiersma and Mills, 2014) and avoiding what Sartre (1957) referred to as acting in 'bad faith' in failing to understand our own essential responsibility for making decisions.

LEADERS IN SUSTAINABILITY

Fisk draws out a helpful distinction between what he terms as a 'new leadership mindset', one centred on the difference sustainability can make, from an outdated leadership mindset that regards sustainability as non-core and a threat (Fisk, 2010).

Below are listed ten of Fisk's new sustainability mindset characteristics with added interpretative notes:

1 Core – the new leadership mindset does not marginalize or overlook the significance of sustainability.
2 Opportunity – the new leadership mindset sees the sustainability agenda as opportunity, not threat.
3 Innovation – the new leadership mindset goes beyond compliance to sustainability norms and standards. It transcends this attitude by innovating around sustainability.
4 Profit – the new leadership mindset recognizes the potential sustainability has for profitability.
5 Breakthrough – the new leadership mindset seeks to see and achieve a breakthrough in the area of sustainability.
6 Global and responsible – the new leadership mindset is allied to wider global and responsible perspectives.
7 Systemic solutions – the new leadership mindset seeks systemic solutions to sustainability challenges.
8 Proactive – the new leadership mindset is proactive not reactive with regard to sustainability.
9 Quantifiable – the new leadership mindset seeks to quantify sustainability gains and targets.
10 Short and long term – the new leadership mindset doesn't regard sustainability as purely a long-term concern.

MODELS OF GOVERNANCE

Here we introduce two models of governance: the shareholder and stakeholder approaches; and the ground-breaking King codes.

Shareholder and stakeholder

You will recall that in Chapter 13 we introduced the distinction made by Andreason (2009) between the shareholder and stakeholder approaches. Out of this differentiation emerge two models of corporate governance outlined in Table 14.1:

Table 14.1 Two models of corporate governance (Andreason, 2009)

Shareholder model	The corporation is viewed as an extension of its owners, and ultimately responsible to them
	Most common in liberal market economies, e.g. United States and the UK
	Sometimes referred to as Anglo-Saxon (or stock market) capitalism

(Continued)

Table 14.1 (Continued)

Stakeholder model	The corporation is viewed as a 'social entity', responsible and accountable to a broader set of actors
	Most common in coordinated market economies, e.g. Germany and Japan
	Sometimes referred to as Rhineland (or welfare) capitalism

In the wake of the Enron crisis highlighting corporate governance failure on a huge scale, business organizations came to recognize the enormous costs involved in such collapses, not only the cost to investors but also the incalculable human costs suffered by workers, their communities and the fallout felt by partners, i.e. supplier businesses, landed with loss of trade and bad debts.

The King codes

Out of a quite different context, post-apartheid South Africa yet another model of governance emerged. Taking their name from Mervyn E. King, the country's three published reports on corporate governance constitute what are often referred to as the King codes:

- King I published in 1994
- King II published in 2002 (Institute of Directors, 2002)
- King III published in 2009 (Institute of Directors, 2009)

Our particular interest in them here is that, as Robinson and Dowson highlight, they put ethics very much at the centre of governance (Robinson and Dowson, 2012).

Andreason (2009) presents the significance of the King reports as follows:

- They attempted to balance a wide array of interests and rights encompassing the company, the government, employees, shareholders and even the environment.
- They constituted a hybrid model combining aspects of both shareholder and stakeholder interests fitted to suit the local and specific context of post-apartheid South Africa.
- They took into consideration key social realities such as uneven development, extreme inequalities and unsettled, uncertain state-business relations.
- King II recommended triple bottom line reporting (see below).

The King reports, Andreason highlights, became 'notable examples of how an emerging market can devise its own solutions to aligning corporate governance with international best practice while also addressing CSR and needs for broad-based development' (Andreason, 2009).

In *Business Ethics in Practice* Robinson and Dowson (2012) provide a detailed overview of King II and King III as well as outlining the significance of the Sabanes-Oxley Act, 2002 and the Combined code (2006 and 2010) as responses to the Enron disaster.

Of particular note, they argue, is King's six-stage process of governing ethical performance summarized below:

1. Identifying through stakeholder engagement the perceptions and expectations that stakeholders have of the ethical performance of a company.
2. Determining the company's ethical values and standards and codifying them in a code of ethics.
3. Institutionalizing the values and code of ethics of a company in terms of both its strategy and its systems.
4. Monitoring and evaluating compliance to the code of ethics.
5. Accounting and auditing ethical performance according to emerging global standards on ethical accounting and auditing.
6. Disclosing ethical performance to relevant stakeholders.

The third stage is significant in its emphasis on companies venturing beyond purely implementing a code of ethics, to make a change to company culture. In King III onus is put on the board to change the culture of the board itself, making it move in the direction of pursuing ethical thinking and in the light of this continually defining and re-evaluating the purpose, aims and values of the organization (Robinson and Dowson, 2012).

Robinson and Dowson also include a section on the philosophy of the King III report. They highlight that in King III leadership is characterized in terms of four core ethical values:

1. responsibility
2. accountability
3. fairness
4. transparency.

Leadership forms a key function, particularly in the South African context, of building a bridge between business and society, where business takes account of its social environment, adopting a stakeholder-inclusive approach.

Significantly, also in King III, sustainability is viewed as the primary ethical and economic imperative of the twenty-first century. Governance is called upon to genuinely integrate nature, society and business and this integration should be reflected in both reporting and development (Robinson and Dowson, 2012).

Perhaps, however, the most exciting thing about the King codes follows on from Andreason's point that they constitute a hybrid 'African model' of governance, suited for its 'hybrid society' (Andreason, 2009). In view of the fluidity and shifting nature of late modernity in Europe and beyond, experiencing hybridity also, the King reports have added significance.

TRIPLE BOTTOM LINE

Robinson and Smith argue that over time corporate social responsibility with its emphasis on the relationship of business to the local community evolved into the so called triple bottom line approach (Robinson and Smith, 2014). This involves an organization reporting not only with respect to its financial performance but also providing an account of its relationship to the social and physical environments as well. The proliferation of these different styles of reporting, Robinson and Dowson say, amounts to 'ethical accounting' (Robinson and Dowson, 2012).

One size does not fit all and there are a number of tools organizations utilize to report on the social and environmental performance of the organization. We shall examine two of these tools below. Firstly, the BIRG (Business Impact Review Group) framework developed by Business in the Community (BITC) and secondly, the international ISO 26000 standard.

The BIRG framework defines key indicators for measuring an organization's social and environmental performance in four impact areas particularly with a view to reporting on performance including:

- the marketplace
- the environment
- the community
- the workplace.

Although only a small selection of indicators for each of the impact areas is shown in Table 14.2, one of the great values of the framework is that it permits organizations to quantify performance, particularly in areas that would have the greatest significance for shareholders and stakeholders. Of course, this form of accounting is open to manipulation, however, there is increasing scrutiny from all quarters as to how organizations are succeeding with respect to the environment and in their treatment of their workforces especially.

Table 14.2 BIRG model example indicators in its four impact areas

Marketplace	Environment
• Customer complaints, about products and services • Customer satisfaction levels • Upheld cases of anti-competitive behaviour	• Overall energy consumption • Water usage • Solid waste produced by weight • Environmental impact over the supply chain
Community	**Workplace**
• Individual value of staff time, gifts in kind and managerial costs • Impact evaluations carried out on community programmes • Perception measures of company as a good neighbour	• Staff absenteeism • Staff turnover • Value of the training and development provided for staff • Number of staff grievances

The ISO 26000 standard developed by the well-respected International Standardization Organization was created to achieve an international consensus on what social responsibility means in practice. Guidance is provided in translating principles into effective actions. The intention was also to disseminate information about what constitutes best practice.

Examination of the standard's subjects (see Table 14.3) organized into seven core areas illustrates how wide is the scope of what is included under the heading of social responsibility. It is therefore more likely that a larger organization rather than a SME would seek to implement ISO26000.

Table 14.3 The scope of ISO26000 and its seven core areas of social responsibility

Fair operating practices

- Fair competition
- Social responsibility in the value chain
- Anti-corruption

Consumer issues

- Sustainable consumption
- Fair marketing
- Consumer data protection

The environment

- Sustainable resource use
- Climate change and business
- Protection of the environment
- Pollution prevention

Organizational governance

- Integrating social responsibility with company strategy and operations
- Regular reviewing of actions and practices
- Internal and external communication on social responsibility
- Internal competency for social responsibility

Human rights

- Adhering to fundamental principles and rights at work
- Upholding economic, social, political and cultural rights
- Avoidance of complicity

Community involvement and development

- Community action and involvement
- Employment creation and skills development

Labour practices

- Work conditions
- Health and safety at work
- Training and development

ETHICAL CODING

Ethical coding comes in all shapes and sizes. In one sense we should probably refer to it as ethical encoding, because a code is a form of communication intended for its reader. It is usually the product of some serious thinking, but it doesn't follow that that thinking is particularly rigorous or the product of real conviction. There are 'hollow' codes as well as ones that display an obvious weight and commitment.

We could also speak of ethical decoding, because at the same time a code is only as strong and as relevant as it is adopted or followed. This is leads us to Paul Ricoeur's profound concept of Mimesis 1, 2, and 3, which is outlined briefly below.

KEY CONCEPT – PAUL RICOUER'S MIMESIS 1, 2, 3

Paul Ricoeur (see Parris, 2002) would refer to a code as a text. Texts are not just pieces of writing but constitute the varied ways in which human beings communicate something and come to communicate with one another. A piece of art, or an item of clothing, or a car, or an example of architecture, or a song are all examples of text. If you think about it these texts are everywhere and in some senses they compete.

The creators or users of these texts are encoding (or communicating) something through the text. Ricoeur refers to this as Mimesis 2. Applied to a business code it is a creation of sorts and it inevitably fulfils a function of what its author or authors intended, or somehow wanted to communicate.

But the profound thing about texts of all kinds is that what results is something more and something different from what the authors intended. Because what is encoded must also be decoded. Ricoeur's Mimesis 3 is the term we can apply to all that emerges from the act of something being communicated and that same something being interpreted and applied by another. So the business code is not just what was communicated (encoded if you like). It is also what is decoded and more particularly how the reader or user of the code transforms it, as they receive it and apply it in their practice. This probably explains why a code that is effectively dead, is one which fails to win the hearts and minds of the decoder. Mimesis 2 has taken place in the production of a text, but Mimesis 3 amounts to little or nothing.

What of Mimesis 1? This is Paul Ricoeur's term for what pertained before the text was created. An example might be, what pertained before the American Declaration of Independence? It was a different world, or put another way, when the text of the Declaration was authored and published (Mimesis 2) it changed the world in a profound manner. Mimesis 3 was startling.

Applied to business, there is the situation that pertains now (Mimesis 1). Into this situation a code might be created and published (Mimesis 2). Its reception and adoption, its very application could be startling (Mimesis 3). Put like this, it is easy to see the significance that a code might have, but in the end only if it is written, unveiled and promoted in such a way that it captures hearts and imaginations. That the reader of the 'text' wants in their freedom to pick it up and run with it.

A good starting reference for Paul Ricoeur's Mimesis 1, 2, 3 is Kim Atkins' entry for Ricoeur in the *Internet Encyclopedia of Philosophy* (2006).

We can speak of there being three types of codes:

- codes of ethics
- codes of practice
- codes of conduct

Codes of ethics

These are determined by those responsible for the governance of an organization. We could refer to those governing the organization, in many organizations functionally fulfilled by a board of directors and shareholders, as the gatekeepers of codes of ethics. Whether a code of ethics is adopted or not, and in what sense it is pursued or promoted, is a responsibility that profoundly rests with the board or the governing function of any organization. The board doesn't have to author a code of ethics, but it must in the end sanction its specific content. It is the responsibility of governance to do this, whether they penned the code or not. The code, as it were, has their names written on it.

Codes of practice

These are determined by external governing bodies. In any professional context there is usually a code of practice. Following a code of practice is what it means to be a professional and it is very important that it constitutes an external reference to the individual who has adopted it and who follows. It is in the professional's mind what the code says, what the code demands of them. It provides guidance, some might say 'wisdom', on how to operate – as to what practice is good practice and what practice falls short of this.

A professional code of practice therefore provides checks and balances and does so in at least two ways. Firstly, as alluded to above, it operates with the humanity and even fallibility of the practitioner who, at the same time as fulfilling a professional function, is a person. A professional code of practice should help the person to give their best to their function. This is not to suggest that this amounts to giving their 'all' as it is sometimes expressed. Professionalism has boundaries and ethical practice recognizes not only the needs of clients and the needs of the organization, but also the needs of the practitioner themselves as a person.

Secondly, a professional code of practice provides checks and balances against the commercial aspects of business. What is most profitable to do is often not the same thing as what is professionally ethical to do. An example of this is how the professional allocates their time. The balance to be achieved here is that the organization is employing the individual, and in addition to this there is the need of the client or customer, and in addition to this there are other demands on the professional's time. One can quickly see here that a code of professional practice, external to the organization and external to the pressure on the professional's time, is a useful and resourceful reference to have.

Codes of conduct

Codes of conduct are determined by HRM departments and again their significance as fulfilling a guiding role is that they are external to the individual. Interestingly also they govern the actions of employees both inside and, often, outside of the organization.

At first sight we probably associate codes of conduct as 'thou shalt not' – as highlighting or underlining the myriad things and behaviours that are not permitted or acceptable in the employment or as an employee of a given organization. A number of areas immediately come to mind:

- one's use of language
- standards of honesty
- matters of sexual ethics
- disrespectful behaviour
- use of company time
- balancing employment responsibilities with one's personal life
- bullying and discrimination
- what it means to be professional.

It is plain to see that there clearly needs to be employee codes of conduct and especially so given the fact that the west has decidedly moved in the direction of upholding appropriate behaviour as a matter of law.

It is, however, increasingly prevalent to see more positively framed codes of conduct or parts thereof in the workplace. These might include:

- posters or displays highlighting traits and positive behaviours the organization is encouraging
- work surrounding what it means to be a '[company name] woman' or '[company name] man' or simply '[company name]', this being a form of employee profiling
- company rituals that communicate the positive behaviours implicitly expected of employees.

CASE STUDY – MÉDECINS SANS FRONTIÈRES

Médecins Sans Frontières (MSF) is a respected name in the international arena and there is no doubt about the organization's and its workers' commitment to a profoundly ethical purpose – to offer medical care to those facing conflict and endemic diseases, irrespective of ethnicity, religion or any other factor.

Founded in 1971 MSF has an annual budget of approximately US $400 million and 19 national offices, known as sections. Our case highlights aspects of its governance which are particularly notable in a number of respects.

MSF has over time produced three core documents outlining its principles and core understandings. This reflects an evolution of core values and the recognition of the need to specify rules of operating.

- The MSF Charter – consisting of four clear statements (Médecins Sans Frontières, 2014). Of particular interest to us here is the paragraph that reads: 'members undertake to respect their professional code of ethics and to maintain complete independence from all political, economic or religious powers'. This puts clear onus on its medics and other workers to operate both professionally and impartially. The core values of neutrality and impartiality are clear in the MSF Charter.
- Chantilly Principles – added in 1994 in the wake of the Rwanda genocide where mass human rights violations occurred under the eyes of humanitarian agency workers, causing MSF to rethink its position and even identity. Witnessing (termed *temoignage*) was added as a core value which involves the duty to raise public awareness of the plight of people in danger and the 'last resort' as it is stated, of denouncing breaches of international conventions (Médecins Sans Frontières, 1994). Practical rules of operating were also specified here including a Section 4 on financial control and transparency.
- La Mancha Agreement – a further 'reference document' as it describes itself, divided into two sections, one Action section and another Governance section, each containing 14 rules to be followed. What is extraordinary about La Mancha is how it expresses a 'self-critical' awareness on the part of MSF who openly acknowledge failures as well as successes and challenges. This is the kind of spirit, if not attitude, on the part of an organization that permits it to produce what we might term a living code. The La Mancha Agreement states that the issues it raises will be regularly reviewed (Médecins Sans Frontières, 2006). Rule 1.12 in the Action section to address any misunderstanding of its purpose states, 'Although justice is essential, MSF differs from justice organizations by not taking on the responsibility for the development of international justice and does not gather evidence for the specific purpose of international courts or tribunals'. Rule 2.12 in the Governance section underlines the value of dialogue given the diversities contained by the organization by stating, 'considering that diversity of opinion in MSF is critical to the vitality of the movement if agreement on a common position is not possible, it is acceptable that a majority and minority position co-exist'.

In 2013, MSF withdrew from Somalia after 22 years working there; 16 staff members had died in violent incidents and many others had been

(Continued)

(Continued)

intimidated, threatened and abducted. According to Simon Allison (2013) MSF had been pushed over its danger threshold. It was of course a governance responsibility to be ever mindful of the safety of MSF teams of workers. This expresses the gatekeeping responsibility of governance, as we described it. This is not just a matter of defining what is acceptable and encouraged, differentiating this from what is not acceptable and discouraged – but also that equally essential role of governance in drawing lines, of stating 'this far and no further'.

APPLIED PERSONAL DEVELOPMENT

The key personal development issue that arises from this chapter is are you a leader and how might you develop your leadership skills along responsible lines? I hope it is clear that leadership takes place in many different contexts and operates on many levels. Reviewing the different theories of leadership highlights that there are many ways of leading or that leadership involves many things.

Undoubtedly Post-Enron and in view of the undeniable need for leaders to engage with issues surrounding multiculturalism and globalization, the responsible leader has come of age. Added to this, the massive emphasis now on sustainability, both environmental and social sustainability, means that business leaders must instinctively think 'triple bottom line'.

Poetically perhaps, Robinson and Smith (2014) caused us to consider the Ulysses myth. There is much about all the dangers and delights of his epic voyage that is akin, in the twenty-first century, to the situation that business leaders find themselves confronted by. A narrow 'transactionalist' or even transformational leadership approach that irresponsibly underestimates complexity inherent in the external and internal business environments will soon be exposed as inadequate. This challenges all leaders to open their eyes to the shifting, fluid (Bauman) realities of late modernity.

How is an organization governed? Consider taking the time to research the often 'shadowy', i.e. little known, figures that direct and guide, particularly sizeable business organizations. It's a huge responsibility and this chapter has revealed all that is involved with the 'gatekeeping' function of governance. To code or not to code, and how to code, are certainly central concerns of governance.

You might have a future in governance. You might find yourself becoming a school governor. Like leadership responsibilities, all personal experience particularly when reflected upon, yields key developmental pointers.

REFERENCES

Alimo-Metcalfe, B. and Alban-Metcalfe, J. (2005) 'Leadership: time of change for a new direction', *Leadership*, 1 (1): 51–71.

Allison, S. (2013) 'Sans Médecins Sans Frontières', *Good Governance Africa*. Available at: http://gga.org/editions/aif-17-taking-the-pulse/sans-medecins-sans-frontieres (accessed 10 March 2014).

Andreason, S. (2009) 'Understanding corporate governance reform in South Africa: Anglo-American divergence, the King reports, and hybridization', *Business Society*, 50: 647–673.

Atkins, K. (2006) 'Paul Ricoeur (1913–2005)', *The Internet Encyclopedia of Philosophy*. Available at: www.iep.utm.edu/ricoeur/ (accessed 27 October 2014).

Bass, B. (2005) *Transformational Leadership*. New York: Erlbaum.

Brown, R. T. and Fields, D. (2011) 'Leaders engaged in self-leadership: can followers tell the difference?', *Leadership*, 7 (3): 275–293.

Burns, J. (1978) *Leadership*. New York: Harper and Row.

Campbell, R. and Kitson, A. (2008) *The Ethical Organisation*. Basingstoke: Palgrave Macmillan.

Ciulla, J. (ed.) (2004) *Ethics, the Heart of Leadership*. Westport: Praeger.

Covey, S. (2009) *Principle Centred Leadership*. London: Simon & Schuster.

Fisk, P. (2010) *People, Planet, Profit: How to Embrace Sustainability for Innovation and Business Growth*. London: Kogan Page.

Gill, R. (2006) *Theory and Practice of Leadership*. London: Sage.

Greenleaf, R. (1977) *The Servant as Leader: A Journey into the Nature of Legitimate Power and Greatness*. New York: Paulist Press.

Institute of Directors (2009) *King III Report on Corporate Governance*. Johannesburg: Institute of Directors in Southern Africa.

Institute of Directors (2002) *King II Report on Corporate Governance*. Johannesburg: Institute of Directors in Southern Africa.

The Internet Encyclopedia of Philosophy (2006) 'Paul Ricoeur (1913–2005)'. Available at: www.iep.utm.edu/ricoeur/ (accessed 22 June 2014).

Laub, J. (2004) 'Defining servant leadership: a recommended typology for servant leadership studies', *Proceedings of the 2004 Servant Leadership Research Round Table*. School of Leadership Studies, Regent University. Available at: www.regent.edu/acad/global/publications/sl_proceedings/2004/laub_defining_servant.pdf (accessed 27 October 2014).

Lips-Wiersma, M. and Mills, A. J. (2014) 'Understanding the basic assumptions about human nature in workplace spirituality: beyond the critical versus positive divide', *Journal of Management Inquiry*, 23 (2): 148–161.

Médecins Sans Frontières (2014) The Médecins Sans Frontières Charter. Available at: http://association.msf.org/Charter (accessed 10 March 2014).

Médecins Sans Frontières (2006) Final – La Mancha Agreement – 25 June 2006, Athens. Available at: http://association.msf.org/sites/default/files/documents/La%20Mancha%20Agreement%20EN.pdf (accessed 10 March 2014).

Médecins Sans Frontières (1994) The Chantilly principles. Available at: http://association.msf.org/sites/default/files/documents/Principles%20Chantilly%20EN.pdf (accessed 10 March 2014).

Parris, D. P. (2002) 'Imitating the parables: allegory, narrative and the role of mimesis', *Journal for the Study of the New Testament*, 25 (1): 33–53.

Robinson, S. and Dowson, P. (2012) *Business Ethics in Practice*. London: CIPD.

Robinson, S. and Smith, J. (2014) *Co-charismatic Leadership: Critical Perspectives on Spirituality, Ethics and Leadership*. Bern: Peter Lang.

Sartre, J. P. (1957) *Being and Nothingness: An Essay on Phenomenological Ontology*. New York: Philosophical Library.

Schwartz, J. (2002) 'Darth Vader. Machiavelli. Skilling sets intense pace', *New York Times*, 7 February.

Sherman, S. (2002) 'Enron: uncovering the uncovered story', *Columbia Journalism Review*, 40: 22–28.

Western, S. (2008) *Leadership: A Critical Text*. London: Sage.

PART IV
HUMANITY AND FUTURES

15 SUPPORTING RESOURCES

Learning outcomes

When you have completed this chapter you will be able to:

- identify what it means to belong to Generation Y
- understand the significance of the so called 'time between times' as experienced by the 19-something student

(Continued)

(Continued)

- appreciate the normality of personal challenges experienced at university
- deconstruct what makes for this being a time that is emotionally super-charged
- see the significance of others in one's flourishing
- story one's way forward.

A GENERATIONAL THING

We must never lose sight of the fact that 'people are people'. The development of an empathic outlook is a two-part process. Part 1 permits a person to identify things of value they have experienced first-hand from others. For example, that being honoured feels good and is better than being dishonoured. Or similarly that being the recipient of kindness trumps unkindness. In Part 2 this learning and experience is extended to others. We consider what we have found valuable and behave similarly towards others.

However, at the same time there is a generational thing going on. One generation is not characteristically the same as the next one, or the one before it. Hansen and Leuty (2011) speak of four generations working side-by-side. For that matter, these four generations are also living together in families, households and neighbourhoods. They can all, for example, be found on a golf course, in the supermarket and enjoying the park on a sunny day. Hansen and Leuty also inform us of what the different generations are known as and critically, in terms of date of birth, where one generation ends and the next generation begins, as shown in Table 15.1.

Table 15.1   A typology of the generations

Generation	Date of birth	Alternative labels
Silent generation	1925–1945	
Baby Boomers	1946–1964	boomers
Generation X	1965–1980	X-ers, the 13th generation
Generation Y	After 1980	millennials, dot.com generation, the internet generation

GENERATION Y

Our focus will be on Generation Y, which includes you if you're reading this and you were born after 1980. Erik Erikson wrote and theorized around the notion of the generations needing one another for people of all ages to develop and flourish. In his book, *Childhood and Society* (1965) he argued it was fashionable to highlight a kind of one-way dependence of a younger generation on an older one, when in reality the dependence is mutual (Erikson, 1965). This has important implications for each generation respecting the significance of not only their own generation but also the significance of others. Ageism in this context might be thought of not only as disregarding and disrespecting those of another generation, but also as profoundly disrupting a significant developmental process and potential.

KEY CONCEPT – HABITUS

Eyerman and Turner (1998) define generation as 'people passing through time who come to share a common habitus, hexis and culture, a function which is to provide them with a collective memory that serves to integrate the generation over a finite period of time'.

Zopiatis et al. (2012) highlight the significance of the distinctive character and experiences of the generations for their achieving a comfortable co-existence in the workplace. This provides a potent way to comprehend the significance of equal opportunities thinking, applied to age and the danger of ageism as a source of disharmony and conflict in the workplace.

Here we want to enlarge on the concept of habitus, most famously associated with the French late twentieth-century sociologist Pierre Bourdieu (1930–2002). This should not be confused with the more familiar term habitat, referring to the material environment.

For Bourdieu, habitus comprised a set of cultural orientations or dispositions resulting from each individual's specific life experiences and membership of a particular social subgroup. The set of dispositions or attitudes not only reflect 'belonging' to a certain subgroup, but also enable individuals to play the game (or their part) within each 'social field' as Bourdieu puts it (Cohen and Kennedy, 2007).

Grace Jantzen, in her penetrating book, *Foundations of Violence* (2004), also highlights the significance of Bourdieu's concept of habitus. For the member of a subgroup their behaviour is what Bourdieu terms 'practical sense' (Bourdieu, 1998). Jantzen (2004) thinks of this as a spontaneous 'common sense' that derives from a whole socialization including the internalization of the subgroup's structure of language, social rules and patterns referred to as the 'symbolic'.

The implications of the habitus, Jantzen argues, are as follows:

- It enables us to make sense of how people in the same society can behave in quite different ways.
- Habitus is not inborn, but socially constructed.

(Continued)

(Continued)

- People are resistant to the disruption of their settled habitus and find ways of avoiding getting into situations where it might be challenged.
- The dispositions as highlighted feel entirely natural, being the product of a long socialization and training.
- It may be accurate to speak of individuals as being in the grip of a dominant symbolic system.

GENERATION Y'S CHARACTERISTICS

The workplace is a good place to begin in identifying the characteristics of Generation Y. Zopiatis et al. (2012) have collated the findings of 48 pieces of research which profile the occupational characteristics of Generation Y placed alongside those of Generation X and Generation Baby Boomers. A selection of research findings is summarized in Table 15.2.

Table 15.2 A selection of research findings on the occupational characteristics of Generation Y (based on Zopiatis et al., 2012)

Occupational factors	Generation Y (selected) research findings
Views on authority	Challenge workplace norms
Attitude towards motivation	Motivated when managers connect their actions to personal and career goals
Views on recognition	More narcissist than other generations – not good at taking criticism
Views on loyalty	Less loyal to the company and more 'me' oriented
Views on work–life balance	Blend work and play
Technological orientation	Intense users of high technology
Attitude towards rewards	Individual development is very important
Views on change	Addicted to change
Individualists or team players	Expect diversity
Lazy v. hard working	Perceived as slackers by other generations
Views on supervision and guidance	Want managers who empower them and who are open and positive
Views on work schedules	Not willing to give up their personal activities due to work
Views on career	Prefer a job that has meaning
Views on management style	Hate micro-management
Views on socialization at and off work	Prefer more frequent social interaction with their managers

Occupational factors	Generation Y (selected) research findings
Attitudes towards respect	Tend to value respect
Views on reliability	If treated professionally they are likely to act professionally
Local or global thinkers	Globally concerned
Views on learning ability	Learn best by collaborating
Views on single/multi-tasking	Multi-tasking is a habit

Even a brief review of Generation Y at work highlights something of their individuality and their departure in style and attitude to previous generations. For example, the research suggests the Baby Boomers generation, when compared to Generation Y is generally in the workplace contrastingly technologically challenged by the digital age (Zopiatis et al., 2012). On global thinking, the research suggests a greater consciousness of concern by Generation Y when compared to Generation X (Zopiatis et al., 2012). Attitude to change shows pronounced change across the generations with Baby Boomers most resistant and Generation X more adaptive, culminating in Generation Y embracing it (Zopiatis et al., 2012).

Below we have distilled these characteristics as observed in the workplace into four generic characteristics:

1 self-consciousness
2 the cult of youth
3 digitally defined
4 plurality.

Self-consciousness

Charles Jencks makes the interesting observation that 'self-consciousness' is a natural consequence of living in a post-Freudian age (Jencks, 1987). Freud kick-started a new way of looking at ourselves and others, allowing for complexity, personal history and even apparent contradiction. You will hear Generation Y sometimes described as 'narcissistic', meaning self-loving and self-absorbed. It might be more accurate to speak of the emergence of a self-project which amounts to managing and directing the multiple and varied self in relationship with equally polymorphous human beings.

Generation Y express this self-project in promoting and presenting themselves as a brand. Facebook and social media sites are, if you think about it, a form of self-advertising and self-promotion. This self-branding implies the possibility of a public persona that is some distance from the authentic self, a model being adopted by some celebrities. Overall, this socialization in putting oneself forward and 'out there' possibly accounts for Generation Y not being shy about expressing a sense of entitlement.

The cult of youth

We might describe Generation Y as the generation of youth, in a wider society that pursues the ideal of youthfulness. This is perhaps expressed in parents as well as their teenagers both enjoying Facebook. Jantzen (2004) speaks of a paradigmatically beautiful virile youth. Although all the generations in western society aspire to youthfulness and unfading beauty/sex-appeal, in Generation Y there is an evident ultra-avantgardism. Generation Y are even more daring and experimental than their seniors, and play and chance and desire figure prominently in all they do (Jencks, 1987).

Digitally defined

Generation Y view mobile technology as being empowering, and facilitating a way of being and operating whereby they can migrate between various roles and identities (Lindgren et al., 2002). Although this is an area of technology that has seen huge advances in recent years, Generation Y more than any generation before it has been able to surf this rapid change. Symbolically Generation Y are almost permanently attached to their mobile devices, suggesting an unyielding appetite for connection to a network of friends and contacts as well as the news, information and gossip they seek. Savage (2014) speaks of their swimming in the media revolution. Everyday interactions extend wider than those they are with in real time, creating a kind of dual existence that must be managed, at least in relation to the use of one's mobile devices.

Plurality

Generation Y has grown up seeing everywhere a fragmented, what Jencks calls 'violent' heterogeneity (Jencks, 1987). Inevitably this radical plurality, evident in myriad ways and styles of living, raises with it both adrenaline and anxiety. It calls for social adaptation and it amounts to the present-time impossibility of viewing the world monolithically. Jumbled living has resulted from globalization and the breakdown and disintegration in Europe of the so called Christian world. Generation Y are better placed than the older generations to both accept and inculcate this social and cultural revolution.

EMPLOYABILITY FOCUS – BOOMERS IN CHARGE

An important thing to keep in mind is that although all the generations are represented in the workplace, the distribution of power across the generations is unequal and it is the Baby Boomers who are, for the time being at least, the dominant generation in terms of occupying positions of senior leadership and management. What might be the implications for employability if the leaders are 'Boomers' and more often than not male?

In terms of getting through the selection process and advancement within organizations this might have significance for the younger generations. It may be prudent for them to understand how Boomers think and know how to relate positively to those born roughly between 1946 and 1964.

Returning to the research of Zopiatis et al. (2012) we have summarized below using key words (where possible) some of the attitudes and ways associated with the Boomers:

- respect authority
- seniority over merit
- loyal to organizations
- live to work
- materialistic
- highly competitive
- celebrate individualism
- hard to gain their respect
- confident task-completers
- weaker on multi-tasking.

If you're in the Generation Y category (born after 1980) perhaps think about parents or other members of your family who are Boomers. Listen out for their attitudes and practise relating to them!

A TIME BETWEEN TIMES

Jon Savage appositely speaks of a time of hiatus, between youthful dependence and adult responsibility (Savage, 2014). Here, we have labelled these late teenage and early-twenties years as a time between times. It represents a time of transition between youth and belonging in every sense to the full-adult order.

Adopting the familiar metaphor of life being likened to a journey we have organized our examination of this unfolding and explorative period of life around a number of sections:

Prominent features – what are the main characteristics of being 19-something? Or put another way, what are the sorts of things that are typical about this time period in a young adult's life?

At that time of the night – as the title suggests, this section comments on some of the exhilarations, or they can be pressure points, for young adults.

We're familiar with the phrase, 'no pressure'. Some appear to breeze through this time. Usually, however, the pressure is felt one way or another.

The landscape of emotions – here we deconstruct some of the feelings that are flying around the world inhabited by young adults at university. You will note that they're universal to being human, nevertheless a 19-year-old inevitably navigates these feelings in a different way to how a 9-year-old or 29-year-old might.

Obstacles – the human experience also presents us with many challenges, which we've labelled here as obstacles. Our purpose remember in this chapter is to highlight for individuals reading it that they are not alone in experiencing their journey and to suggest ways of understanding what's going on for them at a time of huge transition.

Prominent features

Belonging and groupings

The first prominent feature we could summarize with the phrase, 'only connect'. Often leaving a home town behind and venturing to a new city involves a re-ordering of relationships. The student seeks new friendships, which when analysed speak of the importance of connecting to others.

Not only is this a time of new friendships, it often involves attaching oneself to new groups, all of which can make for a sense of belonging. The student becomes a member of a cohort on a course. They will be attached to a particular school of studies and/or a university college. They will probably join a club or a society reflecting an existing or new interest. And last, but certainly not least, they will invariably find a group of people they end up spending a lot of their time with.

Inevitably, there is an element of adventure mixed with some anxiety in all this process of discovery and re-ordering. Some find 'fit' more easily than others. Some gain a new sense of settled 'place', others feel out of place, at least for a time. Often the people one first gets to know at university are not necessarily the people who are one's closest friends by the end of the course. The key here is to try and remember this and give oneself time to settle and connect with others.

Examining their patterns of new studying, social or romantic relationships at university students might ask themselves:

1 Do these reflect ongoing identifications (carried over from school days) or new identifications?
2 Do they reflect new found independence or perhaps even a rejection of parental values?
3 In what ways are these relationships bound up with public image/status?

Relationships and sexuality

Fields of gold to minefield – being 19-something will involve multiple feelings and experiences spanning this spectrum. The student needs to keep one eye here on the phrase, 'sexual health and wellbeing'. This amounts to something along the lines of remembering to be kind to oneself and to others and relates also to risk taking emotionally, sexually and in terms of one's health.

Like friendships one forms and groups one attaches oneself to, romantic relationships and sexuality are also expressions of identity. The young adult is 'finding their way' in this area, as they are in other areas of their life. Contrary to how this is often presented, romantic relationships represent an area of challenge (and often hurt) for adults of all ages.

Relationships and sexuality is a process of trial and error. Some people find what they are looking for; some people find mutuality (where feelings are reciprocated) and love; everybody it seems experiences break-ups and some heartache. There is no straight route to fulfilment here. When embarking on sexual relationships remember the issue of protection.

Universities have counselling services staffed by people who can assist when facing all manner of challenges and difficulties. One of the great generational progresses is that there is no stigma now in asking for help and support.

Adventure and exploration

Most adults beyond their twenties look back at the time around 19 with a degree of nostalgia. University won't necessarily be the time of your life, but university, the first time, is a time that can never be repeated. This again points to it having the quality of a time between times, venturing out into a new environment but as is the case with most (although not all) of those experiencing this life stage, there are fewer responsibilities than in the life stages that follow. The uniqueness of the time that is called 'university' is reflected in a number of key areas:

> *Freedom* – university facilitates multiple choices. Depending on one's cultural, family and school background the degree of freedom one discovers at university can represent a radical discontinuity from what went before. Freedom is invariably squandered to a certain degree, but learning here helps to awake a consciousness of making the most of this special time.

> *Identity formation* – we have made a number of references to the notion of this stage of life constituting a significant step forward in the area of identity formation. In Freudian terms, the individual has journeyed from departing the matrix that is the womb/mother to being dwarfed for a time by father and father figures to finding oneself somehow apart from parental influence/control. The question pops up more strongly than ever before, 'What do you want?' It's a kind of 'over to you now' and it can feel anything from heady to disconcerting.

Ideas formation – university is about exploring ideas. This is done through a process of not being told what one should think, but rather listening to multiple voices as we explore together (for many, as if for the first time) all the possibilities of where we might position ourselves. This is all part and parcel of what we might term 'ideas formation' and it applies not only to academic studies but also areas such as our lifestyles, our politics, our adopted values and our beliefs or religion.

YOUNG MAN LUTHER

You will recall in Chapter 2 we introduced the idea of life stages and looked at Isidore of Seville's division of a young life into infantia (0–7 years), pueritia (7–14 years) and adolescentia (14–28 years). This represents a different way of 'cutting the cake' than Erikson's scheme where the stage of adolescence approximates 13–19 years and the young adulthood stage follows, spanning a person's twenties and thirties.

A contrasting division here may relate to how differently a human life was structured or conceived following the gains made in modernity. The move to cities and away from work allied to the land led through time to increased life expectancy, a delay in the age of marriage and child-rearing and an elongated formal education before the beginnings of full-time employment. In Erikson's scheme the period around late adolescence is a time between times and according to Iverson (2010) was viewed by Erikson as the most critical period for identity development.

In *Young Man Luther* (1958) Erikson presents the emotional crises associated with late adolescence in his famous portrayal of the psychosocial development of Martin Luther. The usefulness of this work is that it not only portrays Luther's wrestling to develop his identity (his identity crises) but does so through telling us something of Luther's story and showing his so called 'inner landscape'. We have outlined some of what Erikson presents as Luther's struggles below:

Negative identity fragment – Erikson suggests that Luther's attitude to German peasants reflected his own ancestry and that in his family this constituted what Erikson terms a negative identity fragment, meaning an identity that Luther and his family wished to live down. Nietzsche, Erikson tells us, referred to Luther as a Bergmannssohn, a miner's son, but he honoured Luther for this.

Oedipus complex – Welchman (2000) says Erikson presents Luther as a young man 'troubled in his relations with his strict and sometimes brutal Father'. Erikson (1958) states clearly that we would most certainly ascribe to Luther an Oedipus complex, reflected in part by a love–hate relationship with his Father. He adds that Luther rebelled against his Father's wishes to join the monastery. This prefigured his later rebellion against the Church.

'I am not' – Erikson relates the story of how the young Luther, when experiencing a fit in the choir, reputedly spoke out the words 'I am not.' Erikson presents this fragment as both the repudiation of the accusation that he was mentally sick and/or what his Father said he was (Erikson, 1958). 'The raving and roaring suggest', argues Erikson, 'a strong element of otherwise suppressed rage'. This episode was part of Luther finding his voice – one that later became heard around the world.

Main executive of his identity – it took Luther some time to find what Erikson refers to as the main executive of his identity – as historical protestor and reformer.

Letting go – Erikson speaks of how Luther in due course 'finally learned to let himself go'. In Luther's case this was expressed not only in powerful oratory but in a 'towering temper'. He adds that Luther was the 'first revolutionary individualist' asserting himself and his ideas against the most powerful institution of his time.

Gathering all these threads together we can say that late adolescence encompasses the themes highlighted above:

- working out what you want to be identified with
- pursuing what you want over what your parents want
- not being pushed into being somebody you're not or pigeon-holed as being something less than you are
- discovering the main executives of your identity
- in authenticity, 'letting go' and being who you are.

Such expressions of individualism, of finding one's voice and expressing one's chosen identity may very well involve struggles of assertion.

At that time of the night

Savage speaks of these years as being 'emotionally supercharged' (Savage, 2014). This is not said from the standpoint of considering the 19-something young adult as over-the-top. It is probably much closer to remembering the pressure of this time, at times seen in emotions spilling over or individuals struggling to contain the sheer volume of emotions within.

It is a time to learn a new literacy in expressing emotions, not just for the approval and convenience of others, but for oneself as an individual. The challenge is double-sided. For some, it involves learning to be assertive and finding one's voice, both of which are enormously significant aspects of personal development. Classically this might be about discovering ways one can be true to oneself in saying 'no thank you' or 'yes please'. Personal boundaries and enlargement are defined through speaking thus. For others, the challenge is not so much outward, but inward – deciding not to suppress feelings as may be the individual's propensity or habit. Instead of 'pushing down' strong feelings that can lead sometimes to depressive and 'controlled' implosions, the new literacy here is about owning up, even to oneself, to what these feelings are about.

Kindlon and Thompson (1999) speak not only of the importance of emotional literacy, but also of the mask of silence and anger. The first takes the individual in the direction of emotional health, the latter in contrast points in the direction of a mental-health issue. They go on to argue that both genders would be fortified by developing language skills in this area (Kindlon and Thompson, 1999). Emotional awareness, they add, means individuals are less likely to inflict hurt on others.

Bringing some literacy to emotions, sometimes overwhelming ones, is not achieved either overnight or in a straight line. Again this is a learned process and older generations have by no means mastered this either. Rather, a pattern of oscillation is often evident in the young adult at university, now expressing angst and disorientation and next a contrasting longing for the approval of a peer or a parent.

'At that time of the night' is perhaps also a suitable heading to examine some aspects of the 'full-on' lifestyles lived by the youngest adults. Carolyn Jackson (2002) provides a vocabulary to examine some of its features.

Hedonistic practices

This term perhaps sounds loaded, however, it may simply betray the perspective of onlookers – an individual, group or generation that doesn't follow the associated 'excesses' from the perspective of the observers. Perhaps a more helpful term is 'experimental hedonism', involving having a laugh, unrestrained alcoholic consumption, a sportingly sexualized arena and overall the pursuit of a fun time. This has now achieved a status of becoming a social discourse followed by many people across the generations.

Competition

The pursuit of such a lifestyle may in an indirect fashion reflect, as Jackson puts it, a certain competition (Jackson, 2002). This might be about:

- wanting to be seen as successful
- enhancing a social media status
- being seen to be the best at dancing or drinking or comedy or 'pulling'
- denying or covering other ongoing concerns or needs not evident on a night out.

Masculinities

This is the term Jackson adopts for the assertion of masculine identity. It is something we'll return to in the ethics box below. At first sight it would appear as only applying to the male gender. Kenway and Fitzclarence (1997) speak of a hegemonic (i.e. ruling or dominant) masculinity and describe this as the standard-bearer of what it means to be a 'real' man. The assertion of this, of course, has huge implications not only for the male gender but for the female gender too.

Given the evident intensity of everything we have introduced in this section it is no wonder that the 19-something young adult tires and reasonably requires much sleep. Our bodies are partners in all our pleasures and sometimes pains. Coming to think of them as 'full partners' in our lives we often need to be reminded to look after them, nourishing them with lifestyles of diet and exercise that invite good health.

ETHICS BOX – MASCULINITIES AND GENDER EQUALITY

Masculinities constitute a more structural way of looking at gender equality. According to Amanda Sinclair (2000), most popular books steer clear of the subject, preferring instead to emphasize what she terms an individual perspective on this key issue. For Karlsson and Karkara (2004) a masculinities approach to gender equality takes us back to how girls and boys in all societies are socialized differently and how the gender-based expectations people grow up with profoundly impact their lives, relationships and careers.

Karlsson and Karkara (2004) argue, 'Boys and young men learn that it is considered masculine to be strong and dominate, violent, sexually active, not to show emotions and inner feelings, and to exercise authority over women and children'. In the workplace, Sinclair suggests that power (and privilege) is often in the hands of men, what she refers to as 'traditional corporate masculinities'.

We outline below the implications of a masculinities perspective for the key matter of gender equality and the health, well-being and flourishing of the sexes in the workplace and beyond:

Denial – Sinclair (2000) suggests that those in positions of authority in the workplace or occupying the dominant group don't experience discrimination and therefore often don't recognize it. The answer here might be to listen to the accounts of those outside the dominant group that have experienced discrimination.

Categorization – the assumption is usually made that matters of gender are about women (Sinclair, 2000). This betrays a tendency in

(Continued)

(Continued)

> organizations to fall short of deconstructing how particular types of masculine cultures overlook the nature and extent of their impact on men as well as women.
>
> *Overarching* – if gender equality is an overarching as well as individual issue in society this highlights that there is a need to examine, as Sinclair puts it, 'how masculinities are produced and perpetuated within the broader social structure' (Sinclair, 2000).
>
> *Self-discovery* – Karlsson and Karkara (2004) argue that the women's movement has pushed men into the same journey of self-discovery. This may suggest why men are often not as able as women in terms of exploration, openness, interaction and expressiveness. Certain masculine cultures may stifle such self-discovery and self-expression. There is of course great significance in men being equipped and able to express themselves and solve their conflicts verbally.
>
> *Sexuality* – Karlsson and Karkara (2004) also mention the notion of male control over female sexuality. What would greater gender equality in the area of sexuality look like? Or put another way, how different would sexuality and sexual expression play out if power was truly shared rather than unequal.

The landscape of emotions

The full landscape of human emotions is of course incredibly varied. Below we outline some of the most typical emotions as commonly experienced.

Anxiety

It is not difficult to discern anxiety in oneself. It makes its presence felt in all sorts of ways in our bodies, registering with us that it wants to be heard. Depending on the individual it might manifest itself in a number of ways:

* tingling face, hands or limbs
* dizziness, difficulty breathing and palpitations
* stomach or chest pains
* exhaustion and feelings of fatigue
* difficulties in sleeping or eating
* difficulties concentrating and making decisions.

Trethowan and Sims (1983) differentiate between normal anxiety and so called morbid anxiety. Normal anxiety is anxiety that is proportionate to the situation that warrants it. In contrast, morbid anxiety Trethowan and Sims describe as 'objectless fear' or 'fear displaced on to some relatively neutral object or situation' and add that it is fear disproportionate to that which gives rise to it. In cases of both normal and morbid anxiety they argue that 'steps must be taken to overcome it' (Trethowan and Sims, 1983).

Lader (1975) distinguishes between 'state anxiety' and 'trait anxiety' where state anxiety refers to feeling anxious at particular times, whereas trait anxiety is a habitual tendency to be anxious. The general anxiety felt in the time between times in young adulthood is probably somewhere in the middle of state and trait. There is plenty of ammunition for young adults to feel in a state of anxiety. This can all too easily bleed into becoming an anxiety trait.

Anger

We all experience anger. It can betray a feeling of exposure. If a person is exposed in some way – in a way that is certainly unwanted – it will result in anger. For example, someone might feel shame or humiliation in the face of something being said or coming to light. Or it might relate to fear of exposure in a social or relational context, heightened where the people really 'matter' to the individual.

Continuing with the exposure theme, anger may be the result of being subjected to all manner of difficulties that leave the individual with a sense of injustice or feeling inadequate, struggling to know how to respond. Alternatively, anger can result from feeling goal-blocked or misunderstood or misrepresented.

Robinson's (2001) treatment of anger is useful here. He speaks of it as being part of a cluster of feelings, which together can be difficult to comprehend or manage. We must, he argues, allow for the possibilities that:

- the person doesn't want to be seen to be angry
- it may feel unacceptable to express it
- it could feel morally wrong to court it
- it could be extremely difficult for the person to appropriately direct it.

Robinson suggests a seven stage process for dealing with anger. We have added interpretations of his summaries:

1 acknowledgement – beginning to say what the feelings are
2 ventilation – releasing the emotion in a safe way
3 identifying – the cluster of feelings
4 understanding – working through the feelings, for example where they come from
5 validating – through sharing the feelings with a trusted figure
6 communicating– dialogue with this person producing a way forward
7 action – moving towards better practice in this area.

With anger, it is perhaps helpful to differentiate between explosion and implosion. The former pushes anger out, the latter holds it in like an underground atomic explosion. Both actions have consequences and as the process above highlights there are better ways to both understand and manage angry thoughts and feelings.

Loss

Loss comes in all shapes and sizes and can be complicated by the experience of multiple loss, where one loss follows after another. Spall and Callis (1997) speak of a number of types of loss including:

> *Major loss* – these are earth shaking losses including the death of close relatives and friends, significant losses of health, a relationship ending, a family divorce, the loss of a cherished pet.

> *Minor loss* – these are generally less traumatic than major losses but still involve the same emotional reactions, all of which are normal, such as, shock, disbelief, 'why me?', anxiety, anger and leading ultimately to a feeling that the loss has been resolved and being able to move on (Spall and Callis, 1997). Examples might be losing all the files stored on a stolen laptop or missing three weeks of the first semester at university due to severe tonsillitis.

> *Loss of 'oughts'* – these are the loss of things that ought to happen but probably never will. Spall and Callis (1997) argue that people often overlook this kind of loss. For example, a parent not attending one's graduation after all.

Lost

Loss is something different from the sense of feeling lost. This is an extremely common feeling when arriving at university. Lack of familiarity in a new locality, being surrounded by strangers (albeit often friendly ones) and commencing a 'new life' can all contribute to feeling disorientated and lost.

Although universities work very hard to help students feel welcome some students struggle to settle. An important thing here is the student pinpointing what is troubling them. Before exiting university early there are a range of possibilities that can be explored including switching courses, or campuses or accommodation and gaining support from mentoring/counselling services.

Heartbreak

University particularly in the first few weeks can feel like heartbreak hotel. Typically even long-standing relationships from school days and 'back home' often break down with the distance and all the adjustments involved in going to university. Perhaps, after all, you want to make the break. Or you might be experiencing your boyfriend or girlfriend having made the decision to end the relationship. This is a hugely difficult and painful time for many. If you're suffering here, look up to see others who are also heart-broken. The National sing:

You didn't see me, I was falling apart

I was a white girl in a crowd of white girls in the park

You didn't see me, I was falling apart

I was a television version of a person with a broken heart. (Berninger and Dessner, 2013)

It is loss. It can bring on feelings of being lost. Emotional support at such times can be enormously significant. Friends are human and can range from being amazing to insensitive. A weekend or two with family support would constitute time well spent. The counselling service is geared to assisting with this issue, like many others.

We might add here that relationships are ever carriers of joy and pain. Furlong (1994) reminds us that both joy and pain can lead to growth.

Obstacles

We could probably compile an A to Z of obstacles that might pop up to frustrate the 19-something young adult, but instead it seems more appropriate to focus on those which commonly represent some of the largest obstacles for young people to deal with while at university.

Body matters

being a woman is tied up with image and being attractive.

So said the young woman interviewed on the radio. How one looks is also an issue for men, reflected for both genders in fashion, consumption of health and fitness pursuits, hair and hygiene products and following celebrities and the media.

Segal suggests, 'gender and sexuality provide two of the most basic narratives through which our identities are forged' (Segal, 2002). The self-fashioning of the body is a matter of how the individual wants to present themselves to others and also reflects gender and sexuality.

Susan Benson speaks of the contemporary gym culture and cult of fitness as well as the mushrooming of body-building. These developments are all bound up with creating 'a body for others to look at' (Benson, 2002).

Problems can emerge around what we might term one's own 'critical gaze' – that is, looking at one's body or body image through anxious self-doubt or dissatisfaction. When the body is tyrannically regarded as potentially unruly or even destructive then we might be on the way to an eating disorder or an obsessional regime of seeking a particular look.

Apter (2001) says as many as 20 per cent of women students are anorexic, but body related anxieties are by no means just a female issue. Body dysmorphia, as it is called, referring to excessive concern about body image, is prevalent in young adulthood.

Depression

This is a much misunderstood phenomenon which is difficult to comprehend if not experienced. It can be linked to a clutch of serious issues including low self-esteem and poor self-image; personal travail that may be 'hidden' from others; a sense of getting stuck and not being able to find a way forward; unresolved issues and anxieties. If we think about it we all probably know a number of individuals who have wrestled with depression and depressive feelings, at the very least for a season (medically referred to as a depressive episode). A major depression is where at least five out of the following nine symptoms are evident:

1 depressed mood
2 loss of interest or pleasure in almost all activities
3 significant weight loss or gain, or change in appetite
4 insomnia or hypersomnia
5 psychomotor agitation or retardation (observed by others)
6 fatigue or loss of energy
7 feelings of worthlessness or excessive or inappropriate guilt
8 diminished ability to concentrate
9 suicidal thoughts or recurrent thoughts of death.

Divorce

Relationship failure is ubiquitous but it still can come as a massive surprise when it happens in one's own family. Young adults who have experienced a family divorce have likened it to a planet falling out of the sky. It can challenge what seemed like secure assumptions. Later, those same people can describe having come to terms with the notion that Mum or Dad is a human being too. Divorce, whether extremely difficult or more amicable, has complex ramifications. From the perspective of a son or daughter it often shifts parents being viewed as a predictable unit, into being separate individuals, which in turn upsets the son's or daughter's view of themselves. It often leads to new relationships for a parent which in turn produces new family patterns and dynamics. Students can be an enormous help to one another in this area. Those who have experienced change in this area some time ago can help others where the news has just broken.

Financial

There can be a huge contrast in people's financial positions at university. Many students have part-time jobs to finance being there. Whatever a student's financial support and situation there is the matter of spending versus income. Everything that is purchased has to be paid for somehow. It would not be news to any student to speak of financial planning and budgeting and exercising prudence in the areas of accommodation, spending on nights out and adopting a certain lifestyle in the areas of spending on food and clothes. Remember employers look favourably on young people, whatever their family means or background, who have held down jobs, serving at tables, or working in shops. This is not wasted time in terms of life and work experience.

Sexuality (and physicality)

This is a massive subject and one of great delight, discovery and sadly sometimes depression for those at university. We have included it in a section entitled obstacles, not because it constitutes challenge for everyone, but rather because it has to be navigated by all teenagers/young adults as part of the process of journeying towards full maturation. Sexuality encompasses relationships, sexual lifestyle choices, sexual health and sexual preferences. Some young people navigate their way to relationships and choices which yield happiness and peace. For others this process is, for a time at least, fraught and unsatisfactory. Again students can be a help and encouragement to one another in this area by being trusted friends. In addition to sexuality the sheer physicality of these years is expressed in the boundless energy of this time of life. Sports and fitness constitute wonderful opportunities to direct energies, have fun and make friends.

Personal futures

In addition to life and career planning (presented in Chapter 9) the notion of storying oneself forward is appositely presented here. Apter highlights the significance of imagination and students visualizing their futures (Apter, 2001). Seeing one's life unfold, as *Bildungsroman*, is proposed in the embodiment box below. This involves:

- exercising courage in seeking and venturing into pastures new
- seeing others as providing help and encouragement and learning
- not underestimating the difference one life can make
- expecting some setbacks, but also wonders
- viewing life as a gift.

EMBODIMENT BOX – STORYING YOURSELF AND YOUR LIFE AS *BILDUNGSROMAN*

Bildungsroman is the name for a coming of age story featuring a protagonist who arrives at maturity via a journey of adventure and difficulty. The best literary examples are Charlotte Bronte's *Jane Eyre* (1847) and Charles Dickens' *David Copperfield* (1850) but perhaps the most well-known contemporary example is Truman Burbank (Jim Carrey) in the film *The Truman Show* (1998).

Taking Jane, David and Truman together we are given a window into their interiority and the true struggle of their path in attaining psychological and

(Continued)

(Continued)

moral growth. In Truman's case the plot centres on him leaving behind a defensively constructed 'false self', what Winnicott (1954) terms a 'caretaker self', and discovering his true self.

Morgenstern (2009) speaks of *Bildungsroman* permitting the reader to observe the protagonist 'develop before our eyes' and seeing him or her strive towards a true maturity by treading a varied path of 'endeavours, battles, defeats, and victories'. Morgenstern argues that Goethe's point of the purpose of true poetry applies here. Namely, that the intention of the writer is to lessen the reader's anxiety and pain through what Goethe terms 'ingenious representation' and providing a 'bird's-eye perspective' to all 'the convoluted errors of the earth'.

Iverson (2010) provides us with a *Bildungsroman* index consisting of close to 100 features and organized into nine sections. A selection of key features are listed below:

- narrator understands more than young protagonist
- protagonist is basically good and willing to help others
- other character(s) essential in making protagonist change and grow
- moves to big city
- family secret of other family revealed
- setting for childhood scenes is countryside or provincial town
- turning point, reversal: protagonist experiences important defeat or failure
- book title includes the name of the protagonist
- the psychological and moral development of the protagonist from youth to adulthood.

Looking at *Bildungsroman* as a resource and particularly by placing oneself in the shoes of the protagonist the following developmental principles emerge.

- In viewing your situation gain the perspectives of trusted people who stand apart from your present and day-to-day challenges.
- Don't lose sight of all you have to offer, including not just skills but strengths and virtues.
- Remember the significance of the people around you in how life unfolds and develops, particularly good friends, supportive family and key professional advocates.
- Think of big moves as being highly significant and strategic.
- Whatever you see, remember there is more going on. Don't underestimate what can happen and what is happening.
- Remember where you've come from. Don't be in denial about good formative influences and experiences. Celebrate what's good about what you have.
- Turning points are inevitable. Everybody faces them. Don't give up when encountering setbacks.
- Story yourself forward. You are interesting and you are all you'll ever have. Don't underestimate your significance in the world.

> - Life is about development and development never ceases. Other transitions will follow.
>
> In summary:
>
> - Look on life as a narrative.
> - Expect some wrong turns and setbacks.
> - You have choices to make.
> - Remember the significance of who you're travelling with.

APPLIED PERSONAL DEVELOPMENT

My hope in this chapter was that something you have read here might adjust your perspective, particularly with respect to appreciating that being a 19-something student is at the same time both exciting and very challenging. A number of specific personal development pointers emerge from looking at what it means to belong to Generation Y and how and why young adults typically experience at the very least some turbulence on entering adult air-space.

It sounds obvious but don't suffer silently and alone. Remember the counselling service available at university (uniquely funded for students) offers someone you can turn to in the event of being confused or shot to pieces by a challenge of some nature. You can even look at it as being a place where you can talk through something that is concerning you.

In addition to this professional resource, remember the significance of friendships at university. Be kind to others and appreciate others as those who are sharing a journey with you. Remember too, the difference you can make not only to fellow students but people you mix with from all the generations. There is a more 'democratic spirit' in adulthood than in childhood and youth where it matters less what specific age you are. At the same time this chapter has highlighted how the generations might differ.

We ended the chapter by looking at storying yourself forward. This is a kind of extension to the prevalent notion in Generation Y as seeing oneself as a brand or 'legend'. A story wouldn't be a story at all, if you never moved, or never met new people, or never had new experiences, or never learned life lessons. Give yourself time. That's what storying oneself amounts to.

REFERENCES

Apter, T. (2001) *The Myth of Maturity: What Teenagers Need from Parents to Become Adults*. New York: W. W. Norton & Co.

Benson, S. (2002) 'The body, health and eating disorders', in K. Woodward (ed.), *Identity and Difference*. London: Sage.

Berninger, M. D. and Dessner, A. B. (2013) *Pink Rabbits*. New York: 4AD.

Bourdieu, P. (1998) *Practical Reason: on the Theory of Action*. Cambridge: Polity.

Cohen, R. and Kennedy, P. (2007) *Global Sociology*. Basingstoke: Palgrave Macmillan.

Erikson, E. H. (1965) *Childhood and Society*. Harmondsworth: Penguin Books.

Erikson, E. H. (1958) *Young Man Luther: A Study of Psychoanalysis and History*. London: Faber and Faber.

Eyerman, R. and Turner, S. B. (1998) 'Outline of a theory of generations', *European Journal of Social Theory*, 1 (1): 91–106.

Furlong, M. (1994) 'Sex before marriage', in J. B. Nelson and S. P. Longfellow (eds), *Sexuality and the Sacred: Sources for Theological Reflection*. Louisville: Westminster/John Knox Press.

Hansen, J. C. and Leuty, M. E. (2011) 'Work values across generations', *Journal of Career Assessment*, 20: 34–52.

Iverson, A. T. (2010) 'Change and continuity: the *Bildungsroman* in English'. Available at: http://munin.uit.no/bitstream/handle/10037/2486/thesis.pdf?sequence=1 (accessed 14 April 2014).

Jackson, C. (2002) 'Laddishness as a self-worth protection strategy', *Gender and Education*, 14 (1): 37–51.

Jantzen, G. M. (2004) *Foundations of Violence*. London: Routledge.

Jencks, C. (1987) *Post-modernism: The New Classicism an Art and Architecture*. London: Academy Editions.

Karlsson, L. and Karkara, R. (2004) 'Working with men and boys: to promote gender equality and to end violence against boys and girls', International Save the Children Alliance. Available at: http://resourcecentre.savethechildren.se/sites/default/files/documents/1516.pdf (accessed 20 April 2014).

Kenway, J. and Fitzclarence, L. (1997) 'Masculinity, violence and schooling: challenging poisonous pedagogies', *Gender and Education*, 9: 117–133.

Kindlon, D. and Thompson, M. (1999) *Raising Cain: Protecting the Emotional Life of Boys*. London: Penguin.

Lader, M. H. (1975) 'Psychophysiology of clinical anxiety', in T. Silverstone and B. Barraclough (eds), *Contemporary Psychiatry*. London: Royal College of Psychiatrists.

Lindgren, M., Jedbratt, J. and Svensson, E. (2002) *Beyond Mobile: People, Communications and Marketing in a Mobilized World*. Basingstoke: Palgrave.

Morgenstern, K. (2009) 'On the nature of the *Bildungsroman*', trans. Tobias Boes, *PMLA*, 124 (2): 647–659.

Robinson, S. (2001) *Agape: Moral Meaning and Pastoral Counselling*. Cardiff: Aureus Publishing.

Savage, J. (2014) 'Time for the teenager', *RSA Journal*, 1: 16–19.

Segal, L. (2002) 'Sexualities', K. Woodward (ed.), *Identity and Difference*. London: Sage.

Sinclair, A. (2000) 'Teaching managers about masculinities: are you kidding?', *Management Learning*, 31 (1): 83–101.

Spall, B. and Callis, S. (1997) *Loss, Bereavement and Grief: A Guide to Effective Caring*. Cheltenham: Stanley Thornes Publishers.

Trethowan, W. and Sims, A. C. P. (1983) *Psychiatry*. London: Baillière Tindall.

Welchman, K. (2000) *Erik Erikson: His Life, Work and Significance*. Buckingham: Open University Press.

Winnicott, D. W. (1954) 'Metaphysical and clinical aspects of regression within the psychoanalytical set-up', in D. W. Winnicott, *Collected Papers Through Paediatrics to Psychoanalysis*. London: Hogarth Press.

Zopiatis, A., Krambia-Kapardis, M. and Varnavas, A. (2012) 'Y-ers, X-ers and boomers: investigating the multi-generational (mis)preceptions in the hospitality workplace', *Tourism and Hospitality Research*, 12: 100–121.

16 FUTURES

● ● ● ● ● ● ● ● ● ● ● ● ●

A NOTE FROM THE AUTHOR

It is said in China, 'May you be cursed to live in interesting times' (Jencks, 1987). Judging from daily reports of current and international affairs, there is nothing dull about the time we are living through or where the world is heading. Obviously, gaining a handle on how it is changing and coming to terms with the implications of this for both business and for us as individuals is a strategic matter of inquiry.

If we knew the future how differently we would approach so many things, including how we lead our lives in the so called 'now' (referring to the present). We cannot know the future, because no one has been there or discovered it ahead of us. Emerging daily news stories also remind us that our powers of prediction as human beings are at best 'blunt', particularly when compared to our staggering ability to present the past through analysis and researched histories.

And yet we must try as individuals and organizations, for all manner of reasons, to anticipate the future. To plan for what lies ahead constitutes a 'guesstimate' of sorts, nevertheless the notion of smart planning suggests there are more intelligent ways of anticipating the future. Sustainability has at its core how we might adopt a future-thinking mentality, acting in relation to what lies in the future and on behalf of future generations. Investments are bound up in futures thinking. Where the markets are heading is a central issue for investors.

'The future is already here – it's just not evenly distributed' (*The Week*, 2013). So said William Gibson. This suggests that although our personal and corporate futures are unknown, there are both signals and emerging trends to discern that can help us as individuals and businesses to in some sense 'see' or 'foresee' what may lie ahead.

This chapter suggests futures thinking is central to personal development. The astute individual or manager anticipates the future not only in their career choices, but also in their professional development and on behalf of their organizations. It provides a vocabulary one can employ to talk meaningfully about futures and concepts which bring into focus what tomorrow may look like.

Learning outcomes

When you have completed this chapter you will be able to:

- acquire a futures vocabulary
- develop a futures consciousness
- understand the concept of zeitgeist applied to futures thinking
- articulate futures trends
- explain what is meant by circular economy.

A FUTURES VOCABULARY

A good place to start futures thinking is by introducing some terms particularly associated with futurists and futures studies. Here we particularly recommend the work of Elina Hiltunen (2006, 2007, 2008).

Futurists and futures – futurists are sometimes referred to as foresight practitioners, implying that the function of these specialists is to provide foresight as to how the future may unfold and facilitate others in thinking in a futures oriented way. This is relevant to all aspects of business but particularly so to business strategy and to product or market development (Hiltunen, 2007). Hiltunen is categorical that we cannot predict the future, which explains, she says, why futurists refer to 'futures' (Hiltunen, 2007).

Scenarios – futurists generate these and they constitute alternative possible futures. Presenting multiple scenarios helps businesses envision what may occur.

Weak signals – these can be defined as 'currently existing small and seemingly insignificant issues that can tell us about changes in the future' (Hiltunen, 2006). Hiltunen (2006) adds that there are clues present today providing hints to the future's possible events and trends. They are, she argues, 'today's earliest form of information' about the future and in retrospect may well prove to have been the first sign or symptom of a big change, even a megatrend (Hiltunen, 2007). Hiltunen speaks of there being three sources of weak signals (Hiltunen, 2008):

1 Human sources – a whole range of people, Hiltunen's research suggests, may be significant here including researchers, scientists, futurists, consultants and artists. She highlights personal networks may be significant as sources of weak signals.
2 Textual sources – the radio and television are key textual sources, as are academic and scientific journals, popular science and economic magazines and educational and scientific books.

3 Online sources – the top online source of weak signals are company and organization websites but blogs and the homepages of individual people/consultants are also good sources.

Wild cards – most often defined according to Hiltunen as surprising events that have significant consequences, the attacks on the World Trade Center towers on 11 September 2001 being a notable example (Hiltunen, 2006). Cornish argues, 'wild cards have the power to completely upset many things and radically change many people's thinking and planning' (Cornish, 2003). If we consider, as Rockfellow (1994) cites, historical wild cards including technological leaps from the horse to the car, the pen to the typewriter and the typewriter to the computer, the over-arching characteristic is one of radical discontinuity. The notion of a wild card raises the intriguing as well as sometimes disconcerting possibility that anything might happen next. Despite their 'out of nowhere' quality, Hiltunen (2006) underlines that it is sometimes possible to anticipate wild cards in advance.

Futures consciousness – drawing together Hiltunen's futures glossary we might propose businesses and individuals adopting a futures consciousness characterized by the following:

- scanning the external environment for weak signals and emerging issues
- looking out for signals from a wide variety of sources
- going beyond the identification of signals to processing them
- generating alternative images of plausible world futures (Wagar, 2002)
- drawing together futures studies
- thinking holistically about the future (Wagar, 2002)
- unlocking a potential to embrace the future.

NEITHER SUN NOR DEATH – PETER SLOTERDIJK WITH HANS-JÜRGEN HEINRICHS

An example of a futures textual source would be a book like *Neither Sun Nor Death* by the German philosopher-intellectual Peter Sloterdijk (2011).

Sloterdijk speaks of the present time as undergoing a change of world-form. He argues that we have shifted into a new epoch – a 'post-post war period' – which exhibits more complexity than what came before. This is due to the presence of a great many what he terms 'coexistent forces' in an expanded globalized space. Psychologically tackling the problems and challenges these coexistent forces generate feels like being, as Sloterdijk puts it, 'kidnapped'. Individuals and even nation states can feel overwhelmed by the intrusive, daunting and complex quality of these coexistent forces, heightening tension and making navigation difficult.

The future Sloterdijk sees is:

- more complex
- more filled with tension
- more pluralistic
- more technological.

By more Sloterdijk means, than went before. Also, more to handle than is straightforward, with overall populations, as Sloterdijk proposes, 'set in synchronous states of alarm and militant rhythms of excitation'.

For Sloterdijk our world situation is post-Christian. He argues, 'science, technology, parliamentarism, the financial economy, art, mass entertainment, medicine, body culture – almost everything that makes up the modern world is devoid of any Christian project and none of its elements have any specific monotheistic presuppositions'. This suggests to him that an emerging world culture would be 'more pluralistic than monotheistic, and more technological than metaphysical'.

His challenge to us as individuals is to seek what he terms '(personal) sovereignty'. This is being able to distance oneself from what he describes as the 'epidemics of opinion', that amount to collective fields of excitation generated by the media. In the future, it will be necessary he says to incessantly raise the following question: 'Am I contributing to a debate, or am I running along with the mob?'

He speaks of this as his philosopher's mission – to show someone that they can be an 'interrupter' and not merely a 'channel' of waves of excitation associated with thematic epidemics. The ancients term this as 'pondering' – which is no easy thing –where as Sloterdijk argues, 'the energies of alignment are stronger than the habits of dissidence'. It is that ability to not irresistibly have to go with the flow of culture or fashionable ways of being.

IDEOLOGICAL UNDERPINNINGS

Warren Wagar (2002) suggests that futures studies and research is rarely if ever value-neutral. Consequently when examining multiple scenarios constituting alternative images of plausible world futures as anticipated by futurists he encourages his students to begin by sorting them into three rough categories, depending on what he describes as their 'ideological underpinnings' as follows:

1 Technoliberal paradigm – encompassing both liberal and conservative futurists 'who put their faith in market economics, representative democracy, and the wizardry of high tech'.

2 Radical or Marxist paradigm – exhibiting commitment to democratic socialism.
3 Countercultural paradigm – espoused by thinkers embracing a new global culture who will assign the 'highest priority to community, self-governance, attunement with nature, and a sustainable economy'.

Wagar says all futurists approach the future with what he calls this 'ideological baggage'. The complexity of the world is reflected in the fact that in addition to these three camps there are other futurists who see the future through religious spectacles, Muslim and Christian thinkers, or those belonging to an overtly technocratic way of thinking. Wagar adds, 'I challenge my students to detect the ideological inspirations informing every text they read and every lecture they hear from the podium' (Wagar, 2002). This approximates Sloterdijk's notion of 'pondering' as outlined above.

But beyond sensitivity to discerning ideological leanings in versions of the future, Wagar presents the added complication that even futurists of similar ideological persuasions often arrive at quite different visions of the future. The purpose of generating and considering many futures is not to be able to say one version is right, but to stimulate dialogue about the future and to equip students to make choices for themselves and their own futures equipped by this more developed futures mindedness. He suggests that this is also fostered by reading novels about the future which in Wagar's teaching approach might form a focus for discussion and dialogue.

ZEITGEIST – 'COMING IN THE AIR TONIGHT'

Zeitgeist is a loanword, which is borrowed from the German language. *Geist* can be translated into English as mind, spirit or ghost and *zeit* translated as time or tide. Putting the two words together, into zeitgeist, the term is used to suggest the attitude or general outlook of a particular time or alternatively its defining spirit or mood, evident in its ideas and beliefs.

Paul Verhaeghe (2011) speaks of feeling 'the end of a season in our bones, together with the start of the new one'. Phil Collins famously sang, 'I can feel it [a future] coming in the air tonight'. What begins as something quite amorphous – a feeling or a mood – given time, takes shape and is reflected in ways of being and living. The spirit of an age or its zeitgeist seems in the end to be reflected everywhere.

In this section we have sought to capture in words a number of these moods that are not only representative of this age or time but have sufficient force to take on significant form and become embodied in activities and actions.

Distress

Mark Savickas speaks of new social arrangements sweeping aside former stabilities and securities and causing people tremendous distress (Savickas, 2011).

This is supported by Zygmunt Bauman who says that contemporary life 'punctuated by new beginnings' is producing 'worry and apprehension'. He adds that life's 'incurable inconclusiveness' results in tension and anxiety (Bauman, 2008). Krishan Kumar casts more light on this in his observation that we are living 'in a world saturated with information and communication' changing everything, including the nature of work with 'unnerving speed' (Kumar, 1995).

Ecoanxiety

Jonah Sachs speaks of another type of anxiety – ecoanxiety as he calls it (Sachs, 2012). This relates to ecological challenges such as:

- climate change – what Al Gore refers to as 'the climate crisis' (Gore, 2007)
- water scarcity – with likely rises in the price of fresh water
- population pressure – an ever-increasing world population chasing finite and depleting natural resources.

Slavoj Žižek (2011) goes further in speaking of the ecological crisis as signalling, as he puts it, 'an apocalyptic zero-point' for the global capitalist system. He adds, 'its four riders of the apocalypse' are comprised of not only the ecological crisis but also:

- biogenetic intrusions into human nature
- imbalances within the capitalist system itself
- explosive growth of social divisions and exclusions.

Narcissism, really?

Is it really fair to speak of an acceleration of narcissism expressed in lack of empathy, lack of reciprocity and lack of adaptability? Narcissus you'll recall was the beautiful son of the river god Cephisus who had no regard for the maiden's hearts he broke, including the fairest of the nymphs, Echo. This displeased the goddess Aphrodite who punished Narcissus for this by inspiring him with a passion for the reflection of himself, which he saw mirrored in a pool. The one who would not love others was lost in love for himself.

Narcissism refers to a way of being that picks out several aspects of this story:

- self-centred, self-loving, self-absorption culminating often in a sense of entitlement
- seeking admiration and bound by vanity (or self-gaze) bespeaking of little to no self-awareness
- short-term focus leading to exploitative patterns of behaviour and disregard for others.

The latter relentless focus on short-term thinking, reflected in transient and self-centred attachments, Louis Sass (1992) speaks of as leaving narcissistic individuals feeling hollow and disgruntled.

Relating to Narcissus and his 'self-gaze', Pedro Pinto astutely refers to this as 'bodily self-surveillance' (Pinto, 2009). Hundley and Shyles (2010) speak of the significance of 'self-presentations', managed with the aid of digital devices. These of course require relentless and continuous updating (Pinto et al., 2012).

CASE STUDY – FUTURE SPOTTING IN *GAME OF THRONES*

You can, so to speak, future-watch by reading fiction or by viewing it in films or television. For example, we'll illustrate this by looking closely at some of the major themes explored in the enormously popular *Game of Thrones* (GOT) series written by the master of character study, George R. R. Martin. Having informally generated a list of 96 thought 'associations' with GOT, ten were selected for their obvious strength. A GOT character was attached to each of the ten major themes, reflecting on how the character embodies or illustrates each futures theme.

Narcissism (Cersei Lannister)

Cersei reminds us of what an ardent 'me' orientation looks like. Interestingly Cersei's narcissism is extended to her familism. The attitude is expressed by Tocqueville who said, 'he exists only in himself and for himself alone ...' (quoted in Ferguson, 2012).

Family (Catelyn Stark)

Alternatively, meaning itself can be concentrated in family loyalty and in loving and protecting one's family, as can be seen in Catelyn Stark. A strong family can provide significant social capital for all family members.

Survival (Sandor 'The Hound' Clegane)

Sandor's life path is never far away from tribulation of one form or another, but 'The Hound' as he is called is determined to survive, even if he has to constantly adapt and keep moving. His strength is in never entertaining self-pity.

Mercenary (Bronn)

Bronn is a survivor too and one who always knows how to earn silver. He earns a good living, doesn't trouble himself by thinking too much and keeps smiling.

Character (Tyrion Lannister)

Tyrion embodies character in both senses of the word. He has a strong but not overbearing personality and the character to usually do the right thing. He's not perfect but he is well liked.

Wealth duality (Missandei)

Wealth duality is reflected in the contrasting lives of the high-born and their servants (sometimes slaves). Missandei is Daenerys Targaryen's hand-maiden, herald and translator. She oozes dignity and respect, including self-respect.

Wounding (Bran Stark)

Game of Thrones begins with young Bran's staggering loss, becoming a cripple as a result of injustice. He overcomes his disadvantage through the support of friends and forges on seeking to fulfil his chosen quest.

Mortality (Ned Stark)

Bad things happen all the time in *Game of Thrones* ... and even the best characters (like Ned Stark) die. No one is 'safe'.

Plurality (Jaime Lannister)

George R. R. Martin says, 'I believe in great characters. We're all capable of doing great things, and of doing bad things ... our lives are a succession of choices' (Gilmore, 2014). Such plurality is evident in his character, Jaime Lannister.

Secrecy (Peter Baelish)

Secrecy is expressed in Peter Baelish's power-play. We know what's going on when we observe Peter but those in the story don't know what he's going to do next.

Financialization

Satyajit Das writes in his book *Extreme Money*:

> The master narrative of the world is now economic and financial as much as social, cultural or political. Identities are defined and reinvented around money. Individual economic futures increasingly depend on financial success. Business and governments define their performance by financial measures. (Das, 2011)

Increasingly in the west we have seen the development of a 'money culture', or to build on Das' quotation, a culture where money dominates. Das speaks of the phenomenon of 'financialization' and observes that financialization has been reinforced by the media, reflected in 24/7 coverage of money matters (Das, 2011).

Anna-Maria Murtola incisively speaks of this as 'the command of capital over life' (Murtola, 2014) There are two aspects of this which have great significance for the future:

1 Corporate nation-state model – Jeffrey Nealon underlines how the nation state has become consumed by this 'market-takes-all' philosophy. Nealon argues, it 'now seeks primarily to hold the door for transnational capital' (Nealon, 2012).
2 Wealth inequality – Das points to the 'new financial superclass that rules the world' (Das, 2011). Charles Eisenstein says that wealth is 'increasingly concentrated in the hands of the few' (Eisenstein, 2011) even within more wealthy nations. Tim Jackson employs the phrase, 'islands of prosperity within oceans of poverty' (Jackson, 2009), which constitutes a metaphor for global inequalities.

The 'patchy' distribution of wealth makes for an almost unnoticed underclass of what Bauman calls 'flawed consumers' (Bauman, 1987). These are whole swathes of people, sometimes whole regional populations, who find themselves 'virtually disenfranchised … outside the consumerist circus' as David Lyon (2000) puts it.

Search for experience

We return to the research of Anna-Maria Murtola (2014) to discern something in the air that both combines the 'me' focus of narcissism and explains the striving for financial wealth – an appetite shared by millions of people for experiences, which heighten the senses and cause people to feel truly alive.

These are experiences that in the end, we buy. From the lifestyle of a new home in the country or an equally desirable locale, to travelling to distant lands with friends. Expressed for some in the thrill of driving off the forecourt in a top-of-the-range auto-symbol of success and luxury, for others in casting off from the shore in their own boat, on what at least feels like their own lake. Pursued on various scales, from major purchases to packing into one's life lots and lots of bite-sized memorable day-adventures, participating in sports and leisure activities, or enjoying them as a spectator. The purchases may be only 'miniatures' of significance like sharing a great night out, or wearing a desirable item of clothing, or having the repeated pleasure of using an ergonomic mobile phone.

These things are clearly what Murtola terms 'subjectivities' and for her they signify what she would term 'the ongoing commodification of experience' (Murtola, 2014). She adds that, 'we are moving from the experience economy to the experience content economy in which the consumer is starting to … demand substance to the experience' (Murtola, 2014). This puts the onus on manufacturers, retailers and event planners to deliver something of substantive value to customers. It is not, she says, about entertaining them, but rather engaging them (Murtola, 2014).

TRENDS

Weak signals embody early information regarding future changes. The information conveyed through weak signals may often seem funny or strange, even cause confusion, because they offer new ways of thinking. As time passes, it may turn out that weak signals were the first signs or symptoms of big changes, growing trends, or even megatrends.

So write Heinonen and Hiltunen in *Futures* (2012). We draw particular attention to a number of important things:

- the connection between weak signals and trends – that the former can develop into the latter
- not to discount something that strikes one as odd, as having no possibility of significance
- the differentiation between growing trends and megatrends.

In this section we will outline a range of trends, some of which represent even megatrends, all of which have some measure of significance for the future. This is not intended to act as a definitive list of futures trends, but rather an illustrative one.

The big gaze – 'I like to watch'

John Berger in *Ways of Seeing* (1972) argues the attitudes and values which informed Renaissance nude oil painting through time were 'expressed through more widely diffused media – advertising, journalism, television' (Berger, 1972). Since its publication in the early 1970s our ways of seeing have extended to the internet.

Berger adds that 'men look at women' and added 'women watch themselves being looked at' (Berger, 1972). This accords with Lacan's use of the term 'gaze' where the eye, as Elizabeth Wright puts it, is not merely an instrument of perception 'but also an organ of pleasure' (Wright, 2000).

The intensity of the gaze remains the same but the objects of one's gaze differ, such that we can speak of the 'spectator's gaze' and the 'sovereign gaze':

Spectator's gaze: in an increasingly sophisticated sports and entertainment culture most people practise spectator's gaze. People like to watch others performing: acting, at concerts and festivals, in live sports of all kinds. Assisted by technology, the trend has been towards greater and closer scrutiny – the big screens, 'behind the scenes', line-technology, iconic stadia, all delivering spectator experiences and memorable spectacles. This close scrutiny reflects the Colosseum of old in Rome with its synoptic design – where the many can gaze at the few.

Sovereign gaze: we are less conscious of another sort of gaze – how the so called sovereign or sovereign state observes us and other states. Again assisted by technological advances, Glenn Greenwald's book, *No Place to Hide* (2014) illustrates the power and reach of (US) state surveillance motivated not just by security concerns but in the United States by 'obtaining an all-purpose global advantage' – security, diplomatic and economic. This constant surveillance or gaze is closer to what architecturally is known as a panoptic design, famously highlighted by Michel Foucault (1979) in Jeremy Bentham's 1785 model for a prison. With its open view cells and overseen by a central tower, there was 'nothing' that could not be viewed. In the United Kingdom, the proliferation of CCTV cameras delivers this near 'panoptic' view of the many, by the few.

The trend is towards the gaze supporting money-making and vested interests feeding an ever increasing appetite for ever more acute visual-based experiences (spectator's gaze) or systems-based ways of leveraging power (sovereign power). All manner of technologies and industries are attached to these endeavours.

ETHICS BOX – POST-POSTMODERNIST INTENSIFICATION AND THE RETURN OF EMPIRE

An important contribution to painting a picture of culture's and capitalism's 'post-post' future is provided by Jeffrey Nealon's book, *Post-postmodernism: Or, the Cultural Logic of Just-in-time Capitalism* (2012). Nealon's analysis of the direction culture and capitalism are moving in is both penetrating and enlightening, with huge ethical implications for all living through this time of great transition.

Nealon argues that the fall of the Berlin Wall in 1989 signalled a millennial defeat of Soviet power leading to a 'market-take-all' ethos and the ascendency of transnational capital. Ubiquitous corporatization followed and with it a corporate emphasis on maintaining a high stock price 'by any means possible' (Nealon, 2012). Nealon highlights the winners and losers in capitalism's 'intensification' as he terms it, with an upward distribution of wealth to the owners of capital and their executives.

Almost imperceptibly, Nealon argues, 'the nation-state's primary reason for being has changed' with it now primarily seeking 'to hold the door for transnational capital' (Nealon, 2012). Pointing to the thinking of Hardt and Negri (2000), this indicates not so much the end of imperialist power, but as Nealon puts it, 'its intensification and transmutation into another kind of power' (Nealon, 2012).

Quoting Deleuze (1995), Nealon suggests that this intensification permits control: 'We're definitely moving toward control societies that ... no longer operate ... [primarily] by confining people but through continuous control and instant communication ... In a control-based system, nothing's left alone for long.'

The internet of everything

Ansorge and Barkawi's (2014) research encourages us in a Foucauldian fashion to look behind an object of technology to observe the power that has produced or supplied it. This serves as a reminder to not regard a given technology as power-neutral, but to look at what Ansorge and Barkawi term its 'world-ordering' and 'world-making' functions. These respectively can be viewed as expressing a certain worldview and as instruments of reordering the world. This may explain why every object of technological advancement is not universally welcomed and prompts the question: 'Whose interests, both economic and non-monetary, are furthered by this latest gadget or system?' The consumer can ask, 'Do I want to buy into what this innovation totally represents?' In the workplace, the questioning and resistance of the latest innovation may be more difficult.

The internet is delivering what *The Economist* (2014) article, 'The onrushing wave', refers to as 'big data', coupled with far-reaching greater access to it. Glenn Greenwald makes the point that the internet represents the 'epicentre of our world' (Greenwald, 2014) – a digital world explains why businesses and individuals, both seeking competitive advantage, display a tendency to valorize the so called 'digital revolution'. Like the gaze we spoke of above, this also reflects a long history, from the enlightenment onwards, of embracing the machine in the name of the labour-saving and command-vantage it promises.

The Economist article goes on to raise the spectre of what John Maynard Keynes termed as 'technological unemployment' (*The Economist*, 2014). Into this pigeon hole we can post a whole clutch of concerning associated trends including:

- more and more job categories being open to automation
- a growing concentration of wealth in the hands of the owners of capital and their 'supermanagers' (*The Economist*, 2014)
- the pronounced challenge of responding to technological innovation flexibly and with cognitive dexterity.

As a response to this toxicity aspect of the digital world expressed in patterns of labour market polarization and the increased need for acute adaptability we will consider later in the chapter Frey and Osborne's (2013) thinking on emerging occupations and cutting edge capabilities.

Benjamin Barber presents us with the gloating Hummer owner who he says:

> may preen with macho pride, unaware or simply uncaring of the fact that he drives an ecological behemoth that squanders fossil fuel resources, pollutes the environment, and makes the United States more dependent than ever on foreign oil resources contributing quite inadvertently to the justification for Middle East interventions he otherwise vehemently opposes. (Barber, 2007)

1 Does Barber's Hummer merely express postmodernity's 'new playfulness' (Lyon, 2000)? Discuss.
2 In Barber's vignette where do your identifications lie:

- with the gloating driver?
- with Barber?
- with ecologists?
- with Middle Easterners?

3 How can we/you change?

Rising inequality

The bottom line of the above article from *The Economist* is that within the conventional capitalist market (with its producers, consumers and workers) there will be winners and losers and, as the article highlights, 'inequality could soar' both in the United States and beyond (*The Economist*, 2014).

Jeffrey Rifkin is an economist and thinker who believes that a replacement economic paradigm, one he terms 'the collaborative commons', is emerging on the world stage and that this will become a powerful challenger to the capitalist market (Rifkin, 2014a).

It is perhaps not conceivable that the existing system based upon the adoption of new labour saving technologies to increase productivity can sustain extending employment and relative prosperity to a large majority. The so called 'hyper-unequal model' *The Economist* (2014) speaks of as pioneering in the United States (where the owners of capital and their senior executives command an ever enlarged share of the wealth) may be a harbinger of a rising inequality within the capitalist market. Pearce and Hallgarten (2000) underline that many people view this inequality as leading even to a social unravelling.

Rifkin himself says, 'I think this is going to be a rough road' (Rifkin, 2014b) but he anticipates a continued rise of a global collaborative commons, where consumers become what he calls 'prosumers' (Rifkin, 2014a) using, he adds, near zero marginal cost internet technology to produce and share all manner of goods and services. This social commons has, he argues, been largely overlooked by economists – a world where social capital is as important as financial capital (Rifkin, 2014c).

Rifkin argues, 'we don't know what the replacement economy might be' (Rifkin, 2014b) but the future he anticipates will be a kind of hybrid system – part capitalist market and part collaborative commons. The vision here could amount to the capitalist market being increasingly and creatively bypassed, particularly by those it has effectively excluded. This will all be a part of what Rifkin describes as a move from geopolitics to what he calls 'biosphere consciousness' – all, he argues, 'in one generation' (Rifkin, 2014b). This is a way of looking at the world squarely in the face of economic crisis, food and water security, the need for green energy, and climate change. The latter he says is 'the elephant in the room' (Rifkin, 2014b).

Another key voice on the emerging new shape of capitalism and the trend of the dualizing inequality dynamics is Saskia Sassen. A key word for Sassen is 'expulsions' – the expulsions of people, places and traditional economies, which she argues we are witnessing as advanced capitalism enters a new global phase (Sassen, 2013). Her mapping of capitalism's systemic transformation suggests that this new phase is what she terms 'post-Keynesian', and it signals the leaving behind of Keynesianism's valuing of people as workers and consumers. This encompasses destruction of traditional capitalisms with their traditional petty bourgeoisies and traditional national bourgeoisies.

The needs of high finance and global capitalist production will in fact result in swathes of 'surplus people' and with them what Sassen calls 'zones of expulsion' (Sassen, 2014), the latter being territories devastated by:

- poverty and disease
- various kinds of armed conflict
- governments rendered dysfunctional by acute corruption
- crippling international debt regime.

The surplus people are disturbingly both 'invisible' (Sassen, 2014) and surprising, given this unforeseen impoverishment and shrinking of the middle classes (Sassen, 2013). The forces at work here are centripetal and centrifugal (Latin for centre fleeing) with concentrations of money and power, as Sassen puts it, 'driving people to the edges' (Sassen, 2014).

The implications here are interesting. Life will go on for those pushed aside:

- where an 'elementary' (Sassen, 2013), that is a simpler rather than complex, way of living will emerge based upon the bartering of goods and services
- social capital, i.e. who you know and the quality of relationships, will take on greater significance
- there will be a multiplication of what Sassen calls 'systemic edges' (Sassen, 2014), i.e. systems will only take you so far before you will need to find new ones

- those in 'the shadows' (Sassen, 2014), beyond the spheres of the relative wealthy, cannot be discounted, that is treated as though they no longer can influence what happens.

EMBODIMENT BOX: 'HAVE A HEART' – FROM A 3D PRINTER

Looking into the future it is well known that, other than significant population increase in Africa and South Asia, Europe and other parts of the world will experience ageing populations resulting in so called 'grey pressure' (Bakas, 2009). The latter demographic is partly the result of scientific and technological advances, meaning older people live longer. The implication for business goods and services should not be overlooked.

3D printing is an emerging technology that Fraser indicates could be utilized to produce in the future for a grateful recipient 'a new heart, or liver or maybe even a brain' (Fraser, 2013). The McKinsey Global Institute (MGI) identify 3D printing as one of 12 so called 'disruptive technologies' that will transform life, business and the global economy' (McKinsey Global Institute, 2013).

Using an array of materials including a broad range of polymers, even converted old plastic, 3D printers can be used to create 'product prototypes, tools, moulds and even final products' (Ellen MacArthur Foundation, 2014). The implications of this new technology, as our new heart example illustrates, could be startling. Joshua Pearce, a Materials Science Professor at Michigan Technological University, talks about how affordable 3D printers combined with widespread internet access mean more people will 'use, study, copy and change a design for free – and share the improvements online' (*The Guardian*, 2014). An article in *The Independent* (2014), 'What's the big deal with 3D printing', highlights the significances of 3D printing for home manufacturing and the return of cottage industries. It predicts, 'the factory can be one person at home again' or perhaps even more profoundly, 'you can make the things you want'.

Circular economy

The future is circular, not linear. This is the core thinking behind what are known as circular economy practitioners and thinkers. The Ellen MacArthur Foundation (2014) report, *Towards the Circular Economy*, provides a clear rationale for a future that is not centred around our current predominantly linear economic system, summarized as 'take-make-dispose'.

Circular economists call into question the notion of continual growth within a world of finite resources (Balch, 2014). The above report suggests that sustained rises in the price of resources and 'unparalleled' resource price volatility highlight that the linear model of production and consumption is not sustainable and proposes a new industrial model characterized as follows:

Design out waste – the last 150 years of industrial evolution, the report argues, has followed a model that wastes all that is produced, with its so called 'end-of-life' concept (Ellen MacArthur Foundation, 2014). Simply put, a circular economy aims instead to design out waste, by reusing materials to the maximum extent possible. The cradle-to-cradle (C2C) approach to technological and biological cycles is significant here.

The sharing economy – with half of the world's ever increasing population living in urban areas the report proposes a reinvention of traditional ownership-based market behaviours towards collaborative consumption models focusing on access rather than ownership.

Replacing one-way products and processes with those more circular in design implies:

- regenerating natural assets
- refurbishment
- remanufacturing
- reuse of goods.

An emphasis on sharing, in the widest sense, has its own set of implications including:

- more social-community based practices such as lending, swapping, bartering and giving
- the expansion of the rental market for goods, hitherto primarily owned
- greater 'tracking' of all resources to prevent them being underutilized or idle
- the monitoring of resource use to prevent excess and unnecessary waste.

Post-Freud orientation

The famous Chilean psychoanalyst Ignacio Matte Blanco spoke of a 'general orientation brought about by Freud'. Freud, he argued, discovered a world – he termed the unconscious – 'ruled by entirely different laws from those governing conscious thinking' (Matte Blanco, 1998). For Freud, the unconscious was a 'true psychical reality', in other words a mode of being (Matte Blanco, 1998).

Victor Hugo famously said, 'an invasion of armies can be resisted but not an idea whose time has come'. Freud's discovery of a realm of contradictory forces and instinctive desires coincided with people in the west coming to terms with the totality of their experiences and of themselves. Freud's thinking was a modern equivalent of the opening of Pandora's box – all manner of things that had long been repressed could now be expressed – Psychological man was born.

Hall speaks of the multiplication of identities in our midst and in our neighbourhoods (Hall, 2000). Bakas describes the United States and Europe becoming a 'salad bowl' of racially and nationally diverse groups living and working side by side (Bakas, 2009). The coming together of these two things – the end of structural repression and multicultural integration – presents almost infinite possibilities for expressions and innovations of plurality.

Hall astutely adds that 'multiculturalism thrives right alongside deep and fundamental forms of racism' where 'one is not exclusive of the other' (Hall, 2000). The implication is that resulting tensions will have to be managed. Mustakova-Possardt (2006) speaks of the simultaneous operation in global civil society of two opposing processes – 'increasing global integration and deepening social disintegration'. The latter is bound up with what she describes as a 'crisis of meaning' in the west, including a 'prevailing philosophy of materialism'.

The return of the religious

In 1993 the famous contemporary philosopher Jacques Derrida spoke of 'the return of the religious' (Raschke and Taylor, 2013). The so called return, as Philippa Berry highlighted, came as something unexpected, especially in view of the prevalence of secularism and hyperrationality (Berry, 2004). Carl Raschke added:

> the postmodern turn that began a quarter of a century ago has opened wide the question of religion in ways that were inconceivable a generation ago. (Raschke, 2005)

The return, Raschke continued, should not be thought of as 'an archaic revival nor a counterpraxis to the trend towards secularisation', but a 'resurgence' (like a wave) made all the more powerful for its alliance with tele-technoscience (Raschke, 2005).

Zygmunt Bauman argues that modernity was all about 'doing without God' (Bauman, 1997). In his book, *Intimations of Postmodernity* (1992) he suggested, as hard as modernity had tried to 'dis-enchant' (or despiritualize) the world, postmodernity ushered in a re-enchantment of the world (Bauman, 1992).

Berry astutely highlights that Derrida's 'return of the religious' referenced 'some spirits', which she suggests amounts to a host of modes of spirituality (Berry, 2004). Clifford Longley describes these as 'self-made' spiritualities, making no claim to philosophical coherence (Longley, 1999). Berry also highlights the hybridity of these typically populist heterodox and highly diffuse forms of belief, drawing on ideas and religious experiences beyond the dogmas of traditional religions (Berry, 2004).

Adjiedj Bakas speaks of the possibility of the emergence of a new religion and adds that the celebrity culture might produce a figure (either a politician or a star) that would achieve a kind of divine status in the eyes of his or her followers (Bakas, 2009).

Raschke, on the other hand, dwells on a new 'war of religion' between on the one hand the Enlightenment force of globalization and telemediatization, as Derrida describes it, and a reactive response of faith groups. Here, fundamentalisms spring up in reaction to the felt 'compression' at the hands of the 'techno-rationalising war machine' of globalization (Raschke, 2005).

Frey and Osborne's (2013) research on the future of employment enables us to anticipate the impact of advances in technology on occupational choice. One trend is towards a job polarization termed as 'lousy and lovely jobs' (Goos et al., 2009) where there will be growing employment in high income cognitive jobs and low income manual jobs, accompanied by a hollowing out of middle income jobs.

Frey and Osborne call for people to respond to this employment challenge by acquiring creative and social skills. They highlight six cutting-edge capabilities.

1 Social intelligence – what they alternatively term as 'social perceptiveness', that is being aware of others reactions, and understanding why they react as they do.
2 Negotiation – a collaborative skill bringing people together with a view to reconciling differences.
3 Persuasion – another collaborative skill helping people to change their minds or behaviour.
4 Personal care – providing specialist emotional support and care.
5 Originality – developing highly creative ways to solve problems.
6 Creative arts – acquiring knowledge of the theory and techniques required in areas such as music, the visual arts and drama.

Examination of this list of capabilities suggests a common theme of what Eric Rayner (1998) would describe as 'intellectual emotionality'. On the one hand, there is a call here for high-order what are traditionally called 'soft skills' coupled with an emphasis on creativity. On the other hand, these are applied in contexts which are pressing or demanding so their rigour is tested, like metal in fire.

Mustakova-Possardt (2006) points to Danesh's (1994) thinking around what is termed as 'optimal consciousness', which brings together three leading human powers:

1 the power to know
2 the power to love (or care)
3 the power to exercise will (choosing between action or inaction).

Awareness, care and will amounting to an optimal consciousness is close to Rayner's intellectual emotionality and suggests a course of personal development along which all can fruitfully travel.

APPLIED PERSONAL DEVELOPMENT

When we look at the subject of futures the notion of radical journeying presents itself. Our sailing into the future combines both adventure and challenge in the great western tradition of Odyssey. Any faint-heartedness must be overcome through studying the present for futures signals and trends and remembering the significance of social capital – of journeying with significant others.

I want to underline here a number of concepts we have introduced in this chapter, starting with Peter Sloterdijk's (2011) notion of sovereignty. You will recall that this is the ability to stand apart from the current of opinion or fashion that has the potential to carry us off in a certain direction, without us either choosing this or even knowing it. Sloterdijk's sovereignty is close to the ancients' practice of pondering – a form of detachment which permits the individual to see the forces that in everyday reality, swirl around them. Roszak spoke of 'spiritual intelligence' which was the ability to tell the greater from the lesser reality (Roszak, 1975). As Sloterdijk's thinking highlights, we need to be sovereign in the face of both.

The notion of discernment would also appear to be central to reading the signs of the times and in the section entitled Zeitgeist I highlighted a fascinating range of emergent attitudes or moods that pop up everywhere. These included the anxieties that attach themselves to different concerns including so called ecoanxiety, prevalent narcissism, money-mindedness and the search for experience. None of us is 'above' such things. The point rather is seeing clearly such things at work in us as individuals and in relation to the direction business will move in.

We are also subject to the trends: multiple forms of gazing, the internet of everything, a widening gap between the haves and those that have a lot more, the new circularity in the way we organize our economies and the full outworking socially of the post-Freud orientation. My identification of trends, like the early warning signals, is not a definitive list – but rather a means of encouraging us to give more time and resources to the serious business of anticipating, plotting and working through the implications of possible futures.

Not only in this chapter but throughout the book I have underlined what it means to be living in a post-post world – post of the post-war period and post of postmodernism. This has enormous implications for patterns of employment and my challenge here is to ask how on earth can we ever expect to get to grips with planning futures, including career planning and business planning, without the sharpest possible comprehension of the context of the world in which we are living?

REFERENCES

Ansorge, J. T. and Barkawi, T. (2014) 'Utile forms, power and knowledge in small war', *Review of International Studies*, 40 (1): 3–24.

Bakas, A. (2009) *World Megatrends: Towards the Renewal of Humanity*. Oxford: Infinite Ideas.

Balch, O. (2014) 'Circular economy practitioners set out views in new book', *The Guardian*, 11 February.

Barber, B. R. (2007) *Consumed: How Markets Corrupt Children, Infantilize Adults, and Swallow Citizens Whole*. New York: W. W. Norton & Co.

Bauman, Z. (2008) *Does Ethics Have a Chance in a World of Consumers*. Cambridge, MA: Harvard University Press.

Bauman, Z. (1997) *Postmodernity and Its Discontents*. Cambridge: Polity Press.

Bauman, Z. (1992) *Intimations of Postmodernity*. London: Routledge.

Bauman, Z. (1987) *Freedom*. Buckingham: Open University Press.

Berger, J. (1972) *Ways of Seeing*. London: Penguin Books.

Berry, P. (2004) 'Postmodernism and post-religion', in S. Connor (ed.), *The Cambridge Companion to Postmodernism*. Cambridge: Cambridge University Press.

Cornish, E. (2003) 'The wild cards in our future', *The Futurist*, 37: 18–22.

Danesh, H. (1994) *The Psychology of Spirituality*. Manotick, Ontario: Nine Pines.

Das, S. (2011) *Extreme Money: The Masters of the Universe and the Cult of Risk*. Harlow: Pearson Education.

Deleuze, G. (1995) *Negotiations, 1972–1990*, trans. Martin Joughin. New York: Columbia University Press.

The Economist (2014) 'The onrushing wave: the future of jobs', 18 January: 18–21.

Eisenstein, C. (2011) *Sacred Economics: Money, Gift and Society in the Age of Transition*. Berkeley, CA: Evolver Editions.

Ellen MacArthur Foundation (2014) *Towards the Circular Economy: Accelerating the Scale-up Across Global Supply Chains*. Available at: www.ellenmacarthur-foundation.org/business/reports (accessed 28 May 2014).

Ferguson, N. (2012) *The Great Degeneration: How Institutions Decay and Economies Die*. London: Penguin Books.

Foucault, M. (1979) *Discipline and Punish: The Birth of the Prison*. New York: Vintage Books.

Fraser, B. (2013) 'Forever young', *Thought: The Art of Investing*, J.P. Morgan, 3Q: 48.

Frey, C. B. and Osborne, M. A. (2013) 'The future of employment: how susceptible are jobs to computerisation', 17 September. Available at: www.oxfordmartin. ox.ac.uk/downloads/academic/The_Future_of_Employment.pdf (accessed 6 May 2014).

Gilmore, M. (2014) 'The power behind the throne', *Sunday Times*, News Review, 4 May.

Goos, M., Manning, A. and Salomons, A. (2009) 'Job polarisation in Europe', *The American Economic Review*, 99 (2): 58–63.

Gore, A. (2007) 'Foreword', in S. L. Hart, *Capitalism at the Crossroads: Aligning Business, Earth, and Humanity*. Upper Saddle River: Wharton School Publishing.

Greenwald, G. (2014) *No Place to Hide: Edward Snowden, the NSA, and the US Surveillance State*. New York: Metropolitan Books.

The Guardian (2014) '3D printing could offer developing world savings on replica lab kit', 21 February.

Hall, S. (2000) 'Multicultural citizens, monocultural citizenship?', in N. Pearce and J. Hallgarten (eds), *Tomorrow's Citizens: Critical Debates in Citizenship and Education*. London: Institute for Public Policy Research.

Hardt, M. and Negri, A. (2000) *Empire*. Cambridge, MA: Harvard University Press.

Heinonen, S. and Hiltunen, E. (2012) 'Creative foresight space and futures window: using weak signals to enhance anticipation and innovation', *Futures*, 44: 248–256.

Hiltunen, E. (2008) 'Good sources of weak signals: a global study of where futurists look for weak signals', *Journal of Futures Studies*, 12 (4): 21–44.

Hiltunen, E. (2007) 'The futures window – a medium for presenting visual weak signals to trigger employee's futures thinking in organisations', Helsinki School of Economics Working Papers W – 423. Available at: http://epub.lib.aalto.fi/pdf/diss/a365.pdf (accessed 9 May 2014).

Hiltunen, E. (2006) 'Was it a wild card or just our blindness to gradual change?', *Journal of Futures Studies*, 11 (2): 61–74.

Hundley, H. L. and Shyles, L. (2010) 'US teenagers' perceptions and awareness of digital technology: a focus group approach', *New Media Society*, 12: 417–433.

The Independent (2014) 'What's the big deal with 3D printing', 25 May.

Jackson, T. (2009) *Prosperity Without Growth: Economics for a Finite Planet.* London: Earthscan.

Jencks, C. (1987) *Post-modernism: The New Classicism an Art and Architecture.* London: Academy Editions.

Kumar, K. (1995) *From Post-industrial to Post-modern Society.* Oxford: Blackwell.

Longley, C. (1999) 'A spiritual land with little time for church', *Daily Telegraph*, 17 December.

Lyon, D. (2000) 'Post-modernity', in G. Browning, A. Halcli and F. Webster (eds), *Understanding Contemporary Society: Theories of the Present.* London: Sage.

Matte Blanco, I. (1998) *The Unconscious as Infinite Sets: An Essay in Bi-logic.* London: Karnac Books.

McKinsey Global Institute (2013) *Disruptive Technologies: Advances That Will Transform Life, Business and the Global Economy.* Available at: file:///C:/Users/Paul/Downloads/MGI_Disruptive_technologies_Executive_summary_May2013.pdf (accessed 29 May 2014).

Murtola, A. (2014) 'Experience, commodification, biopolitics', *Critical Sociology*, 1–20.

Mustakova-Possardt, E. (2006) 'Clash or meeting between east and west: an analysis of the post-9/11 challenges', *Journal of Peace Psychology*, 12 (2): 189–203.

Nealon, J. T. (2012) *Post-Postmodernism: Or, the Cultural Logic of Just-in-time Capitalism.* Stanford, CA: Stanford University Press.

Pearce, N. and Hallgarten, J. (eds) (2000) *Tomorrow's Citizens: Critical Debates in Citizenship and Education.* London: Institute for Public Policy Research.

Pinto, P. (2009) 'From post-feminism to "dildocracy": sex industries and happy woman's biopolitics', *Psychology of Women Section Review*, 11 (2): 3–10.

Pinto, P., Nogueira, C. and Oliveira, J. (2012) 'Minding the body, sexing the brain: hormonal truth and the post-feminist hermeneutics of adolescence', *Feminist Theory*, 13: 305–323.

Raschke, C. A. (2005) 'Derrida and the return of religion: religious theory after postmodernism', *Journal of Cultural and Religious Theory*, 6 (2), Spring. Available at: www.jcrt.org/archives/06.2/raschke.pdf (accessed 9 June 2014).

Raschke, C. A. and Taylor, V. (2013) 'From alchemy to revolution: a conversation with Carl A. Raschke', *Journal of Cultural and Religious Theory*, 12 (3), Spring. Available at: www.jcrt.org/archives/12.3/taylor.raschke.pdf (accessed 9 June 2014).

Rayner, E. (1998) 'Foreword' in I. Matte Blanco, *The Unconscious as Infinite Sets: An Essay in Bi-logic.* London: Karnac Books.

Rifkin, J. (2014a) 'Capitalism is making way for the age of free', *The Guardian*, 31 March.

Rifkin, J. (2014b) 'The zero marginal cost society', *Social Europe Journal*, 25 April. Available at: www.social-europe.eu/2014/04/zero-marginal-cost-society (accessed 30 April 2014).

Rifkin, J. (2014c) *The Zero Marginal Cost Society: The Internet of Things, the Collaborative Commons and the Eclipse of Capitalism*. Basingstoke: Palgrave Macmillan.

Rockfellow, J. (1994) 'Wild cards: preparing for the big one', *The Futurist*, 1: 14–19.

Roszak, T. (1975) *Unfinished Animal: The Aquarian Frontier and the Evolution of Consciousness*. London: Faber and Faber.

Sachs, J. (2012) *Winning the Story Wars: Why Those Who Tell and Live the Best Stories Will Rule the Future*. Boston: Harvard Business Review Press.

Sass, L. (1992) 'The epic of disbelief: the postmodernist turn in contemporary psychoanalysis', in S. Kvale (ed.), *Psychology and Postmodernism*. London: Sage.

Sassen, S. (2014) 'The future of capitalism', *Start the Week*, BBC Radio 4, 28 April.

Sassen, S. (2013) 'Expelled: humans in capitalism's deepening crisis', *American Sociological Association*, 19 (12): 198–201.

Savickas, M. L. (2011) *Career Counseling*. Washington DC: American Psychological Association.

Sloterdijk, P. with Heinrichs, H. (2011) *Neither Sun Nor Death*, trans. Steve Corcoran. Los Angeles: Semiotext(e).

Verhaeghe, P. (2011) *Love in a Time of Loneliness: Three Essays on Drive and Desire*, trans. Plym Peters and Tony Langham. London: Karnac Books.

Wagar, W. W. (2002) 'Past and future', in J. A. Dator (ed.), *Advancing Futures: Futures Studies in Higher Education*. Westport: Praeger.

The Week (2013) 'Wit & wisdom', 24 August.

Wright, E. (2000) *Lacan and Postfeminism*. Cambridge: Icon Books.

Žižek, S. (2011) *Living in the End Times*. London: Verso.

INDEX

NOTE: Page numbers in *italic type* refer to tables.

Bridges, William, 25
Briggs Myers, Isabel, 142
Brown, D., 290
Brown, Marvin, T., 170–4
Brown, R.T., 303
Browning, Don, 190
Buber, Martin, 173
Burnard, Philip, 221
Burns, James, 298
business acumen, 99
business insight, 225, 229
business schools, 30–1

Callahan, Shawn, 195–6
Callis, S., 334
Campbell, R., 297
capacity building, 229
capitalism, 105–6, 352–3, 354–5
career
    meaning of word, 180
    as motivation for university, 21
career anchors, 184–6
career choice
    impact of technology on, 359
    and personality type, 142
career construction theory, 187
career counselling, 186–8
career development, 181
career planning, 182
    DOTS model, 188–9
    and Holland's career theory, 183–4
career theory, Holland's, 183–4
Carnegie, Andrew, 197
categorization, and gender, 331–2
Center for Creative Leadership (CCL), 117–19
Chantilly Principles, 313
chaos, 155
Chapman, Y., 143, 144
character formation, 28–9
    see also identity; personality types
Charcot, Jean-Martin, 251
childhood, Freud on, 252–3
choice points, 181
Christian, Susanne, 73
circular economy, 356–7
civic integrity, 172
clarity, 87
Clark, Martin, 232–3
Clarke, Nita, 290
co-workers, 239–40
codes of conduct, 312
codes of ethics, 163, 311, 313
codes of practice, 311, 313
cognition, 78, 95–6
cogwheeling, 264
Coicaud, J., 31

collaboration, 118
collaborative commons, 354–5
colleagues, 239–40
collective unconscious, 257
Colton, Stephanie, 196
commodification of experience, 350–1
communication
    and individuality, 101
    non-verbal, 66, 215–17
    in presentations, 63–6
    as skill/competency, 99, 117
    typology of, 172–3
    see also written communications
communicator jobs, 76–7
community, 94–5, 104, 108, 276
competencies
    and assessment centres, 220
    definition, 44
    and internships, 240–1
    key competencies, 93–6, 99
    and professionalism, 96–100
    see also skills
competition, 330
complexity, Whyte on, 155–6
complexity theory of leadership, 301
computational thinking, 78
confidence, 101, 103–4
conflict resolution, 175–6
connection/connectedness, 87, 304
Conrad, C.A., 58
conscientization, 144
consciousness, 165, 276
consistency, 164
constructivist practitioners, 187
consumerism, 35
consumers, 97, 278, 282–3
contacts, 75
    see also networking
contention, and integrity, 160
control orientation, 32
conversation, 26, 117
cooperants, 229
Corfield, Rebecca, 222
corporate global citizenship, 114–15
corporate integrity, 160, 170–4, 290
corporate nation-state, 350
corporate responsibility (CR), 271–2
corporate social responsibility (CSR), 116,
    308–9
corporate values, 275–7
cosmopolitan communication, 173
counselling service, 339
cover letters, 195, 207, 211
Covey, S., 295–6
Cox, D., 174, 175
creativity, 87, 289

crises, Erikson's concept of, 167, 261–3, 328–9
Criswell, C., 117–19
critical interculturality, 121
critical theorists, 144
critical thinking, 58–60, 78
cross-cultural skills, 121, 229
cult of youth, 324
cultural competence, 241
cultural integrity, 172–3
Cupitt, Don, 148
customer focus competencies, 97
CVs, 68, 207, 210–11

Daldeniz, B., 230
Daloz Parks, S., 30
Damasio, Antonio, 95–6
Das, Satyajit, 349–50
decision responsibility, 304
deep drivers, 86–7
defence mechanisms, 253–6, 260
defensive reasoning, 144
demographic trends, 356
denial, 256, 331
Department for International Development (DFID), 228
dependability, 160, 276
depression, 336
development
    volunteering for (V4D), 226
    see also life stages; moral development; personal development; young adulthood
developmental motives, for attending university, 22
dialogical self theory, 168–9
dialogue, 172–3, 176
difference, 121, 122, 241
    see also 'other'; strangeness and strangers
digital capitalism, 105–6
digital technology, 324, 353
    see also internet
direction, 87
discourse, of higher education, 84–5
disorientation, 334
dissonance, 235
distress, 346–7
    see also anxiety; uncertainty
Divan, A., 81, 82
divorce, 336
DOTS model, 188–9
double-loop learning, 145
Dowson, Paul, 166, 287, 299–300, 306–7
Drewell, Mark, 116
dynamic cycle, 190
dysfunctional roles, 55–6

e-portfolios, 209
Ebert, A., 138
eco-leadership theory, 301
ecoanxiety, 347
ecology see environmental impact; sustainable development
economic impact of business, 272
economic paradigms, 354–5
    see also capitalism; financialization
ecozoic era, 130–1
educational motives, 22
ego, 253
ego defences, 253–6, 260
egoistic level of development, 279
Elder, L., 58–60
Elford, R.J., 109–10
Ellen MacArthur Foundation, 356–7
embodiment, of integrity, 160
emotion
    managing, 95–6
    see also affective dimension
emotional investment in job applications, 205
emotional literacy, 329–30
emotional pressure, 329–31
empathy, 78, 99–100
employability
    and career choice, 142
    compared with 'in employment', 80
    concept of, 9–10
    and generations, 324–5
    in graduate jobs formula, 74
    and integrity, 163–4
    and internships, 234
    and job applications, 194–5
    and moral imagination, 288–9
    and occupational individuation, 258–9
    PD file/portfolio, 209
    and purpose of university, 28
    skills for, 51–2, 88–9
    and volunteering, 81
employee engagement, 289–90
employees
    co-worker relationships, 239–40
    codes of conduct, 312
    values imposed on, 281
employment
    compared with employability, 80
    future of, 359
    for graduates, 71, 72–3
    transferable skills, 68
    while studying, 71, 336–7
empowerment, for interns, 242–3
engagement
    of employees, 289–90
    and graduate identity, 89
    and placements, 232, 243–4

generativity, 264
Gentile, M.C., 30
Gibbs' reflective cycle, 145
Gieser, T., 168–9
Gill, Roger, 294
global capitalism, 33
global citizenship, 114–15
global ethic, 123–4
global nature of higher education, 85–6
global perspective, 114, 229
global practitioners, 117–23
global/globalization
    concept of, 7, 11–12, 113–14
    and personal development, 131–2
    and progress, 128
globally responsible leadership, 116
glocal worldview, 127
Goldberg, M.L., 85
golden theme, *187*
Gomez, Lavinia, 259
Goodpaster, Kenneth, 165, 175
'goods of life', 190
Gore, Al, 12
governance
    and accounting, *284*
    and codes of practice, 311
    ethical coding, 311–12
    models of, 305–8
    MSF case study, 312–14
    see also standards
graduate identity approach, 88–9
graduate jobs/employment, 71, 72–3
graduate jobs formula, 74–5
graduate networking, 75, 81–3
graduate schemes, 73
graduate skills, 75–80, 88–9
graduates, global nature of, 85–6
grammar, in job applications, 208–9
Grayling, A.C., 198
green issues
    business opportunities, 119
    see also ecoanxiety; environmental impact;
        sustainable development
Greenleaf, R., 299–300
Greenwald, Glenn, 352, 353
Greenwood, M.R., 285–6
group work, in assessment centres, 220–1
groups, and young adulthood, 326
Guptara, Prabhu, 12, 99

Ha-ping Yung, Hilary, 289
habitus, 321–2
Hall, Calvin, 254
Hall, S., 357–8
Hampton, M.P., 230
Hansen, J.C., 320

harassment, 287
hard HRM, 285–6
Hart, Stuart, 106–7
Harvard business school, 30–1
Haste, Helen, 93–6
heartbreak, 334–5
hedonistic practices, 330
Heinonen, S., 351
Hermans, H.J.M., 168–9
Hiebert, Paul, 126–7, 129
hierarchy, Indian worldview of, 129
higher education
    aims of, 27, 28–9
    discourse of, 84–5
    global nature of, 85–6
    views of, 26
    see also university
Higher Education Academy, 88–9
Hiltunen, Elina, 343–4, 351
Holland, John, 183–4
Holmes, J., 260
homework, for interviews, 218
homo economicus, 279
honesty, 108, 163–4, 276
Hopkins, Burt, 257
Howie, George, 29
human resource management (HRM),
    285–90
humanity, 86
Hunt, Geoffrey, 288
Hurding, Roger, 252
hybridity, 36, 307
hysteria, 251

id, 253
ideas formation, 328
identifications, multiple, 168–9
identity, 88–9, 169–70
identity capital, *187*
identity crisis, 167, 261–3, 328–9
identity formation, 327
imagination, 154–5, 183
in-tray exercises, 213–14
inclusion, 171
independence motives, 22
independent learning, 60–1
Indian worldview, 129
individualism, USA worldview of, 129
individuality, 100–3
individuation, 258–9
inequality, 128, 350, 354–6
information sources, and critical thinking, 59
inner journey, *187*
innovation, 118
Institute for Employment Studies, 75–6
instrumental strategy, 25

leadership *cont.*
   sustainability mindset, 304–5
   theories of, 296–302
learning
   from experience, 204, 212, 221, 223
   from placements, 231–2
   high impact internships, 236–42
   and 'making a difference', 280
   single and double loop, 145
   views of higher education and, 26
learning and development, in HRM, 286
learning tribes, 20–1
Lebow, Ned, 169–70
Lederach, John Paul, 118, 288–9
Leeds City Council, 107–9
Lees, John, 215, 217
leeway, 263
legalistic level of development, 279
Leigh, W.A., 58
Leuty, M.E., 320
liberal education, 28
libido, 141, 256
life planning
   as balance, 190–1
   as flourishing, 198
   as story, 191–7
life stages, 22–5, 328
   Erikson's theory of, 23, 24, 167, 261,
      262–3, 328–9
   see also young adulthood
life stories/narratives, 24
life views, 130
lifestyle (LS), 186
LinkedIn, 82–3
Lips-Wiersma, M., 304
liquid modernity *see* late modernity
living contradiction, 165–6, 176–7
Lock, Robert, 183, 184
locus of control, 303
Lonergan, Bernard, 150–1
Lore, N., 31–2
loss, in young adulthood, 334
lost/disoriented, in young adulthood, 334
love
   projection and, 255–6
   see also heartbreak
Luther, Martin, 328–9

McAdams, Dan, 24
McCandless, David, 34–5
MacLeod, David, 290
McMahon, Walter, 28
Macmurray, John, 149–50
macro stories, 218
macro-leadership, 296
macronarrative, *187*

'making a difference', 280
Malcolm, Janet, *255, 256*
management
   compared with leadership, 294–5
   engaging managers, 290
   senior management competencies, 98–9
managing change, 99
Mann, Sarah, 84–5
marketing, 277–83
Martin, A., 117–19
Marx, Karl, 144
masculinities, 331–2
Mason, Geoff, 43–4
match/fit
   and career planning, 183
   and job applications, 204
   of skills with target, 45
Matte Blanco, Ignacio, 357
MBTI (Myers-Briggs Test Indicator), 140
meaning, in work, 273–4, 304
Médecins Sans Frontières (MSF), 312–14
meeting new people, 66
Meine, Dirk, 139–40
meta-leadership, 296
Metcalfe, Valerie, 46
methodology, of ethical practitioners, 110
micro stories, 217–18
micro-leadership, 296
micronarrative, *187*
Middleton, J.R., 34, 35, 128
Mills, A.J., 304
Mimesis 1, 2 and 3, 310
mind-body relationship, 149
modernistic communication, 173
modernity, 33–4, 126–7, 128, 150–1
   see also late modernity
monocultural communication, 173
moral climate, 160, 162
moral development, 279–81
moral imagination, 288–9
moral strivers level of development, *279*
morality, and ethics, 109
moratorium, 24
Morgenstern, K., 338
motivation, for attending university, 21–2
MSF charter, 313
multiculturalism, 358
multiple identifications, 168–9
Murphy, P.E., 277–82
Murtola, Anna-Maria, 350–1
Mustakova-Possardt, E., 358
mutuality, 263
Myers-Briggs framework, 140–2

narcissism, 347–8
narrative

narcissism *cont.*
  aspects of, 192–4
  and career construction, 187
  life narratives, 24
  strategic, 290
  see also story; storying
narrative identity, *187*
narrative learning cycle, 191–2
nation-state, and capital, 350, 352
Naugle, David, 124
Nealon, Jeffrey, 350, 352–3
nerves *see* anxiety
networking, 66–8, 75, 81–3, 206, 226
neuromarketing, 282–3
neurosis, 251
new media literacy, 78
non-verbal communication, 66, 215–17

Oakeshott, Michael, 26
objective career, *187*
occupational choice *see* career choice
occupational individuation, 258–9
occupational motives, 21
one-to-one interviews, 214
open-mindedness, 122–3
optimism, 79
orchestrator jobs, 76
order, chaos and, 155
organizational insight, 225
organizational integrity, 160, 170–4, 290
organizations
  definition, 271
  dynamic cycle applied to, 191
Orr, David W., 119
Osborne, M.A., 359
'other', 93, 100, 149
  see also difference; strangeness and
     strangers
outer journey, *187*
Oxfam, 114

Palmer, Robert, 26
panel interviews, 214
panoptic model, 352
Papapol, Martin, 105–6
paradoxical curiosity, 289
patriarchal attitudes, 287
Paul, R., 58–60
peacebuilding, 288–9
Pearce, W.B., 172–3
Pears, Richard, 62–3
people *see* consumers; students
perceiving/judging scale, 142
Peregrin, Tony, 82–3
performance, and graduate identity, 89
Perrone, Lisa, 43

persona, 258
personal awareness *see* self-awareness
personal development (PD)
  applied
    at university, 38–9
    in career and life planning, 198–9
    and futures, 359–60
    global dimension, 131–2
    and integrity, 177
    and job applications, 223
    leadership and governance, 314
    and placements, 229, 244–5
    and profiling, 156–7
    psychosocial aspects, 266–7
    and responsibility, 291
    and skills, 68–9, 89–90
    values and competence, 110–11
    and young adulthood, 339
  see also self-development
personal development (PD) concept, 8–10
personal development (PD) file, 209
personal development planning (PDP), 46
personal effectiveness, 98
personal futures, storying, 337–9
personal growth, 182
personal and social roles, 54–5
personal statements, 212
personality tests, 213
personality types, 138–42, 183–4
  see also traits
physicality, and young adulthood, 337
Piper, T.R., 30
placements
  internships *see* internships
  in jobs formula, 74–5
  self-reflexive biographies, 231–2
  volunteering, 81, 225–33
plagiarism, 62–3
planning
  action planning, 51
  career planning, 182, 183–4, 188–9
  life planning, 189–98
  personal development planning, 46
play, as psychoanalytical technique, 259–60
plurality, 125, 324, 357–8
poetry, 155–6
political conditions, and integrity, 174
portfolios, 209
  see also profiles
positive thinking, 79
positivist practitioners, *188*
post-Enron phenomena, 297–8
post-Freud orientation, 357–8
post-Keynesian phase, 355
post-postmodernism, 127, 352–3
postmodernity, 34–5, 37–8, 127, *150*, 167–8, 186

stage theory (Erikson), 23, 24, 167, 261,
    262–3, 328–9
stakeholder governance model, 305–6
stakeholder theory, 162
standards
    of expected competence, 96–8
    ISO on social responsibility, 309
    LCC case study, 107–9
    see also governance
status motives, for attending university, 22
Stewart, Mark, 212
story
    job application as, 194–5
    life planning as, 191–7
    life stories, 24
story line, 188
story telling, 195–6, 204–5
storying, 217–18, 337–9
strangeness and strangers, 121, 125–6
    see also difference; 'other'
strategic narrative, 290
strategies, in graduate jobs formula, 75
strengths, 44, 101
    see also competencies; skills
StrengthsFinder 2.0 assessment, 101
students
    as independent learners, 60–1
    learning tribes, 20–1
    motivations, 21–2
    procrastination by, 43
    see also young adulthood
subjective career, 188
subjective experience, 260
sublimation, 256
Sullivan, S., 67
superego, 253
surveillance, 352
sustainable development, 106–7, 115,
    229–30, 272–3, 304–5
    see also ecoanxiety; environmental impact
Sweitzer, H.F., 233–4, 235, 236–43
SWOT analysis, 46–7
symmetry, and integrity, 164
system, and integrity, 174–5

'T-shaped' workers, 78
talents, 44, 101–3
Taylor, Matthew, 99–100
team contributions, 57
team roles, 53–6
teamworking, 53–8, 98, 107–8
technical and functional competence (TF), 185
technology
    and future trends, 353, 356
    and Generation Y, 324
    impact on career choice, 359

technology cont.
    managing, 96
    see also internet
teleopathy, 165
tests, pre-interview, 213–14
theories-in-use, 145
theory and practice, 237–8
thinking/feeling scale, 141
third sector, 227–8
Thurlow, Crispin, 121
Torok, M., 255
trait theory of leadership, 296–7
traits, 86–7
    see also personality types
transactional leadership, 298
transferable skills, 68
transference, 256
transformational leadership, 298–9
transition
    and career development, 181
    concept of, 25
    going to university, 13
    good, 7–8
    graduation, 43–4
    Schlossberg's view on, 151–3
    to independent learning, 60
    see also life stages; young adulthood
transparency, 276
Trelhowan, W., 332–3
triple bottom line, 115, 271–2,
    308–9
true self, 148, 204, 214–15
Truss, C., 285–6
trust, 100, 108, 171
Turner, S.B., 321
'turning up', 204, 205

uncertainty, 11, 35, 93
    see also distress
unconscious, 253, 257, 357
university
    ethical, 37–8, 120
    motives for attending, 21–2
    and personal development, 38–9
    in postmodern context, 37–8
    purpose of, 26–9
    skills acquisition at, 44–5
    and young adulthood see young
        adulthood
university assignments, 56, 62–3
university business schools, 30–1
University of Westminster skills model, 50
'us and them', 100
    see also difference; 'other'; strangeness and
        strangers
USA worldview, 129